D0204025

BANK DEREGULATION
AND
MONETARY ORDER

Can the "invisible hand" handle money? In this collection of essays George Selgin challenges the view that government regulation creates monetary order and stability, and instead shows it to be the main source of monetary and banking crises.

The volume is divided into three sections. Part I describes institutional features of an unregulated banking and payments system, refuting the claims that such a system would be "moneyless" and that it must inevitably lead to the emergence of a central bank. Part II discusses the macroeconomic properties of an unregulated payments system, showing how such a system helps to keep real economic variables at their "natural" levels by stabilizing aggregate spending, while refuting the popular misconception that a monetary system is unsound unless it delivers a stable output price level. Part III draws on both theory and historical experience to show that banking crises, far from being inherent to fractional-reserve banking, are in fact by-products of misguided government intervention in the banking industry.

Written by one of the leading contributors to the debate on free or *laissez-faire* banking, *Bank Deregulation and Monetary Order* is bound to provoke controversy while stimulating further research. It will be of great interest to students and researchers in monetary economics, banking and economic policy.

George Selgin is Associate Professor of Economics at the University of Georgia.

ROUTLEDGE INTERNATIONAL STUDIES
IN MONEY AND BANKING

BANK DEREGULATION
AND
MONETARY ORDER

George Selgin

London and New York

First published 1996
by Routledge
2 Park Square, Milton Park, Abingdon, Oxon, OX14 4RN

Simultaneously published in the USA and Canada
by Routledge
270 Madison Ave, New York NY 10016

Reprinted 2000

Transferred to Digital Printing 2006

Routledge is an imprint of the Taylor & Francis Group

Typeset in Times by
J&L Composition Ltd, Filey, North Yorkshire

British Library Cataloguing in Publication Data
A catalogue record for this book is available from the British Library

Library of Congress Cataloguing in Publication Data
Selgin, George A., 1957–
Bank deregulation and monetary order / George Selgin.
(Routledge international studies in money and banking)
Includes bibliographical references and index.
1. Banks and banking–State supervision. I. Title. II. Series.
HG1725.S44   1996
332.1′0973–dc20   95–53116

ISBN 0–415–14056–0 (hbk)

Publisher's Note
The publisher has gone to great lengths to ensure the quality of this reprint
but points out that some imperfections in the original may be apparent

To Joanne

CONTENTS

Part III The regulatory sources of monetary disorder

LIST OF ILLUSTRATIONS

FIGURES

TABLES

ACKNOWLEDGEMENTS

In looking over the acknowledgements published in the original versions of the essays reprinted here, I see that dozens of persons, many whose names are still unknown to me, contributed in some fashion to my research. I think I ought to thank once more at least those whose names come up repeatedly in my original "thank-yous." Foremost among them is my friend and colleague Lawrence H. White who, besides co-authoring two of the essays, had a hand in all the others as well. Others whom I have often turned to for comments and suggestions are Don Boudreaux, Kevin Dowd, Milton Friedman, Robert Greenfield, George Kaufman, David Laidler, Bill Lastrapes, Kurt Schuler, Anna Schwartz, Dick Timberlake, Bill Woolsey, and Leland Yeager. Obviously they should not be blamed for any of my mistakes, especially since some of them still believe, alas, that my main contentions are themselves mistaken. They are all guilty, nonetheless, of encouraging me in my work.

INTRODUCTION

According to most bank regulators, monetary authorities, and economists today, bank deregulation is a mixed blessing. On one hand, deregulation is said to enhance the competitive efficiency of the payments system, expanding the scope of financial intermediation. On the other, deregulation supposedly undermines central banks' ability to control nominal magnitudes and increases the likelihood of catastrophic payments-system failure. A completely deregulated or "free" banking and payments system is, implicitly at least, portrayed as one that would quickly self-destruct.

Remarkably, this consensus of opinion has been reached with little help from economic theory: the instability of unregulated banking is often simply taken for granted, or is demonstrated through causal references to economic history, with little care taken to distinguish market-based sources of instability from ones connected in crucial ways to government interference.

In view of this, one is entitled to ask whether an explicit inquiry into the nature and operations of a "free" banking and payments system, making consistent appeal to predictable consequences of self-interested behavior, supports prevailing views. This means asking: (1) What sorts of institutions would an entirely unregulated banking and payments system involve? (2) How would nominal magnitudes, including the price level and money stock, behave in such a system? and (3) How vulnerable would such a system be to crises?

Until the mid-1970s, scarcely any attempt had been made to answer such questions. Instead, critics of bank regulation (of which there has never been a shortage) settled for a piecemeal approach, revealing the practical shortcomings (and, on occasion, the unsavory origins) of existing regulatory arrangements, but never questioning the claim that *some kind* of regulation is necessary. That misguided government interference itself might be the *main* source of observed monetary and banking difficulties was not seriously considered. The claim that financial markets and banking in particular are "inherently unstable" was not open to doubt.

During the last two decades, all this has changed. Economists, aroused by Hayek's (1976) pioneering essay on "Choice in Currency," began systematic inquiries into the nature and implications of free banking. The basic intent of this research, including books by Lawrence White (1984), David Glasner (1989), Kevin Dowd (1989, 1992, 1993), Tyler Cowen and Randy Kroszner (1994), Steve Horwitz (1992), Larry Sechrest (1993), and myself (1988), was to reconsider governments' role in monetary and payments systems, by first imagining how these systems might develop in the absence of government interference. Although different assumptions led each investigator to some alternative "vision" of monetary *laissez-faire*, all were led to reject the inherent-instability hypothesis, concluding that problems of existing monetary arrangements were due to *government* (that is, regulatory and central bank) failures rather than market failure.

The essays reprinted here (with minor revisions) are, with two exceptions, articles written by me since the publication of my *Theory of Free Banking*. They are presented here in three parts, corresponding to the three questions posed above. The essays in Part I consider the institutional implications of monetary *laissez-faire*. Chapter 1, "How would the invisible hand handle money," written with Lawrence H. White, sets the stage by reviewing recent research on the implications of monetary deregulation. White and I identify three distinct schools of thought on this subject. The "modern free banking" school, to which White and I belong, insists that an entirely deregulated and privatized payments system of the future would involve many of the same basic institutional features – including a single "outside" base money cum unit of account – found in past, relatively unregulated banking systems.[1] The "competing fiat monies" school, to which Hayek belonged, imagines a world of plural, private fiat monies. Finally, the "New Monetary Economists" believe that deregulation would pave the way to a purely "inside" monetary system, lacking base money altogether. White and I argue that, of these alternative views of monetary *laissez-faire*, only the modern free banking view involves institutional arrangements that are both viable and predictable outcomes of individuals' self-interested behavior.

Chapter 2, "The evolution of a free banking system," also written with White, offers a further defense of the modern free banking view in the form of a "conjectural" history of a typical free banking system. The point of such a conjectural history is to show precisely how the unregulated actions of individual agents give rise to monetary institutions as envisioned in the free banking literature. Although this paper predates my earlier book, and was in fact the prototype for a chapter in that book, I include it here because it is crucial for understanding the institutional assumptions relied upon in my more recent papers. One can, of course, *define* free banking in a strictly negative sense – as a system where bankers are held to the usual laws of contract but where intermediation is not otherwise legally restricted

– but some more positive understanding of the nature of free banking is needed before any conclusions can be reached concerning its practical consequences.

Charles Goodhart (1988) rejects the conclusions White and I reach concerning features of a "typical" free banking system. Noting economies of scale achievable through a centralization of bank reserves, Goodhart argues that reserves will naturally tend to gather in a dominant "bankers' bank." Central banking itself is thus seen as a "natural" development. As I note in Chapter 3, "The rationalization of central banks," some centralization of reserves is in fact assumed in modern discussions of free banking. However, some earlier proponents of free banking appeared to deny any natural tendency for reserves to become centralized. Walter Bagehot (1873), for one, refers to free banking as an arrangement with every bank "keeping its own [cash] reserve" (ibid., pp. 331–2). Goodhart is right to argue that this view is incorrect. It does not follow, though, that reserves will "naturally" accumulate in a "bankers' bank," like the Bank of England. On the contrary: despite his erroneous view of free banking, Bagehot was on solid ground when he called the Bank of England's reserve monopoly "the gradual consequence . . . of an accumulation of legal privileges [which] no one would now defend" (ibid., p. 100). The possibility overlooked by both Bagehot and Goodhart is that free banks can, and indeed historically did, achieve reserve economies while avoiding possible conflicts of interest by establishing branch networks and by joining non-bank clearinghouses. A number of new case studies of free banking (Dowd 1992), published since Goodhart's critique appeared, lend additional support to this modern free banking view.

The same case studies do not, on the other hand, support any of the alternative visions of monetary *laissez-faire*: one finds, for example, no historical instances of freely evolved "moneyless" payments systems of the sort contemplated by the "New Monetary Economists" or of systems relying upon broad index-type accounting units of the sort recommended by Dowd (1989, pp. 98–100) and Glasner (1989, pp. 227–49). Voluntarily accepted, privately issued "fiat" money is likewise unheard of. Instead, simple, single-commodity standards have tended to emerge and to remain in place until their eventual dismantlement by governments; and, although the most sophisticated free banking systems, like Scotland's, were ones in which bank customers rarely converted banknotes into gold or silver, there is no reason to suppose, *pace* Cowen and Kroszner (1994), that consumers' failure to exercise their legal rights heralded a voluntary abandonment of those rights. Indeed, it is more accurate to say that the Scots did not bother to convert banknotes into gold only because they believed banknotes could always be converted in gold.

Part II gathers my papers addressing the implications of free banking for the behavior of nominal macroeconomic magnitudes including the money stock, the price level, and nominal income. Unlike the essays in Part III, these generally take for granted public confidence in the banking system, and so address the behavior of free banks during "normal" (non-crisis) periods.

Surprisingly and, I think, wrongly, some critics of free banking seem inclined to treat these "normal" monetary implications of free banking as a diversion from the "real" issue of banking crises, as if a system's ability to avoid crises were the only thing that mattered, and as if the likelihood of crises itself were not crucially dependent upon the workaday stability of nominal magnitudes. To at least some extent, I suppose, this attitude reflects the simultaneous abatement of inflation and resurgence of banking crises after 1980 as well as the fashion that arose during the same period (known as the "new classical revolution") of downplaying the importance of monetary changes to real activity. Fashions change, of course, and I believe it will not be long before theorists begin to see the behavior of nominal magnitudes during "normal" times as *the* fundamental issue for free banking theory. Much depends, of course, on whether theorists in general become convinced, as I am (for reasons given in Part III), that banking crises themselves are mainly due to unwarranted government interference with market-based monetary arrangements.

More surprising than some critics' lack of interest in the "normal" monetary implications of free banking has been the neglect of these implications by students of free banking themselves. Although it is heartening to see more widespread acceptance of the claim that, under free banking, "the supply of money may adapt naturally to the demand for it" (Deane and Pringle 1994, p. 322), in most of the free banking literature the validity of this claim – as a claim favoring free banking rather than a particular base money regime – is not adequately substantiated. White (1984), for example, studies a free banking system in an open-economy gold standard context, and so is able to assume that the money stock adjusts in the long run to accommodate a "given" international price level. Glasner at one point (1989, p. 19) relies upon a Fullartonian "reflux" of excess bank money as a constraint against aggregate overissuance, suggesting – incorrectly, in my view – that banks will be discouraged from issuing excessive quantities of bank money when such excesses are returned to them in the form of loan repayments.[2] Glasner also assumes (ibid., pp. 227–47), together with Dowd (1989, pp. 98–100), that free banks will denominate their liabilities in units deliberately chosen so as to guarantee the liabilities' long-run purchasing power.[3] In all such schemes, arbitrage is ultimately relied upon to determine the equilibrium stock of bank money. But the very same arbitrage mechanism could also be administered by a single, monopoly bank-of-issue, so that one is left to wonder whether free banking has any advantage over centralized banking when it comes to avoiding short-run episodes of aggregate monetary disequilibrium. What advantage, we are obliged to ask, does, say, a gold or a commodity-basket standard with free banking have over *the same standard* with central banking? Does the decentralized and legally unrestricted issuance of bank money (including paper notes) really help, or is the definition of the unit of account all that matters?

A standard reply is that, under free banking, the clearing mechanism disciplines individual firms, by subjecting them to reserve losses whenever they issue notes or otherwise extend credit beyond their share of the market for money balances. This discipline takes effect without any need for prior changes in the price level, thereby checking overexpansion more rapidly than any arbitrage-based mechanism, which (assuming an environment of less than "perfect" information) can begin to operate only *after* prices have risen. This argument, however, only serves to rule out any short-run overexpansion of individual banks *relative* to other banks. If all banks overexpand in unison, none suffers adverse clearings.

Dowd (ibid., p. 47) and White (1984, p. 18) both observe, correctly in my view, that the sort of uniform overexpansion contemplated here is unlikely to take place. But this observation still leaves a hole in the theory, in so far as the aggregate demand for bank reserves for clearing purposes appears to be indeterminate with respect to both the aggregate quantity of bank money *and its velocity*. Long-run arbitrage appears, after all, to be the only mechanism capable of both stimulating desirable adjustments in the aggregate stock of bank money and of "pinning down" the price level.

The way to patch the whole, which I first proposed in "The stability and efficiency of money supply under free banking" (Chapter 4), is to note that free banks would hold reserves, not only to meet expected net clearing losses, but also as protection against unexpected or random fluctuations in daily net clearings. The demand for such "precautionary" reserves would tend to be proportional to the flow of bank liabilities through the clearing system and, hence (assuming that this flow itself is a fairly constant multiple of aggregate expenditures on final goods), nominal income. Given some stock of the outside reserve medium, a unique equilibrium value of nominal income is implied, with the stock of bank money responding automatically to changes in the demand for (velocity) of bank money. The adjustments depend, crucially, on changes in the excess demand for precautionary reserves, but not on any arbitrage-related changes in the actual stock of bank reserves. Because a central bank has no need for reserves for clearing purposes, this equilibrating mechanism is unique to free banking.

In "Commercial banks as pure intermediaries: between 'old' and 'new' views" (Chapter 5), I relate these findings to previous debates concerning whether banks are merely passive or "pure" intermediaries (and, hence, not independent sources of net additions to aggregate spending) or not. My conclusion echoes James Tobin (1963), who argued that a crucial distinction must be drawn between commercial bank money and "printing press" money, the latter only being capable of expanding independently of the monetary wants of the public. I differ from Tobin, however, in thinking that the crucial distinction is, not so much between bank and "printing press" money, but between competitively issued and monopolistically issued monies: an expansion of central bank deposits, even redeemable ones, is after all quite capable of boosting the aggregate nominal demand for goods and services, even if the central bank is a private institution (like the early Bank of England) whose deposits are backed by private debt. "Printing press" money in the form of competitively issued, redeemable banknotes is, on the other hand, unlikely to expand ahead of the public's monetary needs, unless the issuing banks have somehow managed to get hold of new reserves. I also note that private banks' ability to function as pure intermediaries is typically impaired by legal restrictions, including especially statutory reserve requirements and the outlawing of competitive note issuance – the "purest" intermediation system of all being one in which complete freedom of private banks is combined with a rigid or "frozen" monetary base.

The implications of a frozen base regime, with and without restrictions on private banks, are further explored in Chapter 6, "Free banking and monetary control." This essay gives a formal account of how a demand for precautionary reserves fixes nominal magnitudes in a free banking system. It explains that, with a frozen monetary base, changes in the velocity of bank money will tend to be accommodated by opposite changes in the money stock. Growth in real output may, in contrast, to some extent at least be reflected in falling prices.

Those who regard stability of the general price level as the *sine qua none* of a sound monetary system will view the last conclusion as a distinct drawback of a frozen base free banking regime. However, as I argue in "Monetary equilibrium and the productivity norm of price-level policy" (Chapter 7), there are good reasons for preferring a regime that stabilizes nominal spending (and thereby allows the price level to drift downward in a progressing economy) to one that stabilizes the general price level. Indeed, such a "productivity norm" for price-level behavior was, as shown in Chapter 8, once a serious rival to the alternative (and now clearly dominant) policy goal of "zero inflation."

The emphasis on banknotes running throughout some of the above chapters will strike many readers as archaic or even as quaint, given the declining importance of paper currency relative to other (even narrowly defined) "monetary" assets, which is only likely to accelerate with ongoing innovations in electronic funds transfer. Yet there are reasons for discussing banknotes, the most important being that the capacity of private notes to completely displace public holdings of high-powered money is an established fact: private notes did this in Scotland, where they were preferred to coin; and in Canada, where they were also preferred to government-issued "Dominion" notes. "Smart" cards and other recent developments may in future allow private financial firms to substitute their liabilities for public holdings of fiat money despite the government monopoly of paper currency; but it is only possible to engage in loose speculation concerning the economic implications of as-yet incomplete technologies.[4] To assess the theoretical implications of a fully privatized money stock based on banknotes and checkable deposits only is, in contrast, relatively straightforward. Indeed this approach provides, I think, the best available framework for thinking about potential consequences of electronic money.

A focus on banknotes is, more obviously, also useful for shedding light on banking history. It was central banks' monopolies (or quasi-monopolies) of paper notes that caused their liabilities to become "high powered," allowing central banks to escape the discipline of the clearing mechanism and giving them the power to engineer a general monetary expansion or contradiction independent of prior changes in the stock of specie or the velocity of money. Then, in order to evade the long-run restraint still posed by external drains of specie, central banks suspended the convertibility of their notes – something that no competitive note issuer would have been able to do without severe private repercussions – thus ushering in the modern era of fiat money.

Besides severely limiting the influence of any single banking firm upon the aggregate money stock, competitive note issuance played a crucial role in allowing competing banks to accommodate changes in their clients' demand for money balances. This demand can be decomposed into a demand for transferable deposit credits on one hand and a demand for circulating currency on the other. As long as banks were free to issue notes, they could easily accommodate routine changes in the public's *relative* demand for currency without upsetting an established supply – demand equilibrium for the aggregate money stock. But once note issuance was legally restricted, through its monopolization or otherwise, even routine increases in the relative demand for currency became a potential cause of general monetary contraction, with private banks having to draw on their reserves (instead of issuing more notes) to supply their clients with hand-to-hand means of payment. The extent to which nineteenth- and early twentieth-century banking crises were either caused or aggravated by the legal restriction of competitive note issuance, though generally known by contemporary authorities, today goes unappreciated: modern commentators even claim the very crises in question as proof of the need for a "lender of the last resort," neglecting how such a "lender of last resort" acquires its power to "help" other banks only after depriving them of their ability to help themselves.

Restriction of private note issuance is only one of many ways in which government intervention has made banking systems more vulnerable to crises. Indeed, it is now generally appreciated that many kinds of bank regulation have contributed in one way or another to the likelihood of banking crises, especially by artificially limiting opportunities for bank portfolio diversification and by reducing or eliminating entirely bank customers' incentive to avoid high-risk financial firms.

Such harmful consequences of regulation raise the question whether, in the absence of regulation, banking systems would still be crisis prone. The conventional answer is that banking is "inherently" unstable, and that at least *some* regulations (the favorite candidates are deposit insurance and central bank legislation) are needed to avert disaster.[5] Chapter 9, "Are banking crises free-market phenomena?", takes a critical look at this conventional wisdom, and finds it hopelessly at odds with the historical experience of several countries, including Scotland, Canada, and Sweden during the nineteenth century. Evidently some alternative to the conventional view of banking crises is needed. Chapter 10 ("Legal restrictions, financial weakening, and the lender of last resort") proposes the most obvious candidate: a pure "legal restrictions" theory. According to this theory, fractional-reserve banking systems are not "inherently" crisis prone at all, but have been rendered crisis prone by misguided regulations, including regulations underlying central banking and government deposit insurance.

Care must be taken, of course, in interpreting claims regarding the absence of "crises" in unregulated banking. Individual bank failures, including some spectacular failures, did occur in the absence of restrictive regulations, just as they have continued to occur with alarming frequency *in the presence of* all manner of regulation. The free banking claim is that comprehensive deregulation would reduce the risk of *systemic* failure – that is, it would reduce the threat of general panics leading to a collapse of money and credit multipliers.

The basis for this claim is, first, that even regulated banking systems are less vulnerable to systemic failure than bank regulatory authorities (and some economists) would have us believe and, second, that the removal of regulations (including deposit insurance) would reduce this vulnerability to a negligible level, by giving consumers in all markets ready access to at least a few banks that are either relatively highly capitalized or relatively free of portfolio risk or both. This conclusion assumes, of course, that the monetary base regime itself is reformed in a manner consistent with the avoidance of dramatic swings in the price level and interest rates. According to proponents of free banking, such reform is itself mainly a matter of eliminating central banks' discretionary powers – powers that were, after all, originally acquired as by-products of restrictions on commercial banking.

Although a free banking system would, I think, be relatively immune to systemic crises, one cannot entirely rule out the possibility of such crises occurring: while most empirical evidence points to the unlikelihood of systemwide contagion effects (Kaufman 1994), there is some evidence of limited contagions.[6] And, although deregulation should reduce banks' vulnerability to shocks (including runs), theory itself cannot rule out the possibility of a panic that is both widespread and ill-informed. Could a system of unregulated banks, lacking a lender of last resort, contain such a panic? One reply is that it could do so by making its liabilities conditionally demandable only: banks could reserve the right to "suspend" over-the-counter payments of high-powered money in the event of a run. The very presence of such a right would discourage runs, by eliminating the possibility of run-induced insolvency.

Diamond and Dybvig (1983), however, reject suspension as an alternative to deposit insurance or central bank intervention, arguing that suspension would prevent bank customers from pursuing their normal consumption activity. In "In defense of bank suspension" (Chapter 11) I show that Diamond and Dybvig's conclusion is based on the absence of transactable bank money from their model: as long as banknotes and deposits can be used to purchase goods, suspension need not impair bank customers' ability to go shopping.

Regrettably, most people are much better at imagining catastrophic banking failures than they are at imagining how such failures might be avoided by an open, diverse, and non-hierarchical banking industry. Thus competitive developments that might more properly be seen as reducing the likelihood of crises are instead seen as threats to stability. One example is the "globalization" of banking. Alan Greenspan (1995, p. 6), for one, has said that such globalization *increases* the likelihood of systemic failure by strengthening "interdependencies among markets," meaning, presumably, that as banks become more diversified internationally, more of them will be exposed to shocks in any one region. That any *given* regional shock will affect a relatively small part of any global bank's portfolio goes unmentioned. Technologies allowing a more rapid flow of information are likewise portrayed as a threat (ibid.) – as if such technologies somehow favored the transmission of fear over the transmission of panic-squelching firm-specific information. Financial derivatives are still another *bête noir*, despite the fact that most of them are used to transfer and reduce risk – including especially risk associated with central bank-inspired fluctuations in interest and exchange rates. Regulators' jaundiced attitude toward competitively inspired financial market innovations seems to go hand in hand with their habit of ignoring the more genuine threats to financial markets and consumers posed by their own regulatory and monetary practices.

Just as crises themselves tend to be seen entirely as market-driven phenomena, so too have bank-lending "manias" that supposedly set the stage for many historical crises. I address this popular belief in "Bank-lending 'manias' in theory and history" (Chapter 12), which argues that historical lending "manias" have been based, not on competing bankers' succumbing to "waves of optimism," but on new deposits of high-powered bank reserves supplied, as often as not, by central banks.

I have tried in these essays to answer many of the most frequently heard arguments for continued government involvement in money and banking. The routine voicing of many of these arguments may justify to some extent at least my own repetitions of counterarguments. In any event, such repetitions are difficult to avoid in a collection of this sort.

I do not pretend, on the other hand, to have addressed every important argument against comprehensive bank deregulation. Although it is now beginning its third decade, research on free banking is still in its infancy. Much more work needs to be done, both in refining the theory and in confronting it with empirical evidence. My fondest hope is that this book will encourage some readers to pursue such research; but I will be happy if it merely causes a few more persons to question the conventional view that payments systems are "inherently" unstable.

NOTES

1 The "outside" base money could consist either of a commodity – as was the case in all historical free banking systems – or of some fiat money. In my own (1988) proposed free banking reform, the base money regime consists of a frozen stock of fiat Federal Reserve notes. Strictly speaking, one can also combine free banking with a discretionary central bank-based fiat money regime. But most proponents of free banking, noting the historical origins of central banking in legal restrictions imposed on commercial banks, view free banking as an *alternative* to discretionary central banking arrangements.

2 Strictly speaking, a bank need have no reason to fear a prompt return of its notes or checks through direct *loan repayments*, which might only confront it with excess reserves and, thereby, with an incentive to find new borrowers, for example by lowering its lending rates. Of course, if bank loans are repaid with the liabilities of *other* banks, reserve demands may be generated, just as they may be generated whenever one bank gets hold of some other bank's liabilities. In any case, how a *general* increase in interbank payments is supposed to lead to a general contraction of bank balance sheets still has to be explained.

3 In Glasner, the unit of account is supposed to guarantee a constant wage index, whereas in Dowd the unit serves to maintain a constant output price index.

4 The implications of private banknote issuance, or the lack thereof, in developing countries also deserve consideration: because many persons in poorer countries rely on currency instead of bank deposits, prohibiting access to banknotes amounts to a serious form of "financial repression," overlooked by most of the development literature, which has the effect of diverting to the government sector scarce savings that might otherwise be a source of funds for private investment.

5 Even George J. Benston and George G. Kaufman (1995), despite assigning a crucial role to misguided regulations in generating crises in US banking history, take for granted the need for a central bank acting as a "lender of the last resort." They are thus driven to embrace *implicitly* the conventional view that fractional-reserve banking is "inherently" unstable even as they attempt *explicitly* to refute it!

6 For example, Pozdena (1991). As long as depositors perceive some safe alternatives to stuffing money in mattresses, shocks to individual banks or groups of banks will not have adverse macroeconomic consequences. Even limited spill-over effects are, however, inconsistent with allocative efficiency.

REFERENCES

Bagehot, Walter. 1873. *Lombard Street: A Description of the Money Market.* London: Henry S. King.

Benston, George J., and George C. Kaufman. 1995. "Is the Banking and Payments System Fragile?" *Journal of Financial Services Research 9*(4) (December).

Cowen, Tyler, and Randy Kroszner. 1994. *Explorations in the New Monetary Economics.* Oxford: Blackwell.

Deane, Marjorie, and Robert Pringle. 1994. *The Central Banks.* New York: Viking.

Diamond, Douglas W., and Philip H. Dybvig. 1983. "Bank Runs, Deposit Insurance, and Liquidity." *Journal of Political Economy 91*(3) (June), pp. 401–19.

Dowd, Kevin. 1989. *The State and the Monetary System.* New York: Philip Allan.

———, ed. 1992. *The Experience of Free Banking.* London: Routledge.

———. 1993. *Laissez-Faire Banking.* London: Routledge.

Glasner, David. 1989. *Free Banking and Monetary Reform.* Cambridge, UK: Cambridge University Press.

Goodhart, Charles. 1988. *The Evolution of Central Banks.* Cambridge, Massachusetts: MIT Press.

Greenspan, Alan. 1995. Remarks before The Economic Club of New York, New York City, June 20.

Hayek, F. A. 1976. *Choice in Currency: A Way to Stop Inflation.* London: Institute of Economic Affairs.

Horwitz, Steven. 1992. *Monetary Evolution, Free Banking, and Economic Order.* Boulder, Colorado: Westview Press.

Kaufman, George. 1994. "Bank Contagion: A Review of the Theory and Evidence." *Journal of Financial Services Research 8*(2) (April), pp. 123–50.

Pozdena, Randall J. 1991. "Is Banking Really Prone to Panics?" Federal Reserve Bank of San Francisco *Weekly Letter* 91–35 (October 11).

Sechrest, Larry J. 1993. *Free Banking: Theory, History, and a Laissez-Faire Model.* Westport, Connecticut: Quarum.

Selgin, George. 1988. *The Theory of Free Banking: Money Supply under Competitive Note Issue.* Totowa, New Jersey: Rowman and Littlefield.

Tobin, James. 1963. "Commercial Banks as Creators of 'Money'." In Deane Carson, ed., *Banking and Monetary Studies.* Homewood, Illinois: Richard D. Irwin, pp. 408–19.

White, Lawrence H. 1984. *Free Banking in Britain: Theory, Experience, and Debate, 1800–1845.* Cambridge, UK: Cambridge University Press.

Part I

THE NATURE
OF FREE BANKING

1

HOW WOULD THE INVISIBLE HAND HANDLE MONEY?*

with Lawrence H. White

INTRODUCTION

The last three decades have seen governments around the world remove a number of restrictions from financial markets and payments systems. Technological innovations have reduced the effectiveness of some surviving regulations, and a virtually unrestricted offshore banking market has grown to prominence.

During this same time some economists have become intrigued by the idea of a completely unregulated financial and payments system – the conceptual (if distant) endpoint of deregulation. What are the implications of *laissez-faire* in money and banking? What, in particular, would follow from allowing private institutions to provide all sorts of payment media (including currency) and intermediation services, free from political restrictions and without the supervision of government central banks?

Considerable controversy surrounds attempts to answer such questions. Describing the likely institutional arrangements of a *laissez-faire* monetary regime requires imaginative speculation. Trying to assess the *desirability* of the hypothesized institutions only compounds the speculation. The relevance and even indispensability of such speculation should nonetheless be clear: just as the positive understanding and normative assessment of tariffs require the hypothetical benchmark of pure free trade, so the understanding and assessment of current monetary regimes require the hypothetical benchmark of pure monetary *laissez-faire*. This chapter takes stock of recent attempts to characterize and analyze such a benchmark.

*Reprinted with permission, from the *Journal of Economic Literature*, Vol. XXXII, No. 4 (December 1994).

What is a *laissez-faire* monetary regime?

It is easy to note what is absent from a pure *laissez-faire* monetary regime. There is no government control of the quantity of exchange media. There is no state-sponsored central bank. There are no legal barriers to the entry, branching, or exit of commercial banks (or non-bank financial institutions, assuming any distinction can be drawn). There are no restrictions on the quantities, types, or mix of debt and equity claims a bank may issue, or on the quantities, types, or mix of assets it may hold. Interest rates are not controlled. There are no government deposit guarantees. In general, no restrictions are placed on the terms of contracts made between banks and their customers, beyond the requirement that they adhere to the standard legal principles governing all business contracts.

To say just what sorts of contracts and institutions a modern *laissez-faire* environment would support, and how well those institutions would work, is much more difficult. Nineteenth century proponents of "free banking" could generally share a common vision of *laissez-faire* in money and banking. They could, after all, observe competitive note-issue systems in many countries, including Adam Smith's Scotland, during the eighteenth and nineteenth centuries (Kurt Schuler 1992a).[1] They took for granted that a free market would continue to use silver or gold as its medium of account and most basic medium of exchange (with the most radical among them arguing that private mints could supply the appropriate coins). It took no great effort for them to imagine legally unrestricted and unprivileged banks competing in issuing both transferable deposits and circulating paper currency (banknotes), with competition compelling the banks to make their liabilities contractually and actually redeemable in the standard commodity money.

No similar consensus occurs in modern discussions. Instead, at least three strands of literature can be distinguished according to the different sorts of payment media each predicts would predominate under *laissez-faire*. The strands include: (1) a modern free banking literature that, much like its nineteenth century predecessor, proposes that an unregulated money and banking system would have a single, distinct base money, possibly but not necessarily a precious metal, and private-bank-issued monies in the traditional forms of banknotes and transferable deposits made redeemable in base money; (2) a small but influential group of works that associate the competitive supply of money with parallel private fiat-type monies, that is plural brands of non-commodity base money issued by private firms; and (3) related literatures known as the "new monetary economics" and the "legal restrictions theory" that envision competitive payments systems without any base money, with common media of exchange consisting entirely of claims, paying competitive rates of return, on banks or money-market mutual funds.

These capsule summaries obviously need to be unpacked and explained. In the sections that follow, we attempt to spell out the institutional features proposed by each strand of the modern literature and to consider these features' economic implications. In particular, we seek answers to the following questions: What would *laissez-faire* institutions and exchange media look like? How would the quantity of exchange media be determined, and what does this imply for the maintenance of macroeconomic equilibrium? How would an unregulated system cope with or prevent crises of confidence? We explore answers to these and related questions below, beginning with answers found in the modern free banking literature, and then turning to consider alternative answers found in the literatures on competing fiat-type monies and competitive payments systems without base money.

Sources of modern *laissez-faire* monetary thought

A brief background to the modern literature will further set the stage. Three broad trends in the economics profession, cited by Milton Friedman and Anna Schwartz (1986), have encouraged research on monetary *laissez-faire*: (1) the "rational expectations revolution," with its emphasis on studying the structure of policy regimes; (2) the emergence of public choice theory with its emphasis on constitutional political economy and its skeptical view of government; and (3) the revival of Austrian economics, with its attention to institutional orders formed spontaneously without central design. The most important real-world stimuli have come from ongoing financial deregulation as well as the widely criticized performance of existing central banking regimes. The high inflation rates of the 1970s and the difficult disinflation of the early 1980s prompted many observers to wonder whether alternative regimes might produce better outcomes.

Another source of inspiration can be found in the discussions of monetary optimality in the 1960s and early 1970s. Monetary theorists, originally concerned with the inefficiency of the US government policy prohibiting interest on demand deposits, tried to state precisely the conditions for efficiency or optimality in the holding of money balances. The question naturally arose: Would free competition produce optimal results in the market for money balances, just as it can (under the right conditions) produce optimality in competitive markets for ordinary goods?

In this discussion, Paul Samuelson (1968, 1969) argued the "nonoptimality of money holding under laissez-faire" on the grounds that there is a difference between the (positive) private and (zero) social costs of holding additional real cash balances: an individual's efforts to economize on holding socially costless money end up restricting the purchasing power of everyone's money balances, leaving everyone less well off. M. Friedman

(1969, pp. 38–9), on the other hand, claimed that one route to an optimum quantity of money (an alternative to his better-known proposal for an optimal rate of deflation to alleviate the private costs of holding additional real cash balances) "would be to permit free entry into banking, and to allow banks to issue both currency and deposits and to pay interest on both." Banks would also have to be freed from required holdings of non-interest-bearing reserves. Neither M. Friedman nor Samuelson, nor their critics (Robert Clower 1969, 1970; William P. Gramm 1974), discussed in any detail the likely structural features or practical implications of monetary *laissez-faire*. These writers as a group did, nonetheless, raise the issue for others to explore.

"FREE BANKING" WITH A DISTINCT BASE MONEY

Milton Friedman's competitive banking proposal embraces the main elements of monetary *laissez-faire* as envisioned in the modern free banking literature. Modern free banking theorists believe that *laissez-faire* banks would issue both banknotes and deposits while contractually binding themselves (in ways and for reasons discussed below) to redeem their liabilities in a common base money. This base money would both define the unit of account and serve as the banking system's ultimate means of settlement. The conventional role played by a single base money in such a "free banking" system makes the system more like existing arrangements than the other visions of *laissez-faire*, to be discussed later, which propose either multiple base monies or no base money at all.

Payments institutions and the monetary standard

The most obvious difference between free banking and current arrangements is that banks are allowed to issue currency (banknotes), as was common before the advent of central bank note monopolies in the nineteenth and early twentieth centuries. Currency has since declined in importance relative to deposits, and may continue to do so with the spread of point-of-sale electronic funds transfer. Free banking might not reverse this trend, but it would allow private banks to compete for shares in the market for currency, perhaps ushering in improvements in the quality of currency that could enhance demand for it. Perhaps, as M. Friedman suggests, private notes would bear interest. Alternatively, if transactions costs of collecting small amounts of interest on rapidly circulating hand-to-hand media are prohibitive, banks would compete entirely in non-price dimensions to promote their notes. We return to the question of interest payments below in connection with the legal restrictions theory of money. Of more immediate concern are the implications of competitive banknote issuance for the quality and quantity of money.

A common concern about competitive note issue is that it might give rise to an inconveniently non-uniform currency, with notes issued by different banks circulating at various discounts from par. Critics cite the example of the antebellum United States, which did indeed exhibit such non-uniformity. As discussed below, however, banking in the antebellum United States was hardly free. It was, in fact, based upon a patchwork of state regulatory systems, all of which were a far cry from *laissez-faire*. In particular, interstate (and sometimes even intrastate) branch banking was prohibited. Discounts on out-of-town notes largely reflected the transportation cost and risk of returning them to distant issuers for redemption (Gary Gorton 1991). In a truly unrestricted system, by contrast, banks (and note-issuing banks especially) would tend to branch widely, eliminating the distinction between local and out-of-town notes. Any two reputable banks would have an incentive to agree to accept one another's notes at par, just as US banks today agree to accept one another's ATM cards, because par acceptance at both banks promotes the circulation of both brands of notes (Lawrence H. White 1984a, pp. 19–22). In Scotland notes generally circulated at par once pairwise mutual acceptance pacts merged into a common note-exchange system in the 1770s. Even in New England, which did not allow branch banking, a note exchange organized by the Suffolk Bank of Boston brought par acceptance to banknotes by the 1830s (George Trivoli 1979).

Most discussions of free banking assume that the monetary base does not include currency or deposits issued by an extant central bank. By itself, however, free banking does not uniquely specify the base money regime. Base money could be gold or silver, as would be consistent with the evolution of a monetary system in which government had never intervened.[2] Or it could be some fiat money, with the stock of fiat money permanently frozen (or otherwise determined by a strict rule) to eliminate any scope for discretionary monetary policy (M. Friedman 1984; Selgin 1988).

Money supply and reserve holding

With a frozen monetary base, the behavior of the money stock would depend entirely on the behavior of the money multiplier (the ratio of bank-issued money to bank reserves). More generally, the money-supply implications of free banking are distinct from the implications of any particular monetary standard. For this reason we do not discuss here the money-supply properties of any particular base money regime.

One potential advantage of letting banks issue notes (and possibly token coins), without statutory reserve requirements, is that the banks could then accommodate changes in the public's desired currency–deposit ratio simply by changing the mix of their note and deposit liabilities. In the simplest case, where banknotes alone are normally employed as currency and the desired reserve ratios for notes and deposits are the same, no change would be required in the overall quantity of money or bank credit. Formally, the stock of base money, B, is equal to the stock of bank reserves, R, while the money stock, M, is equal to the stock of bank deposits, D, plus outstanding banknotes, N:

$$B = R \tag{1}$$

and

$$M = D + N, \tag{2}$$

Equilibrium requires that actual reserves equal desired reserves,

$$R = r(D + N), \tag{3}$$

where $r = R/M$ is the desired reserve ratio. Combining (1)–(3) to eliminate D and N gives

$$M/B = 1/r, \tag{4}$$

which shows the independence of the free banking money multiplier, M/B, from the public's desired currency–deposit ratio.

In a conventional central banking arrangement, in contrast, all currency takes the form of base money. This means that, in place of (1) and (2) above, we have

$$B = R + C \tag{1'}$$

and

$$M = D + C, \tag{2'}$$

where C stands for public holdings of base money. Because commercial bank liabilities do not include banknotes, the condition for reserve equilibrium is simply

$$R = r(D). \tag{3'}$$

Letting $c = C/D$ denote the public's desired currency–deposit ratio and substituting to eliminate D and C yields

$$M/B = (1 + c)/(r + c). \tag{4'}$$

The expression on the right-handside is the standard textbook money multiplier. Unlike the free banking multiplier, it implies that, holding B constant, a change in the public's desired currency–deposit ratio alters the equilibrium quantity of money. The public's attempts to draw currency from their deposit accounts cause reserve drains from banks, which forces them to contract their balance sheets, unless the central bank promptly and appropriately increases the monetary base. A centralized currency supply is thus seen to create information (and possibly incentive) problems not necessarily present with a decentralized supply.

The absence of statutory reserve requirements, coupled with free note issue, would not imply an infinite or indeterminate money multiplier, because the desired reserve ratio (r in equations (3) and (4)) would not go to zero. Standard inventory-theoretic models of prudential reserve demand indicate that each bank in a multi-bank system has a well-determined demand for base money reserves in relation to the size and turnover of its liabilities.[3] Even if the public have become so accustomed to banknotes and token coins that they never seek to redeem bank-issued money for base money over the counter, each bank holds reserves to meet its potential interbank clearing obligations. These obligations arise when the quantity of bank j's notes and checks deposited into rival banks, which return them for settlement, exceeds the quantity of rival banks' liabilities collected by bank j between clearing sessions. Bank j optimizes by equating the marginal cost of holding reserves (foregone interest) to the marginal benefit (the value of the reduced probability of default on clearing obligations) at a positive level of reserves. Formally, following Ernst Baltensperger (1980, p. 5), optimization implies a choice of R_j such that

$$r = p \int_{R_j}^{\infty} f(X)dX \qquad (5)$$

where R_j is the quantity of reserves held by bank j at the onset of the planning period, r and p represent the per-dollar opportunity cost of reserve holding and the per-dollar adjustment cost of a reserve deficit, respectively, X represents the net reserve loss of bank j over the course of the period, and $f(X)$ is the density function of X. As Baltensperger notes, where X is symmetrically distributed with a mean of zero, equation (5) implies that R_j will be positive if and only if $p > 2r$. This condition is plausible when p includes all the transaction costs of arranging a loan or liquidating assets on short notice.

The above discussion takes for granted that a free banking system will support several rival banks. Laidler (1992, p. 197) expresses the fear that economies of scale implied by the theory of reserve demand might "prompt unregulated banks to merge into one institution." The ensuing natural monopoly would of course be free from any need for reserves for interbank settlements. Both theory and history suggest, however, that reserve economies tend to be offset in practice by scale diseconomies in other aspects of the banking business (Kevin Dowd 1992c; Schuler 1992a). Instead of exhibiting natural monopoly, past free banking systems (or near-free banking systems) typically supported many banks of issue, most of which captured some reserve-holding economies through extensive branch networks. (The Scottish system in the early nineteenth century, for example, had around twenty banks of issue competing at any moment, most of them widely branched.) These banks in turn often pooled their reserves in one or more clearinghouses, which achieved further reserve economies by arranging multilateral rather than bilateral settlement of interbank clearing obligations.

Some writers, while granting the presence of rising marginal costs of note issue for each bank considered individually, fear that the reserve ratio for a free banking system taken as a whole might be unanchored. If all banks expand in concert, no expanding bank systematically loses reserves. Therefore, the argument goes, concerted expansion and contraction might cause the money multiplier to vary pro-cyclically (Charles P. Kindleberger 1978, ch. 4; Charles Goodhart 1988, p. 50; Laidler 1992). The standard inventory-theoretic model of reserve demand indicates, however, that a bank's prudential or precautionary demand for reserves depends on the anticipated variance and not just the mean or expected value of the bank's reserve losses (Selgin 1993). Although perfect in-concert expansion does not affect any bank's mean clearing losses, it does increase the variance of each bank's clearing losses, and does therefore increase each bank's precautionary demand for reserves. The reserve ratio remains well anchored. To see this in a simple model, let bank j be a representative member of a system of banks starting with identical market shares. Suppose that all purchases are made using banknotes or checks, and that every transaction is for one dollar. Let $X_i \sim (0, \sigma_{x_i})$ be a symmetrically distributed random variable representing the effect of a single transaction on bank j's share of total bank reserves, R, with

$X_i = \$1$ if the transaction involves a withdrawal from bank j;
$X_i = -\$1$ if the transaction involves a deposit to bank j; and
$X_i = 0$ otherwise.

Let

$$X \sim (0, \sigma) = \sum_{i=1}^{T} X_i$$

represent the net reserve loss to bank j over the course of a planning period involving T transactions. If X is approximately normal, optimization requires that

$$R_j = b\sigma = b\sigma_{x_i}(T)^{\frac{1}{2}} \tag{6}$$

where $b = p/r$. If, instead of having a nominal value of one dollar, each transaction is for P dollars, (6) becomes

$$R_j = Pb\sigma_{x_i}(T)^{\frac{1}{2}} \tag{6'}$$

By interpreting P as the "price level," we can relate the optimal reserve condition in (6') to the condition for overall monetary equilibrium as given by the equation of exchange,

$$MV_T = PT \tag{7}$$

where M is the aggregate stock of bank money (assumed to consist of equal quantities of each bank's notes and deposits), V_T is the planning-period value of the transactions velocity of money, and T again represents the number of transactions per planning period. Subsituting to eliminate P and rearranging gives

$$R_j = b\sigma_{x_i} MV_T(T)^{\frac{1}{2}}, \tag{8}$$

which shows that, holding V_T and T (and, hence, the public's real demand for money) and b constant, any increase in M entails a proportionate increase in the representative bank's demand for reserves. A given stock of reserves implies a unique equilibrium quantity of bank money.

What happens, though, if members of a clearing system develop ways to use an interest-earning asset rather than base money for interbank settlements? It is easy to imagine commercial banks using interest-bearing deposit balances in a jointly owned fractional-reserve clearinghouse bank. (The use of securities would raise information costs and would create the problem – perhaps not insoluble – of how the paying and receiving banks would split the difference between a security's bid and asked prices.) In the limit, with clearinghouse reserves of base money economized to zero and hand-to-hand currency entirely bank issued, so that neither the banking system nor the public holds any base money, the purchasing power of base money would depend entirely on non-monetary demand for the substance comprising base money. Under a commodity standard the value of the unit of account (a standard unit of the base money commodity) would still be determinate. Under a fiat standard, the value of the unit of account would go to zero (because there is no non-monetary demand for fiat money), placing the system's viability in doubt.[4] We discuss below alternative proposals of "the new monetary economics" for maintaining a valuable unit of account in a system without base money reserves by separating the unit-of-account function from the medium-of-redemption-and-settlement function.

The theory of prudential reserve demand, extended to notes as well as deposits, has at least one other interesting macroeconomic implication: a free banking system tends to stabilize the flow of money income. Let $y = kT$ and $V = kV_T$, where k is the quantity of real income per monetary transaction ($0 < k < 1$) and y and V are planning-period values of real income and the income velocity of money, respectively. Equation (8) can then be rewritten as

$$R_j = b\sigma_{x_i} MVy^{\frac{1}{2}}k^{-\frac{1}{2}}, \tag{8'}$$

which shows that, for given values of y, k, and R, a change in V will produce an opposite and offsetting change in M to preserve an equilibrium of reserve supply and demand. A fall in velocity, for example, because it reduces the flow of notes through the clearing system and therefore reduces precautionary reserve demand, prompts an offsetting increase in the money multiplier and thereby in the money stock (Selgin 1994b). The "hoarding" of bank money thus does not have the deflationary consequences it tends to have in conventional banking systems. Market forces compel banks to issue more money when, at given prices, more of it is demanded by the public, stabilizing nominal aggregate demand.[5] This stabilizing property is weakened, however, if the public insist on holding base money, as they might during a systemwide crisis of confidence (Carl Christ 1990).

Crises of confidence

The question naturally arises: how will a free banking system prevent or respond to a crisis of confidence, when bank money ceases to be preferred to base money and customers are inclined to run on their banks? A systemic banking crisis is likely if a "contagion effect" causes one bank failure to trigger systemwide runs, implying large-scale demands to redeem bank-notes and deposits for base money. Assuming that banks hold only fractional reserves of base money, systemwide runs can result in widespread bank failures, undermining the payments system. The desirability of preventing or containing systemic banking crises commonly underlies the case for an official lender of last resort or other departures from *laissez-faire*, such as government-sponsored deposit insurance.

Research on the susceptibility of free banking systems to crises of confidence has asked: (1) whether the threat of systemic crises has been as great in real-world banking systems as the contagion-effect argument would suggest; (2) whether legal restrictions have been an important contributing factor to historical crises; and (3) whether private arrangements under *laissez-faire* might be able to eliminate the threat of runs and panics.

Contagion effects are not easy to find in practice. Surveys of global experience show that banking systems outside the United States have rarely suffered genuine banking panics (Bordo 1986; Schwartz 1986, 1988a, 1988b). While some attribute this fact to the presence of more "dependable" central banks in other countries, an alternative explanation is that other countries in the past have benefited from having less regulated banking systems. Many of the countries in question avoided panics even while they lacked central banks or other public lenders of last resort (Selgin 1994a).

Even US experience does not offer strong support for the contagion-effect hypothesis. Antebellum US "free banking" systems did not clearly exhibit contagion effects (Arthur J. Rolnick and Warren E. Weber 1986);[6] and of the five or six major panics (1873, 1884, 1890, 1893, 1907; perhaps also 1896) during the National Banking era, only three involved suspensions of payments. Among them, failure statistics suggest that only the 1893 panic involved a nationwide contagion (George Kaufman 1988, p. 566, 1993). Runs against National Banks appear to have been triggered by news indicating probable bank insolvency, contrary to the theory that depositors stage runs simply out of fear that others might run (Gorton 1985, 1988). Furthermore, bank customers in the National Banking era panics attempted to redeem deposits for currency, but generally did not attempt to redeem banknotes for gold or other legal tender (R. Alton Gilbert 1988, pp. 137–8, n. 3); in northern states holdings of Canadian banknotes also increased. These facts suggest that fear of currency shortage (banknote issue was legally restricted) rather than fear of bank failure was at work.

Contagion effects also appear to have played a more limited role than is usually supposed during the "Great Contraction" of 1930 to 1933. Prior to 1932, bank runs were confined mainly to banks that were either pre-run insolvent themselves or affiliates of other insolvent firms (Elmus Wicker 1980). Serious regional contagions erupted in late 1932, but these were aggravated if not triggered by state governments' policy of declaring bank "holidays" in response to mounting bank failures (George J. Benston et al. 1986, p. 52). The truly nationwide panic that gripped the nation in the early months of 1933 appears to have been more a run on the dollar than a run on the banking system, triggered by rumors that Roosevelt intended to reduce the dollar's gold content (Barrie A. Wigmore 1987).

A second line of historical research finds that an array of legal restrictions on banks has contributed to past clusters of bank failures, suggesting that crises would be even less frequent under *laissez-faire*. The interaction of reserve requirements, anti-branching rules and restrictions on note issue fostered the panics of the National Banking era, because they prevented banks from issuing additional notes or effectively mobilizing reserves to meet peak demands for currency, instead promoting an interbank scramble for base money. The absence of panics in Canada, which lacked the restrictions found in the United States, supports the hypothesis that regulatory restrictions were instrumental in fostering panics (Alexander Dana Noyes 1910; Vera Smith [1936] 1990; Selgin 1989; Richard M. Salsman 1990). Legal restrictions may also have impeded the flow of bank-specific information that could have eliminated contagion effects. In a system where dispersed banks issue notes, a secondary (dealer) market for banknotes arises. Observed discounts in such a market (which functioned in the United States until the Civil War) provide ordinary noteholders with expert information on the soundness of issuers, eliminating information asymmetries that might otherwise encourage contagion effects (Gorton and Donald

J. Mullineaux 1987). By effectively closing the secondary market for banknotes, National Banking regulations made the banking system more susceptible to runs and panics.

A number of analysts have pointed to ways in which US banking regulations have increased the frequency of recent bank failures: restrictions on branch banking have prevented diversification, making banks much more vulnerable to sector-specific shocks; Regulation Q ceilings on deposit interest rates led to the massive deposit outflows of the 1960s and 1970s; federal deposit guarantees have undermined depositor discipline and encouraged banks to take greater risks (Salsman 1990; Benston 1991). Central banks acting as "lenders of last resort" have promoted risk taking by providing life-support to insolvent banks, violating the "classical" rule of providing liquidity to the market only, because of inadequate information and because of a bureaucratic tendency to err in the direction of providing excessive assistance (Arnoud W. Boot and Anjan V. Thakor 1993). The most serious charge against central banks, however, concerns their monetary as opposed to regulatory policies. Many episodes of financial instability have been linked to dramatic movements in the price level and in nominal interest rates (Schwartz 1988a) produced by discretionary central banks.

Evidence of inappropriate regulations or destabilizing central bank policy does not, of course, constitute a case against bank regulation or central banking *per se* (Bordo 1991). Such evidence does, however, suggest a need to distinguish carefully between weaknesses and instabilities that are traceable to regulations and those that are inherent to fractional-reserve banking.

"Inherent" instability and contractual remedies

A third avenue of research argues that observed banking contracts have been significantly influenced by legal restrictions and that modified contracts could relieve or entirely eliminate the threat of panics under *laissez-faire*. Discussion here has centered around Douglas W. Diamond and Philip H. Dybvig's (1983) influential model of bank runs, which has been viewed as showing that a harmful instability is inherent to *laissez-faire* banking. A Diamond–Dybvig bank is unstable because it faces uncertain deposit withdrawals and holds assets that are less liquid than its deposits. This instability spoils the beneficial risk-sharing arrangement provided by the bank.

The Diamond–Dybvig bank operates in a three-period world. In period 0 the bank offers a contract to its depositors (who together contribute all its funds; it has no distinct equity shareholders) and invests the proceeds in production projects that will not come to maturity until period 2. In period 1, a depositor may elect to withdraw a prespecified (debt-like) payment or to wait for a pro-rata (equity-like) share of the bank's investment returns to be paid in period 2. Some depositors randomly discover that they need to withdraw in period 1; others find the payoff to waiting higher unless they anticipate a run. If few enough depositors opt to withdraw during period 1, the scheme makes all of its participants better off. If too many depositors opt to withdraw, however, the bank must liquidate its investments prematurely at a loss, defaulting on late-in-line claims. Running to withdraw is an individually rational strategy if it is the strategy others are playing. Consequently there are two possible outcomes: a good equilibrium, in which only those depositors who really need liquidity withdraw in period 1, and a bad equilibrium, which represents a bank run.

For our purposes, the most fundamental question to ask about the Diamond–Dybvig model is whether the run-prone contract it posits actually represents a plausible *laissez-faire* outcome. Deposits in the model constitute unconditionally demandable debt at the end of period 1, with a first-come-first-served rule for meeting withdrawals (a "sequential service constraint") and with default in prospect for the last claims serviced. This contractual structure is what makes the payoff for running on the bank potentially higher than the payoff for not running. Rather than offer such an insecure contractual arrangement, *laissez-faire* banks would presumably seek to make the claims they issue "run-proof" or at least run-resistant. Logically such run-proofing must involve modifying (1) the debt nature of the banking contract, or (2) the rule for meeting redemption requests, or (3) the likelihood of a diminished payoff for the last customer in line.

A wide array of economists, including both proponents and critics of monetary *laissez-faire*, have noted that the problem of runs on checking accounts can be avoided by linking checking services to equity claims (such as money-market mutual fund accounts) rather than to debt claims (such as demand deposits). There is no point in running on a mutual fund, because there is no greater expected payoff from closing one's account ahead of others. Any fall in the value of a mutual fund's assets is shared immediately by all account holders. A large enough fall in the value of an ordinary bank's assets, by contrast, brings the value of assets below the (unchanged) value of debt claims, in which case depositors who close their accounts first may get a greater payoff than those who close their accounts last.

In light of these considerations, some economists predict that checkable money-market mutual fund accounts, being run-proof, would dominate demand deposits in a *laissez-faire* system without deposit insurance (Tyler Cowen and Randall Kroszner 1990, 1994). But, notwithstanding the advantages of money-market mutual fund accounts, there are countervailing advantages that might allow demandable debt exchange media to survive under *laissez-faire*. Equity shares, with fluctuating values, would be inconvenient to use as currency. Customers might prefer interest-bearing demandable debt (with its prespecified nominal return) for their checking accounts, simply because it makes account balances more predictable and easier to track (White 1984b). Even relatively uninformed agents can trade demandable bank debt conveniently and without loss, making it more widely marketable than equity (Gary Gorton and George Pennacchi 1990). A more sophisticated reason for demandable debt to survive is that it beneficially constrains banks to act in the interest of claimholders, precisely because claimholders have the option of forcing liquidation. This option, in combination with a first-come-first-served rule for meeting redemption requests, gives claimholders an incentive to monitor the bank's financial condition, overcoming a possible free-rider problem (Mitchell Berlin 1987; Charles W Calomiris and Charles M. Khan 1991). As long as it survives for any reason, demandable bank debt can function cheaply and conveniently as a payment medium, holding its own with money-market funds accounts under *laissez-faire* provided that its default risk is sufficiently low (David Glasner 1989, pp. 195–201).

A second type of run-proofing arrangement, much discussed in the modern free banking literature, preserves the demandable-debt nature of bank-issued money but modifies the rule for meeting redemption demands. Discussions of bank runs and panics ordinarily assume that a bank continues to pay out base money until either all demands are satisfied or the bank is declared bankrupt. An alternative exists: a bank may suspend payments of base money before such payments render it insolvent and force it into bankruptcy. Although suspension is often regarded as inherently a violation of a bank's contractual obligations to holders of its demandable debt, the unconditional demandability of banknotes and some deposit liabilities may be the result of legal restrictions rather than market forces (Rockoff 1986, pp. 618–23). Under *laissez-faire*, bank liabilities might be conditionally demandable only. A bank might contractually reserve the option to suspend for a limited time the redeemability of its notes or demand deposits, as Scottish banks did with banknotes before 1765 (when the practice was outlawed) and as banks do today when they include "notice of withdrawal" clauses in deposit contracts. Suspension-clause contracts can benefit both a bank and its customers by interrupting a run that might otherwise lead to "fire-sale" losses and consequent bankruptcy through rapid liquidation of assets (Gorton 1985; Dowd 1988). A mutually beneficial suspension clause must be incentive compatible such that a bank will not choose to suspend when suspension is not in the interests of liability holders. Scottish "optional" notes seem to have been designed with such incentive compatibility in mind when they obligated the issuing bank to pay a high rate of interest on suspended notes.

Diamond and Dybvig (1983) consider suspension contracts a potential arrangement for dealing with runs, but conclude that suspension is undesirable because it interferes with consumption. This conclusion depends on the absence of bank-issued money from the Diamond–Dybvig economy. If demandable bank debt itself functions as a medium of exchange, that is takes the form of banknotes or transferable deposits, then the inability of a bank's customers to redeem bank liabilities during a suspension does not necessarily prevent them from acquiring consumption goods (Selgin 1993). Also, Diamond and Dybvig find government deposit insurance preferable to contractual alternatives only because they impose a sequential service constraint on their bank but not on their proposed government deposit insurance agency. Their deposit insurance scheme is infeasible when the deposit insurance agency faces the same sequential service constraint that the bank faces. When the constraint is not imposed on the bank, the bank can replicate Diamond and Dybvig's deposit insurance privately by making deposit payoffs contingent on the number of depositors who opt to withdraw in a period (Neil Wallace 1988b; J. Huston McCulloch and Min-Teh Yu 1993).

A third category of "run-proofing" arrangements discussed in the modern free banking literature consists of devices for reducing the likelihood that a bank will be unable to provide a full payoff to the last customer in line. The Diamond–Dybvig bank issues only a single hybrid contract under which depositors who wait to withdraw become residual claimants. Such a contract is more run-prone than an ordinary bank deposit, where distinct equity owners insulate depositors against all but extraordinary losses. A bank that issues equity claims to a distinct class of shareholders provides an equity cushion to redeem the deposits withdrawn before the bank's investments mature. Sufficient capital would eliminate the danger of default on deposits and consequently the bank-run equilibrium in the Diamond–Dybvig model (Jurgen Eichberger and Frank Milne 1990; Dowd 1992a). One device for ensuring capital adequacy (though it may not provide for optimal risk sharing between depositors and shareholders), used historically in Sweden and Scotland (Lars Jonung 1989; White 1992), is for bank shareholders to accept unlimited liability for a bank's debts. In Canada, double liability served a similar purpose.

In the (non-*laissez-faire*) postbellum US National Banking system, another device for solvency assurance was observed: commercial bank clearinghouses served as certifying and regulatory agencies and as private lenders of last resort. We discuss these institutions below.

Private deposit insurance might represent still another device for assuring depositors that, even in the event of insolvency, the last depositor in line will get a full payout. Competition in insurance has the advantage of tending to generate genuinely risk-based premiums, avoiding the risk subsidization associated with the flat premium structure of the FDIC. A tax-funded monopoly like the FDIC lacks the profit motive and the competitive-market test that compel private insurers to discover and charge risk-appropriate premiums (Eugenie D. Short and Gerald P. O'Driscoll

1983; O'Driscoll 1988). The question remains, however, whether private insurers could cover the seemingly non-diversifiable risks posed by bank-run contagions and by macroeconomic shocks (William S. Haraf 1988), to the extent that such risks would be present in a *laissez-faire* environment.

HISTORICAL EPISODES OF COMPETITIVE NOTE ISSUE

Of the various theoretical visions of monetary *laissez-faire*, only free banking with a distinct base money has been even approximately realized in history. How well any particular historical experience illustrates the features of *laissez-faire* banking depends of course on how close the approximation was. In the United States, it was not very close. In Scotland and elsewhere, it was closer. A brief review of modern research on historical "free banking" episodes seems in order before moving on to consider alternative, more hypothetical, visions of monetary *laissez-faire*.

America, Scotland and elsewhere

The seminal work by Rockoff (1974) dispels the previously common misconceptions that the "free banking" laws passed by various American state governments between 1837 and 1861 instituted *laissez-faire* regimes and that the laws frequently gave rise to "wildcat" banking. State "free banking" laws may have allowed freer entry into banking, but they required banks to collateralize their notes by lodging specified assets (usually state government bonds) with state authorities. Various state governments also restricted branch banking and outlawed notes that were postdated or that gave the issuer an option to delay redemption. An American state "free banking" regime was thus "a far cry from pure laissez-faire" (Rockoff 1991, p. 75).[7]

As for wildcat banks, Rockoff finds that poorly designed note-collateral regulations actually encouraged them in some states. Wildcatting was nonetheless rare. Subsequent studies of bank failures during the US "free banking" era have minimized the problem of wildcat banking even further (Rolnick and Weber 1983, 1984; Andrew J. Economopolous 1988, 1990).

Although wildcatting was rare, US "free banking" laws had other short-comings. Overall bank failure rates appear to have been relatively high in "free banking" states (James A. Kahn 1985). The reason may have been that free banks, not having to worry about forfeiting a stream of monopoly rents, pursued riskier strategies and were more prone to failure than chartered banks (Siu-ki Leung 1991), though this hypothesis contradicts a finding that the laws appear not to have actually increased entry (Kenneth Ng 1988). The laws certainly did not help state banking systems cope with crises like the panic of 1857 (Rockoff 1991). Because US "free banking" systems were far from *laissez-faire*, such flaws may have been the results of regulation rather than of competitive banking. For example, clusters of "free bank" failures were principally due to falling prices of the state bonds they held, suggesting that bond-collateral requirements caused bank portfolios to become overloaded with state bonds (Rolnick and Weber 1984, 1986; White 1986a).[8]

Naturally, nineteenth century proponents of free banking did not point to banking in the United States generally as a model to be emulated. They pointed instead to the less restricted banking systems of Scotland (1716–1844), New England (1820–60), and Canada (1817–1914). Though the Canadian and New England systems have been the subjects of some recent research (Schuler 1992b; Mullineaux 1987), Scotland has become the most discussed of the three. Attempts to offer Scotland as a model free banking system (Rondo Cameron 1967; White 1984a, 1987) have prompted debate about just how free, competitive, and independent the Scottish system was.[9] Two main questions have arisen:

1 Did the legal privileges of the three Scottish chartered banks, namely their exclusive access to limited liability and the receivability of their notes for payment of government duties (Jack Carr, Sherry Glied, and Frank Mathewson 1989; Cowen and Kroszner 1989) significantly impair competition? Evidence on bank structure and conduct indicates that the answer is no: competition was in fact vigorous. The chartered banks lost any structural dominance they may have previously enjoyed when numerous large joint-stock banks entered after 1810 (Munn 1982). The spread between the interest rate on loans and the rate on deposits was in the highly competitive neighborhood of only 1 per cent (S. G. Checkland 1975, pp. 384–88). Cartel agreements on interest rates could not be sustained (Checkland 1975, pp. 449–50; Munn 1982, p. 122).

2 Was the Scottish system merely a "satellite to the London centre," as Charles Goodhart (1987, p. 131) puts it? In particular, did the Bank of England act as a central bank or lender of last resort for the Scottish banks (Goodhart 1988, pp. 51–2; Larry J. Sechrest 1993, ch. 5; Cowen and Kroszner 1989)? Again, the evidence indicates negative answers. The Scottish banks did buy and sell assets in the London financial market, but they did not hold deposits at the Bank of England nor, it seems, any significant quantity of its notes (Checkland 1975, p. 194). Nor did the Bank of England make last-resort loans to the Scottish banks. The Bank did extend long-term credit to the Royal Bank of Scotland in the calm year of 1830, but required the Royal Bank to repay during the next period of credit stringency, in 1836 – exactly the reverse of last-resort lending (Checkland 1975, p. 444).

Other important episodes of banknote competition took place in Australia, China, Colombia, France, Ireland, Spain, Sweden, and Switzerland. In all, there appear to have been at least 60 countries or colonies that allowed note issue by competing private banks, subject to varying degrees of regulation (Roland Vaubel 1984a; Schuler 1992a; Dowd 1992b). An important question raised by the sheer number of these systems of competitive note issue, all the more puzzling when it is reported that nearly all of them appear to have worked successfully, is why central banking so universally supplanted them.

Private clearinghouses

A related line of historical research asks: how and how well did these past competitive note-issue systems regulate themselves? The Scottish and Suffolk note-exchange systems were often praised in the nineteenth century for tightly regulating the volume of notes circulated by Scottish and New England banks. In addition to their more prosaic functions, nineteenth century clearinghouse associations in the United States served as private bank-certifying and regulatory agencies and even as lenders of last resort (Richard H. Timberlake 1984; Mullineaux 1987; Gorton and Mullineaux 1987). These and other experiences suggest that member banks of a *laissez-faire* clearing system would jointly agree to conform to clearinghouse solvency and liquidity standards, and to allow their enforcement via audits, because each bank wants credible assurance that notes and deposits issued by the other members (which it is accepting at par) will be redeemed in full. The availability of clearinghouse-mediated loans to illiquid member banks helps to insure solvent banks against "fire-sale" losses in the event of liquidity problems, thereby reducing the incentive of customers to stage runs in the first place.

It is not clear just how many of the regulatory or "hierarchical" aspects of the US clearinghouses would survive in a pure *laissez-faire* environment. When banknotes trade at bank-specific discounts, as they do before the formation of an effective par-acceptance and clearing arrangement, note prices embody information about bank-specific risks. Once notes trade at par, clearinghouse or other hierarchical supervision may be needed to overcome information asymmetries between banks and their customers and the consequent danger of contagion effects (Gorton and Mullineaux 1987). But the emergency issuing function of the US clearinghouses, and possibly some of their regulatory functions, were by-products of legal restrictions peculiar to the United States, particularly restrictions on note-issue and branch banking (Dowd 1994; Steven Horwitz 1990; Selgin and White 1988). Clearinghouses appear to have provided less supervision in the less-regulated Scottish and Canadian banking systems, though even these clearinghouses would expel members for unsound practices. These two systems largely managed to avoid crises despite the par acceptance of banknotes. Although the Canadian crises of 1907 and 1914 suggest to some monetary historians the value of a public lender of last resort (Bordo 1990), those crises were due at least in part to legal restrictions, namely restrictions that had become binding on the note issues of Canadian banks (Donald R. Wells 1989; Schuler 1992b).

Goodhart (1988; see also Laidler 1992), in an important critique of monetary *laissez-faire*, argues that private regulation cannot adequately address enforcement and incentive problems present in a system of competing banks of issue. Bank reserves will tend to become concentrated in a dominant commercial bank, transforming it into a "bankers' bank." Conflicts of interest will then naturally lead subservient banks to welcome the replacement of the private bankers' bank with a government central bank. Goodhart's theory is incongruous with the facts in a number of ways. First, except where one bank has enjoyed special legal privileges, the note-issuing banks have relied upon a non-competitive clearinghouse, rather than a rival commercial bank, to manage their reserves while avoiding conflicts of interest. Moreover, in no country has central banking originated from private bankers' petitioning to have their clearinghouse nationalized. As Goodhart's own case studies show, central banks have instead been established unilaterally by governments, without the express consent and often in the face of express disapproval by the banking community (e.g., the Bank of Canada), or have grown out of grants of legal privilege to particular private banks (e.g., the Bank of England) (Bordo and Redish 1987; Dowd 1991). As Smith ([1936] 1990, p. 148) correctly puts it:

> A central bank is not a natural product of banking development. It is imposed from outside or comes into being as a result of Government favours.

Showing that central banking has non-market origins does not, of course, settle the question of whether it is desirable. For most economists, a positive or negative verdict on the desirability of central banking will depend on what theory and history indicate about the likelihood that a government agency will design and implement a more appropriate set of regulations on banking and the money supply than private market institutions will.

COMPETING NON-COMMODITY BASE MONIES

Because it focuses on the implications of competition in the supply of redeemable bank money, the modern free banking literature does not as such address the question of competition in the production of base money. Full-bodied commodity monies can be and historically have been competitively supplied by private mining companies and mints (Donald H. Kagin 1981). The possibility of competitive minting under a metallic standard has been discussed only in passing by academic economists (Murray N. Rothbard 1970, pp. 59–60; Selgin and White 1987), but its implications are fairly straightforward: coins will be manufactured to meet the common standard of weight and fineness for the monetary unit, whatever it may be, and minting services will be priced at marginal cost.[10]

The implications of competition in the supply of a non-commodity base money are far less straightforward. The fiat monies of various governments compete to some extent, though not in an entirely *laissez-faire* environment, as studied by the literature on "currency substitution" (Lance Girton and Don Roper 1981). But one can imagine, as Benjamin Klein (1974) and F. A. Hayek (1978) have, *laissez-faire* competition among multiple brands of "private fiat money."[11]

Is private fiat-type money viable?

The key question concerning private fiat-type money is whether there is a tenable equilibrium in which it has a positive value, given the apparent profitability (whenever its value is positive) of printing more of it. Unlike banks offering redeemable notes and deposits, issuers of non-redeemable paper money would not be constrained by limited reserves. Would anything else effectively constrain them?

An early argument held that competitive issue of fiat-type money could not be viable because any individual issuer would find it profitable to keep printing dollars so long as a 10 dollar bill (or a 10-to-whatever-power dollar bill) was worth more than the paper on which it was printed. In equilibrium the money would be valueless, or would become a literal paper standard (M. Friedman 1960, p. 7). As stated, the argument assumes that anyone has the right to print indistinguishable "dollars." Such an assumption denies a critical feature of ordinary market competition, namely firms' enforceable brand names in their products (Klein 1974, pp. 429–31; Earl Thompson 1974). The suboptimal (hyperinflationary) outcome is not due to competition *per se*, but to poorly defined or unprotected property rights.

Hayek (1978, pp. 43–6) suggests that private producers of fiat-type monies bearing legally protected brand names would outcompete both commodity-based monies and government fiat monies by promising greater stability of purchasing power. Each issuer would pledge to hold the purchasing power of its money constant in terms of a specified price-index basket. But the pledge would not be a legally enforceable commitment of the sort embodied in a redemption contract: "it would be neither necessary nor desirable that [an issuer] tie itself legally to a particular standard" because a particular standard (a specific index basket) might become outdated.

But would the keeping of such a non-enforceable pledge be consistent with profit maximization? A profit-maximizing fiat-type issuer could choose to hyperinflate its own brand of money, and would do so if staying in business promised less than the one-shot profit available from an unanticipated hyperinflation. Klein frames the viability question clearly – without finally resolving it – as the question of whether the present value of staying in business, embodied in an issuer's "brand name capital," would exceed the issuer's profit from "cheating." A private issuer's non-enforceable pledge to hold the purchasing power of its money constant, as envisioned by Hayek, might be "time-inconsistent" in the sense of Finn E. Kydland and Edward C. Prescott (1977).

If money-holders had perfect foresight, cheating by a fiat-type issuer would of course be impossible. Equivalently, if each fiat-type issuer could make an enforceable precommitment with an infinite horizon regarding its money's purchasing power, then free competition would compel each issuer to furnish a money that appreciates in value at a competitive rate. Competition *would* then provide the optimum quantity of money in M. Friedman's sense. Under imperfect foresight, or if precommitment is impossible, private fiat-type money would not be viable; that is, it would hyperinflate and have zero value in equilibrium (Taub 1985a).

Although Klein (1974, pp. 436–7) writes out conditions for a non-hyperinflationary equilibrium (in which private fiat money has a positive value) under "imperfect foresight," his conditions may define only a local profit maximum for a fiat-type issuer, at which profits are less than those from hyperinflation. Klein's equilibrium requires that consumers sufficiently penalize an issuer who surprises them through monetary expansion by reducing the "rental price" they are willing to pay (the difference between the nominal interest on that issuer's brand of money and the nominal interest rate on other assets denominated in the same brand of money). To prevent hyperinflation from being the issuer's global profit-maximizing choice, the rental price must be capable of falling to negative infinity, which has curious implications. Perhaps more importantly, the equivalent of perfect foresight prevails in Klein's "imperfect foresight" equilibrium. In the event of an unexpected expansion, consumers correctly estimate the magnitude by which they must reduce the rental price and make the adjustment instantaneously. To do this, they implicitly must know the size of the surprise expansion, and correctly estimate the potential profit from an unpenalized monetary surprise of that size. It is hard, given these assumptions, to accept Klein's characterization of the equilibrium as one of imperfect inflation-rate foresight.

Redeemability as a "goods-back" guarantee

The time-inconsistency problem in the private issue of name-brand fiat-type money is an instance of the customer-assurance problem that generally faces any producer who attempts to market a copyright-protected durable good (like an artist's lithographs) at a price clearly exceeding its marginal cost of production (Ronald H. Coase 1972; David Glasner 1985,

p. 50). How can a potential customer, thinking of purchasing the good at its initial price, be sure that the producer will not sell a later batch at a lower price? The problem is particularly acute with respect to a medium of exchange, which is acquired solely for later resale.

An enforceable repurchase clause or money-back guarantee is one way to resolve the assurance problem in general. (A pledge not to produce more than a specified number of units is another way, but one that is sometimes more difficult to monitor and enforce.) A bank's contractual commitment to redeem banknote and deposit monies at a specified rate for an asset (like an externally produced or "outside" base money), whose supply the bank cannot cheaply augment, constitutes such a repurchase clause. Redeemability provides a "goods-back guarantee" to assure potential holders of a money that the issuer will not cheat them through overissue. In the case of demandable bank debt the holder can invoke the repurchase clause any time.

If redemption contracts are a cost-effective (because relatively cheap to write and enforce) method for providing customer assurance, then potential holders of private money are likely to insist on redeemability, and *laissez-faire* will not support private fiat-type monies (Thomas Saving 1976; Girton and Roper 1981). Instead, it will deliver some sort of redeemable monies, for example the sort contemplated in the modern free banking literature. The centuries-long survival of redeemable private bank-issued monies, contrasted with the complete historical absence of private fiat-type monies, provides at least prima facie evidence for this view.

An implication of this view is that actual fiat monies in the modern world cannot represent an outgrowth of free market evolution. History indicates that such monies were instead born from the permanent breach of redeemability contracts previously honored on the liabilities of central banks (Taub 1985b, pp. 29–30; Selgin 1994c). Money-holders could not exercise their preference for redeemable monies because their options were legally restricted. Central banks enjoying monopoly note-issuing privileges had their notes declared "legal tender" for debts denominated in what was originally a commodity-money unit.[12]

COMPETITIVE PAYMENTS SYSTEMS WITHOUT BASE MONEY

If money-issuing firms under *laissez-faire* were to offer goods-back guarantees, rather than fiat-type monies, in what good or goods would the firms denominate and redeem their claims? Taking history as its guide, the modern free banking literature assumes that a single "outside" base money serves both as a unit of account and as a medium of redemption and interbank settlement. But other arrangements are conceivable. A group of authors beginning with Fischer Black (1970) has contemplated systems in which the unit of account would be a pure numeraire, distinct from any set of assets serving as the medium (or media) of redemption. No identifiable base money would then exist. Instead, all media of exchange would be bank issued or "inside" money. In such a system, its proponents propose, competition would assure an optimum quantity of money. Macroeconomic disturbances would, at very least, no longer be caused by changes in the supply or demand for base money. This third strand of literature on monetary *laissez-faire* has been dubbed "the new monetary economics," somewhat ironically given that the literature contemplates the abolition of base money as we know it.

Like the "New View" of money and banking associated with James Tobin (1963), the new monetary economics literature finds that under competitive conditions the *real* quantity of bank-issued money is subject to a "natural economic limit" determined by the interaction of demand (depositor preferences) and supply (cost conditions in banking).[13]

This conclusion rests on standard microeconomic considerations and goes through straightforwardly (if unsurprisingly). Tobin (1969, p. 26) and Black (1970, p. 10) have also suggested that there is a natural limit to the *nominal* quantity of bank-issued money. This suggestion is correct only if the monetary system's anchor (e.g., the nominal dollar equivalent of an ounce of gold – the first ratio on the right-hand side of equation (9) below – or the nominal quantity of fiat base money) is fixed. If monetary policy can vary the nominal scalar, it is not true that *laissez-faire* banking by itself leaves (as Tobin says) "no room for monetary policy to affect aggregate demand" even in nominal terms. Black's (1987) puzzling claim that monetary policy is passive and inert even in our current regime is not shared by Tobin or by the other new monetary economists; indeed Greenfield and Yeager (1983, 1989) wish to reform the current regime in a *laissez-faire* direction precisely because they view the present monetary regime as an important source of macroeconomic disturbances. But just how would the elimination of base money serve to make the payments system macroeconomically neutral? And how, exactly, would actual payments be accomplished?

Separation and indirect redeemability

The new monetary economists' vision of a *laissez-faire* payments system is one of a pure "accounting system of exchange." The transactions activities of banks, making computer-entry transfers of ownership of whatever financial assets, have no influence on the purchasing power of the numeraire in terms of which goods and financial assets are priced. Eugene Fama (1980, p. 45) proposes that under *laissez-faire* the Modigliani–Miller theorem on the irrelevance of pure financing decisions applies to banks: "banks hold portfolios on behalf of their depositors because this probably allows them to provide transactions services (the accounting system of exchange) more efficiently, but the portfolio management activities of banks affect nothing, including prices and real activity." Banks are passive suppliers of deposits, and the banking system "is at most a passive force in the determination of prices and real activity."

We can contrast these properties Fama describes to the properties of a conventional gold standard. Where the unit of account is the gold "dollar," price-level determination can be represented simply by

$$P = \$/\text{CPI bundle}$$
$$= (\$/\text{oz. Au})(\text{oz. Au/CPI bundle}) \tag{9}$$

where the ratio ($/oz. Au) defines the gold content of the dollar, and the ratio (oz. Au/CPI bundle) denotes the relative price of gold in terms of the consumer price index bundle of goods. The gold dollar is a base money that serves as a means of settlement and (where the public employ some base money) also as a substitute for bank deposits. Banks holding gold reserves themselves demand the numeraire good, and in providing transactions services they affect the public's demand for the numeraire good (Kevin D. Hoover 1988). Banks therefore play an active role in determining the relative price of gold and, thereby, the level of nominal prices. Fama (1980), by contrast, assumes that a barrel of oil, or a steel ingot, could serve directly as the unit of account – so that P = bbl. oil/CPI bundle – without creating any special difficulty. Greenfield and Yeager (1983) propose that a new unit of account be created that is deliberately "separated" from any medium of redemption and settlement. Yeager (1989) calls the new unit the "valun" (for value unit).[14] To achieve stability in the general level of prices, the valun is supposed to be defined as a broad bundle comprising specific amounts of a variety of standardized commodities: the P = valuns/CPI bundle; the price level is determined by the relative price ratio between the valun and CPI bundles. Although this ratio will not be perfectly stable except where the valun and CPI bundles are identical, Greenfield and Yeager note that it *will* (by the law of large numbers) be more stable than the price ratio between any single commodity (like gold) and the CPI bundle.

Unlike earlier proposals for "commodity reserve currency," which envisioned warehouses full of raw materials (Hayek 1948), the Greenfield–Yeager proposal does not contemplate using the valun bundle itself as either a medium of exchange or a redemption medium. A Greenfield–Yeager bank instead redeems its transaction account balances and currency notes, and settles its interbank clearing balances, in whatever asset it and other banks deem most convenient – possibly gold or platinum or a specific security.[15] A one-valun banknote is a claim to that quantity of the redemption medium equal in value to the valun bundle at the moment of redemption. That is, the redemption rate (valun notes/oz. Pt) varies as necessary to offset changes in the relative price of platinum (oz. Pt/valun bundle), so as to keep their product (valun notes/valun bundle) equal to unity. Notes and transactions balances are in this sense "indirectly redeemable" for the bundle. Thus, even in the event that gold were used as the redemption medium, the system would not be a gold standard because exchange media would be denominated in valuns, not in units of gold. Unlike a gold standard, the nominal (valun) price of a unit of gold would vary to reflect changes in the value of gold relative to the value of the broad commodity (valun) bundle.

The Greenfield–Yeager proposal in some ways resembles Irving Fisher's (1920, 1926; Glasner 1989, pp. 227–36) "compensated dollar" plan, which sought to stabilize the dollar price level by varying the gold content of the dollar ($/oz. Au) to offset changes in the relative price of gold (oz. Au/CPI bundle). There are, however, at least four important differences. First, where Fisher assumed that government would monopolistically provide currency and hold gold reserves, Greenfield and Yeager envision exclusively private issue of notes and transaction accounts. Second, where Fisher proposed periodic discrete changes in the gold content of the dollar, Greenfield and Yeager suggest that the redemption rate can and should be adjusted continuously. For this reason, the valun bundle needs to be composed of goods traded on organized exchanges, and cannot be identical to the CPI bundle. Third, it follows that while Fisher's redemption rate was adjusted to the CPI bundle, Greenfield and Yeager's is adjusted to a different bundle and therefore (unless a Fisher mechanism is added) does not rule out permanent changes in the CPI. Fourth, Fisher's system did not "separate" the unit of account from the redemption medium; at any moment the dollar was to be legally defined as a definite quantity of gold. In the Greenfield–Yeager system, the valun is supposed to be defined in terms of a broad commodity bundle, not in terms of the redemption medium (which could be any asset) or any medium of exchange.

Under a conventional gold or a fiat dollar standard, an excess supply or demand for base money in a closed economy calls for a change in the purchasing power of the monetary unit that can only be achieved through the protracted process of adjusting the nominal prices of goods and services generally.[16] Fisher wanted to render such price adjustments unnecessary by instead adjusting the official gold content of the dollar. Greenfield and Yeager argue that their separated system will likewise allow an excess supply or demand for the redemption medium to be eliminated expeditiously through market adjustment of its unit-of-account price. An excess demand for payment media, meanwhile, is rapidly eliminated by the market's adjustment of their relative yield. The payments system will then be neutral with respect to real activity. A system without base money thus ensures that an excess demand for base money, and a corresponding aggregate excess supply of goods, causing a depression of real activity, cannot arise. With the markets for redemption media and bank accounts clearing rapidly, the aggregate excess supply of other goods stays close to zero.[17]

Greenfield and Yeager (1989, pp. 413, 417) also see a second advantage in monetary separation: a flexible valun price for the redemption medium would supposedly eliminate the danger posed to ordinary fractional-reserve-based payments systems by bank runs. Instead of draining reserves from the banking system, any increased demand for the scarce redemption medium would merely reduce the valun price of the redemption medium, allowing banks to pay out less per valun claim redeemed. This second purported advantage of separation appears, however, to be in conflict with the system's main *raison d'être*: although *some* redemption rate does exist that would allow any Greenfield–Yeager bank to redeem all its liabilities no matter how small its reserves, a Greenfield–Yeager bank cannot individually move to such a rate so long as it honors its obligation to redeem a one-valun note with one-valun-bundle's worth of the redemption medium. The redemption rate is given to the individual bank. For this reason a Greenfield–Yeager banking system cannot simultaneously remain passive with respect to the price level and rule out reserve shortages.[18] The appeal of the Greenfield–Yeager proposal must, then, reside mainly or entirely in its vision of a payments system that remains neutral with respect to real activity as explained above.

Doubts remain, however, concerning whether the system would achieve even this principal aim. Monetary separation of the sort envisioned by Greenfield and Yeager raises the question of how the unit-of-account prices of goods, financial assets, and exchange media are proximately determined. Greenfield and Yeager (1983) indicate that prices would be quoted in terms of the valun bundle unit itself rather than in terms of any distinct bank-issued media of exchange. Banknotes and some transactions accounts would be denominated in valuns, but those that are demandable debt claims could in certain circumstances trade above or below par, that is may need to be priced in valuns, while those that are mutual fund account balances must be continuously repriced in valuns.[19] But just how is it possible in practice to price goods, financial assets, and exchange media all in terms of a numeraire (a bundle) that never actually trades against them? A numeraire truly "separate" from any actual exchange medium appears to require a kind of Walrasian auctioneer pricing mechanism that does not operate in real-world markets. For agents in the real world, information and transactions costs are minimized by quoting prices in units of the dominant medium of exchange (White 1984b).

One way to get around this problem is to resort to a less strict but more coherent version of separation, allowing prices to be quoted in terms of a particular brand of bank-issued exchange media. The market price of the valun commodity bundle can then momentarily diverge from par (i.e., the prices of its constituent commodities can sum to more or less than one valun), until arbitrage returns it to par. But, as Norbert Schnadt and John Whittaker (1993; see also Cowen and Kroszner 1994, pp. 86–8) have argued, this solution poses a problem of its own: when the market price of the valun bundle diverges from par, indirect (bundles-worth) redeemability with continuous adjustment of the redemption rate may be "inoperable."

The nature of the inoperability is as follows. A bank attempting to practice indirect redeemability with continuous adjustment must continuously observe the current price of the valun bundle relative to the redemption medium (say, platinum). Because the market does not directly price bundle items in platinum units, but rather in valun-denominated bank-issued claims, the bank must derive the relative price by observing the current valun prices of all the goods in the bundle and the current valun price of platinum (Schnadt and Whittaker 1993, p. 216). Suppose that increased demand for some of the goods in the bundle momentarily raises the bundle's market price above par without changing the market price of platinum. A bank that continuously adjusts its redemption rate must now offer more ounces of platinum in exchange for each one-valun banknote, to accord with the increased value of the valun bundle relative to platinum. Arbitrage insures that the market price of one ounce of platinum falls correspondingly: no one in the market will accept fewer ounces of platinum per valun than can be gotten at a bank. The fall in the market price of platinum compels the banks to raise the platinum-ounces-per-valun redemption rate once again, pushing the market price of platinum down even further, and so on.

Schnadt and Whittaker (1993, p. 217) conclude that, with banks continuously adjusting the redemption rate, the redemption rate rises and the market price of platinum falls without limit, so long as arbitrage in the platinum market works faster than any forces pushing the bundle price back to unity. They suggest that "in practice" a rising redemption rate will reduce a bank's effective reserve ratio, eventually forcing it to suspend. This suggestion appeals to the limits on the banking system imposed by prudential demands for scarce reserves, the same type of limits present in conventional monetary payments systems. Greenfield and Yeager (1983, pp. 308, 311), however, clearly believe that such reserve-ratio considerations do not apply to their system. One is thus left with a puzzle as to how the system achieves a stable equilibrium.

Periodic adjustment of the redemption rate, as originally proposed by Fisher (1920, 1926), might solve the problem raised by Schnadt and Whittaker by stabilizing the price level over a longer horizon. But periodic adjustment surrenders the ideal of unit-of-account separation, and with it the goal of completely insulating the price level from changes in the supply and demand for exchange media or the medium of redemption. Periodic adjustment furthermore raises still another problem: at least in its ordinary form, it is vulnerable to speculative attack (Glasner 1989, pp. 232–4; Cowen and Kroszner 1994, ch. 3; Dowd 1992c). The anticipation that an issuer is about to lower its redemption rate, because a lower price level is about to be announced, would prompt a run on the issuer.

A "compensated dollar" issuer might avoid speculative attacks by retaining the right to make *ex post* adjustments to the redemption rate, as Glasner (1989, pp. 234–6) proposes. The issuer would swap currency for gold (say) at the current market price of gold, and then make or take a rebate later, after learning the height of the price index (measured with a lag) that prevailed on the day of the swap. The rebate would insure that exactly a constant dollar's worth of gold was finally received for each one-dollar note redeemed. Any speculative profit would have to be returned, eliminating the incentive to stage a redemption run. Because the *ex post* compensation scheme requires the currency issuer to be able to track down and extract a rebate from a note redeemer, however, it does not appear to be feasible for a private issuer. Nor is it clear that currency users under *laissez-faire* would opt for a redemption contract that delayed final settlement of redemption claims for weeks while also depriving them of their anonymity. Glasner, like Fisher, understandably assumes that the federal government is to operate the scheme. The scheme is therefore more appropriately regarded as a reform to be fastened onto a government monopoly issuer than as a likely outcome of monetary *laissez-faire*.

There are other reasons for doubting whether the Greenfield–Yeager system would arise or survive under *laissez-faire*. The system's unit-of-account separation and lack of a base money require breaking from traditional direct redemption arrangements. They may also hinder efficient interbank settlement. Not having base money as a medium of redemption, nor any other asset with an unambiguous unit-of-account value, Greenfield–Yeager banks would seem to face a costly bid-asked spread in each interbank settlement or over-the-counter redemption (White 1984b, 1986b; O'Driscoll 1985, 1986). For these reasons individuals and their banks might prefer an "unseparated" system offering the familiar convenience of a unit of account linked to (rather than separated from) a basic medium of exchange and means of settlement.

The legal restrictions theory

The "legal restrictions theory" of the demand for money – a line of thought distinct from but kindred to the new monetary economics – also predicts that a *laissez-faire* payments system would lack base money of the current sort.[20] Where the new monetary economics focuses on the possibilities opened by unit-of-account separation, the legal restrictions theory derives from an arbitrage argument: base money of the current sort cannot survive under *laissez-faire* because it is dominated in rate of return by interest-bearing instruments. The predicted disappearance of the fiat dollar under *laissez-faire* implies that the economy would have to switch to another unit of account (Wallace 1983), but the legal restrictions theory as such is not concerned with what type of substitute unit might be desirable or how it would be selected.

Like the new monetary economists (and like the modern free banking theorists), Thomas Sargent and Neil Wallace (1982) suggest that *laissez-faire* competition would compel banks to supply only the quantity of liabilities demanded. They identify this proposition (questionably, according to Laidler 1984) with the venerable "real bills doctrine," but it bears a more obvious affinity with Fama's extension of the Modigliani–Miller theorem to banks (Y. C. Jao 1984, p. 15) and with Tobin's "New View."

The legal restrictions theory grew out of the New Classical macroeconomics project "to render monetary theory subject to standard [general equilibrium] modes of analysis" (John Bryant and Neil Wallace 1980, p. 1).[21] With a nod to John Hicks (1935), legal restrictions theorists consider it a crucial task of monetary theory to explain why people hold an asset (money) that is dominated in rate of return. But where Hicks sought an explanation in "frictions," Bryant and Wallace (1980, p. 3) believe that "adequate modeling of the frictions that inhibit the operation of the law of one price has proved refractory." A satisfactory theory of transaction costs not being available, they advocate studying money using the Walrasian zero-transaction-costs or perfect-arbitrage approach of finance theory. In a zero-transactions-cost world, the notion that money has a liquidity advantage over bonds becomes meaningless: assets' pecuniary rates of return are all that matters.

The "legal restrictions theory" is so named because it attributes today's rate-of-return discrepancy between government currency and bonds entirely to legal restrictions against private currency issue. Under *laissez-faire*, the argument goes, financial intermediaries would be free to issue currency-like liabilities in the form of payable-to-the-bearer discount bonds. Competition among intermediaries would eliminate any spread between the rates received on their assets and paid on their liabilities that was wider than the costs of intermediation (estimated to be about 1 per cent). Intermediaries' portfolios could be perfectly maturity matched so that their bearer-bond liabilities carried no greater capital risk or (absent fraud) default risk than their assets. Unless nominal interest rates happen to be close to zero, non-interest-yielding currency would be outcompeted by such interest-yielding bearer bonds (Wallace 1983, 1988a). The view that the demand for base money of the present-day sort rests critically on legal restrictions is the complement to Black's view that *laissez-faire* implies a world without (base) money (O'Driscoll 1985, p. 11).

It is easy to grant the points that the initial establishment of a fiat money regime requires the contravention of *laissez-faire* (because it requires a government monopoly of currency), and that the demand for a fiat money is enhanced by legal restrictions that suppress substitute media of exchange. But the legal restrictions theory makes a stronger prediction that appears to be contradicted by historical evidence. The theory predicts that non-interest -bearing currency cannot coexist with equally risky bearer bonds paying an interest rate above the costs of intermediation. Yet history shows the survival of non-interest-bearing banknotes in regimes where such bonds were available (Gail E. Makinen and G. Thomas Woodward 1986; White 1987; James A Gherity 1993). The survival of ordinary banknotes can be attributed to computation and transactions costs – assumed away by the legal restrictions theory – that make the potential interest on small-denomination circulating claims not worth collecting.

Responding to this critique, legal restrictions theorists have suggested that an economical way of paying a real return on currency might be to have the currency unit continuously rise in real value, that is to have a falling price level (Wallace 1988a; Bryant 1989). Such a deflation would, via the Fisher effect, drive nominal interest rates down close to zero and thereby eliminate any rate-of-return dominance by non-currency assets. This suggestion draws obvious inspiration from M. Friedman's (1969) optimum-quantity-of-money policy. To achieve this result, each competing currency issuer would have to choose or create its own appropriately appreciating unit of account. An important ground for doubting that *laissez-faire* would in fact compel this result is that the unit of account represents a social convention that no individual issuer can easily deviate from or alter (Karl Wärneryd 1990).

CONCLUSION: WELFARE IMPLICATIONS AND REAL-WORLD RELEVANCE

Research on *laissez-faire* conceptions of money and banking provides an opportunity for rethinking both the positive rationales economic theory can offer for the existence of our current payments institutions and the normative rationales it can offer for government involvement with money. In assessing how well the invisible hand would handle money, it is important to avoid the "Nirvana fallacy" criticized in another context by Harold Demsetz (1969). The Nirvana fallacy consists of thinking that one of the options, when choosing among alternative regimes, is a world in which our collective ability to improve on market outcomes is not at all constrained by information or agency costs. *Laissez-faire* does not usher in Nirvana; neither do legal restrictions or government bureaus. Institutional arrangements under any regime must come to grips with the inescapable information and agency costs of securing desired behavior from those who issue money or regulate its issue.

Modern welfare economics offers two standard rationales for government involvement in the provision of a good: externalities and natural monopoly. It is difficult to find a sustained attempt in the literature to establish that either of these rationales applies to base money or the medium of account, though a variety of externality claims are often made in passing.

It is not possible to evaluate specific claims here. But it can be noted generally that while externality arguments lend themselves to support of taxes or subsidies, or more rigorous definition and enforcement of property rights, they are not well suited to justify the sort of barriers to entry by private money producers that are common in modern monetary regimes. Nor are natural monopoly arguments: only by allowing rival issuers to attempt entry can we find out whether a natural monopoly really exists (Vaubel 1984b).

With respect to bank-issued money, confidence externalities (bank-run contagions) are commonly invoked to justify government providing deposit insurance or acting as a lender of last resort. The moral hazard created by deposit insurance and last-resort lending is in turn used to rationalize regulations on bank balance sheets. The theoretical and historical research cited above on whether "inherent instability" would characterize a *laissez-faire* regime casts doubt, however, on the idea that confidence externalities clearly provide a rationale for government intervention. Confidence externalities may be negligible under *laissez-faire* with appropriately evolved "run-proof" banking contracts and mutual-support institutions. Legal restrictions on banks have arguably hindered the development of run-inhibiting arrangements such as branch banking, contractual suspension clauses, and mutual-fund-based payment accounts. Balance-sheet regulation may tend to exacerbate rather than alleviate contagion effects by making banks more uniform.

In light of the potential problems of information asymmetry and moral hazard in banking, one might conclude with Martin F. Hellwig (1985, pp. 585–6) that economic theory does not yield decisive arguments for or against *laissez-faire* in bank-issued money. "We simply do not know very much about how competition among inside monies works," and "it is unclear whether government intervention is harmful or useful." Alternatively, a verdict may be sought by considering historical evidence on how competition among inside (bank-issued) monies has worked, particularly how bankers and their customers have tried to minimize information asymmetry and moral hazard problems, and by considering evidence on whether government intervention has proven beneficial. At least some monetary historians who have taken this second approach have concluded from the record that government intervention into money and banking has been harmful – destabilizing and efficiency reducing – on balance (M. Friedman and Schwartz 1986, p. 40).

Even a consensus among economists that non-regulation would in practice prove better than the current regime (or any realizable regulatory regime) would probably be insufficient to persuade governments to retire from the monetary arena, of course. Governments throughout history have enjoyed fiscal benefits from their monetary roles, namely seignorage revenues and forced loans from the banking system (Glasner 1989, ch. 2).[22] In the twentieth century they have come to value monetary policy for its perceived macroeconomic benefits. Public choice analysis suggests that governments would want to persist in monopolizing base money production and regulating bank-issued money even if it were generally recognized that their involvement fails to improve the quality of money (H. Geoffrey Brennan and James M. Buchanan 1981; Richard Wagner 1986). In the developed countries, the post-Bretton-Woods regimes have experienced neither hyperinflation nor a great depression, and so have not aroused any great public clamor for change (Bennett T. McCallum 1989, p. 349). The prospects for a switch to a *laissez-faire* monetary regime any time soon are, therefore, similar to the prospects Walter Bagehot (1873, p. 332) saw for the abolition of the Bank of England's monopoly privileges twelve decades ago: "Nothing but a revolution would effect it, and there is nothing to cause a revolution."

If a policy revolution is not in prospect, is there any practical value to the literature on *laissez-faire* approaches to money and banking, apart from its intellectual interest for monetary theorists and historians? There are two possible practical values. First, a verdict on the desirability of monetary *laissez-faire* may motivate the direction taken by marginal reforms, within the constraints of the politically possible. Second, as M. Friedman and Schwartz (1986 p. 60) point out, citing the abolition of Regulation Q and the switch to floating exchange rates, crises may after all make conditions ripe for a "revolution" in public policy. When a crisis occurs, "what happens will depend critically on the options that have been explored by the intellectual community and have become intellectually respectable." Extra-ordinary monetary policy research performs a service by "widening the range of options and keeping them available." Views may differ on which if any varieties of *laissez-faire* monetary thought have become "intellectually respectable," but it cannot be denied that the literature discussing them has broadened the range of options, and has enhanced the liveliness of monetary policy debates.

NOTES

1 A number of American state governments instituted so-called "free banking" systems between 1837 and 1861. These were actually much further from *laissez-faire* than regimes in many other nations. We discuss US "free banking" experience below.

2 As a referee has noted, government coinage is ancient. But Arthur R. Burns (1965, p. 136) concludes from his wide-ranging review of anthropological and numismatic evidence that the use of metallic monies and coinage had already evolved before governments monopolized the coinage business: "The use of coins is no more than an improvement upon exchange based upon the transfer of metals by weight, the system common in the East for some thousands of years before the peoples of the Aegean began to make coins. When they began to strike money they naturally used the metal already circulating as a means of payment. When states took over the business of minting they adopted the same course, confirming the choice of a medium of exchange already made by the community at large, and crystallized in contemporary commercial customs." Carl Menger (1892) provides a well-known theoretical account of how, starting from barter, an economy can converge on a generally accepted medium of exchange.

3 The idea that deposit creation is limited naturally by rising marginal costs, reflecting the potential reserve losses that an expanding bank will experience through interbank clearing and settlement is of course common fare in money and banking texts. Modern free banking theory merely extends the same logic to note issue, and thereby to bank-issued money as a whole.

4 One means for guarding against such an outcome would be to impose, as a minimal legal restriction, the requirement that clearinghouses maintain a fixed fraction of their own assets in the form of fiat money. This would not be a statutory reserve requirement in the usual sense, in that prudential considerations alone would continue to govern commercial banks' demands for clearinghouse balances.

5 The desirability of stabilizing nominal aggregate demand can be represented most simply in the aggregate supply and demand framework offered by under-graduate textbooks. With an upward-sloping aggregate supply curve, shifts in the aggregate demand curve cause temporary deviations of real output from its natural rate. These deviations are undesirable because they involve errors by suppliers confused between nominal and relative price changes.

6 Iftekhar Hasan and Gerald P. Dwyer, Jr. (1994, p. 284) examines four state "free banking" episodes in which numerous banks closed. They conclude:

> The evidence is consistent with the existence of contagious bank runs and contemporaries' knowledge of them, but these contagion effects had little or no impact on the number of banks that closed permanently. The evidence indicates that the runs on the banking systems were precipitated by events exogenous to the banking systems.

It is clearly important to distinguish two possible causes of an episode of systemwide runs: (1) an exogenous shock that simultaneously weakens and thereby prompts runs on many banks, an event made more likely by the US "free banking" regulation because it led the banks to hold very similar portfolios; and (2) a contagion effect or confidence externality by which, holding other information constant, a run or failure at one bank prompts runs at other banks. Hasan and Dwyer note that bankers in these episodes were concerned to mitigate *potential* contagion – groups of bankers in two states acted jointly to publicize and certify one another's soundness – but they do not provide any direct evidence, eyewitness or statistical, that contagion actually occurred to any appreciable extent.

7 Despite Rockoff's and other economic historians' clarity on this point, monetary theorists (e.g., Stephen D. Williamson 1992) occasionally still misidentify US "free banking" arrangements as *laissez-faire* regimes.

8 As a referee has pointed out, this explanation rests on the hypothesis that the collateral requirements were binding; that is, that unrestricted banks would have chosen portfolios significantly less vulnerable to shocks, which remains to be shown.

9 The following overview of the debate draws on White (1991), which defends the near-*laissez-faire* view of Scottish banking against its critics. See also the comment by Charles Munn (1991).

10 For an alternative, skeptical view see Kindleberger (1992). Scott Sumner (1993) has recently discussed the advantages of privatizing coin and note production and issue – by auctioning monopoly franchises rather than by allowing free entry – under the fiat dollar standard.

11 The term "private fiat money" is used by Bart Taub (1985a). The conjunction of "private" with "fiat" is somewhat paradoxical, given the dictionary definition of a fiat as "an arbitrary order or decree," presumably backed by non-private power. We shall accordingly refer to "fiat-type" private monies.

12 Neither the literature on private fiat-type monies, nor our historical account of the origins of government fiat monies, provides an analysis of the viability of government fiat money. For critical surveys of work on this fundamental question of monetary theory see Benjamin Friedman and Frank Hahn (1990), especially the chapters authored by Ostroy and Starr, Brock, and Duffie.

13 On the influence of the "New View" see Glasner (1989, pp. 171–5). The modern free banking literature reaches the same conclusion for unregulated banks in the traditional sense (Selgin 1989). In our discussion of the new monetary economics the term "bank" should be understood as a shorthand for any type of financial firm, possibly a mutual fund, producing media of exchange.

14 The "valun" name was first used by E. C. Riegal (1944, 1978). Greenfield and Yeager call the system they envision the "BFH" system, to acknowledge that they have drawn constituent ideas from *B*lack (1970), *F*ama (1980), and Robert *H*all (1982).

15 Against Greenfield and Yeager's suggestion that there might be a varied list of redemption media, White (1986b) argues that transactions costs are minimized by using a single common medium of redemption. On the need for ultimate settlement see Hoover (1988).

16 Invoking the aggregate supply and demand framework again, we characterize Greenfield and Yeager's concern as the concern that short-run equilibria off the long-run aggregate supply curve (which is vertical at the natural rate of output) not persist due to "sticky prices." Persistence is particularly undesirable when real output is below the natural rate.

17 In other words, "Say's law" – in the sense of zero aggregate excess demand for non-money goods – tends strongly to hold because the market for "money" tends to clear continuously. On valid and invalid versions of "Say's law" see Robert Clower and Axel Leijonhufvud (1981).

18 Elsewhere Greenfield and Yeager (1989, p. 416) do recognize that an individual bank might default in their system.

19 Cowen and Kroszner (1994, p. 82) argue that the Greenfield–Yeager system "requires that exchange media are priced explicitly." The value of a particular bank's notes or checking balances may, according to their view, bear a discount or premium in terms of valun bundles.

20 For a sympathetic overview that makes the legal restrictions theory an integral part of the new monetary economics see Ian R. Harper and Andrew Coleman (1992). In fact the two schools of thought are distinct. Greenfield and Yeager's analysis of the properties of a radically different monetary regime, for example, is orthogonal to Neil Wallace's analysis of the current regime. The two schools are "kindred" in proposing the absence of base money under *laissez-faire*, and in pursuing Walrasian or finance-theoretic modes of analysis.

21 See also John H. Kareken and Neil Wallace (1980), who link the overlapping generations model of fiat money to this project. The legal restrictions theory resolves the question of why agents in an overlapping generations model would hold an asset (fiat money) that is dominated in rate of return by bonds.

22 The seignorage of the US federal government, measured as the change in the monetary base, was about $40 billion in the most recent twelve months available (February 1993 to February 1994). This is "only" 3.5 per cent of total federal receipts for fiscal 1993, but it is unlikely that the Treasury would be indifferent to its loss. Nor would the Federal Reserve be indifferent, according to the analysis of Mark Toma (1982), because its own budget is financed by taking a share of the seignorage. Other countries rely on seignorage for substantially larger percentages of government revenue. We are not suggesting that seignorage alone motivates any government's role in the monetary system; we are only suggesting that it is one tangible motive, which would remain in place even if other welfare-based reasons for government involvement became discredited.

REFERENCES

Bagehot, Walter. *Lombard Street: A description of the money market.* London: Henry S. King 1873.

Baltensperger, Ernst. "Alternative Approaches to the Theory of the Banking Firm," *Journal of Monetary Economics*, January 1980, 6(1), pp. 1–37.

Benston, George J. "Does Bank Regulation Produce Stability? Lessons from the United States," in Forrest Capie and Geoffrey E. Wood, eds. 1991, pp. 207–32.

Benston, George J. et al. *Perspectives on safe and sound banking.* Cambridge, MA: MIT Press, 1986.

Berlin, Mitchell. "Bank Loans and Marketable Securities: How do Financial Contracts Control Borrowing Firms?" *Federal Reserve Bank of Philadelphia Business Review*, July/August 1987, pp. 9–18.

Black, Fischer. "Banking and Interest Rates in a World Without Money: The Effects of Uncontrolled Banking," *Journal of Bank Research*, Autumn 1970, *1*(3), pp. 9–20.

————. *Business cycles and equilibrium.* Oxford: Basil Blackwell, 1987.

Boot, Arnoud W. and Thakor, Anjan V. "Self-Interested Bank Regulation," *American Economic Review*, May 1993, *83*(2), pp. 206–12.

Bordo, Michael D. "Financial Crises, Banking Crises, Stock Market Crashes and the Money Supply: Some International Evidence, 1870–1933," in Forrest Capie and Geoffrey E. Wood, eds. 1986, pp. 190–248.

————. "The Lender of Last Resort: Alternative Views and Historical Experience," *Federal Reserve Bank of Richmond Economic Review*, January/February 1990. *76*(1), pp. 18–29.

————. "Comment" [on Benston 1991], in Forrest Capie and Geoffrey E. Wood, eds. 1991, pp. 233–5.

Bordo, Michael D. and Redish, Angela. "Why Did the Bank of Canada Emerge in 1935?" *Journal of Economic History*, June 1987, *47*(2), pp. 405–17.

Brennan, H. Geoffrey and Buchanan, James M. *Monopoly in money and inflation.* London: Institute of Economic Affairs, 1981.

Bryant, John. "Interest-bearing Currency, Legal Restrictions, and the Rate of Return Dominance of Money: A Note," *Journal of Money, Credit, and Banking*, May 1989, *21*(2), pp. 240–5.

Bryant, John and Wallace, Neil. "A Suggestion for Further Simplifying the Theory of Money." Unpublished ms., Federal Reserve Bank of Minneapolis and University of Minnesota, 1980.

Burns, Arthur Robert, *Money and monetary policy in early times.* New York: Augustus M. Kelley, 1965.

Calomiris, Charles W. and Kahn, Charles M. "The Role of Demandable Debt in Structuring Optimal Banking Arrangements," *American Economic Review*, June 1991, *81*(3), pp. 497–513.

Cameron, Rondo. *Banking in the early stages of industrialization.* New York: Oxford University Press, 1967.

Capie, Forrest and Wood, Geoffrey E., eds. *Financial crises and the world banking system.* London: Macmillan, 1986.

————, eds. *Unregulated banking: Chaos or order?* London: Macmillan, 1991.

Carr, Jack, Glied, Sherry and Mathewson, Frank. "Unlimited Liability and Free Banking in Scotland," *Journal of Economic History*, December 1989 *49*(4), pp. 974–8.

Checkland, S. G. *Scottish banking: a history, 1695–1973.* Glasgow: Collins, 1975.

Christ, Carl. "When is Free Banking More Stable than Regulated Banking?" Unpublished ms., Johns Hopkins University, 1990.

Clower, Robert W. "What Traditional Monetary Theory Really Wasn't," *Canadian Journal of Economics*, May 1969, 2(2), pp. 299–302.

————. "Is There an Optimal Money Supply?" *Journal of Finance*, May 1970, *25*(2), pp. 425–33.

Clower, Robert W. and Leijonhufvud, Axel. "Say's Principle, What It Means and Doesn't Mean," in *Information and coordination*, by Axel Leijonhufvud. New York: Oxford University Press, 1981, pp. 79–101.

Coase, Ronald H. "Durability and Monopoly," *Journal of Law Economics*, April 1972, *25*(1), pp. 143–9.

Cowen, Tyler and Kroszner, Randall. "Scottish Banking before 1844: A Model for Laissez-Faire?" *Journal of Money, Credit, and Banking*, May 1989, *21*(2), pp. 221–31.

————. "Mutual Fund Banking: A Market Approach," *Cato Journal*, Spring/ Summer 1990, *10*(1), pp. 223–37.

————. *Explorations in the new monetary economics.* Oxford: Basil Blackwell, 1994.

Demsetz, Harold, "Information and Efficiency, Another Viewpoint," *Journal of Law and Economics*, April 1969, *12*(1), pp. 1–22.

Diamond, Douglas W. and Dybvig, Philip H. "Bank Runs, Deposit Insurance, and Liquidity," *Journal of Political Economy*, June 1983, *91*(3), pp. 401–19.

Dowd, Kevin, "Option Clauses and the Stability of a Laisser Faire Monetary System," *Journal of Financial Services Research*, December 1988, *1*(4), pp. 319–33.

————. "The Evolution of Central Banking in England, 1821–90," in Forrest Capie and Geoffrey E. Woods, eds. 1991, pp. 159–95.

————. "Models of Banking Instability: A Partial Review of the Literature," *Journal of Economic Surveys*, April 1992a, *6*(2), pp. 107–32.

————, ed. *The experience of free banking*. London: Routledge, 1992b.

————. "Is Banking a Natural Monopoly?" *Kyklos*, April 1992c, *45*(3), pp. 379–92.

————. "The Mechanics of Indirect Convertibility." Unpublished ms., University of Nottingham, 1992d.

————. "Competitive Banking, Bankers' Clubs, and Bank Regulation," *Journal of Money, Credit, and Banking*, May 1994, *26*(2), pp. 289–308.

Economopoulos, Andrew J. "Illinois Free Banking Experience," *Journal of Money, Credit, and Banking*, May 1988, *20*(2), pp. 249–64.

————. "Free Bank Failures in New York and Wisconsin: A Portfolio Analysis," *Explorations in Economic History*, October 1990, *27*(4), pp. 421–41.

Eichberger, Jurgen and Milne, Frank. "Bank Runs and Capital Adequacy," Unpublished ms., Australian National University, 1990.

England, Catherine and Huertas, Thomas, eds. *The financial services revolution*. Boston: Kluwer, 1988.

Fama, Eugene. "Banking in the Theory of Finance," *Journal of Monetary Economics*, January 1980, *6*(1), pp. 39–57.

Fisher, Irving. *Stabilizing the dollar*. New York: Macmillan, 1920.

————. *The purchasing power of money*. 2nd edn. New York: Macmillan, 1926.

Friedman, Benjamin M. and Hahn, Frank H., eds. *Handbook of monetary economics, Vol. 1*. Amsterdam: North-Holland, 1990.

Friedman, Milton. *A program for monetary stability*. New York: Fordham University Press, 1960.

————. "The Optimum Quantity of Money", in *The optimum quantity of money and other essays*. Chicago: Aldine, 1969, pp. 1–50.

————. "Monetary Policy for the 1980s," in *To promote prosperity*. Ed.: John H. Moore, Stanford: Hoover Institution Press, 1984, pp. 23–60.

Friedman, Milton and Schwartz, Anna J. "Has Government Any Role in Money?" *Journal of Monetary Economics*, January 1986, *17*(1), pp. 37–62.

Gherity, James A. "Interest-Bearing Currency: Evidence from the Civil War Experience. A Note," *Journal of Money, Credit, and Banking*, February 1993, *25*(1), pp. 125–31.

Gilbert, R. Alton, "A Re-examination of the History of Bank Failures, Contagion, and Banking Panics," in *The financial services industry in the year 2000: Risk and efficiency: Proceedings of a conference on bank structure and competition*. Chicago: Federal Reserve Bank of Chicago, 1988, pp. 128–39.

Girton, Lance and Roper, Don E. "Theory and Implications of Currency Substitution," *Journal of Money, Credit, and Banking*, February 1981, *13*(1), pp. 12–30.

Glasner, David, "A Reinterpretation of Classical Monetary Theory," *Southern Economic Journal*, July 1985, *52*(1), pp. 46–67.

————. *Free banking and monetary reform*, Cambridge: Cambridge University Press, 1989.

Goodhart, Charles A. E. "Review of White [1984a]," *Economica*, February 1987, *54*(213), pp. 129–31.

————. *The evolution of central banks: A natural development?*. Cambridge MA: MIT Press, 1988.

Gorton, Gary B. "Clearinghouses and the Origins of Central Banking in the United States," *Journal of Economic History*, June 1985, *45*(2), pp. 277–83.

————. "Banking Panics and Business Cycles," *Oxford Economic Papers*, December 1988, *40*(4), pp. 751–81.

————. "The Enforceability of Private Money Contracts, Market Efficiency, and Technological Change," NBER Working Paper No. 3645, 1991.

Gorton, Gary B. and Mullineaux, Donald J. "The Joint Production of Confidence: Endogenous Regulation and Nineteenth Century Commercial-Bank Clearing-houses," *Journal of Money, Credit, and Banking*, November 1987, *19*(4), pp. 457–68.

Gorton, Gary B. and Pennacchi, George. "Financial Intermediaries and Liquidity Creation," *Journal of Finance*, March 1990, *45*(1), pp. 49–71.

Gramm, William P. "Laissez-Faire and the Optimum Quantity of Money," *Economic Inquiry*, March 1974, *12*(1), pp. 125–32.

Greenfield, Robert L. and Yeager, Leland B. "A Laissez-Faire Approach to Monetary Stability," *Journal of Money, Credit, and Banking*, August 1983, *15*(3), pp. 102–15.

————. "Can Monetary Disequilibrium Be Eliminated?" *Cato Journal*, Fall 1989 *9*(2), pp. 405–21.

Hall, Robert E. "Explorations in the Gold Standard and Related Policies for Stabilizing the Dollar," in *Inflation, causes and effects*, ed. Robert E. Hall, Chicago: University of Chicago Press, 1982, pp. 111–22.

Haraf, William S. "Toward a Sound Financial System," in Catherine England and Thomas Huertas, eds. 1988, pp. 181–5.

Harper, Ian R. and Coleman, Andrew, "New Monetary Economics," in *The new Palgrave dictionary of money and finance*, ed. John Eatwell, Murray Milgate, and Peter Newman. New York: Stockton Press, 1992, pp. 28–31.

Hasan, Iftekhar and Dwyer, Gerald P., Jr. "Bank Runs in the Free Banking Period," *Journal of Money, Credit, and Banking*, May 1994, *26*(2), pp. 271–88.

Hayek, Friedrich, A. von. "A Commodity Reserve Currency," in *Individualism and economic order*, by Friedrich A. von Hayek, Chicago: University of Chicago Press, 1948, pp. 209–19.

————. *Denationalisation of money*, 2nd edn. London: Institute of Economic Affairs, 1978.

Hellwig, Martin F. "What Do We Know about Currency Competition?" *Z. Wirtschafts. Sozialwissen.*, 1985, *105*(5), pp. 565–88.

Hicks, John. "A Suggestion for Simplifying the Theory of Money," *Economica, NS*, February 1935, *2*(5), pp. 1–19.

Hoover, Kevin D. "Money, Prices and Finance in the New Monetary Economics," *Oxford Economic Papers*, March 1988, *40*(1), pp. 150–67.

Horwitz, Steven. "Competitive Currencies, Legal Restrictions, and the Origins of the Fed: Some Evidence from the Panic of 1907," *Southern Economic Journal*, January 1990, *56*(3), pp. 639–49.

Jao, Y. C. "A Libertarian Approach to Monetary Theory and Policy," *Hong Kong Economic Paper*, 1984, *15*, pp. 1–24.

Jonung, Lars. "The Economics of Private Money: The Experience of Private Notes in Sweden, 1831–1902." Unpublished ms., Stockholm School of Economics, 1989.

Kagin, Donald H. *Private gold coins and patterns of the United States*. New York: Arco, 1981.

Kahn, James A. "Another Look at Free Banking in the United States," *American Economic Review*, September 1985, *75*(4), pp. 881–5.

Kareken, John H. and Wallace, Neil. "Introduction," in *Models of monetary economies*, ed. John H. Kareken and Neil Wallace. Minneapolis: Federal Reserve Bank of Minneapolis, 1980, pp. 1–9.

Kaufman, George. "Bank Runs: Causes, Benefits, and Costs," *Cato Journal*, Winter 1988, 7(3), pp. 559–87.

————. "Bank Contagion: Theory and Evidence." Unpublished ms., Loyalo U of Chicago, 1993.

Kindleberger, Charles P. *Manias, panics, and crashes.* New York: Basic Books, 1978.

————. "Free Minting," in *Privatization: Symposium in honor of Herbert Giersch,* ed. Horst Siebert. Tubingen: J. C. B. Mohr, 1992, pp. 11–22.

Klein, Benjamin. "The Competitive Supply of Money," *Journal of Money, Credit, and Banking,* November 1974, 6(4), pp. 423–53.

Kydland, Finn E. and Prescott, Edward C. "Rules Rather Than Discretion: The Inconsistency of Optimal Plans," *Journal of Political Economy,* June 1977, 85(3), pp. 473–91.

Laidler, David. "Misconceptions about the Real-Bills Doctrine: A Comment on Sargent and Wallace," *Journal of Political Economy,* February 1984, 92(1), pp. 149–55.

————. "Free Banking Theory," in *The new Palgrave dictionary of money and finance,* ed. John Eatwell, Murray Milgate, and Peter Newman. London: Macmillan, 1992, pp. 196–7.

Leung, Siu-ki. "The American Free Banking Experience Re-examined." Unpublished ms., University of South Carolina, 1991.

Makinen, Gail E. and Woodward, G. Thomas. "Some Anecdotal Evidence Relating to the Legal Restrictions Theory of the Demand for Money," *Journal of Political Economy,* April 1986, 94(2), pp. 260–5.

McCallum, Bennett T. *Monetary economics: Theory and policy.* New York: Macmillan, 1989.

McCulloch, J. Huston and Yu, Min-Teh. "Government Deposit Insurance and the Diamond-Dybvig Model." Unpublished ms., Ohio State University, 1993.

Menger, Carl. "The Origin of Money," *Economic Journal,* June 1892, 2(2), pp. 239–55.

Mullineaux, Donald J. "Competitive Monies and the Suffolk Bank System," *Southern Economic Journal,* April 1987, 53(4), pp. 884–98.

Munn, Charles W. "The Development of Joint-Stock Banking in Scotland, 1810–1845," in *Business, Banking, and Urban History,* ed. Anthony Slaven and Derek H. Aldcroft. Edinburgh: John Donald, 1982, pp. 112–28.

————. "Comment" [on White 1991], in Forrest Capie and Geoffrey E. Wood, eds. 1991, pp. 63–7.

Ng, Kenneth. "Free Banking Laws and Barriers to Entry in Banking, 1838–1860," *Journal of Economic History,* December 1988, 48(4), pp. 877–89.

Noyes, Alexander Dana. *History of the national-bank currency.* Washington, DC: US GPO, 1910.

O'Driscoll, Gerald P., Jr. "Money in a Deregulated Financial System," *Federal Reserve Bank of Dallas Economic Review,* May 1985, pp. 1–12.

————. "Deregulation and Monetary Reform," *Federal Reserve Bank of Dallas Economic Review,* July 1986, pp. 19–31.

————. "Deposit Insurance in Theory and Practice," in Catherine England and Thomas Huertas, eds. 1988, pp. 165–79.

Riegel, E. C. *Private enterprise money: A non-political money system.* New York: Harbinger House, 1944.

————. *Flight from inflation: the monetary alternative.* Los Angeles: Heather Foundation, 1978.

Rockoff, Hugh. "The Free Banking Era: A Re-examination," *Journal of Money, Credit, and Banking*, May 1974, *6*(2), pp. 141–67.

————. "Institutional Requirements for Stable Free Banking," *Cato Journal*, Fall 1986, *6*(2), pp. 617–34.

————. "Lessons from the American Experience with Free Banking," in Forrest Capie and Geoffrey E. Wood, eds. 1991, pp. 73–109.

Rolnick, Arthur J. and Weber, Warren E. "New Evidence on the Free Banking Era," *American Economic Review*, December 1983, *73*(5), pp. 1080–91.

————. "The Causes of Free Bank Failures: A Detailed Examination," *Journal of Monetary Economics*, November 1984, *14*(3), pp. 267–91.

————. "Inherent Instability in Banking: The Free Banking Experience," *Cato Journal*, Winter 1986, *5*(3), pp. 877–90.

Rothbard, Murray N. *Power and market: Government and the economy*. Menlo Park, CA: Institute for Humane Studies, 1970.

Salsman, Richard M. *Breaking the banks: Central banking problems and free banking solutions*. Great Barrington, MA: American Institute for Economic Research, 1990.

Samuelson, Paul. "What Classical Monetary Theory Really Was," *Canadian Journal of Economics*, February 1968, *1*(1), pp. 1–15.

————. "Nonoptimality of Money Holding Under Laissez-faire," *Canadian Journal of Economics*, May 1969, *3*(2), pp. 324–30.

Sargent, Thomas J. and Wallace, Neil. "The Real-Bills Doctrine versus the Quantity Theory: A Reconsideration," *Journal of Political Economy*, December 1982, *90*(6), pp. 1212–36.

Saving, Thomas R. "Competitive Money Production and Price Level Determinancy," *Southern Economic Journal*, October, 1976, *43*(4), pp. 987–95.

Schnadt, Norbert and Whittaker, John. "Inflation-proof Currency? The Feasibility of Variable Commodity Standards," *Journal of Money, Credit, and Banking*, May 1993, *25*(2), pp. 214–21.

Schuler, Kurt. "The World History of Free Banking," 1992a in Kevin Dowd, ed. 1992b, pp. 7–47.

————. "Free banking in Canada," 1992b in Kevin Dowd, ed. 1992b, pp. 79–92.

Schwartz, Anna J. "Real and Pseudo-financial Crises," in Forrest Capie and Geoffrey E. Wood, eds. 1986, pp. 11–31.

————. "Financial Stability and the Federal Safety Net," in *Restructuring banking and financial services in America*, ed. William S. Haraf and Rose Marie Kushmeider. Washington, DC: American Enterprise Institute, 1988a, pp. 34–62.

————. "Bank Runs and Deposit Insurance Reform: Comment on Kaufman," *Cato Journal*, Winter 1988b, *7*(3), pp. 589–94.

Sechrest, Larry J. *Free banking: Theory, history, and a laissez-faire model*. Westport, CT: Quorum Books, 1993.

Selgin, George A. *The theory of free banking: Money supply under competitive note issue*. Totowa, NJ: Rowman & Littlefield, 1988.

————. "Legal Restrictions, Financial Weakening, and the Lender of Last Resort," *Cato Journal*, Fall 1989, *9*(2), pp. 429–59.

————. "In Defense of Bank Suspension," *Journal of Financial Services Research*, December 1993, *7*(4), pp. 347–64.

————. "Are Banking Crises a Free-Market Phenomenon?" Unpublished ms., University of Georgia, 1994a.

————. "Free Banking and Monetary Control," *Economic Journal*, November 1994b, *104*(4), pp. 1449–59.

————. "On Ensuring the Acceptability of a New Fiat Money," *Journal of Money, Credit, and Banking*, November 1994c, *26*(4), pp. 808–26.

Selgin, George A. and White, Lawrence, H. "The Evolution of a Free Banking System," *Economic Inquiry*, July 1987, *25*(3), pp. 439–57.

————. "Competitive Monies and the Suffolk Bank System: Comment," *Southern Economic Journal*, July 1988, *55*(1), pp. 215–19.

Short, Eugenie D. and O'Driscoll, Gerald P., Jr. "Deregulation and Deposit Insurance," *Federal Reserve Bank of Dallas Economic Review*, September 1983, pp. 11–12.

Smith, Vera C. *The rationale of central banking*. Indianapolis: Liberty Press, [1936] 1990.

Sumner, Scott. "Privatizing the Mint," *Journal of Money, Credit, and Banking*, February 1993, *25*(1), pp. 13–29.

Taub, Bart. "Private Fiat Money with Many Suppliers," *Journal of Monetary Economics*, September 1985a, *16*(2), pp. 195–208.

————. "Equilibrium Traits of Durable Commodity Money," *Journal of Banking and Finance*, March 1985b, *9*(1), pp. 5–34.

Thompson, Earl. "The Theory of Money and Income Consistent with Orthodox Value Theory," in *Trade, stability, and macroeconomics: Essays in honor of Lloyd A. Metzler*, ed. George Horwich and Paul A. Samuelson. New York: Academic Press, 1974, pp. 427–53.

Timberlake, Richard H. "The Central Banking Role of Clearinghouse Associations," *Journal of Money, Credit, and Banking*, February 1984, *16*(1), pp. 1–15.

Tobin, James. "Commercial Banks as Creators of Money," in *Banking and monetary studies*, ed. Deane Carson. Homewood, IL: Irwin, 1963, pp. 408–19.

————. "A General Equilibrium Approach to Monetary Theory," *Journal of Money, Credit, and Banking*, February 1969, *1*(1), pp. 15–29.

Toma, Mark. "Inflationary Bias of The Federal Reserve System: A Bureaucratic Perspective," *Journal of Monetary Economics*, September 1982, *10*(2), pp. 163–90.

Trivoli, George. *The Suffolk Bank*. London: The Adam Smith Institute, 1979.

Vaubel, Roland. "The History of Currency Competition," in *Currency competition and monetary union*, ed. Pascal Salin. Boston: Martinus Nijhoff, 1984a, pp. 59–73.

————. "The Government's Money Monopoly: Externalities or Natural Monopoly?" *Kyklos*, 1984b, *37*(1), pp. 27–58.

Wagner, Richard E. "Central Banking and the Fed: A Public Choice Perspective," *Cato Journal*, Fall 1986, *6*(2), pp. 519–38.

Wallace, Neil. "A Legal Restrictions Theory of the Demand for 'Money' and the Role of Monetary Policy," *Federal Reserve Bank of Minneapolis Quarterly Review*, Winter 1983, *7*(1), pp. 1–7.

————. "A Suggestion for Oversimplifying the Theory of Money," *Economic Journal*, Supplement, 1988a, *98*(390), pp. 25–36.

————. "Another Attempt to Explain an Illiquid Banking System: The Diamond and Dybvig Model with Sequential Service Taken Seriously," *Federal Reserve Bank of Minneapolis Quarterly Review*, Fall 1988b, *12*(4), pp. 3–16.

Warneryd, Karl. "Legal Restrictions and Monetary Evolution," *Journal of Economic Behaviour and Organization*, January 1990, *13*(1), pp. 117–24.

Wells, Donald R. "The Free Banking Model Applied to Pre-1914 Canadian Banking," *Studies in Economic Analysis*, Fall 1989, *12*(2), pp. 3–21.

White, Lawrence H. *Free banking in Britain: theory, experience and debate, 1800–1845*. Cambridge: Cambridge University Press, 1984a.

————. "Competitive Payments Systems and the Unit of Account," *American Economic Review*, September 1984b, *74*(4), pp. 669–712.

————. "Regulatory Sources of Instability in Banking [Comment on Rolnick and Weber]," *Cato Journal*, Winter 1986a, *5*(3), pp. 891–97.

————. "Competitive Payments Systems: Reply," *American Economic Review*, September 1986b, *76*(4), pp. 850–3.

————. "Accounting for Non-interest-Bearing Currency: A Critique of the Legal Restrictions Theory of Money," *Journal of Money, Credit, and Banking*, November 1987, *19*(4), pp. 448–56.

————. "Banking without a Central Bank: Scotland before 1844 as a 'Free Banking System'," in Forrest Capie and Geoffrey E. Wood, eds. 1991, pp. 37–62.

————. "Free Banking in Scotland Before 1844," in Kevin Dowd, ed. 1992b, pp. 157–86.

Wicker, Elmus. "A Reconsideration of the Causes of the Banking Panic of 1930," *Journal of Economic History*, September 1980, *40*(3), pp. 571–83.

Wigmore, Barrie A. "Was the Bank Holiday of 1933 Caused by a Run on the Dollar?" *Journal of Economic History*, September 1987, *47*(3), pp. 739–55.

Williamson, Stephen D. "Laissez-Faire Banking and Circulating Media of Exchange," *Journal of Financial Intermediation*, June 1992, *2*(2), pp. 134–67.

Yeager, Leland B. "A Competitive Payments System: Some Objections Considered," *Journal of Post Keynesian Economics*, Spring 1989, *11*(3), pp. 370–7.

2

THE EVOLUTION OF A FREE BANKING SYSTEM*

with Lawrence H. White

INTRODUCTION

Monetary theorists' assumptions concerning the institutional features of a completely unregulated monetary system have ranged from the proliferation of numerous competing private fiat currencies at one extreme to the complete disappearance of money at the other.[1] While these assumptions have generated clear-cut and provocative conclusions, their plausibility or realism in light of historical experience is open to serious doubt. These doubts may unfortunately suggest that any discussion of an unregulated monetary system (or "free banking" system) must be tenuous and highly speculative. This chapter trys to show, to the contrary, that important institutional features of a free banking system, in particular the nature of payment media, can be realistically grounded by constructing a logical explanation of its evolution.

The method of logical evolutionary explanation has previously been applied to monetary institutions by Hicks (1967) and Menger (1892), among others. The present study integrates and extends work along their lines. The method is employed here in the belief that it has been unduly neglected in recent work, not that it is the only valid method for theoretically explaining institutional arrangements. The more standard method of building explicit transactions costs or informational imperfections or asymmetries into an optimization model has unquestionably been useful in the task of explaining why banks exist as intermediaries (Santomero (1984, 577–80) surveys this literature).

Our investigation derives arrangements that would have arisen had state intervention never occurred. The results should therefore help to identify the degree to which features of current monetary and banking institutions are rooted in market forces and the degree to which they have grown out of regulatory intervention. Such information gives important clues about how

*Reprinted, with permission, from *Economic Inquiry*, Vol. XXV, No. 3 (July 1987).

future deregulation would modify institutions. We show that sophisticated monetary arrangements, whose institutional features are described, emerge in the absence of regulation. No strong claims are advanced here about the welfare properties of these arrangements.[2] We aim to establish the most credible path for unrestricted monetary evolution, but certainly not the only possible path. Economists who find other institutional outcomes more plausible for an unregulated system will, we hope, similarly try to explain why and how those outcomes would emerge.

The evolution of a free banking system, following the emergence of standardized commodity money, proceeds through three stages. These are, first, the development of basic money-transfer services which substitute for the physical transportation of specie; second, the emergence of easily assignable and negotiable bank demand liabilities (inside money); and third, the development of arrangements for the routine exchange ("clearing") of inside monies among rival banks. The historical time separating these stages is not crucial. The path of development, rather than being one of steady progress as pictured here, may in practice involve false starts or creative leaps. What is essential is that each stage is the logical invisible-hand outgrowth of the circumstances that preceded it. In other words, each successive step in the process of evolution originates in individuals' discovery of new ways to promote their self-interest, with the outcome an arrangement at which no individual consciously aims.

COMMODITY MONEY

Because the use of money logically and historically precedes the emergence of banking firms, we begin with an account of the origin of money. Our account follows that of Menger (1892), who furnished an invisible-hand explanation, consistent with historical and anthropological evidence, of how money originated as a product of undesigned or spontaneous evolution.[3] Menger's theory shows that no state intervention is necessary in order to establish a basic medium of exchange or unit of account. It also provides a useful prototype for our explanations of how subsequent banking institutions evolve in spontaneous fashion.

In premonetary society, traders relying upon barter initially offer goods in exchange only for other goods directly entering their consumption or household production plans. The number of bargains struck this way is small, owing to the well-known problem of finding what Jevons termed a "double coincidence of wants." Before long some frustrated barterer realizes that he or she can increase his or her chances for success by adopting a two-stage procedure. The barterer can trade his or her wares for some good, regardless of its direct usefulness which will more easily find a taker among those selling what he or she ultimately wants. It follows that the earliest media of exchange are simply goods perceived to be in relatively widespread demand. The widening of demand for these things owing to their use as media of exchange reinforces their superior salability. Other traders eventually recognize the gains achieved by those using indirect exchange, and emulate them, even though they may be unaware of the reason for the advantages from using a medium of exchange. This emulation further enhances the acceptance of the most widely accepted media, elevating one or two goods above all others in salability. The snowballing of salability results in the spontaneous appearance of generally accepted media of exchange. Eventually traders throughout an economy converge on using a single commodity as a generally accepted medium of exchange, i.e., as money.

Historical evidence on primitive monies indicates that cattle were often the most frequently exchanged commodity, and that a standardized "cow" was the earliest unit of account. Cattle were a poor general medium of exchange, however, because of their relative nontransportability and nonuniformity. Not until the discovery of metals and of methods for working them did the use of money replace barter widely.[4] According to Jacques Melitz (1974, 95), common attributions of moneyness to primitive media, especially nonmetallic "moneys" (with the exception of cowries in China), warrant skepticism because many of these media (e.g., the Yap stones of Melanesia) do not meet any reasonably strict definition of money.

The emergence of coinage can also be explained as a spontaneous development, an unplanned result of merchants' attempts to minimize the necessity for assessing and weighing amounts of commodity money received in exchange. Merchants may at first mark irregular metallic nuggets or pieces after having assessed their quality. A merchant recognizing his or her own or another's mark can then avoid the trouble and cost of reassessment. Marking gives way to stamping or punching, which eventually leads to specialists' making coins in their modern form. Techniques for milling coin edges and covering the entire surface with type provide safeguards against clipping and sweating and so allow coinage to serve as a guarantee of weight as well as of quality. Arthur R. Burns (1927a, 297–304; 1927b, 59) has illustrated this process with evidence from ancient Lydia, where coins of electrum (a naturally occuring silver–gold alloy) came into early use.

Absent state interference, coinage is a private industry encompassing various competing brands. Under competition coins are valued according to bullion content plus a premium equal to the marginal cost of mintage. The demand for readily exchangeable coins promotes the emergence of standard weights and fineness. Nonstandard coins must circulate at a discount because of the extra computational burden they impose, so that their production is unprofitable. States seem to have monopolized coinage early in history, but not by outcompeting private mints. Rather, the evidence suggests that state coinage monopolies were regularly established by legal compulsion and for reasons of propaganda and mono-poly profit. State-minted coins functioned both as a symbol of rule and as a source of profits from shaving, clipping, and seignorage. For these reasons coinage became a state function throughout the world by the end of the seventh century (Burns 1927a, 308; 1927b, 78).

BANKING FIRMS

The counting and transporting of coins entail considerable inconvenience. Traders, particularly those frequently making large or distant exchanges, will naturally seek lower-cost means of transferring ownership of money. One likely locus for development of such means is the market where local coins are exchanged for foreign coins. Standard coins may differ interlo-cally even in the absence of local state interventions because of geographic diseconomies in reputation building for mints. A coin-exchange market then naturally arises with interlocal trade. A trader who uses a money changer must initially count and carry in local coin each time he or she wants to acquire foreign coin, or vice versa. The trader can reduce costs by establishing a standing account balance, to build up at his or her conve-nience and draw upon as desired. The money changer's inventories equip him or her to provide such accounts, which constitute demand deposits, and even to allow overdrafts. These deposits may originally be nontransferable. But it will soon be apparent, where one customer withdraws coins in order to pay a recipient who redeposits them with the same exchange banker, that the transfer is more easily made at the banker's place of business, or more easily yet by persuading the banker to make the transfer on his or her books without any handling of coins. Thus trading individuals come to keep money balances with agencies which can make payments by ledger-account transfers.

Money-transfer services of this sort, provided by money changers and bill brokers in twelfth century Genoa and at medieval trade fairs in Champagne, mark the earliest recorded forms of banking.[5] In time all the major European trading centers had "transfer banks," as Raymond de Roover (1974, 184) calls them; he comments that "deposit banking grew out of [money-changing] activity, because the money changers developed a system of local payments by book transfer." In our view, however, the taking of deposits on at least a small scale logically *precedes* the devel-opment of book-transfer methods of payment.

Money-transfer services may also develop in connection with deposits made for safekeeping rather than for money changing. The well-known story of the origins of goldsmith banking in seventeenth century England illustrates this development. Wealthy persons may temporarily lodge commodity money with scrivemers, goldsmiths, mintmasters, and other reputable vault-owners for safekeeping. Coin and bullion thus lodged must be physically withdrawn and transferred for its owner to use it as a means of payment. Exchanges in which the recipient redeposits it in the same vault (like redeposits with a money changer or bill broker) create obvious advantages in making the transfer at the vault, or better yet in simply notifying the vault's custodian to make the transfer on his or her books. In England, scriveners were the earliest pioneers in the banking trade; in Stuart times they were almost entirey displaced by goldsmith bankers. English goldsmiths evidently became transfer bankers during the seventeenth century, when they "began to keep a 'running cash' for the convenience of merchants and country gentlemen" (de Roover 1974, 83–4). The confiscation by Charles I of gold deposited for safekeeping at the Royal Mint ended that institution's participation in the process of banking development. Private mints, had they been permitted, would have been logical sites for early banking activities.

Transfer banking is not connected with intermediation between borrowers and lenders when the banker acts strictly like a warehouse, giving deposit receipts which are regular warehouse dockets. The strict warehouse banker is a bailee rather than a debtor to depositors and can make loans only out of his or her personal wealth. Two conditions make it possible, however, to take advantage of the interest income available from lending out depositors' balances, even while satisfying depositors' desire to have their funds withdrawable on demand: (1) money is fungible, which allows a depositor to be repaid in coin and bullion not identical to that brought in, and (2) the law of large numbers with random withdrawals and deposits makes a fractional reserve sufficient to meet actual withdrawal demands with high probability even though any single account may be removed without notice. (Interestingly, these conditions may also be met in the warehousing of standard-quality grain, so that fractional reserve "banking" can likewise develop there, as Williams (1984) has shown.) The lending of depositors' balances is an innovation that taps a vast new source of loanable funds and alters fundamentally the relationship of the banker to the depositor customers.

Historically in England, according to Richards (1965, 223), "the bailee . . . developed into the debtor of the depositor; and the depositor became an investor who loaned his money . . . for a consideration." Money "warehouse receipts" became merely ready promissory notes. W. R. Bisschop (1910, 50n) reports that English warehouse bankers had become intermediaries by the time of Charles II (1660–85): "Any deposit made in any other shape than ornament was looked upon by them as a free loan." Competition for deposits prompted the payment of interest on deposits, and the attractiveness of interest on safe and accessible deposits in turn apparently made the practice of depositing widespread among all ranks of people (Powell 1966, 56–7).

TRANSFERABLE INSTRUMENTS

Under these circumstances the effective money supply obviously becomes greater than the existing stock of specie alone. The most important banking procedures and devices, however, have yet to develop. Many purchases are still made with actual coin. Bank depositors, in order to satisfy changing needs for money at hand, make frequent withdrawals from and deposits into their bank balances. These actions may in the aggregate largely cancel out through the law of large numbers. But they require the banks to hold greater precautionary commodity money reserves, and consequently to maintain a larger spread between deposit and loan rates of interest, than is necessary when payments practices become more sophisticated. Greater sophistication comes with the emergence of negotiable bank instruments, able to pass easily in exchange from one person to another, which replace coin and nonnegotiable deposit receipts in transactions balances. The use of coin is also superceded by the development of more efficient means for the bank-mediated transfer of deposits.

Assignability and negotiability may develop through several steps. Initially the assignment of deposited money (whether "warehoused" or entrusted to the banker for lending at interest) by the depositor to another party may require the presence of all three parties to the exchange or their attorneys. Money "warehouse receipts" (or promissory notes) and running deposit balances cannot be assigned by the owner's endorsement without the banker acting as witness. An important innovation is the development of bank-issued promissory notes transferable by endorsement. Assignable notes in turn give way to fully negotiable banknotes assigned to no one in particular but instead payable to the bearer on demand. A parallel development is the nonnegotiable check enabling the depositor to transfer balances to a specific party, in turn giving way to the negotiable check which can be repeatedly endorsed or made out "to cash."[6] Thus the modern forms of inside money – redeemable bearer banknotes and checkable deposits – are established. Once this stage is reached it is not difficult for bankers to conceive what Hartley Withers (1920, 24) has called "the epoch-making notion" – in our view it is only an incremental step – of giving inside money not only to depositors of metal but also to borrowers of money. The use of inside money enhances both customer and bank profits, so that only the possible reluctance of courts to enforce obligations represented by assigned or bearer paper stands in the way of its rapid development.

In England bearer notes were first recognized during the reign of Charles II, about the time when warehouse banking was giving way to fractional reserve transfer banking. At first the courts gave their grudging approval to the growing practice of repeated endorsement of promissory notes. Then after some controversy, fully negotiable notes were recognized by Act of

Parliament. In France, Holland, and Italy during the sixteenth century merchants' checks "drawn in blank" circulated within limited circles and may have cleared the way for the appearance of banknotes (Usher 1943, 189; Richards 1965, 46, 225).

REGULAR NOTE EXCHANGE

Further economies in the use of commodity money require more complete circulation of inside money in place of commodity money, and more complete development of banknote and check clearing facilities to reduce the need for commodity money reserves. It is relatively straightforward to show that bankers and other agents pursuing their self-interest are indeed led to improve the acceptability of inside money and the efficiency of banking operations.

At this stage, although banknotes are less cumbersome than coin, and checkable deposits are both convenient for certain transactions and interest paying, some coin still remains in circulation. Consumers trust a local bank's notes more than a distant bank's notes because they are more aware of the local notes' likelihood of being honored and more familiar with their appearance (hence less prone to accepting forgeries). It follows that the cost to a bank of building a reputation for its issues – particularly regarding note convertibility – is higher in places further from the place of issue and redemption. The establishment of a network of bank branches for redemption is limited by transportation and communication costs. In the early stages of banking development the par circulation of every bank's notes and checks is therefore geographically relatively limited.[7] People who generally hold the inside money of a local bank but who do business in distant towns must either take the trouble to redeem some of their holdings for gold and incur the inconvenience of transporting coin, or suffer a loss in value on their notes by carrying them to a locale where they are accepted only at a discount, if at all. (The alternative practice of keeping on hand notes from each locality they deal with is likely to be prohibitively costly in terms of foregone interest.) In general, a brand of inside money will initially be used only for transactions in the vicinity of the issuer, and coin will continue to be held alongside notes of like denomination. The use of commodity money in circulation requires banks to hold commodity reserves greater than those required by the transfer of inside money, because the withdrawal of commodity money for spending generates more volatile reserve outflows than the spending of notes or deposits.

In this situation, profit opportunities arise which prompt actions leading to more general acceptance of particular inside monies. The discounting of notes outside the neighborhood of the issuing bank's office creates an arbitrage opportunity when the par value of notes (i.e. their face redemption value in commodity money) exceeds the price at which they can be purchased for commodity money or local issues in a distant town plus (secularly falling) transaction and transportation costs. As interlocal trade grows, "note brokers" with specialized knowledge of distant banks can make a business, just as retail foreign currency brokers do today, of buying discounted nonlocal notes and transporting them to their par circulation areas or reselling them to travelers bound for those areas. Competition eventually reduces note discounts to the level of transaction and transportation costs plus a factor for redemption risk. By accepting the notes of unfamiliar banks at minimal commission rates, brokers unintentionally increase the general acceptability of notes, and promote their use in place of commodity money.

To this point we have implicitly assumed that banks refuse to accept one another's notes. This is not unreasonable; banks have as many reasons as other individuals do to refuse notes unfamiliar to them or difficult to redeem. They have in addition a further incentive for refusing to accept notes from rival banks, which is that by doing so they help to limit the acceptability of these notes, thereby enhancing the demand for their own issues. To cite just one historical illustration of this, the Bank of Scotland and the Royal Bank of Scotland – the first two banks of issue located in Edinburgh – refused to accept the notes of "provincial" banks of issue for a number of years (see Checkland 1975, 126).

Nevertheless note brokerage presents opportunities for profit to bankers. Banks can outcompete other brokers because, unlike other brokers, they can issue their own notes (or deposit balances) to purchase "foreign" notes and need not hold costly till money. Each bank has an additional incentive to accept rival notes: larger interest earnings. If the notes acquired are redeemed sooner than the notes issued, interest-earning assets can be purchased and held in the interim. This profit from "float" can be continually renewed. In other words, a bank can maintain a permanently larger circulation of its own notes by continually replacing other notes with its own, and correspondingly can hold more earning assets than it otherwise could. If other banks are simultaneously replacing Bank A's notes with their own, there may be no absolute increase in A's circulation compared to the situation in which no bank accepts rival notes. But there will be an increase compared to Bank A not accepting, given whatever policies rivals are following, so that the incentive remains. (We argue below that in fact an indirect consequence of *other* banks' par acceptance of Bank A notes will be an absolute increase in A-note holding in place of specie holding.) Where transaction and transportation costs and risks are low enough, competition for circulation will narrow the brokerage fee to zero, i.e., will lead the banks to general acceptance of one another's notes at par. The development of par acceptance by this route does not require that the banks explicitly and mutually agree to such a policy.

An alternative scenario, which assumes strategic behavior by the banks, leads to the same result. A bank may aggressively purchase foreign notes in the market, and then suddenly return large quantities to their issuers for redemption in commodity money, hoping to force an unprepared issuer to suspend payments. The aggressor hopes to gain market share by damaging a rival's reputation or even forcing it into liquidation. These tactics, historically known as "note picking" and "note duelling," initially provoke the other issuers to respond in kind. Collecting and redeeming the first bank's notes not only returns the damage, but helps replenish the other banks' reserves. Purchasing its rivals' notes at par allows a bank to collect them in greater quantities, and may therefore be adopted. (Arbitrage-redemption of notes paid out precludes paying a price above par.) In the long run, nonaggression among banks should emerge, being less costly for all sides. Note picking and note duelling are costly and ineffectual ways to promote circulation when others do likewise. Banks thus find it profitable to take rivals' notes only as these are brought to them for deposit or exchange, and to return the collected notes to their issuers promptly in exchange for commodity money reserves. This result is contrary to Eugene Fama's (1983, 19) suggestion that note duelling will persist indefinitely. It is an example of the "tit for tat" strategy, as discussed by Robert Axelrod (1984), proving dominant in a repeated-game setting.[8] Again, no explicitly negotiated pact is necessary. It only takes a single bank acting without cooperation from other banks to nudge the rest towards par acceptance (zero brokerage fees) as a defensive measure to maintain their reserves and circulation.

In New England at the beginning of the nineteenth century the Boston banks gave the nudge that put the whole region – with its multitude of "country" banks of issue far removed from the city – on a par-acceptance basis (Trivoli 1979). In Scotland the Royal Bank, when it opened for business in 1727, immediately began accepting at par the notes of the Bank of Scotland, at that time its only rival, and instigated a short-lived note duel. One response by the Bank of Scotland, later widely adopted, is notable: the Bank inserted a clause into its notes giving it the option (which it did not normally exercise) of delaying redemption for six months, in which event it would pay a bonus amounting to 5 per cent per annum (Checkland 1975, 60, 67–8). In both places established banks, even after they had begun accepting each other's notes at par, sometimes refused to take the notes of new entrants. They soon changed their policies because the new banks that accepted and redeemed their notes were draining their reserves, while the established banks could not offset this without engaging in the same practice.

Banks that accept other banks' notes at par improve the market for their own notes and, unintentionally, for the notes that they accept. This makes a third scenario possible: if two banks both understand these circulation gains, they may explicitly enter a mutual par-acceptance arrangement. Others will emulate them, leading to general par acceptance. This explanation, previously offered by White (1984a, 19–21), assumes slightly more knowledge on the part of banks than the first two scenarios. Historical evidence of such explicit arrangements in Scotland is provided by Munn (1975).

Statistics from Boston dramatically illustrate the mutual circulation gains from par-acceptance arrangements. From 1824 to 1833 the note circulation of the Boston banks increased 57 per cent, but the Boston circulation of country banks increased 148 per cent, despite the Boston banks' intent to drive the country banks out of business (Lake 1947, 186: Trivoli 1979, 10–12). There is room for all banks to gain because the spread of par acceptance makes inside money more attractive to hold relative to commodity money. Since notes from one town are now accepted in a distant town at par, there is no longer good reason to lug around commodity money. As par note acceptance developed in Scotland, Canada, and New England – places where note issue was least restricted – during the nineteenth century, gold virtually disappeared from circulation. (Small amounts of gold coin were still used in these places at least in part because of restrictions upon the issue of "token" coin and of small denomination notes. In an entirely free system, such restrictions would not exist.) In England and the rest of the United States, where banking (and note issue in particular) were less free, gold remained in circulation.

Even the complete displacement of commodity money in circulation by inside money does not, however, exhaust the possibilities for economizing on commodity money. Much of the specie formerly used in circulation to settle exchanges outside the banks may still be needed to settle clearings among them. Banks can substantially reduce their prudentially required holdings of commodity money by making regular note exchanges which allow them to offset their mutual obligations. Only net clearings rather than gross clearings are then settled in commodity money. The probability of any given-sized reserve loss in a given period is accordingly reduced (by the law of large numbers) and each bank can prudently reduce its ratio of reserves to demand liabilities.

The gains to be had from rationalization of note exchange are illustrated by the provincial Scottish banks before 1771, which practiced par acceptance without regular exchange. Note duelling among these banks was not uncommon (Leslie 1950, 8–9; Munn 1981, 23–4), and to guard against redemption raids they had to keep substantial reserves. Munn's figures (1981, 141) show that their reserves during this period were typically above 10 per cent of total liabilities. This contrasts with reserve ratios of around 2 per cent that were typical after note clearings became routine. The advantages of regular note exchange are great enough to have secured its eventual adoption in every historical instance of relatively free plural note issue.

CLEARINGHOUSES

The most readily made arrangements for note exchange are bilateral. In a system of more than two issuers, however, multilateral note exchange provides even greater economies. Reserve-holding economies result from the offsetting of claims that would otherwise be settled in specie. Multilateral clearing also allows savings in time and transportation costs by allowing all debts to be settled in one place and during one meeting rather than in numerous scattered meetings.

The institutional embodiment of multilateral note and deposit exchange, the clearinghouse, may evolve gradually from simpler note-exchange arrangements. For example, the note-exchange agents of banks A and B may accidentally meet each other at the counter of bank C. The greater the number of banks exchanging bilaterally, the less likely it is that such an encounter could be avoided. It would be natural for these two agents to recognize the savings in simple time and shoe-leather costs from settling their own exchange then and there, and from agreeing to do it again next time out, and then regularly. From a set of three pairwise settlements around one table it is not a large step toward the computation and settlement of combined net clearing balances. Once the advantages of this become clear to management, particularly the reserve-holding economies which may not have concerned the note porters, the institution will spread. Fourth, fifth, and subsequent banks may join later meetings. Or similar, regular few-sided exchanges may be formed among other groups of banks, either independently or by one of the first three banks, whose meetings are later combined with the meetings of the original group. Eventually all the banks within an economy will be connected through one or a small number of clearinghouses.

The histories of the best-known early clearinghouses, in London, Edinburgh, and New York all conform to this general pattern. Gibbons (1858, 292) reports that in New York the impetus for change from numerous bilateral exchanges to combined multilateral exchange came from note porters who "crossed and re-crossed each other's footsteps constantly." Among the London check porters, as related by Bisschop (1910, 160), "occasional encounters developed into daily meetings at a certain fixed place. At length the bankers themselves resolved to organize these meetings on a regular basis in a room specially reserved for this purpose."

The settlement of interbank obligations is initially made by physical transfer of commodity money at the conclusion of clearing sessions. Banks will soon find it economical to settle instead by means of transferable reserve accounts kept on the books of the clearinghouse, echoing the original development of transfer banking. These accounts may be deposits or equity shares denominated in currency units. As a transfer bank, the clearinghouse need not hold 100 per cent reserves, and can safely pay its members a return (net of operating costs) by holding safe earning assets. This development reduces a member bank's cost of holding reserves, but does not eliminate it because alternative assets yield a higher return. Unless regulated directly by the clearinghouse, a bank's reserve ratio is determined by precautionary liquidity considerations depending mainly on the volume and volatility of net clearings and the clearinghouse penalty for reserve deficiency (see Baltensperger 1980, 4–9; Santomero 1984, 584–6).

Once established, a clearinghouse may serve several purposes beyond the economical exchange and settlement of interbank obligations. It can become, in the words of James G. Cannon (1908, 97), "a medium for united action among the banks in ways that did not exist even in the imagination of those who were instrumental in its inception." One task the clearinghouse may take on is to serve as a credit information bureau for its members; by pooling their records, banks can learn whether loan applicants have had bad debts in the past or are overextented to other banks at present, and can then take appropriate precautions (Cannon 1910, 135). Through the clearinghouse banks can also share information concerning bounced checks, forgeries, and the like.

The clearinghouse may also police the soundness of each member bank in order to assure the other member banks that notes and deposits are safe to accept for clearing. As part of this function, banks may be required to furnish financial statements and may have their books audited by clearinghouse examiners. The Chicago clearinghouse insisted on statements as early as 1867, and in 1876 gained the right to carry out comprehensive examinations whenever desired, to determine any member's financial condition (James 1938, 372–3, 499). Regular examinations began in 1906 (Cannon 1910, 138–9). Other clearinghouses, such as the Suffolk Bank and the Edinburgh clearinghouse, took their bearings mainly from the trends of members' clearing balances and traditional canons of sound banking practice. Those two clearinghouses enjoyed such high repute as certifying agencies that to be taken off their lists of members in good standing meant a serious loss in reputation and hence business for an offending bank (Trivoli 1979, 20; Graham 1911, 59).

It is possible that a clearinghouse may attempt to organize collusive agreements on interest rates, exchange rates, and fee schedules for its members. However, rates inconsistent with the results of competition would tend to break down under unregulated conditions, for the standard reason that secretly underbidding a cartel has concentrated benefits and largely external costs. A clear example of this comes from Scottish experience (Checkland 1975, 391–427). The Edinburgh banks set up a committee in 1828 to set borrowing and lending rates. The Glasgow banks joined a new version of the committee in 1836, at which time it represented the preponderance of Scottish banks in number and in total assets. Though not a clearinghouse association itself, the committee had much the same membership as the Edinburgh clearinghouse. In spite of repeated formal agreements, the committee could not hold members to its recommended interest rates. Not until after entry to the industry was closed in 1844 did the agreements become at all effective.

Perhaps the most interesting of all the roles a clearinghouse may perform is to assist its members in times of crisis (see Canon 1910, 24). If a bank or group of banks is temporarily unable to pay its clearing balances, or if it experiences a run on its commodity money reserves, the clearinghouse can serve as a medium through which more liquid banks lend to less liquid ones. It provides the framework for an intermittent, short-term credit market similar to the continuous federal funds market from which reserve-deficient American banks presently borrow. Another possible emergency function of clearinghouses is note issue. This function is called for when member banks are artificially restricted from issuing, as for example US banks were by the bond collateral requirements of the National Banking Acts, so that the banks are not able independently to fulfill all of their depositors' requests for hand-to-hand means of payment. Currency shortages occurred frequently in the United States during the second half of the nineteenth century, and clearinghouses helped to fill the void caused by deficient note issues of the National Banks.[9]

THE MATURE FREE BANKING SYSTEM

We have now reached the stage of mature development of a stylized free banking system, insofar as historical evidence illuminates its likely structural and operational characteristics. Evidence on industry structure from Scotland, Canada, Sweden, and elsewhere indicates that unregulated development does not produce natural monopoly, but rather an industry consisting of numerous competing banking firms, most having widespread branches, all of which are joined through one or more clearinghouses. In Scotland there were nineteen banks of issue in 1844, the final year of free entry. The largest four banks supplied 46.7 per cent of the note circulation. In addition to their head offices the banks had 363 branch offices, 43.5 per cent of which were owned by the largest (measured again by note issue) four banks.[10]

The banks in the mature system issue inside money in the shape of paper notes and demand deposit accounts (checkable either by paper or electronic means) that circulate routinely at par. Banks may also issue redeemable token coins, more durable but lighter and cheaper, to take the place of full-bodied coins as small change. Each bank's notes and tokens bear distinct brand name identification marks and are issued in the denominations the public is most willing to hold. Because of the computational costs that would be involved in each transfer, interest is not likely to accrue on commonly used denominations of banknotes or tokens, contrary to the hypothesis of Neil Wallace (1983) that all currency would bear interest under *laissez-faire*.[11] Checkable accounts, however, provide a competitive yield reflecting rates available on interest-earning assets issued outside the banking system.

Checkable bank accounts are most familiarly structured as demand deposits, i.e., liabilities having a predetermined payoff payable on demand. An important reason for this structure is that historically a debt contract has been easier for the depositor to monitor and enforce than an equity contract which ties the account's payoff to the performance of a costly-to-observe asset portfolio. The predetermined payoff feature, however, raises the possibility of insolvency and consequently of a run on the bank if depositors fear that the last in line will receive less than a full payoff. One method of forestalling runs that may prevail in an unregulated banking system is the advertised holding of a large equity cushion, either on the bank's books or off them in the form of extended liability for bank shareholders. If this method were inadequate to assure depositors, banks might provide an alternative solution by linking checkability to equity or mutual-fund type accounts with postdetermined rather than predetermined payoffs. The obstacles to such accounts (asset-monitoring and enforcement costs) have been eroded over the centuries by the emergence of easy-to-observe assets, namely publicly traded securities. Insolvency is ruled out for a balance sheet without debt liabilities, and the incentive to redeem ahead of other account holders is eliminated. An institution that linked checkability to equity accounts would operate like a contemporary money-market mutual fund, except that it would be directly tied into the clearing system (rather than having to clear via a deposit bank). Its optimal reserve holdings would be determined in the same way as those of a standard bank.

The assets of unregulated banks would presumably include short-term commercial paper, bonds of corporations and government agencies, and loans on various types of collateral. Without particular information on the assets available in the economy, the structure of asset portfolios cannot be characterized in detail, except to say that the banks presumably strive to maximize the present value of their interest earnings, net of operating and liquidity costs, discounted at risk-adjusted rates. The declining probability of larger liquidity needs, and the trade-off at the margin between liquidity and interest yield, suggest a spectrum of assets ranging from perfectly liquid reserves, to highly liquid interest-earning investments (these constitute a "secondary reserve"), to less liquid higher-earning assets. Thus far, because the focus has been on monetary arrangements, the only bank liabilities discussed have been notes and checking accounts. Unregulated banks would almost certainly diversify on the liability side by offering a variety of time deposits and also travelers' checks. Some banks would probably become involved in such related lines of business as the production of bullion and token fractional coins, issue of credit cards, and management of mutual funds. Such banks would fulfill the contemporary ideal of the "financial supermarket," with the additional feature of issuing banknotes.

Commodity money seldom if ever appears in circulation in the mature system, virtually all of it (outside numismatic collections) having been offered to the banks in exchange for inside money. Some commodity money will continue to be held by clearinghouses so long as it is the ultimate settlement asset among them. In the limit, if inter-clearinghouse settlements were made entirely with other assets (perhaps claims on a super-clearinghouse which itself holds negligible commodity money), and if the public were completely weaned from holding commodity money, the active demand for the old-fashioned money commodity would be wholly nonmonetary. The flow supply formerly sent to the mints would be devoted to industrial and other uses. Markets for those uses would determine the relative price of the commodity. The purchasing power of monetary instruments would continue to be fixed by the holder's contractual right (even if never exercised) to redeem them for physically specified quantities of the money commodity. The problem of meeting any significant redemption request (e.g., a "run" on a bank) could be contractually handled, as it was historically during note-duelling episodes, by invoking an "option clause" that allows the bank a specified period of time to gather the necessary commodity money while compensating the redeeming party for the delay. The clause need not (and historically did not) impair the par circulation of bank liabilities.

This picture of an unregulated banking system differs significantly in its institutional features from the visions presented in some of the recent literature on competitive payments systems. The system described here has assets fitting standard definitions of money. Banks and clearinghouses hold (except in the limit), and are contractually obligated to provide at request, high-powered reserve money (commodity money or deposits at the clearinghouse), and they issue debt liabilities (inside money) with which payments are generally made. These features contrast with the situation envisioned by Black (1970) and Fama (1980), in which "banks" hold no reserve assets and the payments mechanism operates by transferring equities or mutual fund shares unlinked to any money.

Bank reserves do not disappear in the evolution of a free banking system, as analyzed here, because the existence of bank liabilities that are promises to pay presupposes some more fundamental means of payment that is the thing promised. Individuals may forego actual redemption of promises, preferring to hold them instead of commodity money, so long as they believe that they will receive high-powered money if they ask for it.

Banks, on the other hand, have a competitive incentive to redeem one another's liabilities regularly. So long as net clearing balances have a positive probability of being nonzero, reserves will continue to be held. In a system without reserve money it is not clear what would be used to settle clearing balances. In an evolved system, the scarcity of the money commodity and the costliness of holding reserves moreover serve to pin down the price level and to limit the quantity of inside money. In a moneyless system it is not clear what forces limit the expansion of payment media nor what pins down the price level. Nor are these things clear, at the other extreme, in a model of multiple competing fiat monies.[12]

Our analysis indicates that commodity-based money would persist in the absence of intervention, for the reason that the supreme salability of the particular money good is self-reinforcing. This result contradicts recent views (see Black 1970; Fama 1980; Greenfield and Yeager 1983; Yeager 1985) that associate complete deregulation with the replacement of monetary exchange by a sophisticated form of barter. (To be sure, Greenfield and Yeager recognize that their system would be unlikely to emerge without deliberate action by government, particularly given a government-dominated monetary system as the starting point.) In a commodity-based-money economy, prices are stated in terms of a unit of the money commodity, so the question of using an abstract unit of account does not arise as it does in a sophisticated barter setting.[13] Even if actual commodity money were to disappear from reserves and circulation, the media of exchange would not be "divorced" from the commodity unit of account; they would be linked by redeemability contracts. We can see no force severing this link. Contrary to Woolsey (1985), the renunciation of commodity redemption obligations is not compelled by economization of reserves. Thus we find no basis for the spontaneous emergence of a multicommodity monetary standard or of any pure fiat monetary standard, such as contemplated in works by Hall (1982), Woolsey (1984), Klein (1974), and Hayek (1978). In short, unregulated banking would be much less radically unconventional, and much more akin to existing financial institutions than recent literature on the topic suggests.

One important contemporary financial institution is nonetheless missing from our account, namely the central bank. We find no market forces leading to the spontaneous emergence of a central bank, in contrast to the view of Charles Goodhart. (For this discussion a central bank is closely enough defined, following Goodhart (1985, 3–8), as an agency with two related powers: monetary policy, and external regulation of the banking system.) Goodhart (1985, 76) argues that the development of a central bank is "natural" because "the natural process of centralization of inter-bank deposits with leading commercial banks tends toward the development of a banks' club" which then needs an independent arbiter. But even on his own account the forces that historically promoted centralized interbank deposits were *not* "natural" in any *laissez-faire* sense. They stemmed crucially from legal restrictions, particularly the awarding of a monopoly of note issue or the suppression of branch banking. Where no legislation inhibits the growth of branched banking firms with direct access to investment markets in the economy's financial center, and able to issue their own notes, it is not at all apparent that profit seeking compels any significant interbank depositing of reserves. Walter Bagehot (1873, 66–8) argued persuasively that "the natural system – that which would have sprung up if Government had let banking alone – is that of many banks of equal or not altogether unequal size" and that in such a system no bank "gets so much before the others that the others voluntarily place their reserves in its keeping." None of the relevant historical cases (Scotland, Canada, Sweden) shows any significant tendency toward interbank deposits.

We have seen that reserves do tend to centralize, on the other hand, in the clearinghouses. And clearinghouses, as Gorton (1985a, 277, 283; 1985b, 274) has recently emphasized, may take on functions that are today associated with national central banks: holding reserves for clearing purposes, establishing and policing safety and soundness standards for member banks, and managing panics should they arise. But these functional similarities should not be taken to indicate that clearinghouses have (or would have) freely evolved into central banks. The similarities instead reflect the pre-emption of clearinghouse functions by legally privileged banks or, particularly in the founding of the Federal Reserve System (Gorton 1985a, 277; Timberlake 1984), the deliberate nationalization of clearinghouse functions. Central banks have emerged from legalization contravening, not complementing, spontaneous market developments.[14]

NOTES

1 See for example Black (1970), Klein (1974), Hayek (1978), Fama (1980), Greenfield and Yeager (1983), Wallace (1983), White (1984b), O'Driscoll (1985a), and Yeager (1985).

2 We have each made normative evaluations of free banking elsewhere: Selgin (1988, chs. 8–10); White (1984a, ch. 5, 1984b).

3 See also Menger (1981, 260–2). The same view appears in Carlisle (1901, 5), and Ridgeway (1892, 47). A more recent version of Menger's theory is Jones (1976). For a secondary account of Menger's theory see O'Driscoll (1985b).

4 See Menger (1981, 263–6); Ridgeway (1892, 6–11), and Burns (1927a, 286–8). On some alleged nonmetallic monies of primitive peoples see Quiggin (1963).

5 See Usher (1943), de Roover (1974, chs. 4–5), and Lopez (1979).

6 On the historical development of banknotes and checks in Europe see Usher (1943, 7–8, 23).

7 See White (1984a, 84–5) for nineteenth century views on geographic diseconomies in note circulation.

8 An example of the explicit adoption of "tit for tat" by an exhausted note-duelling bank is given by Munn (1981, 24).

9 See Cannon (1908), Andrew (1908), Smith (1936), Timberlake (1984), and Gorton (1985a).

10 These figures are based on data in White (1984a, 37). A recent econometric study of economies of scale in banking is Benston, Hanweck, and Humphrey (1982).

11 See White (1984a, 8–9, 1987).

12 Taub (1985) has shown that a dynamic inconsistency facing issuers in Klein's (1974) model will lead them to hyperinflate. Cf. Chapter 1.

13 This point is emphasized by White (1984c). For additional criticism of the Black–Fama–Yeager literature see O'Driscoll (1985a), Hoover (1985a), and McCallum (1984).

14 On the appearance of central banks in several nations see Smith (1936); on Canada in particular see Bordo and Redish (1987).

REFERENCES

Andrew, A. Piatt. "Substitutes for Cash in the Panic of 1907." *Quarterly Journal of Economics*, August 1908, 497–516.

Axelrod, Robert. *The Evolution of Cooperation*. New York: Basic Books, 1984.

Bagehot, Walter. *Lombard Street. A Description of the Money Market*. London: Henry S. King, 1873.

Baltensperger, Ernst. "Alternative Approaches to the Theory of the Banking Firm." *Journal of Monetary Economics*, January 1980, 1–37.

Benston, George J., Gerald A. Hanweck, and David B. Humphrey. "Scale Economies in Banking: A Restructuring and Reassessment." *Journal of Money, Credit, and Banking*, November 1982, 435–54.

Bisschop, W. R. *The Rise of the London Money Market, 1640–1826*. London: P. S. King & Son, 1910.

Black, Fischer. "Banking and Interest Rates in a World Without Money: The Effects of Uncontrolled Banking." *Journal of Bank Research*, Autumn 1970, 9–20.

Bordo, Michael and Angela Redish. "Why Did the Bank of Canada Emerge in 1935?" *Journal of Economic History*, June 1987, 405–17.

Burns, A. R. "Early Stages in the Development of Money and Coins," in *London Essays in Economics in Honour of Edwin Cannan*, edited by T. E. Gregory and Hugh Dalton. London: George Routledge & Sons, 1927a.

―――. *Money and Monetary Policy in Early Times*. New York: Alfred E. Knopf, 1927b.

Cannon, James G. "Clearing Houses and the Currency," in *The Currency Problem and the Present Financial Situation*. New York: Columbia University Press, 1908.

―――. *Clearing Houses*. Washington, DC: Government Printing Office, 1910.

Carlisle, William. *The Evolution of Modern Money*. London: Macmillan, 1901.

Checkland, S. G. *Scottish Banking: A History, 1695–1973*. Glasgow: Collins, 1975.

de Roover, Raymond. *Business, Banking, and Economic Thought in Late Medieval and Early Modern Europe*, edited by Julius Kirshner. Chicago: University of Chicago Press, 1974.

Fama, Eugene F. "Banking in the Theory of Finance." *Journal of Monetary Economics*, January 1980, 39–57.

―――. "Financial Intermediation and Price Level Control." *Journal of Monetary Economics*, July 1983, 7–28.

Gibbons, J. S. *The Banks of New York, Their Dealers, the Clearing House, and the Panic of 1857.* New York: D. Appleton Co., 1858.

Goodhart, Charles. *The Evolution of Central Banks: A Natural Development?* London: Suntory-Toyota International Centre for Economics and Related Disciplines/London School of Economics and Political Science, 1985.

Gorton, Gary. "Clearinghouses and the Origin of Central Banking in the United States." *Journal of Economic History*, June 1985a, 277–83.

————. "Banking Theory and Free Banking History: A Review Essay." *Journal of Monetary Economics*, September 1985b, 267–76.

Graham, William. *The One Pound Note in the History of Banking in Great Britain*, 2nd edn. Edinburgh: James Thin, 1911.

Greenfield, Robert L. and Leland B. Yeager. "A Laissez Faire Approach to Monetary Stability." *Journal of Money, Credit, and Banking*, August 1983, 302–15.

Hall, Robert. "Explorations in the Gold Standard and Related Policies for Stabilizing the Dollar," in *Inflation Causes and Effects*, edited by Robert Hall, Chicago: University of Chicago Press for the National Bureau of Economic Research, 1982.

Hayek, F. A. *Denationalisation of Money*, 2nd edn. London: Institute of Economic Affairs, 1978.

Hicks, John. "The Two Triads, Lecture I," in *Critical Essays in Monetary Theory*. Oxford: Clarendon Press, 1967.

Hoover, Kevin D. "Causality and Invariance in the Money Supply Process." Doctoral dissertation, Oxford University, 1985.

James, F. Cyril. *The Growth of Chicago Banks*. New York: Harper & Brothers, 1938.

Jones, Robert. "The Origin and Development of Media of Exchange." *Journal of Political Economy*, November 1976, 757–75.

Klein, Benjamin. "The Competitive Supply of Money." *Journal of Money, Credit, and Banking*, November 1974, 423–53.

Lake, Wilfred S. "The End of the Suffolk System." *Journal of Economic History*, November 1947, 183–207.

Leslie, J. O. *The Note Exchange and Clearing House Systems*. Edinburgh: William Blackwood, 1950.

Lopez, Robert S. "The Dawn of Medieval Banking," in *The Dawn of Modern Banking*. New Haven, CT: Yale University Press, 1979.

McCallum, Bennett T. "Bank Deregulation, Accounting Systems of Exchange, and the Unit of Account: A Critical Review." Carnegie-Rochester Conference Series on Public Policy, Autumn 1984, 13–45.

Melitz, Jacques. *Primitive and Modern Money*. Reading, MA: Addison-Wesley, 1974.

Menger, Carl. "The Origin of Money." *Economic Journal*, June 1892, 239–55.

————. *Principles of Economics* [1871]. New York: New York University Press, 1981.

Munn, Charles W. "The Origins of the Scottish Note Exchange." *Three Banks Review* 107, 1975, 45–60.

————. *The Scottish Provincial Banking Companies, 1747–1864*. Edinburgh: John Donald, 1981.

O'Driscoll, Gerald P., Jr. "Money in a Deregulated Financial System." *Economic Review*, Federal Reserve Bank of Dallas, May 1985a, 1–12.

————. "Money: Menger's Evolutionary Theory." Unpublished manuscript, Federal Reserve Bank of Dallas, 1985b.

Powell, Ellis T. *The Evolution of the Money Market, 1385–1915.* New York: Augustus M. Kelley, 1966.

Quiggin, A. Hingston. *A Survey of Primitive Money: The Beginning of Currency.* London: Methuen, 1963.

Richards, R. D. *The Early History of Banking in England.* New York: Augustus M. Kelley, 1965.

Ridgeway, William. *The Origin of Metallic Currency and Weight Standards.* Cambridge: Cambridge University Press, 1892.

Santomero, Anthony M. "Modeling the Banking Firm: A Survey." *Journal of Money, Credit, and Banking,* November 1984, 576–602.

Selgin, George A. *The Theory of Free Banking.* Totowa, NJ: Rowman and Littlefield, 1988.

Smith, Vera C. *The Rationale of Central Banking.* London: P. S. King, 1936.

Taub, Bart. "Private Fiat Money with Many Suppliers." *Journal of Monetary Economics,* September 1985, 195–208.

Timberlake, R. H. "The Central Banking Role of Clearing-House Associations." *Journal of Money, Credit, and Banking,* February 1984, 1–15.

Trivoli, George. *The Suffolk Bank: A Study of a Free-Enterprise Clearing System.* London: Adam Smith Institute, 1979.

Usher, Abbott Payson. *The Early History of Deposit Banking in Mediterranean Europe.* Cambridge, MA: Harvard University Press, 1943.

Wallace, Neil. "A Legal Restrictions Theory of the Demand for 'Money' and the Role of Monetary Policy." *Federal Reserve Bank of Minneapolis Quarterly Review,* Winter 1983, 1–7.

White, Lawrence H. *Free Banking in Britain: Theory, Experience, and Debate, 1800–1845.* Cambridge: Cambridge University Press, 1984a.

————. "Free Banking as an Alternative Monetary System," in *Money in Crisis,* edited by Barry N. Siegel. San Francisco: Pacific Institute, 1984b.

————. "Competitive Payments Systems and the Unit of Account." *American Economic Review,* September 1984c, 699–712.

————. "Accounting for Non-Interest-Bearing Currency: A Critique of the 'Legal Restrictions' Theory of Money." *Journal of Money, Credit, and Banking,* November 1987, 448–56.

Williams, Jeffrey C. "Fractional Reserve Banking in Grain." *Journal of Money, Credit, and Banking,* November 1984, 488–96.

Withers, Hartley. *The Meaning of Money.* London: John Murray, 1920.

Woolsey, Warren W. "The Multiple Standard and the Means of Exchange." Unpublished manuscript, Talladega College, Talladega, AL, 1984.

————. "Competitive Payments Systems: Comment." Unpublished manuscript, Talladega College, 1985.

Yeager, Leland B. "Deregulation and Monetary Reform." *American Economic Review,* May 1985, 103–7.

3

THE RATIONALIZATION OF CENTRAL BANKS*

INTRODUCTION

There has never been any shortage of criticisms of particular central banks and their policies. Moreover, central banking in general has recently been criticized as an undesirable and ultimately unnecessary intrusion of government into what some think would otherwise be well-working and stable capitalist monetary systems. What *has* been lacking in the economics literature has been any systematic effort to justify the presence of central banks by pointing to particular respects in which free banking – where numerous banks issue distinct brands of redeemable currency free from political regulation – would prove deficient.

The shortage of scholarly arguments for central banking undoubtedly reflects the view of most economists that central banks are now a permanent feature of the economic landscape that no amount of debate will ever budge. In this regard I am reminded of a letter from a Federal Reserve spokesman, who assured me that the need for a central bank for the United States had been proven once and for all by a congressional vote in 1913.

To his credit, Charles Goodhart of the London School of Economics refuses to take the desirability of central banking for granted. Instead, he has shouldered the burden of showing how central banks came into being and why they are necessary. In the process Goodhart confronts many arguments for free banking. His resulting work on *The Evolution of Central Banks* (Cambridge, MA: MIT Press, 1988) represents, in consequence, an unusual attempt to spell out the failings of the free market in the realm of money.

The first chapters of Goodhart's book grew out of a set of working papers examining the arguments for and drawbacks of free banking. Chapter 2 reviews traditional arguments for free banking that treat it as a wholly decentralized arrangement. Chapter 3 reviews the role of clearinghouses,

*Reprinted, with permission, from *Critical Review*, Vol. 7, Nos. 2–3 (Spring–Summer 1993).

which may, according to more sophisticated arguments for free banking, provide a private (i.e., nonlegislative) basis for regulation and centralization of reserves. Chapters 4 and 5 describe what Goodhart perceives to be inherent instabilities of free banking, including its tendency to fuel business cycles. In chapter 6, private deposit insurance is critically assessed as a means for preventing crises under free banking.

Goodhart's pro-central banking arguments are stated and recapitulated in chapters 7 and 8, which also draw on a 1987 article. Chapter 8 is followed by a lengthy appendix, reviewing the nineteenth-century record of central banking in Europe and Japan.

Goodhart is amply qualified to undertake his self-assigned challenge. Formerly an economist for the Bank of England, he is familiar with the details of actual central bank operations. At the same time, he is thoroughly acquainted with theoretical writings on money and banking, as is evident from his own frequently insightful contributions to this literature. Finally, Goodhart, unlike many other monetary economists, is both familiar with monetary history and aware of the crucial role institutions have played in that history. The result of these exceptional qualifications is a work for which all monetary economists should be grateful. Nevertheless, this work offers no occasion for rejoicing on the part of central bankers of the world, for Goodhart's scholarly defense of central banks mainly succeeds in showing that the case to be made in favor of them is, after all, surprisingly weak.

THE CASE FOR FREE BANKING

The need for various kinds of legislative interference in banking, and for legislation establishing central banks in particular, has been taken for granted by most monetary writers at least since the passage of the English Bank Act of 1844. Peel's Act eventually guaranteed the Bank of England a complete monopoly of paper currency in Great Britain, effectively ending the monetary controversies of preceding decades with a verdict in favor of a (rule-bound) central bank. Yet a few stalwarts continued to insist upon the theoretical superiority of free banking, where numerous banks of issue are "regulated" by competitive pressures only. One of them was Walter Bagehot who, while editor of *The Economist* in 1873, published his highly influential book on *Lombard Street*.[1] Bagehot viewed free banking as an ideal that was both more stable and more "natural" than central banking. In contrast, he viewed the concentration of legal privileges in the Bank of England of his day as both unnatural and dangerous to economic stability. When it came to offering practical advice, however, Bagehot did not propose taking away the Bank's special privileges: that, he said, would be like proposing a "revolution," and just as fruitless. Instead, Bagehot hoped that the Bank could be persuaded to manage its affairs in a manner more conducive to the avoidance of financial crises (and, by implication, less conducive to maximizing the Bank's profits).[2]

In presenting his case for free banking, Goodhart draws heavily on Bagehot's particular vision of a free banking system. Although Goodhart also refers to works by Benjamin Klein and Friedrich Hayek, these have to do with hypothetical arrangements involving competing private issuers of irredeemable fiat money, which are a far cry from free banking in its conventional and traditional (Bagehotian) meaning. In a traditional free banking system, rival banks issue notes redeemable in some "outside" money, like gold, that none of them can create.

Bagehot's defense of free banking suffers, unfortunately, from his unwarranted assumption that a *laissez-faire* regime would involve having (gold) bank reserves scattered evenly throughout the banking system. Goodhart is quick to point out the fallacy in this view: economic considerations, including simplification of interbank payments and a reduced overall need for reserves, would favor some centralization of reserves even under *laissez-faire*. From this indisputable truth Goodhart draws the conclusion that centralization of reserves *in the Bank of England* was itself an inevitable and therefore "natural" feature of the late-nineteenth-century British monetary system. The (Bagehotian) case for free banking is thus seen to rest upon a false dichotomy of free versus centralized banking. In reality, Goodhart suggests (17), freedom itself sponsors a centralization of reserves in particular banks. Those "bankers' banks" then naturally evolve into noncompetitive central banks, charged with managing the total quantity of reserves (and, indirectly, money) in the public interest. Central banking thus appears to be a natural and perhaps inevitable development.

IS CENTRAL BANKING NATURAL?

Goodhart's view of central banking as an inevitable development depends crucially on his belief that bank reserves will naturally tend to gather in and be managed by some *particular* bank. In support of this belief Goodhart refers to the views of economist Henry Thornton. Thornton, as interpreted by Goodhart, claimed at the outset of the nineteenth century that the centralization of reserves in the Bank of England resulted "from its superior credit (not just from the advantages endowed by legislation)" (19). Thornton's claim begs at least two questions. First, if "advantages endowed by legislation" are not crucial, why have there been so few examples of reserves being concentrated in banks not enjoying such special advantages? Reserves did not accumulate in particular banks in Scotland, Canada, China, Australia, Sweden, Ireland, or Switzerland until those countries passed laws favoring particular banks, usually by restricting other banks' ability to issue notes. The one well-documented instance of banks depositing most of their reserves in a single rival bank *not* enjoying any special legal privileges is the case of the Suffolk Bank of Boston, which held reserves for and redeemed notes of other New England banks between 1825 and 1858. Even this one instance was, moreover, no reflection of *laissez-faire* policies: it probably would never have emerged had the laws allowed branch banking, thereby letting individual banks issue and redeem their own notes at numerous locations throughout New England.

Second, what, if not "advantages endowed by legislation," was the source of the Bank of England's "superior credit"? What allowed the Bank eventually to dominate all the other London banking firms, including many much older than it? Contrary to the impression conveyed by Thornton and Goodhart, the superior credit commanded by the Bank of England's notes, which caused other bankers to hold the notes in place of gold, can only be explained by referring to the Bank's enjoyment of legal privileges. After 1697 these privileges included a monopoly of government accounts and limited liability status (a status denied to other banks for another one and a half centuries). In 1709 the Bank obtained an official monopoly in joint-stock banking, meaning that all other banks were thereafter limited to having fewer than seven partners. (After 1826, the establishment of other joint-stock banks of issue was allowed, but only outside a 65-mile radius from the center of London; after 1833, the establishment of joint-stock banks was allowed in London, but only on the condition that they cease issuing notes. Both of these relaxations of the Bank's special privileges left its monopoly of London paper currency essentially intact.) Private bankers' habit of treating Bank of England notes rather than gold as their primary reserve medium was reinforced during the Bank Restriction of 1797 to 1819, when the Bank was allowed to suspend gold payments. In short, had it not been for the Bank's special privileges, there is no reason to suppose that other banks would have been inclined to favor it by treating its notes as primary reserves and reissuing them, instead of pushing notes of their own, as happened everywhere where several banks of issue shared the same legal status.

CLEARINGHOUSES AND BRANCH BANKING

The point of these remarks is to suggest that it is not at all natural for any one bank, in a *laissez-faire* arrangement, to become the custodian of other banks' reserves. This happens only under regulated circumstances, and especially where the law favors a particular bank while restricting its competitors. How, then, would banks in an unregulated system take advantage of economies associated with centralized reserves? They could do so, without paying tribute to any of their rivals, through a combination of branch banking and the establishment of private nonbank clearinghouses. In a typical branch-banking arrangement, a number of large banks have branch offices nationwide. After branch offices exchange checks and notes locally, interbank debts are settled at the head offices in major financial centers. Reserves can thus be concentrated in the head offices, where the need for them is greatly reduced through the "netting out" of most local interbranch debts. Branching alone can often achieve all genuine economies from reserve centralization. Where further economies are desired, however, a group of rival banks can obtain them without elevating one of its members to superior status by establishing a private nonbank clearinghouse.[3] Such clearing houses were an important feature of most nineteenth-century banking systems. They were especially important in the United States, where many state governments prohibited branch banking. Where laws did not favor particular banks, as they did in England after the Bank of England was established, banks relied for the most part on branch banking or private clearinghouses, but *not* on any embryonic central bank or "bankers' bank," as means for economizing on reserves.

Although his chapter 2 summary of "The Case for Free Banking" suggests misleadingly that the only choice is between central banking and arrangements involving "no central reservoir of reserves" (25), in chapter 3 Goodhart does get around to discussing clearinghouses and branch banking. He continues, however, to view bankers' banks as the evolutionary norm, treating systems relying on nonbank clearinghouses and branch banking alone as exceptional mutants. Thus, in discussing private clearinghouses, he focuses on the Suffolk arrangement, which did indeed involve the concentration of reserves and clearing facilities in a firm that was itself a bank. The Suffolk thus serves better than other private clearinghouse arrangements in illustrating "centripetal forces" which, according to Goodhart, naturally allow a single bank to dominate a nation's monetary system. But what about the many other systems that relied entirely on branch banking and *nonbank* clearinghouses to save on scarce reserves? Goodhart mentions Scottish and Canadian free banking regimes only to dismiss them as "oligopolistic." But these examples are not so easily brushed aside for several reasons. First, it is not obvious that the Scottish and Canadian systems were oligopolistic in any economically relevant sense. At one time there were 29 note-issuing banks in the Scottish system, with 19 remaining at the end of the free banking era in 1845. At the peak of its free banking era in 1875, Canada had 51 note-issuing banks. Although attempts were made to form price-fixing cartels in these and other free banking systems, none of them appears to have been successful.[4] Second, even if the charge of oligopoly stuck, it would still leave us to wonder whether oligopoly might itself be more "natural" than central banking. Finally, many other banking systems that were by no means oligopolistic, including that of the United States (excluding the Suffolk system), relied for the most part on nonbank clearinghouses to centralize bank reserves. These instances suggest that Goodhart is not justified in viewing bankers' banks as typical outgrowths of *laissez-faire*.

Goodhart's equally casual dismissal of branch banking, which he also links to oligopoly, is no more satisfactory. He upholds the nineteenth-century US arrangement of unit banks joined by correspondent relationships as a more natural alternative (34–7). This account will, I think, strike most American experts as perverse: most of us tend, I think with ample reason, to regard our arrangement as being a quite unnatural outgrowth of legal barriers to branch banking, which have only recently been tumbling down. Had such barriers not been present throughout most of US history, it is practically certain that we would have had fewer, larger banks, many with nationwide branches, and with a considerably reduced dependence upon either interbank deposits or clearinghouses.

I have devoted so much attention to Goodhart's claim that *laissez-faire* would lead inevitably or naturally to the concentration of bank reserves in a private bankers' bank because it undergirds his principal defense of central banks. According to Goodhart, a fundamental conflict of interest makes it unlikely that any unregulated bankers' bank can be relied upon to manage the stock of bank reserves in a manner consistent with the public interest: rather than act as a lender of last resort during a crisis, a private bankers' bank might prefer to see even its solvent rivals fail. This was, as Bagehot emphasized, a major defect of British monetary arrangements in the last half of the nineteenth century. The practical solution, to which Bagehot pointed the way, was to reform established bankers' banks (like the Bank of England), ensuring that they would serve the public interest as well as possible. Ultimately this would involve making them into full-fledged central banks, possessed with monopolies of paper currency but forbidden to compete with other banks in the business of making commercial loans. I would agree with both Bagehot and Goodhart that an unreformed bankers' bank is a dangerous thing. Nevertheless, because I am not at all convinced that bankers' banks are themselves natural developments, I do not see this fact as constituting an adequate rationalization of central banking. On the contrary, I see it as warranting the condemnation of laws that allowed bankers' banks to develop in the first place.

FISCAL MOTIVES, MONETARY CONSEQUENCES

Of course, the merits of any particular monetary system cannot be inferred from the system's origins, natural or otherwise: even if central banking was not at all inevitable or natural it might still be better than free banking. The way in which particular central banks emerged historically does, nonetheless, yield important clues concerning their merits compared with free banking. Consider again the Bank of England. Established in 1694 for purely fiscal reasons (to pay for William III's war with France), the Bank was not intended to serve as an instrument of monetary policy: it could hardly have been, since there was no such thing as "monetary policy" at the time. Indeed, the Bank's founders gave no thought to any role it might eventually play in managing Britain's money supply. Goodhart acknowledges this fact. But he fails to address a related and equally relevant fact, namely that the Bank's founders also did not consider or realize how special privileges embodied in the Bank's charter would, in strengthening the Bank itself, weaken other English banks and thereby make them quite *un*naturally dependent upon the Bank of England's largesse for their very survival.

The free bankers' view is this: by stripping privileges from other English banks and concentrating them in the Bank of England, the Act of 1694 and other legislation that followed ruined any prospect for the development of a healthy and self-regulating competitive English-banking industry. By securing the use of its own notes as other banks' reserves, the Bank gained unprecedented lending power – power that allowed it to involve the entire English monetary system in inflationary episodes. These would eventually lead to an "external" drain of gold reserves to other countries, obliging the Bank to respond with a sudden contraction of credit. Tragically, the same legislation that allowed the Bank of England to expose the British financial system to previously unknown shocks also left its would-be rivals legally and economically emasculated: limited to six partners or less, they were undercapitalized and underdiversified. Their fragility was such that they were prone to succumb to economic shocks that would have left larger banks – like those that flourished freely at the time in Scotland – unscathed. It was this emasculation of the English "country" banks – a counterpart of the legislation that empowered the Bank of England – that ultimately made it appear desirable to have the Bank serve as a lender of last resort, the central pillar without which the English (and later the British) financial system would collapse.[5]

Just how strong would England's banking system have become had Parliament not interfered with its development in 1694 and after? The experience of Scotland, where banking privileges were relatively widely and generously distributed until 1845 (when Peel's Act was extended to it), is instructive. As Lawrence H. White has shown, the Scottish free banking system did not seem to suffer at all from its lack of a central bank; indeed, the Scottish system appears to have outperformed its English counterpart in every crucial respect. Total per capita deposit and note-holder losses from Scottish bank failures were fewer. Scottish bank crises and suspensions were less frequent; and the overall quality of Scottish bank services was superior.[6]

Goodhart, as I have noted, downplays the significance of Scotland's success: he attributes this success not to the system's relative lack of regulation, but to its reliance upon branch banking and its low ratio of gold reserves to monetary liabilities (52). Here again, it must be stressed that branch banking is not peculiar to "oligopolistic" arrangements (assuming Scotland's was one of these) but has emerged in most settings where it has not been precluded by legal restrictions. It therefore makes no sense to suggest, as Goodhart does, that the Scottish system was strong because it had branch banking *rather than* because it was free. As for reserve ratios being low, this was not a sign of Scottish banks' weakness or dependence on outside support but, on the contrary, a symbol of their extraordinary efficiency and command of public confidence. That, at least, is the view expressed by Rondo Cameron, whose reserve-ratio statistics are cited by Goodhart.[7]

Besides the Scottish example, we now know of dozens of other instances of relatively free banking episodes. Most of these have only very recently been investigated, so that Goodhart could not refer to research concerning them when writing his book. The fact remains, nevertheless, that these systems also appear in general to have performed well, thereby posing an even greater challenge to arguments concerning the necessity and desirability of central banking.

WOULD FREE BANKS OVERISSUE CURRENCY?

Ultimately theory as well as empirical evidence must be weighed in assessing the need for central banks. Goodhart's own understanding of theory causes him to conclude that any banking system without a central bank must eventually display grave defects, including an inability to contain supplies of money and credit within economically desirable bounds. The free bankers' case hinges, Goodhart observes, on the ability of interbank "clearings" – routine requests for payment of each other's notes and checks – to correctly constrain competing issuers. Net payments must be settled in some scarce, outside reserve medium, such as gold or (as in Scotland) London bills of exchange. The clearing mechanism serves to discourage any individual bank in a free banking system from overexpanding its balance sheet relative to its rivals, by confronting the overexpanding bank with net clearing debits that can eventually bankrupt it by exhausting its reserves. This constraint differs markedly from the situation under central banking, where central bank liabilities tend to displace outside assets as a reserve medium and means of settlement, rendering the central bank peculiarly immune from clearing-system-based limits on its lending and money-creating activities.

Goodhart thinks the clearing mechanism incapable of adequately constraining a free banking system for two reasons. First, Goodhart argues, routine clearings under free banking will "tend to lead all banks to expand, or to contract, at a broadly similar rate" *without* limiting the rate of expansion for the system as a whole. Second, individual banks can defeat the clearing mechanism's ability to limit their expansion relative to that of rival banks "by making their own liabilities [including notes] more attractive" (30).

I think the first of these two arguments is mistaken, and the second irrelevant. Routine clearings *do* limit the overall extent of money creation in a free banking system, by forcing banks to maintain some definite ratio of precautionary reserves of outside money relative to their note and deposit liabilities. This ratio will vary as the banking environment varies, but it is not arbitrary. The demand for precautionary reserves reflects random variations in net balances owed by individual banks at the end of a clearing session: even if a banker is certain that his or her bank will gain deposits equal to its losses from withdrawals over the course of some series of clearing sessions, the banker will want to have some safety cushion of reserves to protect the bank against the odds of being a net debtor to other banks at the conclusion of any *one* clearing session. The greater the total value of transactions faced by a bank in a typical clearing session, the greater will be its need for precautionary reserves, other things being equal. Since the volume of transactions depends on the volume of bank money in existence, no bank having limited reserves will want to issue more than a certain limited amount of money. This view of things is, incidentally, not original with proponents of free banking but is, rather, implied by standard theoretical writings on reserve demand. Goodhart's opposite view reflects a popular misconception which has, unfortunately, been propagated even by such luminaries as John Maynard Keynes and Chicago economist Lloyd Mints.

Goodhart's second argument must refer to a situation where (1) an individual bank submits to losses in order to temporarily increase its market share, or (2) one bank profitably increases its market share relative to others, or (3) the *overall* demand for bank money has increased, implying a general fall in the velocity (rate of circulation) of bank money. Case 1 contradicts the usual view that firms are profit maximizers. As for cases (2) and (3), neither implies any change in total spending or any threat to bank liquidity; therefore neither can be said to represent a threat to macroeconomic stability indicating a flaw of free banking. On the contrary, both of the latter situations could represent desirable (and predictable) manifestations of competitive efficiency.

THE UNINFORMED POOR

Goodhart also fears that, under free banking, ordinary people – poor people especially – "will generally have neither the expertise nor the time to maintain a continuous assessment of the standing, riskiness, and reputation of the several alternative banks" (57). In consequence, market discipline will not serve to weed out inferior banks and reward superior ones. The contrary opinion of free bankers reflects, according to Goodhart, their erroneous assumption that information about banks in a free banking system is "costless."

There are several problems with this argument. First, the case for freedom in banking is no more dependent on the assumption that information about banks is costless than the case for freedom in, say, the automotive industry is dependent on the assumption that information about different brands of automobiles is costless. What the success of free banking requires is not costless information, but information that is sufficiently inexpensive to make its acquisition by prospective bank customers practical.

Organized asset markets may help to disseminate bank-specific information easily and cheaply. Goodhart recognizes this, observing that "developments in the conditions of individual banks" may be "quickly [and relatively costlessly] signaled in changes in their equity market shares" (65). However, Goodhart observes, "it would still be costly in time and effort for individuals to monitor and to seek to interpret changes in the market value of all the alternative banks" (66). The complaint here overlooks the possibility of bank customers referring to secondary-market prices, not of bank equity, but of bank *liabilities*: bank certificates of deposit are today also traded in secondary markets. Of even greater significance are the organized markets in banknotes that were present when such notes were issued on a competitive basis. Because banknotes do not typically bear interest, their secondary market "price" serves as a clear indicator of bank-specific risk. Normally, if all is well, a bank's notes will trade at par or face value.[8] If, however, the bank is judged to be in trouble by market experts, including private note brokers, other banks, and clearinghouse authorities, the notes will trade at a discount. The limitation of note-issuing powers to central banks has thus served to cut off an important source of bank-specific information that would be available under free banking.

Also, and despite what Goodhart implies, it is not at all true that bank customers, to protect themselves against getting stuck with bad bank money, must acquire information about each and every bank. They need only convince themselves that one bank is safe, and then agree to accept only checks and notes of other banks that are on the list of "bankable" (i.e., trustworthy) monies that their own bank offers to receive routinely on deposit at par. By this means the greater part of the burden of information acquisition is placed, not on individual consumers, but on the banks themselves. Bad banks are weeded from the system by having their notes refused by other banks, or by a nonbank clearinghouse.[9]

Secondary markets for bank liabilities and equity would not necessarily provide information on all banks: many smaller banks today are private companies; and some banks (small ones again, mainly) might not issue notes even under free banking. Such concerns lead Goodhart to observe that information about *some* banks must necessarily be limited or very costly to acquire in a free market setting (66–8). The observation is, of course, correct, but its relevance is unclear. As long as the market informs agents of the existence of some safe banks, continued patronage of other banks can only signify either customers' risk-loving behavior or their possession of information not available through markets. I see no reason why a healthy banking system should not be able to cater to such customers so long as it also can meet the needs of less financially sophisticated ones.

To suggest that the public could have adequate information concerning the soundness of banks in a free banking system is not to deny that unsound banks have ever existed. It is to suggest, rather, that legislated regulations and restrictions are typically to blame for past information problems. A case in point is the circulation of poor-quality country banknotes in early-nineteenth-century England, complained about by Henry Thornton in a passage quoted by Goodhart. Goodhart overlooks the fact that the survival of such poor-quality notes, that is of notes issued by undercapitalized and underdiversified banks, was a direct consequence of the previously mentioned laws restricting banks, other than the Bank of England, to six partners or less. This legal restriction of competition gave English consumers little choice but to accept notes of little-known country banks, the Bank of England having refused (until well after Thornton wrote) to extend its own business into the countryside. Had English banking enjoyed the same freedom as Scottish banking did at the time, there would undoubtedly have been, not hundreds of small private English banks of issue, but perhaps a few dozen much larger joint-stock banks with nationwide branches and direct access to the London money market. In that case, the English public would have had little trouble locating and discriminating in favor of relatively "sound" bank monies.

The "information problem" that undermined the quality of banknote currency in the United States prior to the Civil War was likewise a direct result of government interference. This time it was not a six-partner rule but barriers to branch banking that led to the proliferation of undercapitalized and geographically isolated banks of issue. Today in the United States yet another information problem stemming from regulation afflicts the banking industry. The problem here has not been that information costs are excessively high but rather that bank customers have lacked the incentive to acquire any information at all concerning bank safety. The cause of this is deposit insurance, which protects bank customers from losses they might otherwise suffer in patronizing risky banks. It is useful, by the way, to contrast the present US banking situation with that in the still relatively unregulated and uninsured mutual fund industry, where information on the performance of individual funds is abundant (and is routinely sought by investors, who sometimes pay a high price for it). While it is true, as Goodhart notes, that mutual funds invest mainly in marketable securities whose riskiness and market value are easier to ascertain than that of bank loans, it is also true that banks could (if they had any incentive to do so) strengthen their own portfolios with marketable securities, collateralized loans, and capital to win the confidence of risk-averse consumers.

It is also sometimes forgotten that bank customers are not risk minimizers but seek a certain balance of risk and (expected) return. Indeed, lower-income depositors are often most willing to accept high risks, presumably for the same reason that the poor buy a disproportionate share of lottery tickets. In Hong Kong, where bank deposits are still uninsured, poor persons often prefer to keep deposits at relatively risky "native" banks, even though they could keep their money at one of several large and apparently safer "foreign-style" banks, including the Hong Kong and Shanghai Bank. The reason cannot be ignorance, since the relative safety of the foreign banks has been made abundantly clear over the years. It is simply that the clients of native banks are, like it or not, more interested in earning potentially high rates of return than in protecting their investments from default risk. Incredibly, "experts" from the Bank of England cannot see this, and so have been trying to foist on Hong Kong a government deposit-insurance scheme like the one that has wrecked the US banking industry.

THE CONTAGION BOGEY

Still another worry expressed by Goodhart about free banking has to do with the possibility that bank failures will lead people to hoard currency, "thereby precipitating a general run on bank reserves" (61). This belief is crucial to the traditional case for central banks acting as the lenders of last resort, as it points to the central bank as the only potential source of funds to quell a panic. If, instead of hoarding currency, customers of failed or failing banks merely switched to holding notes or deposits of other (competitive) banks, individual bank failures might not be a problem calling for government intervention.

It seems to me, though, that the only basis for the widespread belief that individual bank failures and runs are bound to spread, contagion-like, throughout a banking system is repeated incantations of the belief by central bankers and their defenders. In fact, empirical evidence of bank-run contagion effects is surprisingly thin – too thin, I believe, to justify the creation of such dangerous institutions as central banks have turned out to be.[10] The theoretical basis for the belief in contagion effects is weak as well. In this connection Goodhart, quoting John Kareken, refers to a well-known article by Douglas Diamond and Philip Dybvig as the one "rigorous and detailed argument" for the existence of a bank contagion.[11] But to really understand the Diamond and Dybvig model (no easy task, even for economists) is to appreciate how it serves to justify central banking only in the eyes of those who already are convinced that central banks are necessary, but who are intellectually honest enough (as Goodhart obviously is) to worry about a lack of "rigorous" theorizing to back up their case. Suffice it to say that in the Diamond and Dybvig model (1) banks and producing firms are one and the same; (2) banks do not make loans; (3) goods are available only through banks; (4) there is no money; (5) many bank "depositors" are residual claimants, that is they are not promised a fixed return on their deposits; and (6) bank panics are random events characterized by shortages of *goods*. Relaxing only a few of these patently *ad hoc* assumptions in the direction of greater realism – for example, by introducing bank capital – overturns the model's anti-free-banking implications.[12] One is forced to wonder whether *any* meaningful policy implications can be drawn from such a far-fetched model.

THE BORROWERS

Goodhart, however, does not rest his case for central banking solely on the usual contagion-effect argument. Indeed, his repetition of that argument in chapter 5 is followed in chapter 7 by his admission that recent bank runs "have *not* involved an attempt by the public to move . . . into cash but have merely produced a flight of depositors from banks seen as excessively dangerous to some alternative placement (not cash)" (96). Goodhart recognizes, furthermore, that the ongoing substitution of run-proof, equity-based mutual funds for conventional bank deposits makes the contagion-effect argument less relevant than ever. Awareness of such facts might be expected to imply rejection of the whole lender-of-last-resort rationale for central banks. But Goodhart disagrees, arguing that even large-scale interbank movements of deposits would be extremely damaging to bank *borrowers*, and so "would require a continuing support role for a Central Bank to prevent and, if necessary, to recycle such flows" (97).

This argument in defense of central banking, though novel, is to me unconvincing, lacking as it does any reference to the kinds of problems usually thought necessary to establish the existence of a market failure and consequent need for action by the government. Despite his reference to effects of bank failures that "could be extremely damaging for the economy," Goodhart's appeal here is, not to any truly *macroeconomic* (i.e., economywide) consequences of bank failures, nor even to some limited third-part ("external") consequences, but to mere *second*-party consequences, which point to no market failure of any kind. This does not mean that such consequences are unimportant: depositors may suffer a great deal if their (uninsured) bank fails. Also, as Goodhart stresses, a failed bank's investment in information and goodwill with regard to particular borrowers may be lost, making it harder for those borrowers to secure credit elsewhere. But to allow a central bank to rescue failing commercial banks solely in order to avoid such second-party losses is a cure worse than the disease: like deposit insurance, Goodhart's preferred central bank strategy undermines normal incentives for bank customers to "shop around" for better banks or to establish credit with several (rather than just one), encouraging them to focus instead on obtaining the highest possible returns and the cheapest loans, regardless of risk. In short, if it were indeed the case, as Goodhart claims, that high information costs alone sometimes lead bank customers to deal with overly risky banks, Goodhart's approach would exacerbate rather than mitigate the problem. All things considered, the quality of banks would be better, and the extent of customer losses smaller, if central banks did not offer to rescue clients of failed banks.

Goodhart believes that central banks could aid failing banks without subsidizing bad ones by making use of their superior knowledge to "penalize inadequate and improper managerial behavior" (101–2). The problem with this argument is that it would have central banks "punish" bad banks only once they became so bad that they failed; otherwise the system would still tend to punish *good* banks while *rewarding* bad ones. Because it does not seem reasonable to impose special punishments (apart from those normally associated with failure) on managers who are merely "inadequate," and because the line between "inadequate" and "improper" is not easily drawn, it appears likely that the overall effect of Goodhart's arrangement (considered as a substitute for *laissez-faire*) would still be to encourage rather than discourage bad banking. In short, the price we would have to pay to avoid mere second-party losses from bank failures would still be too high, although it might be less than it is under our present system of deposit insurance.

CENTRAL BANKING IN EUROPE

The last part of Goodhart's book – more than a third of the total – consists of an appendix reviewing developments leading to the establishment of European central banks. The appendix relies almost entirely on information from volumes issued by the US National Monetary Commission following the financial crisis of 1907. It is, indeed, largely a synopsis, with some critical comments, of the Commission's findings.

The danger of relying on a single source – or group of sources sponsored by a single governing committee – is, of course, that the source may be biased in favor of a particular point of view. Although Goodhart writes that the National Monetary Commission was set up "to consider . . . the need for Central Banks," the fact is that the experts chosen to head the Commission were already convinced of the necessity of a central bank for the United States well before they commissioned any studies. As James

Livingston bluntly puts it, the Commission's research stands as "a monument to the proposition that facts and values are indissoluble."[13]

I do not mean to deny that there is much useful information contained in Commission volumes. Nevertheless the authors of those volumes were chosen, and information selected and presented to the public, with a particular reform program in mind. Therefore, to be really helpful in objectively reconsidering the case for central banking, the Commission's findings should be read critically and together with information contained in other sources, especially more recent studies of European banking history. Among these I would include Vera Smith's important and fairly recently reprinted study, which is cited in various places by Goodhart but only once (in passing) in his appendix.[14] Other important studies, all of which to some extent contradict the pro-central bank conclusions reached by the National Monetary Commission, include those gathered by Rondo Cameron in *Banking in the Early Stages of Industrialization* and *Banking and Economic Development*.[15] Finally, there is a recent collection, edited by Kevin Dowd, of case studies favorable to free banking entitled *The Experience of Free Banking*.[16] (This last, however, appeared too recently to have been available to Goodhart.) These surveys, together with studies of individual country experiences too numerous to list here but cited in the above works, present a far different view of the necessity of central banks than the one offered to the American public in 1910 and now redisplayed by Goodhart. In many cases the differences are so great that it is hard to believe that the new studies refer to some of the same historical episodes covered by the Commission. For example, Goodhart, relying on a National Monetary Commission source, claims that the Franco-Prussian War of 1870 denied Swiss banks of issue access to the lender-of-last-resort facilities of the Bank of France, forcing the Swiss banks to run for cover and restrict credit. The resulting crisis, he contends, "persuaded the Swiss that they needed a Central Bank of their own" (52). In contrast, Ernst Weber, writing in the Dowd volume, finds that both nominal and real issues of Swiss banknotes *rose* throughout the 1870s, and especially just following the outbreak of the war, when stable-value Swiss currency was demanded in France to replace depreciating French currency.[17] If anything, the Franco-Prussian War appears, in Weber's study, to have given a boost to free banking in Switzerland.

One is tempted to wonder, indeed, what might have been the progress of banking in the United States after 1907 had the American public been presented with the findings contained in recent sources instead of, or at least in addition to, those offered by the National Monetary Commission. Perhaps the thousands of bank failures and violent contraction of the money stock in the 1930s, or the wholesale bankruptcy of much of the banking industry in the 1980s, might have been avoided.[18]

NOTES AND REFERENCES

1 Walter Bagehot, *Lombard Street* (London: Henry S. King, 1873).

2 Sir Robert Giffen, the economist and Bagehot's contemporary, held remarkably similar views. See "Fancy Monetary Standards" in Giffen's *Economic Inquiries and Studies* (London: George Bell and Sons, 1905), 177–86.

3 According to a nineteenth-century Canadian banking expert, banks with branch networks had little to gain from establishing clearinghouses in cities with fewer than seven banks. See Kurt Schuler, "The World History of Free Banking," in Kevin Dowd, ed., *The Experience of Free Banking* (London: Routledge, 1992), 17.

4 See ibid., 18–19.

5 See Vera Smith, *The Rationale of Central Banking* (Indianapolis: Liberty Press, 1990), ch. 2; and Kevin Dowd, "The Evolution of Central Banking in England, 1821–90," in Forrest Capie and Geoffrey E. Wood, eds., *Unregulated Banking: Chaos or Order?* (London: Macmillan, 1991), 159–95.

6 Lawrence H. White, *Free Banking in Britain: Theory, Experience, and Debate, 1800–1845* (Cambridge: Cambridge University Press, 1984). Goodhart, along with several other writers, claims that Scottish banks no less than English ones ultimately relied on the Bank of England as a lender of last resort. In truth, prior to 1845 the Bank of England never offered to serve as a lender of last resort to Scottish bankers, who in any case seldom borrowed from it. See Lawrence H. White, "Banking without a Central Bank: Scotland before 1844 as a 'Free Banking' System," in Capie and Wood, eds., 49–59.

   Goodhart also claims that Canadian banks prior to World War I looked upon New York City banks as a source of emergency funds. This does not prove much, since the United States also had no central bank at the time. Moreover, Canadian banks were generally net *creditors* to New York City banks, just as Scottish banks were generally net creditors to London. It is only natural for banks legally isolated from important financial centers to lend to those centers through correspondents.

7 Rondo Cameron, *Banking in the Early Stages of Industrialization* (New York: Oxford University Press, 1967), 92, 98.

8 This assumes that the costs of redeeming the notes are trivial, as tended to be the case in banking systems (like the Scottish and Canadian systems of the nineteenth century) with well-formed branch and clearinghouse networks.

9 The potential for private ("club") supervision of banks is recognized by Goodhart. However, because he believes that the club is likely to be dominated by a competitive bankers' bank, he concludes that private supervision will tend to be undermined by conflicts of interest.

10 See George Kaufman, "Bank Contagion: A Review of the Theory and Evidence," *Journal of Financial Services Research*, 8, no. 2(1994): 123–50.

   The US banking crisis of 1933, which seems to fit the general contagion scenario, actually involved a general run on the dollar, sparked by (justified) fears that it was about to be devalued, rather than any wholesale loss of confidence in banks. See Barrie Wigmore, "Was the Bank Holiday of 1933 Caused by a Run on the Dollar?" *Journal of Economic History* 47, no. 3 (September, 1988): 739–55.

11 Douglas Diamond and Philip Dybvig, "Bank Runs, Deposit Insurance, and Liquidity," *Journal of Political Economy* 91, no. 3 (1983): 401–19.

12 See Kevin Dowd, "Models of Banking Instability: A Partial Review of the Literature," *Journal of Economic Surveys* 6, no. 2 (1992): 107–32.

13 James Livingston, *Origins of the Federal Reserve System: Money, Class, and Corporate Capitalism, 1890–1913* (Ithaca, NY: Cornell University Press, 1986).

14 Smith, n5 above.

15 Cameron, n7 above.

16 Schuler, n3 above.

17 Ernst Juerg Weber, "Free Banking in Switzerland after the Liberal Revolutions in the Nineteenth Century," in Dowd, n3 above, 187–205.

18 For arguments blaming the banking crises of the 1930s and 1980s, among others, on regulations and central banks, see Chapters 9 and 10 below.

Part II

MACROECONOMIC CONSEQUENCES OF DEREGULATION

4

THE STABILITY AND EFFICIENCY OF MONEY SUPPLY UNDER FREE BANKING*

INTRODUCTION

Recent studies of historical free banking systems suggest that the absence of government regulation and centralized monetary control does not lead to monetary chaos.[1] In addition to these historical works there have also been exercises in pure theory, showing how hypothetical, unregulated banking systems might avoid some macroeconomic shortcomings of existing arrangements.[2] Unfortunately, a wide gap separates these theoretical studies from the aforementioned historical works: the theorists generally deal with "moneyless" or fiat money-producing banking systems that differ radically from any unregulated "free banking" system of the past. This chapter attempts to close this gap by explaining the operation of a money-based, unregulated fractional-reserve banking system.[3] It shows that such a system promotes monetary stability, and in doing so reaffirms some of the well-known (but still controversial) conclusions of Cannan (1935) and Tobin (1963). However, it also extends these conclusions by emphasizing the crucial role of competition in currency supply. It is because such competition is absent in central banking systems that they (and not free banking) *are* "inherently unstable".[4] The difference made by competition is especially evident when a commodity-money-based system in which note issue is monopolized is compared to one in which numerous banks compete in the unregulated issue of redeemable notes.

Because this study deals with the case of a commodity base money it should be viewed as a theoretical exercise intended to shed light on certain episodes of monetary history, and not as a ready proposal for monetary reform.

*Reprinted, with permission, from the *Journal of Institutional and Theoretical Economics*, Vol. 143, No. 3 (September 1987).

GENERAL ASSUMPTIONS

To examine in depth the creation of bank money under free banking, and to render comparisons with centralized banking most meaningful, a closed or "world" system of competing note issuers will be compared to one in which a single bank possesses a world monopoly of note issue.[5] Apart from these differences in the conditions of note issue no other special constraints are assumed to exist in either system[6]; it is only assumed that in both systems there exists a commodity "outside" money into which all monetary bank liabilities are convertible upon demand. This assumption is justified by historical precedent as well as by consideration of the evolutionary process, discussed below, by which bank money emerges in an unregulated system. No assumptions are made concerning the exact nature of the outside-money commodity except that it is scarce and reproducible only under increasing average costs.[7]

THE EVOLUTION OF BANK MONEY

To motivate further assumptions, we turn to the evolutionary origins of bank money.[8] Typically, banking originates with the issuance of 100 per cent-backed "money certificates" by goldsmiths or bill-brokers who receive deposits of commodity money.[9] Such deposits take the form of *bailments*, for safekeeping; they are not intended to be at the goldsmith's or bill-broker's disposal. The depositors must pay a storage fee, since this is the only source of compensation to the providers of the bailment service.

Out of such primitive arrangements two important innovations arise. First, the deposit keepers discover that they can safely lend a portion of their deposits at interest and, second, the depositors find that their money certificates can serve in place of money proper as media of exchange. The two innovations complement one another: the first involves the discovery that depositors' holdings of bank promises can be a source of loanable funds; the second means a general increase in the use of such promises. The modern institution of fractional-reserve banking grows out of these innovations. Its effect is to dramatically alter the status of the "depositor" of money: rather than being a *bailee*, the depositor becomes a *lender* of funds to the bank, and what had formerly been money certificates in the depositor's possession become instruments of credit. Modern forms of bank money are matched on the balance sheet almost entirely by bank lending. The modern banker receives revenues from interest on loans and investments; the "depositor", rather than paying a fee for the safekeeping of his or her money, becomes under competitive circumstances the chief recipient of this interest revenue.

Thus even in its earliest stages of development a free bank – i.e. a fractional-reserve bank free from regulation – performs an intermediary function. It recognizes credit granted to it by holders of its bank money (notes and demand deposits) and makes the involved funds available for loans and investments.[10] As confidence in the demand liabilities of individual banks grows, the entire demand for media of exchange may be fulfilled by them, so that all commodity money is withdrawn from circulation and placed at the disposal of the banks.[11] This leads to a decline in the real demand for and exchange value of the money commodity. Stock equilibrium is reached when the demand for the money commodity for non-circulation purposes (i.e. for bank reserves and industrial/consumptive uses) is sufficient to absorb the surplus created by the use of bank money. The size of the stock of bank money (denominated in commodity units) is then determined by the demand to hold bank money at the new (lower) equilibrium value of the money commodity. From this stage additional supplies of bank money will appear only insofar as the aggregate demand for real balances happens to expand. (This is demonstrated below.)

It will be assumed hereafter that all users of media of exchange prefer bank money to commodity money and have enough confidence in the monies of *particular* banks to enable them to hold these liabilities instead of holding clumsier commodity money. Therefore, the public demand for media of exchange or for real money balances is equivalent to the demand to hold quantities of bank money. It is assumed, however, that banks continue to demand commodity money for their reserves. Another important assumption is that free banks routinely send the notes of rival banks back to their issuers for redemption. The reasons for this are similar to those responsible for the routine clearing of checks: by returning its rivals' notes, a bank only gives up assets that do not earn interest, and in return receives either its own notes held by other banks (which protects it from unexpected redemptions) or, alternatively, commodity money, which is a more liquid and risk-free asset. The implications of this assumption are far reaching and form a large part of the analysis to follow.

THE LAW OF ADVERSE CLEARINGS

In the standard theory of a central banking system the creation of new demand deposits by an individual bank is limited by the bank's holdings of excess reserves. The system as a whole, however, is able to expand its liabilities by some multiple of the total of this amount. In a free banking system, the availability of excess reserves limits both individual banks' expansion of demand deposits and their ability to extend credit via the issue of banknotes. It will be shown here that (1) the scope for the existence of excess reserves is much smaller under free banking than under monopoly issue; and (2) when there is competitive note issue the value of the reserve multiplier adjusts to accommodate changes in the public's demand for bank-money balances.

The fundamental principle governing expansion of liabilities under free banking may be dubbed the "law of adverse clearings". According to this law, any bank that creates demand liabilities in *any* form in excess of the demand to *hold* such liabilities at a given price level is soon faced with adverse clearings and, hence, with a loss of commodity-money reserves equal to its overissue. The principle at work here is routinely acknowledged in discussions of the creation of demand deposits.[12] It applies equally, however, to the issue of banknotes: at any moment, with a given price level, there exists a limited demand to hold bank money in general and the bank money of any individual bank in particular. Suppose these demands are entirely satisfied. Then any notes received from a free bank as a result of additional credit granted by it represent excess bank-money balances and are therefore spent. These notes rapidly find their way into the hands of banks competing with the issuing bank, because clients of competing banks who receive the notes exchange them for their own banks' liabilities. As was shown above, the recipient banks are driven by considerations of profit to return the notes to their issuer in exchange for commodity money. The issuing bank then suffers a loss of reserves which (unless it had excess reserves to sponsor the additional note issue in the first place) compels it to contract credit in compensation for its previous overissues.[13] Once a free bank reaches its optimum reserve level it can profit from new note issues only to the extent that the notes remain in some individual's balances; that is, only to the extent that they do not enter the clearing mechanism by being deposited or exchanged at competing banks.

An important implication of the law of adverse clearings is that no individual free bank can profitably undertake a loan pricing policy cheaper than its competitors simply by issuing notes gratuitously. It can accomplish nothing by attracting additional borrowers via cheap lending rates except the exhaustion of its liquid reserves and, ultimately, of its capital. There will be more to say regarding this in a later section.

The law of adverse clearings does not apply to a monopoly note issuer

This is what gives monopoly issuers their special influence on total money supply. Consider a system where note issue is monopolized but demand deposit creation is competitive. Not all of the demand for bank money can be satisfied by way of demand deposits; there is a need for currency (e.g., banknotes) as well, since currency can be used for transactions where checks are not acceptable. Thus the public will want to hold a definite portion of its bank-money balances as currency. The division of its holdings between currency and demand deposits is, moreover, subject to change.[14] In order to fulfill their clients' demands for currency all the non-issuing banks must therefore always have on hand a ready supply of the notes of the monopoly issuer. A contest for the notes (and deposits convertible into notes) of the monopoly bank takes the place of the contest for commodity money that occurs under free banking. As a result, the deposit banks are able to settle clearings with notes or deposit credits from the monopoly issuer.[15] If there is no public demand for commodity money, the deposit banks' reserves can consist entirely of the monopoly bank's demand liabilities. Commodity money can then be released for industrial and consumptive uses, with consequent impact upon its exchange value.

Under such conditions the law of adverse clearings cannot influence a monopoly note issuer's creation of demand liabilities. The notes and demand deposits of such a bank are treated as reserve *assets* by the deposit banks; there is no reason for banks to request their redemption, even if they are issued without regard to the monetary needs of the public. A world monopoly bank of issue would for this reason be able to expand its demand liabilities without any immediate limit.[16] To do so it merely has to add to its investments or attract additional borrowers by lowering its loan interest rates or credit standards. It need not fear a clearing loss because the new liabilities thus created become lodged in the reserves of the deposit banks. The resulting multiplicative expansion of system-wide deposit balances is not restrained by the public's limited demand to hold bank money at the existing price level. In the long run there will be a general upward shift of the price level together with all nominal magnitudes (although under present assumptions the nominal "price" of commodity-money – the conversion rate – remains the same). Thus the supply of bank money is not promptly self-regulating under monopoly issue. To be effectively limited it must be controlled by way of special rules and restrictions applied to the issuer. In other words, monopolized note issue creates the need for a monetary policy.

The remaining sections of this chapter examine the implications of the law of adverse clearings under free banking and offer criticism of monetary policies based upon monopolized note issue.

THE MARKET FOR BANK MONEY AND THE MARKET FOR CREDIT

In a mature free banking system, a tight link connects the market for bank liabilities to the market for bank assets (loanable funds). The exact nature of this connection has often been misunderstood: often the demand for loanable funds has been confounded with the demand for bank money. The demand for loanable funds is for the most part a demand to acquire producers' and consumers' goods, with bank money serving only as a go-between. The true demand for bank money as such is the demand to *hold* it as a particular form of wealth.[17]

Under free banking, the demand to hold bank money is far from being the same as a demand for loanable funds. On the contrary, it represents a contribution to the *supply* of loanable funds: every holder of demand liabilities issued by a free bank grants that bank a loan for the value of their holdings. Accordingly, any increase in the public's willingness to hold bank money (*given* some level of nominal income and prices) is tantamount to an outward shift in the supply schedule of loanable funds to be intermediated by the banking system.[18]

It is true that the time dimension of loans made to banks by money-holding individuals is not formally stipulated. The estimation of the average duration of such loans is a practical problem that confronts bank management. The banker must be prepared to deal with adverse clearings that will result when clients dispose of the bank's liabilities by exchanging them for goods and, eventually, for the liabilities of other banks. Such adverse clearings represent former liability-holders' termination of their loans. Older banking literature summarized the problem confronted by bank management as one of "matching the maturity dates of assets and liabilities". A similar problem is involved in the management of passbook savings accounts: although a formal stipulation of minimal loan duration typically exists (the "notice of withdrawal" clause), it is rarely used in actual practice, since it is inconsistent with customer convenience and hence with competitive policy. In practice passbook savings accounts, while not checkable, are nonetheless withdrawable upon demand; the difference in duration between them and demand deposits is merely one of degree.

Because the demand to hold bank money represents a granting of credit by individuals it follows that any issue of bank money consistent with this demand accords with the availability of voluntarily supplied, real savings. In other words, if a credit expansion under free banking is consistent with equilibrium in the market for bank money – that is, if the supply of liabilities does not (at given prices) exceed or fall short of the quantity demanded – then it does not disturb equilibrium in the market for loanable funds. To adopt Wicksell's terminology, interest rates remain at their "natural" levels.[19] The same circumstances that prevent free banks from issuing greater quantities of bank money than the public is willing to hold also ensure that the terms under which free banks extend credit are in agreement with wealthholders' willingness to lend funds. Once again it is the law of adverse clearings that ensures these results. This law, it has been shown, does not apply to a monopoly bank of issue.

The maintenance of loan market and bank-money market equilibria under free banking has important implications. In the market for bank money it means that individuals never hold insufficient or excessive balances of bank money in the aggregate. In the loan market it means that banks make loans and investments only on the basis of voluntary (planned or *ex ante*) savings, so that there is no redirection of the means of production due to forced savings or false profit signals (based upon distorted bank rates of interest) that disappear once the redundancy or deficiency of bank money has had its effect upon nominal magnitudes. The disequilibrium situations depicted by monetary business cycle theories, such as Hayek's (1935), are avoided. The long-run implication for both markets is that alterations of commodity prices (both absolute and relative) due to monetary disequilibrium are avoided.

In summary, competitive banks of issue are usually not independent sources of nominal demand for goods and services. This means that they cannot be independent generators of demand for bank money either, because their issues do not influence the general level of prices. Under free banking there is no "Wicksellian indeterminancy" of prices or of demand for money. The same is not true of an unregulated system based upon monopolized note issue.[20]

CHANGES IN THE DEMAND FOR BANK MONEY[21]

So far we have described the self-correcting responses in a free banking system to the creation of bank money in excess of some *given* demand for it. We must now consider how a free banking system responds to changes, positive or negative, in the aggregate demand for bank-money balances; that is, we will examine the mechanisms of dynamic adjustment of demand liabilities under competitive note issue.

Consider first a circumstance where the demand for bank money has grown. It is useful to think of individual demands as "sumps" or "reservoirs" along a flowing stream of bank-money income. An increase in demand is analogous to a deepening of these reservoirs (an intensification of existing demands) or to an increase in their number (a multiplication of money-holding firms and individuals). In either case, the existence of greater demand for bank money means that the community will absorb further fiduciary issues without causing such issues to overflow into the stream of nominal income. Consequently, such new issues do not find their way into the clearing mechanism. They do not result in reserve losses to the banks responsible for them. In this case banks are able to lend profitably beyond what they previously considered their excess reserves.

Persons are not indifferent among various bank monies; everyone tends to hold a definite portfolio of monies. For illustrative purposes we assume that each person prefers the liabilities of one bank with which that person does business. We must investigate the circumstances that allow a competitive bank of issue to take advantage of an extension of demands for its money. The most obvious place to begin is with the bank's borrower customers. Most bank demand liabilities come into being via new loan and asset purchases. Clearly, to the extent that bank borrowers *hold* their borrowed balances rather than spend them, the bank that creates the balances suffers no negative clearings from them. Such balances include "compensating balance requirements" and are the simplest instance of bank-money creation that does not lead to adverse clearings.[22]

A less trivial case is where borrowers' expenditures of bank money find their way into the hands of other individuals who are or who choose to become clients of the issuing bank. This factor is only relevant when there is an actual increase in "permanent" money holdings; otherwise, the issuing bank soon suffers a clearing loss. When bank-money demand has not permanently increased – that is, when a marginal increase in bank issues would lead to an increase in aggregate, nominal incomes as excess issues are spent off – the only asset that is suitable backing for the new liabilities is commodity money. We thus return to the traditional case where only receipt of new outside money by the system will make possible further issues of bank money.

What has been said regarding the expansion of liabilities of individual banks also applies to the free banking system as a whole: Whenever there is a *general* decline in the rate of turnover of bank money, as follows an increase in the demand to hold it, the banks are able to expand their total outstanding liabilities relative to their holdings of outside-money reserves. In other words, there is an increase in the reserve multiplier. Bank-money creation can continue only when there are unexploited "reservoirs" of bank demand. Any issues beyond this lead to additions to the stream of payments, and hence to an increase in total bank clearings and reserve needs.[23]

Now consider what happens when there is a reduction in demand for bank money. Just as new extensions of credit are the occasion for expansion of bank liabilities, retirements of loans and investments are the occasion for their extinction. Bank demand liabilities are reduced whenever new issues cannot offset the absorption of previous liabilities via loan repayments because a fallen demand for bank money renders new issues (or even the "rolling over" of old credits) unsustainable. Let us examine this process at the level of the individual bank of issue.

First of all, a reduction in the demand to hold the bank's liabilities is postulated. Suppose that the surplus liabilities are paid over to someone who is indebted to the issuing bank, who in turn uses them to repay the loan. What is the net result of these transactions? The bank suffers no clearing loss (i.e. no loss of reserves) and no change in its volume of clearings; however, the sum of its outstanding liabilities falls. If it attempts to recover its previous business by extending new credit it suffers adverse clearings to the extent of the new issues. Since its reserve holdings were at the optimum determined by the volume and variance of clearings it faced, such new extensions of credit are unprofitable. Similar results follow if the liabilities of one bank are used to repay loans at another bank when there is a decline in the demand for the liabilities of the first bank with no offsetting increase in the demand to hold the liabilities of its rival.

The process described in the preceding example operates as well when there is a *general* reduction in the demand for bank money. Here there is a system-wide increase in the rate of turnover of demand liabilities, which means that bank assets must be made to "turn over" more rapidly as well. The liquidity needs of the banking system increase, and higher ratios of reserves to liabilities are needed. The reserve multiplier falls because of reduced demand for bank-money balances.

CONFUSION ABOUT THE "RESERVE RATIO"

The individual bank of issue must monitor two statistics related to bank clearings: the *average* of net clearings over a given period and the *variance* of net clearings over the same period. The variance indicates minimum long-run reserve needs. Its value tends to increase absolutely (albeit as a decreasing percentage) with increases in gross bank clearings even if average net clearings remain constant.[24] This means that a bank must add to its reserves, other things being equal, whenever its gross clearings with other banks increase. Otherwise it faces a higher risk of failing to meet the adverse clearings it suffers on any particular day. The banking *system*, in turn, can only sustain an increase in its gross clearings if it improves the efficiency of its clearing arrangements (thereby reducing minimum reserve needs relative to clearings) or if it increases its total holdings of outside commodity money (the primary means of interbank settlement under free banking).

Textbook and other discussions of banking theory tend to devote undue attention to the ratio of reserves to total bank money as a limit to fiduciary issues by individual banks and by the banking system. This emphasis is partly due to focus on legal reserve requirements (which are often stipulated in terms of this ratio) rather than economic reserve requirements. The latter have only an indirect relationship to the total amount of bank money; they are not linked to it by a constant ratio. While total bank clearings (and their variance) are not unrelated to total outstanding liabilities, changes in money demand make it possible for total liabilities to change without at all affecting total clearings. These changes do not alter the banking system's total reserve needs. Therefore, the ratio of reserves to bank money (and hence, the reserve multiplier) in a free banking system alters in response to consumer demands. Variations would be apparent in comparing different banks of issue cross-sectionally and in observing an individual bank (or the banking system) over time.[25] The amount of bank money outstanding is determined, both for individual banks and for the banking system, by the public's demand to hold bank money, through the influence of money demand on optimal bank reserve holdings. Reserve demand will not rise in step with the volume of bank money when the latter grows in response to increased demand to hold bank money. Other things being equal, increased demand to hold bank money leads to a transitional *fall* in individuals' expenditures relative to their total income. This in turn reduces total bank clearings, inviting a compensating expansion of liabilities. Decreased demand to hold bank money has the opposite effect. In these circumstances bank clearings and the demand to hold bank money move in opposite directions. To maintain an optimal ratio of reserve to total *clearings* the banks must allow their ratios of reserves to total *liabilities* to change.[26]

In the theory of monopoly issue or central banking it is customary to overlook changes in the reserve multiplier. This multiplier is treated as a constant. Attention is then drawn to what happens when the monopoly issuer's liabilities expand and the excess comes into the deposit banks' possession. The resulting change in the *system*'s demand liabilities is supply determined. The chain of causation is (1) expansion of monopoly bank liabilities, (2) multiple expansion of deposit bank liabilities to the extent allowed by a fixed reserve multiplier, (3) increased spending prompted by an excess supply of money, (4) higher prices, (5) greater (nominal) demand to hold bank money, and, finally, (6) a new equilibrium with all nominal magnitudes proportionately scaled upward. Under free banking supply-induced expansions of bank money do not occur except when there are expansions in the stock of the commodity money.[27] The chain of causation generally appropriate to monetary expansion under free banking is (1) increased demand to hold bank money, (2) a change in the reserve multiplier, (3) expansion of bank demand liabilities, and (4) a new equilibrium with the scale of prices unchanged. For example, imagine a free banking system with commodity money reserves of $1,000. Suppose that the supply of bank money is $50,000, which equals the public's initial demand for bank money. The reserve multiplier is, therefore, 50. Now imagine that the demand for bank money falls by $10,000, to $40,000. Bank demand liabilities will then be forced to contract by $10,000, so that the reserve multiplier falls to 40; that is, the ratio of reserves to demand liabilities rises from 2 per cent to 2.5 per cent.

The above arguments could have been stated in terms of changes in the "income velocity of circulation" of bank money (which is simply another means of referring to the demand for bank money relative to expenditure), or in terms of the determinants of equilibrium in the market for loanable funds. As has been shown, changes in the demand to hold bank money affect the availability of loanable funds: when more bank money is demanded, the supply of loanable funds is increased, and competitive banks of issue can reduce their lending rates until the demand for credit is sufficient to absorb the greater supply. Opposite adjustments take place when the demand for bank money falls.

That the supply of bank money in a free banking system responds automatically to changes in demand to hold bank money means that equilibrium in both the market for loanable funds and the market for media of exchange is maintained with minimal disturbance of prices from their initial positions even when the demand for bank money changes. The "invisible hand" adjusts supply to demand in a free banking system just as it does in other industries where goods are produced on a competitive basis.

CREDIT EXPANSION "IN CONCERT"

The arguments raised in the previous section also help to refute the traditional view that, if all banks (in an unregulated setting) expand credit "in concert", they will not face any liquidity constraint, and so can expand credit without limit. Picture a situation where every bank has *average* net clearings equal to zero, because every bank's share of the market for bank money is stable, and no bank is expanding "out of step" with its competitors. Assume, furthermore, that the total supply of bank money is at first equal to the wants of the public. Do the banks hold reserves in such a circumstance? They do hold *precautionary* reserves, because although net debit clearings for any bank have a *mean value* of zero, they also tend to vary from this mean over the course of any series of clearings. Therefore every bank holds reserves to protect itself against the possibility of above-average adverse clearings it may suffer in any one clearing session. The demand for precautionary reserves is what limits expansion for the system as a whole.

Now imagine that, starting from the above equilibrium situation, all the banks expand their balance sheets in unison by an equal amount, although the demand to hold bank money (and its distribution across banks) has not changed. The "in concert" expansion might be a result of formal agreements, or it might be spontaneous. Will it leave the banks unscathed? It will not, because, although every bank would find its *average* clearinghouse credits and debits increased by the same amount over the course of numerous clearing sessions, the *variance* of net debit and net credit clearings faced by any bank would also increase, by a factor approximately equal to the square root of the percentage increase in *gross* clearings. In consequence, each bank would soon discover that its precautionary reserve holdings, though formerly adequate to protect it against above-average adverse clearings in any one clearing session, are no longer sufficient. The increased clearing activity brings with it a greater probability of single-session net debit clearings exceeding a bank's reserves. For this reason, "in concert" expansion will not be profitable or sustainable (assuming banks insist on spot payment of clearing balances). Therefore, each bank will have to reduce its liabilities to their previous equilibrium level. Moreover, only *one* bank has to determine that by expanding with the others it has overstretched its precautionary reserves, since contraction by any one bank will immediately force some of its rivals to contract as well, setting off a system-wide correction.

STABILITY OF THE MONETARY UNIT

Because the supply of bank money under free banking is demand elastic, changes in prices that would otherwise arise from changes in demands for real money balances are avoided. The exchange value of the money commodity (and, therefore, of the unit of account) is stabilized. This stabilization takes place without displacement of relative prices or bank interest rates from their equilibrium levels. It is guided by the banks' desires to maximize profits, which inspire them to take advantage of any opportunity to safely expand their liabilities. The law of adverse clearings, in turn, ensures that any bank expanding credit without warrant suffers an unsustainable drain of reserves.

A second important implication of demand-elastic bank money supply under free banking is that any sharp general increase in individuals' bank-money demand (i.e. any "hoarding" of bank money) need not result in a short-run interruption of bank-money income flows with consequent involuntary accumulation of goods inventories and trade disruption. Instead, hoarding (because it constitutes an increase in the supply of loanable funds) is met by the expansion of bank loans and liabilities. Otherwise bank loan rates would be forced temporarily *above* their equilibrium levels (the excess demand for money would imply an excess supply of bonds) until a general decline of incomes and prices led to a downward adjustment of the nominal demand for loanable funds, thereby returning the rates to their appropriate levels. Under free banking, not only is loan market disequilibrium avoided, but the total supply of loanable funds (in real terms) is greater than it would be were the supply of bank money demand inelastic. (There will be more to say about this in the next section.)

The above results depend upon the operation of the law of adverse clearings; none of them apply to systems of discretionary monopoly note issue. Whether monopoly is preferable depends on whether deliberate State management of a monopoly issuer (i.e., central banking and monetary policy) can duplicate or improve upon results achieved automatically by a free banking system.

Many theorists believe that a central bank can properly regulate its issues by stabilizing the general price level (as measured by some price index).[28] Since a monopoly issuer can generate excess or deficient supplies of bank money, and since these excess or deficient supplies should, *ceteris paribus*, reveal themselves in changes in prices of many goods and services, these theorists reason that eliminating changes in the general price level is equivalent to eliminating central bank under- and overexpansions. They fail to recognize that changes in the price level may occur for reasons other than maladjustment of the supply of bank liabilities to demand. Most important are price level changes due to changes in production per capita, which reflect changes in unit cost of production of goods. Attempts to offset, by money-supply changes, movements in the price level stemming from such non-monetary causes are actually disruptive. Because unwarranted monetary injections never affect prices uniformly or simultaneously, they add to or subtract from aggregate nominal income, temporarily prevent relative prices from reaching their equilibrium levels, and disrupt the flow of goods and investment.[29, 30]

Some advocates of central banking realize that changes in the price level are not always due to exogenous changes in the demand for bank money. Accordingly, they have suggested formulae or "rules" for managing the supply of central bank money based on estimates of secular growth in aggregate demand. The most famous, of course, is Milton Friedman's – although Friedman himself has become a proponent of free banking.[31] Sometimes these rules reflect a rough estimate of population growth; other times they are based on much more elaborate estimates from econometric models. Unfortunately, such methods provide only a very crude and unsatisfactory alternative to a demand-elastic supply of bank money.[32] Most of them do not even attempt to deal with seasonal or cyclical changes in demand.

Rules for monetary management generally fail to rule out disequilibrating price disturbances; in particular, an improper supply of central bank money disturbs interest rates, because the extension of loanable funds by the banking system ceases to agree with the voluntary savings decisions of individuals. This particular variety of relative-price distortion, a distortion of intertemporal rates of exchange, results either in a boom-and-bust cycle (inflationary case)[33] or in more immediate depression (deflationary case). Obviously, advocates of a monetary rule desire neither consequence.

If it were true that the public's demand for money could always be satisfied with demand deposits, so that "free" deposit banking could by itself secure a demand-elastic supply of bank money, then one could make a system founded on monopoly note issue function satisfactorily simply by doing away with the issue and use of currency altogether.[34] Automatic alterations in the sum of deposits would then meet needs for money balances. There would be no problems of disequilibrium in either the bank money or the credit markets of such a system.

Unfortunately, not all demands for money can be satisfied by deposit balances: a definite portion of money demand is wanted in the form of currency, and the size of this portion changes frequently. The challenge of monopoly issue is to meet this specific demand for currency notes as it fluctuates seasonally and secularly without unnecessarily altering deposit bank reserves and without thereby causing a multiplicative (inflationary or deflationary) change in the *total* supply of bank money.[35]

Successful monetary management requires some means for identifying changes in the public's demand for bank money, so that bank liabilities expand as demand increases, and diminish as it subsides. Under central banking automatic adjustments will not occur. Overextensions of credit by the monopoly issuer do not reveal themselves by way of adverse clearings suffered by any of the deposit banks. Underexpansion by the monopoly issuer does not invite compensating expansion by the deposit banks because the latter cannot independently fulfill that part of the demand for money consisting of demand for currency. Thus, in a monopolized system the demand for money often must adjust to supply, rather than vice versa. No predetermined rule for monetary management can enable banks in a monopolized system to find the proper limits of credit expansion. Monopolization of currency issue destroys the adverse-clearing mechanism and in doing so creates a vast calculation problem that no a priori formula can solve.

To summarize: a demand-elastic supply of bank money has desirable properties. Free banking provides it automatically; monopolized banking cannot. Central banks and monetary management, usually supposed to solve the problem of controlling the supply of bank money, instead create the problem.

THE EFFICIENCY OF BANK-MONEY SUPPLY
UNDER FREE BANKING

A further consequence of the demand-elastic supply of bank money under free banking is that the use of resources in producing the basic money commodity is less affected by changes in the demand for media of exchange. Elimination of the public's demand for commodity money means significant reductions in the production of the money commodity for monetary uses. Here is the most important secular advantage of the use of fiduciary media under free banking: would-be investments in the money commodity become investments in other things. They are transformed via bank-money holdings into increased supplies of loanable funds. Savings that would, in a 100 per cent reserve system, accumulate as commodity money manifest themselves instead as holdings of credit instruments (which, in the case of demand deposits, are interest bearing). This continuing spur to capital accumulation comes in addition to the initial, once-and-for-all savings associated with the adoption of fiduciary media and resulting release of the money commodity for non-monetary uses. The once-and-for-all savings can, as was noted earlier, actually be increased by monopolizing note issue (since, ideally, *no* commodity-money reserves are needed to settle clearings in a monopoly system). However, against this one-time gain must be weighed the costs that result from a monopoly bank's frequent under- and overissue of fiduciary media. (These costs are further discussed below.) Moreover, the absolute value of the gain is not great, since the reserve needs of a developed free banking system are modest to begin with,[36] and tend to diminish over time as clearing arrangements improve. Such improvements proceed whenever their marginal contributions to bank revenues exceed their marginal costs.

So far we are still operating under the assumption that bank money has completely replaced commodity (outside) money in circulation, and that individuals' confidence in bank money is absolute. To complete our analysis it is necessary to relax this assumption.

If commodity money still circulates, note-issuing bankers consider three margins when deciding the volume of their investments: (1) the marginal cost of attracting new deposits or permanent note holdings; (2) the marginal cost of reducing holdings of non-earning reserve assets (e.g. by running higher risks or by improving the clearing system); and (3) the marginal gain in interest revenues from acquiring earning assets. Ultimately, it is the demanders of media of exchange who determine the direction and extent of economies undertaken with respect to commodity money, through their desires for interest-yielding *versus* low-risk money balances. The investments made by free bankers are, therefore, cost minimizing from the consumers' point of view. In this (subjective) sense the use of bank money under free banking is efficient: bank money is employed (or "produced") instead of commodity money only so far as the anticipated marginal benefits exceed the anticipated marginal opportunity costs; and the banks are driven to supply bank money at the least possible expense. The first conclusion, at least, does *not* apply in the case of monopoly issue: a monopolized system can create excess bank money, and the monopoly issuer will maximize its profits by doing so. Since such an excess does not contribute to the flow of real goods and services (and may even obstruct this flow by disturbing the price system), its production is inefficient even though the direct resource costs involved (paper, ink, etc.) are minor. The overissue is not in accord with the public's desired portfolio mix of commodity money and bank money. In a world of less than complete confidence in bank money this might lead people to redeem excess bank-money holdings. This could necessitate a multiplicative contraction of bank demand liabilities as deposit banks seek to protect their reserves, undoing some of the economies that were achieved using fiduciary media. *Under*issues of bank money under monopoly issue are also inefficient, because they cause the exchange value of the money commodity to rise directly, intensifying production of it. To these costs connected with unnecessary production of the money commodity must be added the costs of disequilibrium resource allocation due to displacement of prices and interest rates.

THE SPECIFIC DEMAND FOR CURRENCY

So far we have dealt with problems of supply and demand respecting bank money in general. Now it is necessary to consider the implications of a change in the demand for one form of bank money – currency – assuming the *total* demand for bank money remains unchanged. The specific demand for currency increases whenever the proportion of payments that can be made by check declines.[37]

The directors of a competitive bank of issue have no special difficulty meeting their clients' demands for currency. If a depositor wants to convert a portion or even all of his or her balance, the bank has only to supply the depositor with notes from its own printing press, as it were. If many customers come forward for the same reason, the bank prints more notes for the occasion. What matters to a free bank is not the form of its demand liabilities but their total value. When customers convert existing deposits into notes, there is merely a reduction of one balance sheet item and an equivalent increase in another. Assuming that the total demand for money remains unchanged, and that the variance of note and deposit clearings is the same at the margin, there need be no change in the bank's total clearings nor in its reserve holdings.

Under monopoly note issue the situation is radically different. When clients of a competitive deposit bank in a currency monopoly system convert portions of their balances into currency, what they receive is not the bank's own currency (which it is prohibited from issuing) but rather the notes of the monopoly bank of issue. These notes are also the deposit bank's reserve media. To pay out notes to its customers, a deposit bank must acquire them in the interbank market, or from the bank of issue. If no additional notes are made available from the issuing bank to the system as a whole (e.g. if the "discount window" is closed or the rate charged is prohibitively high), reserves become deficient and the banks must contract their liabilities to avoid default on clearing balances. In this event the supply of loanable funds is curtailed, and lending rates rise above their equilibrium levels. A scarcity of credit results even though individuals' demand to hold bank money in the broad sense has not changed.

If the monopoly bank of issue provides the desired "reserve compensation" it prevents a credit shortage from happening.[38] However, there is no guarantee that a monopoly issuer will cooperate, especially if it is bound by a statute or rule limiting its ability to create reserves. And if the statute or rule is relaxed, so that the monopoly bank of issue can provide the needed notes, how can the issuer ensure that notes issued for emergency reasons are *retired* once the public no longer needs them? Unless it can take this precaution the surplus notes may return to the vaults of the deposit banks, where they will serve as the basis for a multiplicative, inflationary expansion of bank credit.

The problem of note supply for reserve compensation under monopoly issue may not be insuperable. Nevertheless it is certainly too complex to be solved by any simple rule or formula. It calls for an element of discretion, which creates dangers of its own. In contrast, this same problem simply does not arise under free banking.

THE INADEQUACY OF "KNOWLEDGE SURROGATES" UNDER MONOPOLY ISSUE[39]

The general problem of economic calculation is one of discovering individuals' and firms' demands for particular services and commodities. Where there are market prices this problem is solved by entrepreneurial reactions to signals of profit and loss. Price and profit signals act as "knowledge surrogates"; that is, they lead entrepreneurs and producers to adjust their actions *as if* they actually knew consumers' preferences.

The particular calculation problem that a well-managed banking system is supposed to solve involves estimating the demand for bank money (including the specific demand for currency). Under free banking the incidence of clearings, through its influence upon profits and losses, make these demands known to banks: the clearing mechanism leads profit-maximizing free banks to adjust their outstanding loans and investments *as if* they had direct knowledge of individuals' willingness to hold bank money, via their attempts to maintain optimal reserves with respect to notes and deposits. Consequently interest rates are made to reflect the true state of individuals' time preference.

Under monopoly note issue the clearing mechanism is undermined, since excess issues by the monopoly bank are treated as reserve assets by deposit banks instead of being redeemed by them. In a monopoly system there are no spontaneous knowledge surrogates to guide production. Thus conscious, centralized planning of the supply of bank money becomes necessary. Such planning suffers from an inherent incapacity for using localized (dispersed) information. Monetary policy is nothing more than a crude, makeshift knowledge surrogate erected in place of the vastly more effective knowledge surrogates that function under free banking, and most monetary reform proposals (e.g. "price rules", velocity-adjusted money growth rate rules) offer only different makeshifts and not a solution. Rather than encouraging more complete use of available information, the adoption of central banking in place of free banking results in the complete abandonment of adequate means for gauging the demands for bank money.

A defender of central banking might point out that a central bank has access to information *superior* to that available to competitive banks of issue, including such things as elaborate econometric estimates of money demand and of seasonal fluctuations in the demand for currency. But this would be beside the point. Although free banks may not avail themselves of such information, they also do not *need* it; their attention to reserve drains is sufficient to guide them to supply bank money precisely in accordance with consumers' demands for it.

The absence of adequate knowledge surrogates under monopoly note issue leads to errors that are far more serious than those that would follow from centralized administration of any other industry. This is because money enters into practically all exchange and economic calculation, so that its disequilibrium supply distorts a wide array of price and profit signals, that is distorts other knowledge surrogates. The dislocation of interest rates is perhaps the most important example of this.

In summary, the clearing mechanism enables competitive banks of issue to discover their clients' demand for bank money. It rapidly translates banks' errors of judgement into suboptimal reserve positions and thereby into economic losses. A central bank cannot avail itself of a similar discovery procedure; it must rely upon knowledge surrogates of a decidedly inferior sort.

CONCLUSION

Although several writers in the past have stressed a pure intermediary view of commercial banking, few would argue that banking systems today function according to the pure intermediary ideal or that they do not require centralized supervision of one kind or another. Moreover, traditional textbook treatments do not question the need for central management of the money supply even though (and several economists, notably Friedman, have made this point) it is the central bank itself, and not commercial banks, that is a major source of monetary instability. The present chapter has attempted to show that a free banking system is a perfect embodiment of the pure intermediary view of money-supply processes. In comparison, central banking systems are inherently unable to function in the manner suggested by the pure intermediary view. These results suggest the need for a radical revision of conventional views on free *versus* central banking. Free banking should be regarded as a potential solution to monetary instability, and not as a likely cause of such instability. In contrast, centralized currency supply should be regarded as a likely cause of instability and not as a cure.

NOTES

1 The most relevant of these are Jonung (1985), Rockoff (1974), Rolnick and Weber (1982, 1983), White (1984b), and Vaubel (1984).
2 See for example Black (1970), Fama (1980), Greenfield and Yeager (1983), Sargent and Wallace (1982), and Wallace (1983). Hayek (1978) and Klein (1974) offer theories of the competitive production of irredeemable fiat monies.

3 The arguments in this study are developed in much greater detail in Selgin (1988). Other theoretical studies of free banking which, however, fail to recognize some of its important properties are White (1984b) Chapter 1, and White (1984a). There are also some scattered remarks in Smith (1936).

4 It is important to recall in this connection that in most instances monopolization of currency supply historically preceded the idea of centralized money-supply management. Thus, it is not accurate to say that central banking developed in response to the instability of *decentralized* banking; typically it developed in response to the instability of already centralized systems that lacked any systematic mechanism for regulating monopolistic institutions. In other cases it was imposed as an instrument of state finance. On this see Smith (1936).

5 Discussion of a world monopoly issuer is all the more relevant in that some present-day theorists advocate such a system. See for example Mundell (1983, pp. 207–209).

6 Of course, this is not to suggest that particular *policies* of credit expansion on the part of monopoly issuers will not be considered.

7 The "money commodity" could even be a defunct fiat money, in which case costs of production (absent counterfeiting) are infinite once all specimens have been unearthed.

8 This section summarizes Chapter 2 above.

9 See Powell (1966, pp. 56 ff.) and Richards (1965, Chapters II and IX).

10 The controversial "pure intermediary" view of banking institutions is defended here and in what follows *only* for the free banking case. Gurley and Shaw (1955, 1956) have attempted a more universal application of the "pure intermediary" approach. Their views are ably criticized in Aschheim (1959). See also Poindexter (1946) and Chapter 5 below.

11 The issue of notes of small denominations and token coins (for use in the making of change) is necessary for the complete displacement of commodity money from circulation.

12 For example, Phillips (1920).

13 The extent and rapidity of the reserve drain is usually less for notes than for deposits (how much less depends upon particular conditions). Nevertheless, under all but the most improbable assumptions it will be adequate to deter overexpansion.

14 Problems that arise under monopoly issue as a consequence of variations in this proportion are discussed below.

15 See Rist (1966, p. 208). Note that this argument does not rest upon the presence of "legal tender" status for the notes of the monopoly issuer.

16 Eventually a check occurs in the shape of an increased industrial demand for gold prompted by the fall in its relative price. This "internal drain" is analogous to the "price-specie-flow" that confronts monopoly overissuers of convertible liabilities in an open system. These are long-run sources of restraint, which operate only once prices have been generally influenced.

17 This crucial point is emphasized by Cannan (1921). See also Rothbard (1970, pp. 118–123 and 662–667).

18 See Brown (1910).

19 It is assumed here that the non-commercial bank segment of the loanable funds market is not a source of disequilibrium.

20 Wicksell himself (1935, pp. 188–189) practically acknowledges this in his criticism of the views of Adolf Wagner. Wagner's position, which depends on the clearing mechanism, is of course vitiated if banks expand credit in unison via formal agreements. Yet such agreements are not, Wicksell concedes

(ibid., p. 190) in evidence. So Wicksell undermines his own criticism of Wagner.

21 This section draws heavily upon Cannan (1935). Cannan's reasoning may be accepted without qualification only for the special case of competitive note issue.

22 Borrowers, insofar as they hold rather than spend borrowed bank-money balances, are simultaneously debtors and creditors to the lending bank. On compensating balances see Davis and Guttentag (1962).

23 The determinants of economic reserve requirements are discussed in the next section.

24 By the law of large numbers. See Edgeworth (1888) and Orr and Mellon (1961).

25 For evidence on cross-sectional and temporal variation in Scottish free banks' reserve ratios see Munn (1981).

26 For an argument, within the context of central banking, for allowing *legal* reserve requirements to vary with differing rates of (deposit) turnover, see Jacoby (1963). Jacoby does not note any connection between his recommended legal requirements and the economic requirements of an unregulated system.

27 Increases in the stock of monetary gold are only disequilibrating if they involve shifts in its supply schedule. In fact, many historic "discoveries" of gold were movements along, not of, the long-run gold supply curve. See Rockoff (1984).

28 See for example Hall (1984).

29 This is not to deny that movements in prices due, for example, to increased production do not themselves *influence* the nominal demand for bank money. For one thing, there is a "real balance" effect. However, with respect to it the necessary adjustment of demand liabilities (in the case of falling prices) is *downwards*.

30 See Fisher and Hayek (1935), and Chapters 7 and 8.

31 See Friedman and Schwartz (1986).

32 The search for a stable money demand function to guide monetary policy has been among the more frustrated enterprises of contemporary monetary economics. See Judd and Scadding (1982), and Cooley and Leroy (1981).

33 As in Hayek (1935).

34 A "freeze" on currency issue, even if accompanied by a freeze on deposit creation by the monopoly issuer, would not by itself be adequate, because currency could still influence the supply of credit independently of demand as it passed in and out of bank vaults. On this see the section after next.

35 The full extent of this challenge for monopoly issue is outlined in the section after next.

36 In the Scottish free banking era, reserve ratios of between 2 per cent and 10 per cent were typical, and banks occasionally operated with ratios as low as 0.5 per cent. Were it not for prohibitions upon the issue of small notes the figures might even be lower. See White (1984b, p. 148).

37 An extreme case would be a general loss of confidence in "checkbook" money, which is to be distinguished from a loss of confidence in bank money in the broad sense. The former involves distrust of individual check writers; the latter would imply distrust of the banks of issue themselves. For a statistical analysis of variations in the specific demand for currency see Cagan (1958).

38 Of course, if what is "compensated" is not a true "currency drain" but only a transfer of funds from one bank to another, overissue of credit is involved. Under monopoly issue it is not always possible to tell, even *ex post*, whether a

currency withdrawal warrants reserve compensation or not. Under free banking, notes withdrawn for use in circulation do not cause reserve losses; those withdrawn for redeposit in other banks do.

39 On the general problem of economic "knowledge administration" as faced by central planners see Hayek (1948).

REFERENCES

Aschheim, J. (1959), "Commercial Banks and Financial Intermediaries, Fallacies and Policy Implications", *Journal of Political Economy*, 67, 59–71.

Black, F. (1970), "Banking and Interest Rates in a World Without Money: The Effects of Uncontrolled Banking", *Journal of Bank Research*, 1, 9–20.

Brown, H. G. (1910), "Commercial Banking and the Rate of Interest", *Quarterly Journal of Economics*, 24, 743–749.

Cagan, P. (1958), "The Demand for Currency Relative to Total Money Supply", *Journal of Political Economy*, 66, 303–328.

Cannan, E. (1921), "The Application of the Theoretical Apparatus of Supply and Demand to Units of Currency", *Economic Journal*, 31, 453–461.

———— (1935), "Growth and Fluctuations of Bankers' Liabilities to Customers", *The Manchester School*, 6, 2–17.

Cooley, T. F., and LeRoy, S. F. (1981), "Identification and Estimation of Money Demand", *American Economic Review*, 71, 825–844.

Davis, R. G. and Guttentag, J. M. (1962), "Are Compensating Balance Requirements Irrational?", *Journal of Finance*, 17, 121–126.

Edgeworth, F. Y. (1888), "The Mathematical Theory of Banking", *Journal of the Royal Statistical Association*, 51, 113–127.

Fama, E. (1980), "Banking in the Theory of Finance", *Journal of Monetary Economics*, 6, 39–57.

Fisher, A. G. B. (1935), "Does an Increase in Volume of Production Call for a Corresponding Increase in Volume of Money?", *American Economic Review*, 25, 197–211.

Friedman, M. and Schwartz, A. (1986), "Has Government any Role in Money?", *Journal of Monetary Economics*, 17, 37–62.

Greenfield, R. L. and Yeager, L. B. (1983), "A Laissez-Faire Approach to Monetary Stability", *Journal of Money, Credit, and Banking*, 15, 302–315.

Gurley, J. G. and Shaw, E. S. (1955), "Financial Aspects of Economic Development", *American Economic Review*, 45, 415–418.

———— (1956), "Financial Intermediation and the Saving-Investment Process", *Journal of Finance*, 11, 257–276.

———— (1965), "Financial Intermediaries and the Savings Investment Process", *Journal of Finance*, 11, 257–276.

Hall, R. E. (1984), "A Free-Market Policy to Stabilize the Purchasing Power of the Dollar", pp. 303–321, in: B. N. Siegel (ed.), *Money in Crisis*, San Francisco.

Hayek, F. A. (1935), *Prices and Production*, London.

———— (1948), "The Use of Knowledge in Society", Ch. 4 of: *Individualism and Economic Order*, Chicago.

———— (1978), *Denationalisation of Money – The Argument Refined*, 2nd edn, London.

Jacoby, N. (1963), "The Structure and Use of Variable Bank Reserve Requirements", pp. 213–233, in: D. Carson (ed.), *Banking and Monetary Studies*, Homewood, II.

Jonung, L. (1985), "The Economics of Private Money: The Experience of Private

Notes in Sweden, 1831–1902", *Paper presented at the Monetary History Group Meeting, London, Sept. 27, 1985.*

Judd, J. P. and Scadding, J. L. (1982), "The Search for a Stable Money Demand Function: A Survey of the Post-1973 Literature", *Journal of Economic Literature*, 20, 993–1023.

Klein, B. (1974), "The Competitive Supply of Money", *Journal of Money, Credit, and Banking*, 6, 423–453.

Mundell, R. A. (1983), "International Monetary Options", *Cato Journal* 3, 189–210.

Munn, C. (1981), *The Scottish Provincial Banking Companies, 1747–1864*, Edinburgh.

Orr, D. and Mellon, W. G. (1961), "Stochastic Reserve Losses and Expansion of Bank Credit", *American Economic Review*, 51, 614–623.

Phillips, C. A. (1920), *Bank Credit*, New York.

Poindexter, J. C. (1946), "Some Misconceptions of Banking and Interest Theory", *Southern Economic Journal*, 13, 132–145.

Powell, E. T. (1966), *The Evolution of the Money Market*, New York.

Richards, R. D. (1965), *The Early History of Banking in England*, New York.

Rist, C. (1966), *History of Monetary and Credit Theory from John Law to the Present Day*, trans. Jane Degras, New York.

Rockoff, H. (1974), "The Free-Banking Era: A Re-Examination", *Journal of Money, Credit, and Banking*, 6, 141–167.

————— (1984), "Some Evidence on the Real Price of Gold, Its Costs of Production, and Commodity Prices", pp. 613–649, in: D. Bordo and A. J. Schwartz (eds), *A Retrospective on the Classical Gold Standard, 1821–1931*, Chicago.

Rolnick, A. J. and Weber, W. E. (1982), "Free-Banking, Wildcat Banking, and Shinplasters", *Federal Reserve Bank of Minneapolis Quarterly Review*, 6, 10–19.

————— (1983), "New Evidence on Laissez-Faire Banking", *American Economic Review*, 73, 1080–1091.

Rothbard, M. N. (1970), *Man, Economy, and State*, Los Angeles.

Sargent, T. J. and Wallace, N. (1982), "The Real-Bills Doctrine versus the Quantity Theory: A Reconsideration", *Journal of Political Economy*, 90, 1212–1236.

Selgin, G. (1988), *The Theory of Free Banking: Money Supply Under Competitive Note Issue*, Totowa, NJ.

Smith, V. (1936), *The Rationale of Central Banking*, London.

Tobin, J. (1963), "Commercial Banks as Creators of Money", pp. 408–419, in: Deane Carson (ed.), *Banking and Monetary Studies*, Homewood, Il.

Vaubel, R. (1984), "Private Competitive Note Issue In Monetary History", pp. 59–73, in: P. Stalin (ed.), *Currency Competition and Monetary Union*, The Hague.

Wallace, N. (1983), "A Legal Restrictions Theory of the Demand for 'Money' and the Role of Monetary Policy", *Federal Reserve Bank of Minneapolis Quarterly Review*, 7, 1–7.

White, L. H. (1984a), "Free Banking as an Alternative Monetary System", pp. 269–302, in: B. Siegel (ed.), *Money in Crisis*, San Francisco.

————— (1984b), *Free Banking in Britain: Theory, History, and Debate, 1800–1845*, Cambridge, UK.

Wicksell, K. (1935), *Lectures on Political Economy Vol. 2*, London.

5

COMMERCIAL BANKS AS PURE INTERMEDIARIES*

Between "old" and "new" views

INTRODUCTION

A long-standing debate in monetary economics concerns the role of commercial (demand–liability-creating) banks in the saving–investment process. According to the "New View," commercial banks are pure intermediaries: they act as brokers of, rather than creators of, loanable funds and are not an independent cause of investment in excess of *ex ante* saving. In the words of Gramley and Chase [12, 1385],

> the quantity of deposits a bank sells depends on the willingness of the public to purchase its deposits. Since this is true for each and every bank in the system, the constraint on bank deposits – and hence on bank asset holdings – is derived from the public's desire to hold bank deposits.

Changes in the nominal supply of bank money are therefore responses to prior changes in the public's demand for balances of bank money. According to the "Old View," commercial banks *do* create loanable funds and *are* capable of causing investment to exceed *ex ante* saving: as Yeager [34, 49 and 51–52] puts it,

> there is no problem of [banks] lending and spending new demand deposits into existence. No one need be persuaded to invest in them before they can be created . . . people's initial unwillingness to *hold* all newly created actual money would not keep them from accepting it and would not prevent its creation.

Changes in the supply of bank money are matched by changes in demand only in the long run, by way of changes in the price level.[1] Of these two

---

*Reprinted, with permission, from the *Southern Economic Journal*, Vol. 56, No. 1 (July 1989).

views the new view is more controversial, and in the eyes of many theorists plainly false. It appears, at very least, to be irreconcilable with the fact that bank liabilities expand to some multiple of the supply of (primary) bank reserves, which informs much of the conduct of monetary policy.

This chapter offers a qualified defense of the new view while retaining the old view emphasis on the reserve multiplier and abstracting from the role of price-induced substitution among financial assets. Starting from these old view premises, it shows how the nominal supply of bank money and the reserve multiplier are capable of responding positively to changes in the monetary wants of the public through the influence of the latter on banks' demands for precautionary reserves. Since changes in the public's willingness to hold bank money (at a given price level) represent changes in its *ex ante* desire to lend funds through the banking system, demand-responsive changes in the supply of bank money are consistent with banks' having a pure-intermediary role.

THE SQUARE-ROOT LAW

Our analysis refers to a competitive banking system in which banks issue demand liabilities (bank money) in the form of deposits or banknotes and hold, in addition to interest-earning assets, non-interest-earning reserves. In the real world, of course, banks also finance their assets by issuing liabilities other than bank money, including certificates of deposit and money market accounts. Moreover, it is *generally* agreed (even by proponents of the old view) that banks behave as "pure intermediaries" with respect to these non-money liabilities, issuing only as many as the public wishes to hold at prevailing price and income levels. So we abstract from changes in the desired and actual quantity of these other sources of bank-intermediated financing; our aim is to show that the quantity of bank money in the narrow sense may also be determined by the wants of the public.

Bank reserves are needed to settle adverse clearings among rival banks, arising from unpredictable differences between actual net clearings and the expected value of net clearings, where the latter is assumed to be zero for all banks (because bank market shares are assumed to be unchanging). The nominal quantity of the reserve asset is exogenously given; we shall assume that it is constant. The public makes payments using bank money only and does not hold the reserve asset. Finally, there are no statutory reserve requirements, so that the demand for the reserve asset depends solely on the banks' prudentially determined needs.

A well-known proposition of banking theory, known as the "square-root law" of precautionary reserve demand, holds that, for any given, desired level of security against default, a bank's demand for primary reserves for any fixed planning period will be proportional to the square root of bank-money payments made by its clients during the planning period.[2] The demand for reserves by the banking system obeys the same law since it may be treated as equal to the sum of the reserve demands of individual banks.[3] Thus if G represents the total volume of payments of bank money (i.e., gross bank clearings) the demand for precautionary reserves will be

$$R^d = \theta G^{\frac{1}{2}} \tag{1}$$

where θ (> 0) is a factor of proportionality, which is assumed to be positively related to the per-dollar cost of default at the clearinghouse (p) and negatively related to the per-dollar opportunity cost of reserve holding (r), where r is measured by the loan rate of interest net of all costs of extending credit. Following Leijonhufvud [18, 358] we assume here that r and p move together proportionately, so that θ may be treated as a constant. This implies that changes in the loan rate of interest will generally not induce banks to hold a different level of reserves relative to their outstanding liabilities. The assumption is supported by empirical evidence of a low interest-rate elasticity of reserve demand, e.g., Hancock [15]. It is also analytically convenient and consistent with the old view, which minimizes the role of price-induced substitution among financial assets.

The functional form in equation (1) has also been chosen for its simplicity. A more general form might easily be substituted without altering the results of the analysis.

The intuition behind the square-root law is straightforward. As the volume of gross bank clearings increases, so do random fluctuations in their distribution among banks. This causes variations in net clearings of individual banks around their expected value (which is assumed for simplicity to be zero) to increase as well, only less than in proportion to the increase in gross clearings (because of the law of large numbers). The square-root result is implied if gross clearings alter by virtue of a change in the total *number* of payments (with no change in the average payment size).[4]

Though the square-root law is well known, some of its implications have gone unappreciated. Yet it is easy to show how the law implies that, even absent the conventional portfolio-substitution effects stressed by proponents of the new view, the supply of bank money may respond positively to the monetary wants of the public.

DEMAND-ACCOMMODATING CHANGES IN BANK MONEY

Given some fixed, nominal supply of bank reserves, $R^s = \bar{R}$, the square-root law implies that there is some maximum value of nominal bank-money payments per fixed planning period that can be supported by those reserves.

(This assumes that the structure of payments, e.g., their average size, is unchanging.) That maximum is simply:

$$G^* = (R/\theta)^2 = P^*T^* \tag{2}$$

where P is the average value of payments – the "price level" – and T is the number of payments in a planning period. Let us assume that the value of bank-money payments per planning period in a banking system with fixed reserves equals $\bar{R}$ and some given, real demand for money balances has grown to this maximum sustainable level. Let us also assume that the values of P^* and T^* are such that $M^s = M^d$, where M^s and M^d are the nominal stock of and nominal demand for bank money. This situation can be called "full monetary equilibrium." (See Figure 5.1.)

For a banking system in a state of full monetary equilibrium, the reserve-equilibrium condition is simply

$$R^d = \theta(G^*)^{\frac{1}{2}} = R^s = \bar{R}. \tag{3}$$

Now consider the effect of an autonomous change in the demand for bank money. Starting from full equilibrium any change in demand implies a non-zero excess supply of bank money. During any positive but finite planning period this leads to a temporary change in total bank-money payments (hence a change in the "velocity" or "turnover" of bank money) equal to some multiple of the excess supply of bank money. This reflects

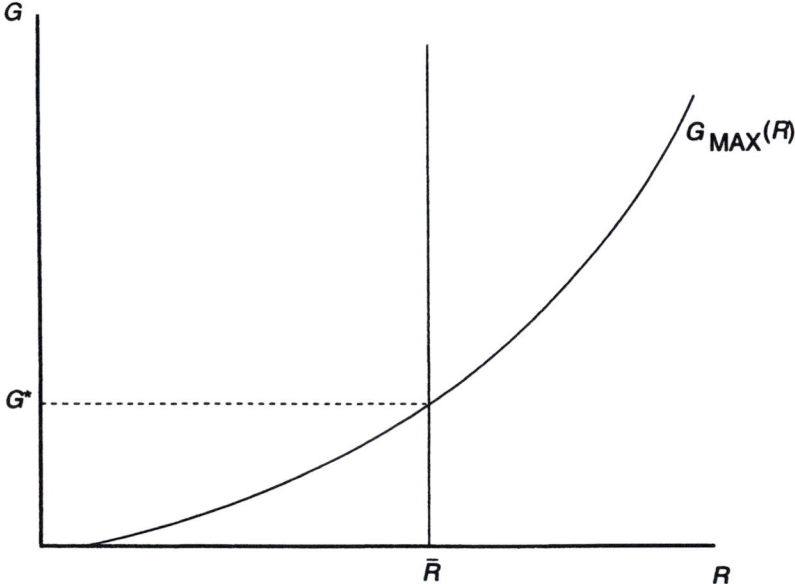

Figure 5.1 Maximum sustainable values of gross bank-money payments (G) per planning period as a function of banking system reserve holdings (R).

the old view assumption that a unit of bank money in excess supply becomes a "hot potato" until the excess is eliminated by an increase in the price level or by contraction of the nominal money supply. The assumption is predicated on the view that at least a part of any lasting excess demand for bank money must be equilibrated in the commodities market. The same applies whenever changes in M^s occur without offsetting changes in M^d.[5] The total change in payments resulting from disequilibrating changes in the supply of or demand for bank money is, therefore,

$$\Delta G = \lambda (M^s - M^d) \tag{4}$$

where $\lambda > 1$. Since $G = G^* + \Delta G$, substituting this in (1) gives

$$R^d = [\theta G^* + \lambda (M^s - M^d)]^{\frac{1}{2}}$$
$$> R^s \ (\text{if } M^s > M^d) \quad \text{or} \quad < R^s \ (\text{if } M^s < M^d). \tag{5}$$

This means that the public's excess-demand function for bank money is an argument in the banking system's excess-demand function for precautionary reserves. An excess demand for bank money leads to a proportionate excess *supply* of bank reserves, and an excess supply of bank money generates excess *demand* for bank reserves. To keep $R^d = R^s$, the banks must keep $M^s = M^d$. That is, the nominal stock of bank money will grow only in response to prior growth in the public's willingness to hold bank money, and will fall only in response to a fall in willingness-to-hold. This agrees with the new view. Given some *fixed* nominal supply of bank reserves, $R^s = \bar{R}$, the reserve multiplier ($m = M^s/\bar{R}$) must adjust to accommodate changes in the demand for bank money. In terms of the equation of exchange, changes in V will lead to opposite, offsetting changes in M (where M is the nominal stock of bank money) rather than to changes in P; the product MV – nominal income or spending – is automatically stabilized.

It would be relatively simple to incorporate these results into an explicit cost-minimization or profit-maximization model of the banking industry, showing how changes in the wants of the public (for balances of bank money) alter the costs and profitability of bank loan and deposit expansion, thereby affecting the equilibrium stock of bank money.

COMMENTS AND QUALIFICATIONS

Though the above results are straightforward, they are not part of orthodox banking theory. Writings on the determinants of the demand for precautionary reserves have not drawn attention to the potential for demand-accommodating changes in the nominal money supply because they have failed to note explicitly how the public's excess-demand function for bank money may (through its influence on the volume of payments) be an argument in the banks' demand function for reserves. Champions of the new view, in contrast, have not attempted to state their theory in a manner consistent with the traditional view that banks face a liquidity constraint and that they will expand their liabilities until this constraint becomes binding. Instead, they have argued their case in terms of banks' responding to changes in the structure of interest rates, including changes in the spread between the marginal revenue on loans and marginal bank operating and borrowing costs, without going into the mechanics of how changes in the wants of the public influence these marginal determinants of the profitability of bank expansion.[6] Finally, many defenders of the old view think it satisfactory merely to point out that bank lending depends on the available supply of reserves and on the size of the reserve multiplier. They do not consider how these variables (which are typically held to be exogenous) may themselves be influenced by the wants of the public.[7]

Our defense of the new view does, however, rest on a number of assumptions which may be, and usually are, violated in real-world banking systems. In addition to employing assumptions standard to the literature on precautionary-reserve demand, it has assumed:

1 that the supply of the reserve medium is fixed;
2 that reserve demand is a function of total payments only, i.e., that changes in the structure of interest rates or in clearing arrangements do not influence reserve demand;
3 that all payments by the public are made with inside (bank) money, so that the public does not hold the reserve asset (this requirement would be satisfied if all payments were made by check or if competitively issued banknotes were used in place of the reserve asset as currency);
4 that the structure of the probability distribution of payments made by the public is constant – a less demanding assumption that would still support new view conclusions is that P (the average payment size) and T (the number of payments in a planning period) always adjust in the same direction during any planning period; and
5 that some part of any excess demand for (supply of) bank money will be equilibrated in the commodities market, via changes in nominal spending and, eventually, commodity prices, unless the excess demand is eliminated through appropriate changes in the nominal money stock.

Though these assumptions have helped us to conclude that banks may be pure intermediaries, none of them is radically in conflict with orthodox money and banking theory, and assumption 5 is clearly in the old view tradition. Moreover, the need for assumption 1 implies that we are not able to defend more extreme versions of the new view, which suggest that changes in the supply of the reserve asset (high-powered money) do not lead to changes in the money stock. On the contrary, our analysis agrees with the conventional view that changes in the supply of bank reserves will cause the supply of bank money to alter independently of changes in the monetary wants of the public. However, insofar as bank reserves *do not* change, our analysis implies that changes in the money stock will still occur, and that these changes will be entirely consistent with the pure-intermediary emphasis of the new view.[8]

In another respect, also, our defense of the new view is conservative: unlike Black [3] and Fama [10], it has not had to posit a "moneyless" world, where banks do not need to hold definite amounts of some monetary reserve asset. Instead it serves as a bridge connecting the old and new views by explicitly acknowledging the old view assumptions (1) that banks face a reserve constraint and (2) that changes in the excess demand for money will affect the nominal volume of payments. The key to constructing the bridge has been to show how the volume of payments and the position of the reserve constraint are related to one another.

NOTES

1 Representatives of the new view include Tobin [28], Gramley and Chase [12], Black [3], Fama [10], and numerous post-Keynesian writers. Defenders of the old view include Aschheim [1], Guttentag and Lindsay [14], and Yeager [34: 35]. In fact the views in question are not as recent as these references suggest. According to Schumpeter [27, 1113] what we now label the new view was typical around the turn of the century. Its last eloquent champion prior to its revival by Tobin was Edwin Cannan [5: 6]. Though it also had proponents during the 19th century (who often exaggerated the capacity of banks to create loanable funds by confusing the powers of individual banks with those of the banking system) the old view first came to dominate the profession with the writings by Withers [32], Phillips [24], and Crick [8]. The old view still serves as the foundation for most textbook discussions of the money-supply process.

The interpretation offered here of the new and old views of commercial banks does not link these views to any particular position concerning the "uniqueness" of commercial banks among financial institutions. As Wood observes [33, 105], "Both the traditional approach (with its emphasis on reserve and other asset ratios and its abstraction from rates of return) and the 'new view' (with its emphasis on substitution among assets) may, under different assumptions, lead either to the result that banks are unique or that they are not unique." Thus, though new view writers, who by our definition regard commecial banks as pure intermediaries, typically downplay the differences between them and other financial firms, while old view writers typically insist upon a sharp distinction between banks and other financial institutions, there are exceptions to this. For example, Gurley and Shaw [13, 202 and 218] argue that banks are *not* pure intermediaries and that they *do* create loanable funds in excess of *ex ante* savings (which agrees with our definition of the old view). Yet they also claim that non-bank financial institutions are not pure intermediaries, and so they also deny that commercial banks are "unique." Conceptually it is also possible (though I know no example of this) for a theorist to insist that commercial banks *are* pure intermediaries (the new view) while claiming that they are also "unique" in this respect because non-bank financial institutions alone are capable of creating loanable funds.

2 Discussions of the determinants of banks' demand for precautionary reserves

include Edgeworth [9], Wicksell [31, 82–84], Orr and Mellon [22], Morrison [19, ch. 2], Poole [25], Frost [11], Olivera [21], Baltensperger [2], Knobel [17], Niehans [20], and Weinrobe [31].

3 As Olivera notes [21, 1100] the extension of the square-root law from individual banks to the banking system assumes "that the number of reserve-holders, as well as their shares of the expected market demand [for reserves], remain stationary when the latter grows."

4 As Patinkin observes [23, 86–88 and 576–577] when a change in total payments is due entirely to a change in average payment size (rather than to a change in the number of payments) reserve demand adjusts proportionately (i.e., with no economies of scale). Thus the square-root law gives a *conservative* estimate of the impact of changes in payments on banks' demand for precautionary reserves.

5 That this approach may be justified even for a pure bank ("inside") money arrangement, where there is no question of any wealth effect due to an excess supply of or demand for money, is argued by Gurley and Shaw [13, 74–75]. Here it is claimed that a "portfolio mix" or "diversification effect" will still lead in the general case to a change in the demand for goods.

6 But see Gramley and Chase [12], Saving [26], and Coughlan [7] for attempts in this direction. All of these studies emphasize the effects of changes in interest rates and in the currency–deposit ratio on the equilibrium money stock. On the consistency of such effects with what we are calling the old view of commercial banking see note 7 below.

Towey [29] tries to give the old view a firm foundation in an explicit model of banking-industry optimization. He does so by assuming that there are binding statutory reserve requirements and that banks hold no excess reserves. In other words, he abstracts entirely from considerations of precautionary reserve demand crucial to the defense of the new view presented here.

7 The last statement needs to be qualified. Proponents of the old view do recognize that the public can alter the supply of bank reserves by adding to its holdings of currency. They also recognize that the reserve multiplier may be influenced by changes in the rate of interest, which is also an endogenous variable. But these endogenous determinants of the nominal supply of bank money do not cause its supply to adjust in a manner consistent with the monetary wants of the public. On the contrary, they generally imply changes in money supply contrary to, rather than consistent with, the new view – necessitating alterations in the price level to restore full equilibrium. What the new view (as interpreted here) asserts is, not just that the nominal supply of bank money responds to actions by the public, but that it responds in a manner consistent with the preservation of monetary (financial portfolio) equilibrium, and hence that the old view pays insufficient attention to the potential influence of the will of the people. Compare Johnson [16, 200–201], who argues that the old view "has incorporated all the relevant influences of the choices of the public among competing monetary and near monetary liabilities and of the financial institutions (both bank and non-bank) among reserves and other assets in the theory of the relation of the conventionally-measured money supply to the cash base provided by the central bank."

8 Thus we are in agreement with Brunner [4, 173] who concludes that "a money supply theory actually constructed along Tobin's [new view] lines . . . yields a useful explication of the 'natural scale.' But it also demonstrates that with or without reserve requirements the money stock and the natural scale respond unambiguously to the base."

REFERENCES

1 Aschheim, Joseph, "Commercial Banks and Financial Intermediaries: Fallacies and Policy Implications." *Journal of Political Economy*, February 1959, 59–71.

2 Baltensperger, Ernst, "The Precautionary Demand for Reserves." *American Economic Review*, March 1974, 205–210.

3 Black, Fischer, "Banking and Interest Rates in a World Without Money: The Effects of Uncontrolled Banking." *Journal of Bank Research*, Autumn 1970, 9–20.

4 Brunner, Karl, " 'Yale' and Money." *Journal of Finance*, March 1971, 165–174.

5 Cannan, Edwin, "The Meaning of Bank Deposits." *Economica*, January 1921, 28–36.

6 ———, "Growth and Fluctuations of Bankers' Liabilities to Customers." *The Manchester School*, 1935, 2–17.

7 Coghlan, Richard T., "Analysis within the 'New View'." *Journal of Money, Credit, and Banking*, August 1977, 410–427.

8 Crick, W. F., "The Genesis of Bank Deposits." *Economica*, June 1927, 191–202.

9 Edgeworth, Francis, "The Mathematical Theory of Banking." *Journal of the Royal Statistical Association*, March 1988, 113–127.

10 Fama, Eugene F., "Banking in the Theory of Finance." *Journal of Monetary Economics*, January 1980, 39–57.

11 Frost, Peter A., "Bank's Demand for Excess Reserves." *Journal of Political Economy*, July/August 1971, 802–825.

12 Gramley, Lyle, and Samuel B. Chase, Jr., "Time Deposits and Monetary Analysis." *Federal Reserve Bulletin*, October 1965, 1380–1404.

13 Gurley, John G., and Edward S. Shaw. *Banking in a Theory of Finance.* Washington: The Brookings Institution, 1960.

14 Guttentag, Jack M. and Robert Lindsay, "The Uniqueness of Commercial Banks." *Journal of Political Economy*, September/October 1968, 991–1014.

15 Hancock, Diana. "The Financial Firm: Production with Monetary and Nonmonetary Goods." *Journal of Political Economy*, October 1985, 859–880.

16 Johnson, Harry G. *Selected Essays in Monetary Economics.* London: George Allen & Unwin, 1978, pp. 181–209.

17 Knobel, A., "The Demand for Reserves by Commercial Banks." *Journal of Money, Credit, and Banking*, February 1977, 32–47.

18 Leijonhufvud, Axel. *On Keynesian Economics and the Economics of Keynes.* New York: Oxford University Press, 1968.

19 Morrison, George R. *Liquidity Preferences of Commercial Banks.* Chicago: University of Chicago Press, 1966.

20 Niehans, Jürg. *The Theory of Money.* Baltimore: The Johns Hopkins University Press, 1978.

21 Olivera, J. H. G., "The Square-Root Law of Precautionary Reserves." *Journal of Political Economy*, September–October 1971, 1095–1104.

22 Orr, Daniel, and W. G. Mellon, "Stochastic Reserve Losses and Expansion of Bank Credit." *American Economic Review*, September 1961, 614–623.

23 Patinkin, Don. *Money, Interest, and Prices,* 2nd edn. New York: Harper & Row, 1965.

24 Phillips, Chester Arthur. *Bank Credit.* New York: Macmillan, 1920.

25 Poole, William, "Commercial Bank Reserve Management in an Uncertain

World: Implications for Monetary Policy." *Journal of Finance*, December 1968, 769–791.

26 Saving, Thomas R., "A Theory of the Money Supply with Competitive Banking." *Journal of Monetary Economics*, July 1977, 289–303.

27 Schumpeter, Joseph. *History of Economic Analysis*. New York: Oxford University Press, 1949.

28 Tobin, James. "Commercial Banks as Creators of 'Money'," in *Banking and Monetary Studies*, edited by Deane Carson. Homewood, IL: Richard D. Irwin, 1963, pp. 408–419.

29 Towey, Richard E., "Money Creation and the Theory of the Banking Firm." *Journal of Finance*, March 1974, 57–72.

30 Weinrobe, Maurice D., "A Simple Model of the Precautionary Demand for Money." *Southern Economic Journal*, July 1972, 11–18.

31 Wicksell, Knut. *Lectures on Political Economy*, vol. 2. London: George Routledge & Sons, 1935.

32 Withers, Hartley. *The Meaning of Money*, 2nd edn. New York: E. P. Dutton & Co.

33 Wood, John H., "Two Notes on the Uniqueness of Commercial Banks." *Journal of Finance*, March 1970, 99–108.

34 Yeager, Leland B., "Essential Properties of the Medium of Exchange." *Kyklos*, 1968, 45–68.

35 ————, "What are Banks?" *Atlantic Economic Journal*, December 1978, 1–14.

6

FREE BANKING AND MONETARY CONTROL*

INTRODUCTION

Despite growing interest in competitive payments systems and the continuing progress of bank deregulation, relatively little is known about the macroeconomic implications of completely unregulated or "free" banking. Its advocates view free banking, where competing banks freely issue monetary liabilities redeemable in base money,[1] as a means for "depoliticising" the money stock by replacing public holdings of government money with private bank money while limiting changes in the monetary base. Such a programme begs many crucial questions. How would the (unregulated) stock of bank money be determined? Would free banking enhance or reduce macroeconomic stability compared to regulated banking? What implications would free banking have for the proper conduct of monetary policy?

Lawrence H. White (1984, ch. 1) employs a model of a free banking system to answer some of these questions. However, because it concerns free banking as practised in Scotland in the nineteenth century, White's model assumes an open economy operating in an international gold standard, where the price level is given and there is no such thing as monetary policy in its modern sense.

Were free banking to re-emerge today, it would probably be based, not on a gold standard, but on irredeemable paper ("fiat") base money issued by a former or extant central bank. Under this form of free banking, the price level is no longer given, and conventional monetary policy questions remain relevant. In particular, would free banking on a fiat standard simplify or complicate the control of nominal variables, including the price level and nominal income? Would it be easier or more difficult to adhere to a simple monetary rule? What would happen if the stock of base money were frozen as a means for ruling out discretion altogether?

*Reprinted, with permission, from *The Economic Journal*, Vol. 104, No. 4 (November 1994).

Answers to such questions require an analysis of determinants of the money stock in a closed free banking system with a centrally determined stock of base money. Here I offer some preliminary answers based upon Carl Christ's (1989) formal interpretation of Selgin (1988). The features of free banking stressed here because they bear most on questions of monetary control include (1) the freedom of banks to issue notes as well as deposits, where banknotes are a more perfect substitute for base money;[2] (2) a tendency for banknotes (including redeemable token coins) to displace completely base money in the currency holdings of the non-bank public; and (3) the absence of statutory reserve requirements.

A MODEL FREE BANKING SYSTEM

Imagine a closed economy with b price-taking banks, free from statutory reserve requirements and unrestricted in offering various kinds of financial instruments to the public. For convenience, let the banks' only liabilities be banknotes and chequeable deposits. The banks begin each planning period with identical market shares. Notes issued by different banks are distinct but redeemable at equivalent par values in (fiat) base money. Consumers favour particular brands of notes, not by accepting them at favourable exchange rates, but by retaining them as part of their asset portfolios, spending or depositing unwanted notes. The banks keep widespread branch networks and join a central clearinghouse, and competing issuers redeem rather than reissue notes from rival banks: that is, they treat them in the same manner as contemporary banks treat cheques. All of these assumptions are consistent with historical free banking experience (Selgin, 1988, pp. 23–6; Dowd, 1992).

Assume also that, owing to the availability of close substitutes, the public does not *ordinarily* demand base money. This assumption is also consistent with historical free banking experience. During its free banking episode (1716–1845) Scotland was "a country almost without gold," the first object of anybody getting hold of a gold sovereign being "to get quit of it in exchange for a bank note" (Checkland, 1975, p . 382). Virtually all cash payments were made in banknotes or (when small change was needed) in token copper or silver coins, despite the outlawing of notes under £1 by the Act of 1765. Canada in the nineteenth century exhibited a similar tendency towards full substitution of fractionally backed bank money for commodity base money.[3] Today's public demand for currency in the form of base money is by and large a byproduct of legal restrictions that have prevented banks from offering close substitutes. Complete substitution of bank money for base money requires that every consumer has confidence in at least one bank, which we take for granted in this and the next section.

The payments process

The banks adjust their balance sheets after several discrete payment periods. Each period involves N payments and clearing transactions, where cheques and notes received from rival banks are returned through the clearinghouse to their issuers for redemption.[4]

Payments to and from individual banks are governed by a random process. This process drives individual banks' demands for reserves, in turn establishing an equilibrium value for the banking system reserve ratio. Although many alternative random processes might be considered, most share a number of common attributes and implications. Here we assume a process similar to that described long ago by Edgeworth (1888). Suppose that an urn contains tickets or "cheques," e.g. a cheque ordering the transfer of £1 from bank i to bank j. (The same "cheque" can also stand for bank j's receipt of a £1 note issued by bank i.) There are b^2 cheques in the urn, each representing one possible type of transaction among the b banks, including the transfer of £1 from a bank to itself. We are interested in the net value of negative transactions (reserve losses) for a representative bank after a series of N transfers or drawings with replacement. This value can be shown to be a symmetrically distributed random variable with zero mean and standard deviation $\sigma = (1/b) \sqrt{[2N(b-1)]}$. The formula for σ has to be modified to allow for payments greater than £1. For simplicity, let us assume that the real value of each transaction is a constant, to which a value of £1 is assigned.[5] Then, if P is the price level, the nominal value of total transactions per payment period is PN. Although the standard deviation of a bank's net reserve losses varies in proportion to the square root of the number of payments, it varies in *strict* proportion with the nominal value of each payment. Thus

$$\sigma = \frac{P}{b} \sqrt{[2N(b-1)]}. \tag{1}$$

The value of σ is shown below to be a main determinant of the representative free bank's demand for reserves, which in turn plays a crucial role in determining the equilibrium quantity of bank money in a free banking system.

Reserve equilibrium

Although the public holds no base money, the banks must settle their net reserve losses in base money at the end of each payment period. Because payments and consequent reserve losses are random, individual banks faced with sufficiently high short-run reserve adjustment costs will want to begin each payment period with positive base-money reserves (or clearinghouse reserve credits) even when the expected value of net reserve losses is zero. The total planned demand for reserves is, in this case, entirely a precautionary demand.[6]

A well-known conclusion of the literature on precautionary reserve demand, beginning with Edgeworth, is that a bank's demand for reserves will be proportional to the standard deviation of its net reserve losses (Baltensperger, 1980, p. 9; Laidler, 1991, p. 186). If we denote a bank's demand for reserves as σq, then the factor of proportionality, q, reflects the representative bank's desired level of security against the prospect of a settlement default, chosen to equate the marginal opportunity costs (forgone interest) and marginal benefits (reduced anticipated costs of reserve shortages) of reserve holding. The value of q will in general be positively related to reserve shortage penalties and negatively related to the rate of interest (Olivera, 1971, pp. 1102–3).

Suppose that each bank starts out with a reserve endowment of R/b, where R is the (exogenous) stock of base money, all of which may be held by the clearinghouse. Equilibrium of reserve demand and supply for the representative bank then requires that $\sigma q = R/b$. If a representative bank's reserve demand (σq) exceeds its reserve endowment (R/b), the bank will attempt to increase its reserves by contracting its loans. With fixed R it is, of course, impossible for the banks collectively to add to their nominal reserve holdings. Yet in trying individually to do so the banks will contract their loans and the money stock, lower the nominal value of transactions (= PN), and thereby collectively reduce σ to the point where their unchanged reserve endowments become optimal. In a like manner, were a representative bank's reserve demand to fall below its reserve endowment, the banks, in trying to rid themselves of excess reserves, would expand loans, the money stock, and the volume of bank clearings until their reserve needs became equal to their reserve endowments.

The reserve-equilibrium condition for the banking system is

$$R = \sigma bq, \tag{2}$$

where σbq represents the total demand for bank reserves.[7]

MONETARY EQUILIBRIUM

We have yet to show precisely how nominal clearing transactions are related to, and influenced by, the quantity of bank money. We can do this by referring to the equation of exchange,

$$MV = Py, \tag{3}$$

where M is the stock of bank money and y and V are exogenous "permanent" or "natural" planning period values of real output or income and the income velocity of money. By treating velocity as an exogenous variable, we avoid making any specific assumptions concerning overall determinants of money demand. It is assumed, however, that changes in velocity involve uniform changes in real demand for every bank's notes and deposits.

The equation of exchange shows the relation between the money stock and the nominal value of *income*. Let ϕ represent the proportion of real income transactions to total transactions, where $0 < \phi < 1$. Then

$$y = \phi N. \tag{4}$$

The equation of exchange can then be rewritten as $MV = \phi PN$, showing clearly the relation between nominal clearing transactions (PN) and the money stock. The equation also demonstrates a frequently overlooked point, namely that the volume of clearing transactions (and, hence, the demand for bank reserves) does not just depend on the outstanding quantity of bank money. The public can influence the demand for bank reserves by altering the volume of transactions arising from a given money stock – that is, by altering the velocity of money.[8]

Equations (1)–(4) constitute an equilibrium system that is a more explicit version of Christ's (1989) system. The solutions for the price level and money stock in terms of R, V, y, q, b and ϕ are

$$P^* = \frac{R}{yq} \left[\frac{\phi y}{2(b-1)} \right]^{\frac{1}{2}} \tag{5}$$

and

$$M^* = \frac{R}{Vq} \left[\frac{\phi y}{2(b-1)} \right]^{\frac{1}{2}}. \tag{6}$$

Equation (6) implies that the stock of money adjusts in inverse proportion to changes in velocity. If velocity falls to one-half its former level, the money stock will double, whereas if velocity doubles the money stock will fall to one-half its original value, other things being equal. To see why, consider equation (3) (the equation of exchange) and equation (1). Monetary equilibrium requires that a doubling of V be accompanied *either* by a halving of M *or* (output being assumed constant) by a doubling of P. The latter alternative would, however, lead to a proportional increase in σ and hence to a proportional increase in aggregate reserve demand. Given a fixed stock of reserves, banks must contract their balance sheets to prevent the demand for reserves from exceeding the available stock.

The price level, on the other hand, is shown by (5) to be invariant to changes in velocity, i.e. to changes in the demand for money relative to real income. Nominal income is likewise invariant, as is seen by multiplying both sides of (6) by V, taking (3) into account. This manoeuvre also shows the relation between nominal and real income: nominal income grows in proportion to the square root of growth in real income, holding ϕ constant. This result reflects economies of scale in reserve demand.

These results assume that the other variables – R, q and b – remain unchanged. The effects of *ceteris paribus* changes in each of these are readily ascertained. An increase in R – the total quantity of base money – leads to proportional increases in the money stock and the price level, with no change in the equilibrium reserve ratio, R/M. An increase in q, due to an increase in the penalty cost of default relative to the loan rate of interest, leads to a proportional fall in the money stock and the price level and to a proportional increase in the reserve ratio, while a decline in q has the opposite effect. A doubling of b leads to a fall in σ but (somewhat surprisingly) to a *decline* in the price level, money stock, and nominal income by a factor just less than $\sqrt{2}$. The explanation has to do again with economies of scale in reserve holding: with P, M and MV unchanged, the demand for precautionary reserves of the new entrants would exceed the reduction (due to the fall in σ) in aggregate precautionary reserve demand of the established banks. Hence with fixed R, N, and y the new equilibrium requires monetary contraction. At the opposite extreme, if there is only one bank, no interbank debts have to be settled, so that reserve demand falls to zero and the bank money multiplier becomes infinite. Both theory and history suggest, however, that free banking is not likely to result in any such natural monopoly (Dowd, 1992; Schuler, 1992, pp. 15–19; compare Podolski, 1986, p. 196).

Two further implications of free banking deserve notice. First, the system money multiplier, M/R, is independent of changes in the desired currency–deposit ratio. This result follows directly from the assumption that currency in the hands of the public consists of banknotes only, which are not base money and which are assumed to require the same fractional-reserve backing as deposits. If the public insists on holding some fraction, z, of base money in its money portfolio in addition to banknotes and deposits, then the money multiplier will adjust inversely with changes in z, as in conventional textbook models (Christ, 1990). The point, however, is precisely that under free banking consumers can employ, and historically have employed, competitively issued banknotes in place of base money to accommodate most of their routinely changing currency needs. In consequence, the money supply multiplier is stabilised.[9] (The possibility of a run for base money under free banking is considered in the next section.)

Second, the banking-system reserve ratio is determined even where every bank's net reserve loss has an expected value of zero for the planning period. This finding implies, *contra* Goodhart (1989) and others, that free banks could not expand their balance sheets at will simply by acting in concert. Such a concerted effort would not be expected to lead to long-term reserve losses by any particular bank or group of banks. It would, nonetheless, increase the precautionary reserve needs of every bank by causing an increase in clearing transactions, and hence an increase in the standard deviation of net reserve losses faced by individual banks.

PANICS AND RESTRICTION OF PAYMENTS

The discussion so far has abstracted from consumer demands for base money by taking public confidence in the banking system for granted. So long as such confidence is widespread, the public has no reason to hold base money in a closed free banking system where banknotes are a convenient form of hand-to-hand money. "Routine" (non-panic-driven) demands for currency are readily satisfied by issues of banknotes, with no drain of base money from bank reserves.

A loss of confidence in one bank, or in a limited subset of banks, by itself does not motivate any lasting increase in public demands for base money. Instead such a loss of confidence would typically lead to a redistribution of reserves and demand for bank money to the remaining banks. The implied fall in the total number of banks would in fact have a somewhat *expansionary* effect on M, P and MV, for reasons described previously. A deflationary increase in public demand for base money must be due to some *general* loss of confidence in banks – a banking panic.[10]

Such a panic could lead to the collapse of a fractional-reserve banking system restricted by law to issuing unconditional demand liabilities. Banks in a free banking system might, however, avoid such a fate by issuing liabilities contractually subject to a "restriction" of base money payments. When a bank restricts payments, it temporarily stops redeeming its notes and cheques over the counter in base money, while continuing to receive them on deposit along with cheques and notes from other banks. The option-clause notes issued by Scottish banks from 1730 to 1765 are one example (White, 1984, pp. 26–30). By restricting payments banks can insulate the money stock and other nominal magnitudes from panic-related effects. According to Dowd (1988) and Gorton (1985), because restriction would be very costly to any banker who resorted to it unnecessarily, it tends to be resorted to only under panic conditions when its use serves both banks' and bank customers' interest.[11] Bank-initiated restrictions of payment need not (and historically did not) interfere with the regular settlement of *interbank* debts, and so would not reduce banks' demands for precautionary reserves for clearing settlements. The primary effect of restriction is to prevent any increase in public holdings of base money. The results described in the preceding section would therefore continue to apply to a free banking system in which payments have been temporarily restricted. Also, because restriction typically would not apply to interbank transactions, an ill-managed bank could still fail despite having restricted payments. Liabilities subject to restriction would therefore continue to embody the beneficial incentives attributed to demandable banking debt by Calomiris and Kahn (1991) and others.

135

EFFECTS OF LEGAL RESTRICTIONS

Statutory reserve requirements

Statutory reserve requirements and the prohibition of private banknotes are two reasons why real world banking systems do not function like a free banking system. The model is easily modified to show the consequences of a statutory reserve requirement by rewriting (2) as

$$R = (1 - \pi)\, \sigma b q + \pi M, \qquad (2')$$

where $0 < \pi < 1$ is the minimum legal ratio of reserves-to-bank-issued money. Equation (2') shows total reserve demand to be the sum of net precautionary and legal requirements. Solving for M gives

$$M^* = \frac{R}{Vq(1-\pi)} \left[\frac{\phi y}{2(b-1)} \right]^{\frac{1}{2}} + \frac{R}{\pi},$$

which shows that velocity-induced adjustments in the money stock are more limited than in the free banking case. Consider, for example, a situation where the stock of base money is frozen and velocity is declining. Under free banking the money stock could, as we have seen, grow in response to a fall in velocity sufficiently to prevent any contraction of aggregate money income. If a statutory reserve requirement is imposed, however, marginal changes in velocity are only partly offset by opposite changes in the money stock, with the price level (and, by implication, real output if prices are "sticky") bearing the burden of the remaining equilibrium adjustment. With a given reserve base, or a base growing at a fixed rate, statutory reserve requirements lead to greater instability of nominal income and a greater likelihood of deflation in response to secular or cyclical declines in velocity. Statutory reserve requirements may, therefore, increase rather than reduce the perceived need for discretionary monetary policy.

Prohibition of banknotes

The effects of prohibiting banknote issuance are more complicated. When banks cannot issue notes, the public's "routine" demand for currency becomes a demand for base money. To allow for this, our system of equations must include

$$\sigma = \frac{P}{b}\, \sqrt{[2N(1-c)(b-1)]}$$

$$R = \sigma b q + c M,$$

where c represents the public's desired currency–deposit ratio, and it is assumed that the ratio of currency to deposits reflects the ratio of currency transactions to transactions conducted by cheque. The standard deviation of bank clearings now depends upon the frequency of deposit transactions only. Solving the new system for M gives

$$M^* = \frac{R}{Vq} \left[\frac{\phi y}{2(1-c)(b-1)} \right]^{\frac{1}{2}} + \frac{R}{c}.$$

An increase in the currency ratio (unlike an increase in the reserve ratio) has an indirect expansionary effect because it reduces total clearing activity and, hence, banks' precautionary reserve needs. But this indirect effect is slight compared to the direct contractionary (reserve-reduction) effect of an increase in c. The latter effect accounts for much of the "inherent instability" of fractional-reserve banking systems that rely exclusively or primarily on base money to satisfy routine public demands for currency.

IMPLICATIONS FOR MONETARY CONTROL

We are now prepared to state some general implications of free banking for monetary control. Assuming that ϕ, q, y and b remain unchanged, money income is a constant multiple of the stock of base money, unaffected by changes in the desired currency–deposit ratio or the income velocity of money. The banking system automatically accommodates changes in velocity with offsetting changes in the money stock. Otherwise, if the monetary base is held constant, the money stock remains constant. Bank money is endogenous in the strict "cloakroom" or pure-intermediary fashion once described by Edwin Cannan (1935) and more recently revived by exponents of the "New View" of commercial banking and of "moneyless" or "pure-accounting" payments systems.[12]

Yet a free banking system is *not* "moneyless." We can therefore consider its compatibility with particular monetary policies. By minimising the destabilising effects of changes in velocity and the currency–money ratio, a free banking system would obviate problems that traditionally rationalise discretion in central banking systems. Free banking thereby remedies some of the more obvious drawbacks in proposals (e.g. Friedman, 1984; Timberlake, 1986, pp. 760–2) for freezing the monetary base. It also complements more "moderate" and popular policy rules aimed at targeting the growth of money income. Under free banking such targeting would be simplified. The authorities would be relieved from the difficult task of responding to velocity-induced changes in income or from having to compensate for reserve losses due to changes in the public's requirements for hand-to-hand money. The range of the authorities' discretion could be curtailed accordingly.

If real output is growing, free banking still succeeds in offsetting changes in velocity. Both the money stock and nominal income will be positively (though less than proportionately) related to real output. The price level, on the other hand, will tend to decline.[13] These results suggest that a free banking system in a growing economy with a frozen monetary base would offer something of a compromise between constancy of nominal income and constancy of the price level, regardless of the behaviour of velocity and currency demand. This range of outcomes, plus others that could be achieved by allowing the base to grow at some constant rate, suggest that free banking may promote rather than endanger monetary stability, and that it could contribute towards the success of a strict, simple and enforceable monetary rule.

This conclusion appears to contradict the more frequently encountered view that deregulation tends to "alter unpredictably the relationships between variables, upon whose stability the effectiveness of monetary control depends" (Podolski, 1986, p. viii). In particular, deregulation is supposed to undermine "the stability of the links between certain monetary aggregates and nominal income" which provides the empirical basis for monetary targeting (Goodhart, 1986, p. 79). The apparent contradiction is resolved by observing that past discussions have focused mainly on the implications of financial liberalisation for the behaviour of the demand for money, concluding that deregulation would tend to destabilise the demand for any particular monetary aggregate. We have not questioned this last claim. Indeed, in treating velocity as an exogenous variable we have scrupulously avoided making any assumptions concerning the stability of the demand for money. Where our results differ is in heeding the implications of complete deregulation for the behaviour of the money *supply*. Although free banking may well loosen the links connecting velocity to variables like the rate of interest, and although it tends as well to loosen the links connecting the monetary base to broader monetary aggregates, it makes for a relatively *tight* link connecting the monetary base to nominal income.[14] Because the monetary base is itself relatively easily controlled, and because the stability of nominal income is ultimately more important than that of any monetary aggregate, the presence of this one tight link under free banking serves to improve rather than reduce the overall prospects for monetary control. In short, although free banking makes monetary targeting in the traditional sense of controlling the growth of some monetary aggregate more difficult, it also makes such targeting unnecessary.

NOTES

1 For example, a commodity money like gold or a frozen stock of irredeemable paper money. "Free banking" is used here in the sense meant by the British free banking school, i.e. as a synonym for unregulated banking, including free competitive note issue.

2 The term "banknotes" need not be taken literally: it may refer to any bank-issued means of payment capable of supplanting public holdings of base money, e.g. deposit credits subject to point-of-sale electronic transfer.

3 National Monetary Commission (1910, p. 53). Although commodity money may be uniquely risk free, this advantage may be outweighed by the greater convenience of paper substitutes. Certain classical economists, including Smith and Thornton, believed prohibition of small-denomination banknotes necessary to keep gold and silver in circulation. Full "fiduciary substitution" is also possible under a fiat money regime, where it might be aided by interest payments to holders of bank-issued currency (McCulloch, 1986, p. 75). See Selgin (1988, pp. 169–70). Christ (1990) presents alternative models of free banking in which the public holds base money.

4 Notes may complete multiple transactions between trips through the clearing system. Assuming, however, that the multiple is more or less constant, it can be ignored.

5 A more complete model would allow the real value of an individual transaction to vary. Later we shall introduce a variable, ϕ, representing the proportion of real *income* transactions to total transactions.

6 If banks establish clearing-account reserve credits by depositing base money with the central clearinghouse in lieu of holding their own reserves, competitive pressures might in turn induce the clearinghouse to trade some of its holdings of base money for interest-earning assets. Under a commodity standard this process could in principle continue until all of the base-money commodity became absorbed in non-monetary uses. The system would then become a full-fledged Wicksellian "pure credit" system (1936 [1898], p. 68), with the value of bank money determined by the non-monetary value of the numéraire commodity. Under a fiat standard a similar process would lead to hyperinflation, since there would be no well-defined non-monetary demand for fiat money. It may, therefore, be necessary to require that a fixed fraction of clearinghouse balances be backed by fiat money to preserve a fiat money standard in an otherwise free banking system. This would *not* be a reserve requirement in the usual sense.

7 The argument that aggregate reserve demand is simply equal to b times a representative bank's demand for reserves is valid given the assumption of stationary bank market shares. Using (1), total reserve demand can be written more explicitly as $\sigma bq = Pq \sqrt{[2N(b-1)]}$, which agrees with the well-known "square root law" of precautionary demand. Reserve demand varies in proportion to the square root of the number of gross clearing transactions per period. Olivera (1971) demonstrates the robustness of the square root result for diverse stochastic payments processes.

8 Most discussions of the theory of bank money supply treat the standard deviation of expected reserve deficits as being proportionate to the square root of the *quantity* of bank money only. Morrison (1966, p. 17) acknowledges, however, that in the presence of transaction costs "the amount of [reserves] banks desire to hold might be expected to vary directly with the frequency of transactions." An empirical test, performed using Frost's (1971) model and data and substituting debits for deposits, confirms Morrison's conjecture (see Chapter 12).

9 See the next section and Selgin (1988, ch. 8). Lloyd Mints (1950, p. 186) long ago noted that the instability of fractional-reserve banking "is due in part to a wholly unnecessary legal restriction," namely the prohibition of banknotes. In a more complete model a variety of instruments, including travellers' cheques and electronically transferable funds, would be allowed to serve as substitutes for base money. Compare note 14 below.

10 On the relatively low probability of a general banking panic under free banking conditions see Chapters 9 and 10 and Dowd (1988).

11 Diamond and Dybvig (1983) consider private deposit contracts allowing for restriction of payments as a market-based alternative to deposit insurance for protecting a banking system from panic-related withdrawals. They argue, however, that restriction prevents bank withdrawals for non-panic-motivated consumption. In Chapter 11 I argue that this conclusion rests on the absence of bank-issued money in the Diamond Dybvig model: claims on a bank cannot be used to *buy* the consumption good, but instead are *redeemed* for the consumption good.

12 On the "New View" see above, Chapter 5; on "moneyless" payments systems see Hoover (1989, ch. 5).

13 In Chapter 7 I argue that such a deflationary result is actually preferable to the more widely acclaimed desideratum of "zero inflation."

14 Some tightening of the link between the monetary base and nominal income has already been observed in connection with financial innovations in the United Kingdom during the late 1970s and early 1980s (Johnston, 1984). This appears to have been due in large part to the public's increased resort to bank cheques and electronic funds transfer in place of base money. The use of private banknotes as currency under free banking is viewed here as providing a basis for *complete* substitution of bank for base money. Although Goodhart (1986, p. 97) correctly observes that there has been "no attempt by financial intermediaries to chip away directly at the authorities' monopoly in the provision of currency," he neglects to add that such attempts might be illegal under existing banking laws.

REFERENCES

Baltensperger, E. (1980). "Alternative approaches to the theory of the banking firm." *Journal of Monetary Economics*, vol. 6, pp. 1–37.

Calomiris, C. W. and Kahn, C. M. (1991). "The role of demandable debt in structuring optimal banking arrangements." *American Economic Review*, vol. 81, pp. 497–513.

Cannan, E. (1935). "Growth and fluctuations of bankers' liabilities to customers." *The Manchester School*, vol. 6, pp. 2–17.

Checkland, S. G. (1975). *Scottish Banking: A History, 1695–1973*. Glasgow: Collins.

Christ, C. (1989). Review of Selgin (1988). *Market Process* (publication of the Center for the Study of Market Processes at George Mason University), vol. 7, pp. 5–10.

————— (1990). "When is free banking more stable than regulated banking?" Unpublished ms., Johns Hopkins University.

Diamond, D. and Dybvig, P. (1983). "Bank runs, deposit insurance, and liquidity." *Journal of Political Economy*, vol. 91, pp. 401–19.

Dowd, K. (1988). "Option clauses and the stability of a laissez faire monetary system." *Journal of Financial Services Research*, vol. 1, pp. 319–33.

————— (1989). *The State and the Monetary System*. Oxford: Philip Allan.

————— (1992). "Is banking a natural monopoly?" *Kyklos*, vol. 45, pp. 379–92.

Edgeworth, E. Y. (1888). "The mathematical theory of banking." *Journal of the Royal Statistical Society*, vol. 51, pp. 113–27.

Friedman, M. (1984). "Monetary policy for the 1980s." In John H. Moore, ed., *To*

Promote Prosperity: U.S. Domestic Policy in the Mid-1980s. Stanford, CA: The Hoover Institution.

Frost, P. A. (1971). "Banks' demand for excess reserves." *Journal of Political Economy,* vol. 79, pp. 805–23.

Goodhart, C. A. E. (1986). "Financial innovation and monetary control." *Oxford Review of Economic Policy,* vol. 2, pp. 79–102.

———— (1989). *The Evolution of Central Banks.* Cambridge, MA: MIT Press.

Gorton, G. (1985). "Bank suspension of convertibility." *Journal of Monetary Economics,* vol. 15, pp. 177–193.

Hoover, K. D. (1989). *The New Classical Macroeconomics.* London: Basil Blackwell.

Johnston, R. B. (1984). "The demand for non-interest-bearing money in the United Kingdom." Government Economic Working Paper No. 66.

Laidler, D. (1991). *The Golden Age of the Quantity Theory.* Princeton, NJ: Princeton University Press.

McCulloch, J. H. (1986). "Beyond the historical gold standard." In Colin Campbell and William R. Dougen, eds., *Alternative Monetary Regimes,* pp. 73–81. Baltimore, MD: Johns Hopkins University Press.

Mints, L. (1950). *Monetary Policy for a Competitive Society.* New York: McGraw-Hill.

Morrison, G. R. (1966). *Liquidity Preferences of Commercial Banks.* Chicago: University of Chicago Press.

National Monetary Commission. (1910). *Interviews on the Banking and Currency Systems of Canada.* Washington, DC: Government Printing Office.

Olivera, J. H. G. (1971). "The square-root law of precautionary reserves." *Journal of Political Economy,* vol. 79, pp. 1095–104.

Podolski, T. M. (1986). *Financial Innovations and the Money Supply.* Oxford: Basil Blackwell.

Schuler, K. (1992). "The world history of free banking: an overview." In K. Dowd, ed., *The Experience of Free Banking.* London: Routledge, pp. 7–47.

Selgin, G. A. (1988). *The Theory of Free Banking: Money Supply under Competitive Note Issue.* Totowa, NJ: Rowman & Littlefield.

Timberlake, R. H., Jr. (1986). "Institutional evolution of federal reserve hegemony." *Cato Journal,* vol. 5, pp. 743–63.

White, L. H. (1984). *Free Banking in Britain: Theory, Experience, and Debate.* London: Cambridge University Press.

Wicksell, K. (1936) [1898]. *Interest and Prices,* trans. R. Khan. London: The Royal Economic Society.

7

MONETARY EQUILIBRIUM AND THE PRODUCTIVITY NORM OF PRICE-LEVEL POLICY*

To a simple fellow like myself it seems that the lower prices which increased production makes possible would benefit everybody, but I recognize there must be a flaw in my thinking, for increased productivity has not brought – and does not seem likely to bring – lower prices. Presumably there is some good reason for this. Will someone explain?[1]

INTRODUCTION

Now that the Phillips curve has disappeared, leaving an "empty place where it used to be" (Leijonhufvud 1981, p. 276), economists must come face to face with the problem of deciding how the price level ought to behave. They can no longer treat price-level policy as incidental to employment policy. Yet, rather than becoming an object of economic controversy, the place left vacant by the Phillips curve has become the exclusive, if somewhat barren, grazing ground of advocates of a stable consumer price level. These advocates appear to be winning the macroeconomic policy battle by default. The only challenge now facing them seems to be that of implementing price-level stabilization by means of a strict and unambiguous policy mandate.

Robert Black (1986, p. 790), for example, argues that price stability should be "the preeminent and perhaps even the unique goal of monetary policy." He adds that it should be enforced in an "automatic or quasi-automatic way" (p. 793). Others who have held similar views include Reynolds (1982, pp. 37–41), Barro (1986), Hetzel (1985), Meltzer (1986), Hall (1982, 1984a, 1984b); and Yeager (1986a). A strict policy of price-level stabilization is also supported by several well-known policy makers, including Jack Kemp, Richard Rahn of the US Chamber of Commerce, and some members of the Board of Governors of the Federal Reserve System.[2] A recent Joint Resolution (H. R. J. Res. 409) introduced

*Reprinted, with permission, from the *Cato Journal*, Vol. 10, No. 1 (Spring/Summer 1990).

by the House Subcommittee on Domestic Monetary policy would, if adopted, require the Fed to achieve a stable price level ("zero inflation") within five years.

Although price-level stabilization is the only widely endorsed price-level policy today, there was a time, just over half a century ago, when prominent economists from numerous schools favored a different approach – the "productivity norm" of price-level behavior. Under this approach, the consumer price level is allowed to vary with changes in unit real costs of production. In theory, the productivity norm is equivalent to stabilization of a price index of factors of production; in practice, it is roughly equivalent to the stabilization of per capita nominal income.

This chapter offers a highly preliminary reconsideration of the case for a productivity norm of price-level policy as against price-level stabilization. In so doing, the chapter also revives and expands upon some forgotten early criticisms of price-level stabilization, and it shows the shortcomings and potential dangers inherent in proposals for the strict enforcement of a constant price level.[3] Because the chapter is meant to compare the productivity norm to the alternative of price stabilization, it should not be construed as an attempt to demonstrate that the productivity norm is an optimal or first-best policy.

THE RATIONALE OF PRICE-LEVEL STABILIZATION

The alleged benefits of price-level stability – generally taken to mean stability of a consumer's price index – include avoidance of debtor–creditor injustice and avoidance of macroeconomic disequilibrium. Debtor–creditor injustice is caused by unexpected changes in the value of long-term debts. Falling prices increase the burden of indebtedness, conferring a windfall gain on creditors, whereas rising prices do the opposite. Price-level stabilization prevents this injustice. However, because indexation schemes such as the tabular standard also avoid changes in the real value of debt, the prinicpal advantage of a stable price level must be sought in its ability to combat short-run macroeconomic fluctuations.[4]

Leland Yeager has eloquently argued for the macroeconomic benefits of a stable price level. According to Yeager (1986b, p. 370), macroeconomic fluctuations – which can be taken to refer to fluctuations of employment and output around their "full information" or "natural" levels – are caused by monetary disequilibrium; that is, by "a discrepancy between actual and desired holdings of money at the prevailing price level." The occurrence of monetary disequilibrium implies (in the absence of instantaneous or even anticipatory price adjustments) a violation of Say's law (though Yeager himself does not use this term): an excess demand for money implies a deficient effective demand for goods with concomitant windfall losses to producers; an excess supply of money implies an excessive effective demand for goods with concomitant windfall profits to producers. Because an excess supply of money leads to rising prices and a deficient supply leads to falling prices, general price changes can be viewed as "symptoms or consequences" of monetary disequilibrium (Yeager 1986b, p. 373). It follows that macroeconomic fluctuations will be avoided or reduced by a policy that adjusts the nominal money stock in such a way as to keep the price level stable.

Although it ultimately rests on a quantity-theoretic foundation, Yeager's macroeconomic defense of price-level stabilization contradicts simpler versions of the quantity theory in a crucial respect: It rejects the view that changes in the money supply or in its velocity of circulation lead to instantaneous, uniform, and costless adjustments in all prices. Were such a simple interpretation of the quantity theory valid, monetary disequilibrium could never exist for more than an instant, and there would be no macro-economic reason for advocating any particular money supply or price-level policy. Rather than accepting this view, Yeager and like-minded propo-nents of price-level stabilization argue that general price adjustments "do not and cannot occur promptly and completely enough to absorb the entire impact of monetary change and so avoid quantity changes" (Yeager 1986b, p. 373).

A number of reasons account for the sluggishness of general price changes. These include the presence of long-term contracts not subject to indexation and other psychological sources of price rigidities such as implicit contracts and money illusion. Perhaps the most fundamental reason, though, has to do – according to Yeager (1986b, p. 377) – with the "public-good" nature of general price adjustments. This stems from money's role as a general medium of exchange that, "unlike other goods, lacks a price and a market of its own":

> No specific "money market" exists on which people acquire and dispose of money, nor does money have any specific price that straightforwardly comes under pressure to clear its (nonexistent) mar-ket. Money's value (strictly, the reciprocal of its value) is the average of individual prices and wages determined on myriads of distinct though interconnecting markets for individual goods and services. Adjustment of money's value has to occur through supply and demand changes on these individual markets.

The consequence is a diffusion of the impact of monetary disequilibrium across various markets, where each affected transactor regards the value of money "as set beyond his control, except to the utterly trivial extent that the price he may be able to set on his own product arithmetically affects money's average purchasing power" (Yeager 1986b, p. 392). Optimal adjustments in individual prices do not take place because their social value may exceed their perceived value to the persons who have to make them. This outcome is all the more likely given that particular price adjustments, rather than being costless as they are often portrayed, frequently involve lump-sum or "menu" costs – of printing, labeling, and negotiations. In consequence, rather than being achieved automatically following a monetary disturbance, a market-clearing general price level has to be "groped towards" by means of a "decentralized, piecemeal, sequential, trial and error" process (Yeager 1986b, p. 375).

Because price adjustments may be slow, they are also likely to be uneven – a result, in part, of the differing degrees of sluggishness of different prices. It is generally assumed that input prices adjust more slowly than product prices. This lag implies that excess demands for money will be a cause of painful short-run losses, whereas excess supply will lead to profit inflation.

A further cause of unevenness of price adjustments is the monetary "transmission mechanism" by which monetary disequilibrium makes its presence felt, not in all markets at once, but first in particular markets from which it slowly spreads to the rest of the economy (Yeager 1990). Thus, a disequilibrium increase in the money supply on the basis of open-market purchases will first raise the value of government securities and then will affect general interest rates through an increase in the volume of commerical bank loans. From there, the monetary expansion will raise the demand for capital goods and increase wages. Only afterward will it lead to a more general increase in the prices of commodities. And this pattern will occur even if prices all along the way are fairly flexible.[5]

Such imperfect price adjustments in response to monetary disequilibrium cannot fail to involve many temporary relative price effects that, by introducing "noise" into price signals, "degrade the information conveyed by individual prices" (Warburton [1946] 1951, p. 374) and provoke unwarranted changes in real activity. A shortage of money will lead to deflation, with reduced sales and production cutbacks in certain sectors of the economy leading to reduced demand for the products of other sectors and finally to general unemployment. An excess supply of money, on the other hand, causes inflation that, because it does not merely imply a uniform increase in prices, can also involve substantial malinvestment of resources.[6]

Responding to the potential dangers from imperfect adjustment of general prices, proposals for stabilizing the price level aim at *minimizing the burden placed on the price system* by maladjustments in the money supply. Adjusting the nominal quantity of money to keep the price level constant in the face of changing demands for real money balances is supposed to achieve this goal in two ways: first by reducing the overall requirement for permanent money-price changes, and second by reducing the extent of temporary, though ultimately unnecessary, relative price changes involved in the monetary transmission mechanism. These changes include disequilibrium movements in interest rates. In the absence of appropriate adjustments of the nominal money stock, both types of price changes must occur to some extent, and each will be a cause of disturbances to real activity. Only the permanent price changes will disturb real activity (apart from "menu-cost" effects) insofar as they fail to occur completely and uniformly, whereas relative price changes will disturb real activity to the extent that they occur at all.

Implicit in these arguments for price-level stabilization is the assumption that changes in real money demand or nominal money supply, and consequent needs for general price adjustments, cannot be perfectly anticipated by economic agents. Although long-term tendencies in the movement of the equilibrium price level may come to be anticipated, short-run disturbances are likely to be completely unexpected and, hence, unrecognized for what they are. Knowledge of the pattern or policy of nominal money-supply changes (assuming this knowledge can be had) is not sufficient to avoid surprises; there may also be unexpected changes in real money demand for which scant public information is available.[7] This predicament brings to bear two further arguments for stabilizing the price level. One is that such stabilization reduces the uncertainty encountered by economic agents, allowing them better to capture potential gains from long-term contracts and production processes. The other is that it puts the monetary authorities on a tight leash by committing them to an unambiguous rule, violations of which are easily detected. The last argument is, however, more prominent and valid today than it was earlier in this century when monetary authorities were disciplined by the gold standard. In that context, price-level stabilization represented, at best, the substitution of one kind of monetary rule for another; at worst, it was a stepping stone from reliance upon a rule to reliance upon unrestrained authority.

THE PRODUCTIVITY NORM

The productivity norm in the history of thought

The productivity norm had many proponents before the ascendancy of Keynesian thought.[8] Perhaps its earliest champion was Samuel Bailey in his *Money and Its Vicissitudes in Value* (1837). Later British economists who at one time or another defended the productivity norm included Marshall, Edgeworth, Giffen, Hawtrey, Pigou, and Robertson.[9] In Sweden the norm was defended by David Davidson in a protracted debate with Wicksell (who in the end partially acquiesced), and also by Lindahl and Myrdal. Elsewhere in Europe the norm was embraced by German, Austrian, and Dutch writers of the neutral money school, including Roepke, Mises, Hayek, Haberler, Machlup, N. G. Pierson, and J. G. Koopmans.

New Zealand economist Allen G. B. Fisher (1935) defended the productivity norm at length in the *American Economic Review*. Finally, in the United States the norm was endorsed by Taussig, Laughlin, and Simon Newcomb in the 1890s and by John Williams in the 1930s. Some American champions of a stable price level, including Mints (1950, pp. 132–34) and Warburton ([1946] 1951, p. 308n), also conceded that price-level stability was not necessarily superior to the productivity norm.

In short, by the 1950s the productivity norm had received serious attention from economists of most schools. There was even a period – the first half of the 1930s – when it seemed to rival price-level stabilization as an ideal for monetary policy. Its popularity was short-lived, however, as it and all other prescriptions for macroeconomic stability were eclipsed by the views contained in Keynes's *General Theory*. The (perhaps unintended) consequence of Keynes's contribution was to detract attention from price-level policy altogether. What mattered was the achievement of full employment, regardless of what this required in the way of movements in the price level. In the end, this approach proved to be a recipe for inflation, which eventually drew economists' attention once more to the question of price-level policy. Only by then – in the 1970s – the productivity norm had fallen by the wayside, and price-level stabilization emerged by default as the sole, popular option for price-level policy.

The rationale of the productivity norm in formal theory

The productivity norm rests upon the same tenets that underlie the norm of price-level stability. Both norms take for granted the desirability of a monetary policy that will combat monetary disequilibrium, while rejecting attempts to employ monetary policy to divert the economy from its natural or full-information levels of employment and output. The two norms also hold in common the assumption that the public's expectations may be less than fully correct in that individuals may fail to anticipate fully changes in income, real output, or the price level. More particularly, the norm of price-level stability implicitly assumes that individuals expect the price level to be *stable* – or at least that it is easiest for the public to form correct forecasts of price-level movements when such movements are altogether avoided.

The argument for the productivity norm, as opposed to a stable price-level norm, is that even in a situation where the price level has been kept stable for some time – say from t_1 to t_n, so that the public is firmly convinced that the price level will again remain unchanged at t_{n+1} – deviations from the natural rate of output will be smaller under a policy that allows the public to be surprised by a difference between p_{n+1} and p_n, provided the difference reflects a change in aggregate productivity. In this case an unanticipated change in the price level serves to compensate for an unanticipated change in real productivity. A formal demonstration of this is offered by Bean (1983), who models labor-market disturbances in an economy where money wages are set one period in advance and where there is uncertainty as regards both the price level and productivity. The goal of policy is to minimize the difference of output from its full-information level. Output obeys the expression:

$$y_t - y_t^* = \beta[(p_t - {}_{t-1}p_t) + \phi(u_t - {}_{t-1}u_t)]$$

with $(0 < \beta < 1)$, where y_t and y_t^* are the logs of the actual and "natural" values of real output and $p_t, {}_{t-1}p_t$ and $u_t, {}_{t-1}u_t$ are the actual and expected values of the price level and productivity per worker $({}_{t-1}u_t + {}_{t-1}p_t$ thus equals the nominal wage).

If the supply of labor is inelastic with respect to changes in productivity, then $\phi = 1$ and changes in the price level should be fully proportionate to opposite changes in output. Such a policy is equivalent to one of stabilizing money income, $p_t + y_t$.

If $\phi < 1$ (i.e., if the supply of labor is elastic), the price level should adjust *less* than in proportion with changes in output, to allow for changes in the size of the full-information labor force.

In general, the price level should vary so as to stabilize *money income per laborer*, $p_t + y_t - l_t^*$, where l_t^* is the size of the full-information labor force. This condition is equivalent to saying that the price level should reflect changes in productivity: A *negative* productivity shock should be offset by a *positive* price-level shock, and a *positive* productivity shock should be offset by a *negative* price-level shock. A policy of stabilizing some measure of per capita money income $(p_t + u_t)$ represents a practical approximation of this theoretical rule.

If the size of the full-information labor force is unchanging and if the demand for real money balances is unit elastic with respect to changes in real income (and does not increase or decrease owing to causes not related to any change in real income), then adherence to the productivity norm will require that the nominal quantity of money be held *constant*. Unless otherwise stated, this case is the one considered in the arguments to follow. If, however, the demand for money is elastic with respect to changes in real income, then (other things being equal) an *increase* in productivity will require an *increase* in the nominal quantity of money, and a *decline* in productivity will require a *reduction* in the nominal quantity of money *to prevent prices from falling or rising more than in proportion to the change in productivity*. In contrast, if the demand for money is inelastic, relative to changes in real income, a productivity norm policy will require that changes in productivity be accompanied by opposite changes in the nominal quantity of money.

Of course, changes in productivity need not always come as a surprise to economic agents. A secular increase in productivity, for example, may be perfectly anticipated in principle. But then the price-level trend (accompanying a productivity-norm policy) would also be perfectly anticipated and would, therefore, be no less desirable than any other fully anticipated price-level trend. Moreover, as will be argued below, a productivity-norm-based trend in prices is likely to be more consistent with the aim of allowing individual, *relative* prices to move in response to changes in productivity where such changes do not occur uniformly and predictably in all industries but are at any moment greater in certain industries than in others.

We now turn to consider how the above arguments hold up against two particular and intuitively appealing arguments for price-level stabilization: (1) that price stability is needed to preserve debtor–creditor equity, and (2) that it is desirable for avoiding difficulties connected with sluggish price adjustment.

The productivity norm and debtor–creditor equity

Consider first the matter of debtor–creditor equity, where "debtors" include all persons who have committed themselves to making fixed-money payments in the future, and "creditors" include all persons who have agreed to receive these fixed-money payments. In a stationary economy where productivity is constant, it is generally agreed that debtors will suffer unjustified losses if the price level falls unexpectedly, and that creditors will realize unjustified gains. If, on the other hand, the price level is held constant, neither debtors nor creditors will (on the whole) have any reason to regret their involvement in contracts fixed in money terms.

But if productivity is changing, a stable price level may no longer achieve this desirable result. Assume, for example, that the public expects both the price level and productivity to remain stable. Then, if the price level is kept constant in the face of unexpected improvements in productivity, readily adjusted money incomes – including profits, dividends, and some wage payments – will increase; their recipients will benefit exclusively from the improvements in real output. Creditors, on the other hand, will not be allowed to reap any gains from the same improvements. Although a constant price level may fulfill their price-level expectations, creditors may still regret their involvement in fixed-money contracts, for they may rightly sense that, had they anticipated the widespread improvement in other persons' real (and, in this case, money) earnings, they could have successfully negotiated better terms. On the other hand, if the price level is allowed unexpectedly to fall to reflect improvements in productivity, creditors will automatically enjoy a share of the gain, while debtors will have no reason to complain: although the real value of their obligations rises (along with everyone else's), so does their real income. The burden of nominal payments imposed upon them is, however, unchanged.

The debtors' only cause for regret is their missed opportunity to enjoy – owing to creditors' lack of perfect foresight – an undeserved windfall at the creditors' expense; their loss, as Haberler (1931, p. 21) put it, is only *lucrum cessans* and not *damnum emergens*.

Some people have objected (e.g., Mints 1950, pp. 132ff, and Haberler 1931, pp. 15–16) that this argument rests entirely on the premise that creditors deserve a share of improvements in productivity, and that no scientific grounds can be given in support of the argument. This objection leads to the conclusion that considerations of equity alone cannot provide any basis for choosing between the productivity norm and a stable price level.

But this conclusion appears to hold only if *improvements* in productivity alone are considered. In his 1889 memorandum to the Committee to Investigate Variations in the Value of the Monetary Standard, Edgeworth (1925, p. 222) observed that those who plead for stabilizing the money value of nominal debts in times of increasing prosperity "might be embarrassed if the principal were extended to the case of declining prosperity." Indeed, if productivity is falling – as during a negative supply shock – the inequity of a price-level stabilization rule cannot easily be denied, for in this case to keep the price level from rising requires a *contraction* of all nonfixed money incomes. This contraction adds to the burden of payment borne by debtors, increasing the likelihood that some or many of them will be unable to meet their obligations. As Lindahl, the Swedish follower of Davidson, observed, a price-level policy that may encourage parties to engage in unfulfillable agreements cannot be judged as equitable in any reasonable sense of the term (cited in Caplan 1942, p. 210).[10] In such cases it is clear that the productivity norm, rather than a norm of price stability, best allows debtors and creditors to accomplish their goals and to avoid inequity when relying upon contracts fixed in money terms.

The productivity norm and price adjustment

The question still remains whether the productivity norm is superior to price-level stabilization in preserving short-run macroeconomic equilibrium. It may be recalled that a major advantage claimed for price-level stabilization in this regard is its alleged ability to minimize the burden of general adjustments borne by the price system. Here again, however, the advantage is no longer present when productivity changes, for *both the extent of necessary "permanent" price changes and the extent of temporary, but ultimately unnecessary, price changes are likely to be greater under price-level stabilization than they would be under the productivity norm.*

Suppose, for example, that 1,000 final goods are produced using three distinct factors of production only. A technological improvement causes the output per period of good x, which formally had a price (included in the price index) of one dollar, to double. Assuming (1) a constant money supply and velocity of circulation of money, (2) that x has a unitary price elasticity of demand, and (3) that demand for goods other than x is independent of real purchases of x, holding nominal income unchanged (thus abstracting from the need for any "secondary" relative price adjustments), the price of x will fall to 50 cents. This implies a slight decline in the price index. Prices of all other goods, including the three factors of production, remain unchanged. The new equilibrium price structure requires one price adjustment only and represents an application of the productivity norm.

Now suppose, instead, that the price level is to be held stable under identical circumstances. To accomplish this, the authorities must expand the supply of money to achieve a uniform, though very slight, increase in the prices of 999 goods and of the three factors of production. The sole exception is good x, the price of which must (as in the previous case) still be allowed to fall, only less than in proportion with the improvement in its rate of output. This approach alone serves to keep the price index stable while also allowing needed adjustments in *relative* prices.

It is possible to construct examples in which the burden of price adjustment (reckoned in terms of the required number of permanent price changes) under price-level stabilization is *less* than what would be required under the productivity norm. This would be true, for instance, if there were a uniform increase in productivity for *all* final goods, and if the number of different factors of production were less than the number of final goods. But such cases are so exceptional that they may safely be ignored in practice.[11]

Admittedly, arguments such as those made here concerning the burden of price adjustments under various price-level policies are distressingly dependent upon artificial assumptions. One must admit that, in reality, any single relative price adjustment can be expected to have secondary effects. These effects lead to an all-round adjustment in relative prices and leave no grounds for preferring any one policy as minimizing the total number of required price adjustments. Nevertheless, I have tried to show that, insofar as *any* case can be made (by appropriately stringent assumptions) for a particular price-level policy using the price-adjustment criterion, it is one that favors the productivity norm rather than a stable price level. To the extent that it requires more price adjustments than the productivity norm, price-level stabilization increases the odds of price adjustments being imperfectly accomplished. It, therefore, tends to promote more widespread, undesirable changes in quantities from their full-information levels.

Another difference between price adjustments made necessary by unaccommodated changes in productivity and those made necessary by changes in the flow of money income (as must occur if the price level is to be kept stable in the face of productivity changes) is that the former are brought about through a more direct stimulus than the latter. The stimulus provided by productivity changes to equilibrium price movements is either immediate, as in the case of prices of goods the rate of output of which is altered (where price changes are a direct response to shifting supply schedules), or of the second order of mediacy, as when changes in output of one group of goods lead to changes in demand for other goods because of the nonunitary price elasticity of demand of goods in the first group.

In contrast, the effects of changes in the flow of money income on equilibrium prices tend to be indirect. These effects involve shifts in demand schedules through a whole series of markets (depending on the precise nature of the monetary transmission mechanism) before relative prices and the distribution of demand reach their final, equilibrium levels. As Warburton ([1946] 1951, pp. 298–99) observed,

> The first change occurs at the point where the additional money is introduced into or taken out of the economy and is expressed in an increased or decreased demand for the goods and services desired by the persons directly affected by the change in the quantity of money.

Such monetary injection effects are another source of unnecessary and undesirable adjustments in quantities, which will be greater under a policy of price-level stabilization than under a productivity-norm policy. The greater the degree of price and wage-rate rigidity, the more extensive such undesirable quantity adjustments will be.

Besides being relatively direct and few in number, price adjustments in response to changes in productivity are also relatively easy and painless compared to price changes made necessary by changes in effective demand or in the flow of money income. This ease of responding to changes in productivity is still another reason why price adjustments are more likely to occur promptly. The reason is that productivity changes imply changes in unit costs of production. For a product with unitary price elasticity of demand, a change in the product's selling price equal to a change in its cost of production leaves the producer's revenues and profits unaffected. Such a change also does not place the producer under any pressure to negotiate new wage rates and salaries or to change the size of the work force. Figure 7.1 illustrates the case of a *general* increase in productivity caused, for example, by widespread technological innovation. Here, a doubling of real output per period, from "a" to "b," with a fixed quantity of factors of production and with an unchanged unit-elastic aggregate demand schedule, leads to a halving of the market-clearing price level. This result is consistent with an unchanged stock of money under the standard assumption that the demand for money is unitary elastic with respect to real income. If the elasticity of demand for money relative to

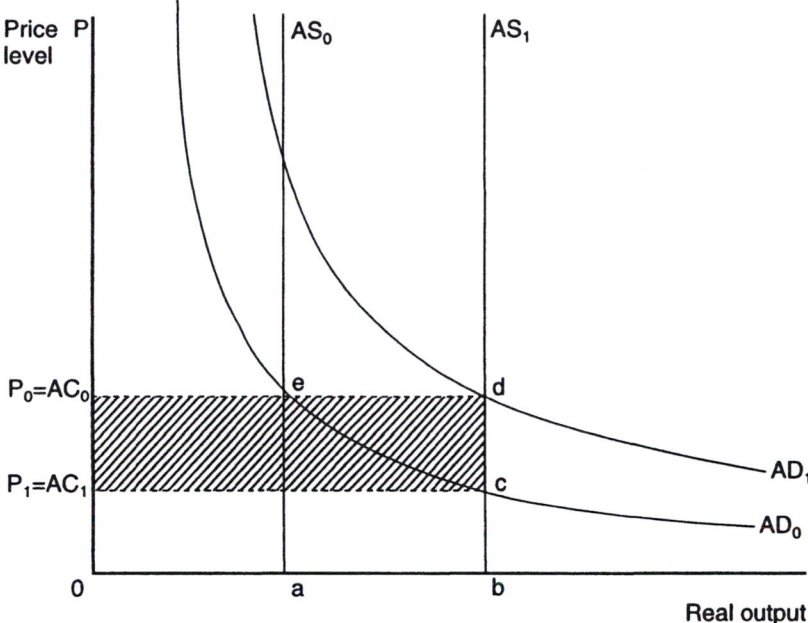

Figure 7.1 A general increase in productivity with unit-elastic aggregate demand

real income is greater than or less than unity, the productivity norm requires expansion or contraction of the money supply to keep aggregate demand (MV, where M is the nominal money stock and V its velocity of circulation) from changing. Producers' aggregate revenues, formerly P_0Oae, afterwards P_1Obc, are not affected, and they suffer no losses. Because the reduction of prices required here is painless, there is no reason for producers to resist competitive pressures to undertake it.

A policy of price-level stabilization, in contrast, would require an expansion of money supply to shift aggregate demand to the right, from AD_0 to AD_1. This shift would make total revenues expand to P_0Obd, causing profits to swell by the amount P_0P_1cd until factor costs adjust upward to eliminate the surplus. This upward adjustment of factor costs may be considerably more difficult and painful for producers to allow than the downward adjustment of prices required by the productivity norm. It is one thing to ask producers to pursue a pricing policy that serves merely to protect them from competition without affecting their profits; it is quite another to expect them to submit meekly to parting with extraordinary profits – even if only paper profits – once they have begun to enjoy them.

Figure 7.2 shows the contrasting case where the market-clearing price level falls by one-half because of an unanticipated decline in aggregate demand, from AD_0 to AD_1, with constant real output. Here, producers' aggregate revenues also shrink by one-half, from P_0Oac to P_1Oab. The loss

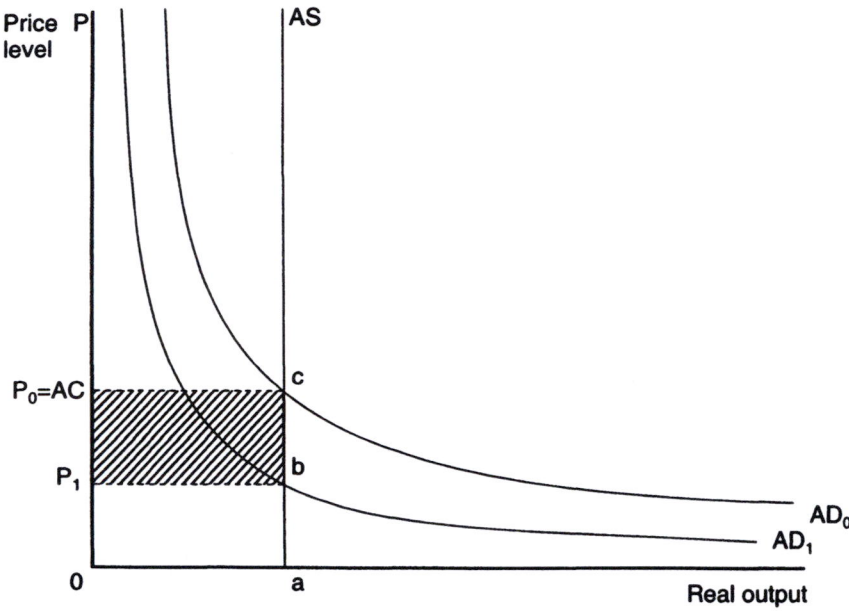

Figure 7.2 An unanticipated decline in aggregate demand

on current output, represented by the shaded rectangle P_0P_1bc, will continue until nominal factor costs adjust downward. The process of price adjustment is evidently a painful one in this case. A policy of monetary expansion to keep aggregate demand and the price level at their original levels appears clearly preferable to one that would require them to fall.

By way of similar reasoning it can be seen that, although a rise in the price level resulting from expansion of aggregate demand should be avoided, a rise in prices of equal magnitude in response to a fall in productivity should be permitted. The only difference is that, in this case, the increase in prices in accordance with the productivity norm cannot be said to be truly painless, in that it represents a fall in real income and output. Nevertheless, to keep the price level stable under identical circumstances would be even *more* painful and discouraging to producers, because it would cause them to suffer temporary, nominal losses – incurring more than their fair share of the overall burden of reduced production – until laborers and other sellers of inputs are convinced that they must accept (painful) cuts in wages and other factor prices.

In further support of these conclusions, we may note that many studies – both theoretical and empirical – of price rigidity incline to the view that product prices are rigid only because factor prices are rigid, and because product prices are often set according to a fixed percentage markup from costs.[12] Although this view accounts for the ill-adjustment of product prices in response to changes in effective demand, it does not predict any ill-adjustment in situations of changing productivity. In the latter case, unit costs of production are themselves changing, so that adjustments in product prices must take place, even as factor prices and the total outlay for factors stay the same, to preserve a constant markup. Implicit contracts between sellers of final goods and sellers of inputs are not necessarily violated when prices change in accordance with the productivity norm.[13]

Until now we have been assuming that changes in the market-clearing price level, whether caused by changes in productivity or by changers in aggregate demand, are completely unanticipated, which adds to the likelihood of needed price adjustments being for a time incomplete. But this assumption is less appropriate for price-level adjustments associated with changes in productivity, for the simple reason that changes in productivity are far less likely to be unanticipated *by price-setting agents in directly affected markets* than changes in aggregate demand. The reason, as Haberler (1931, p. 20) has observed, is that improvements in productivity are often (if not always) consciously aimed at by producers, who pursue the improvements precisely because they seek opportunities to profitably lower their prices compared to their rivals' prices. That downward price adjustments, caused by improvements in productivity, are often sought after by producers and are, therefore, anticipated is another reason for not regarding them as sluggish or incomplete.

All of the above considerations point to the fact that, under the productivity norm, aggregate producer revenues are more likely to keep in line with aggregate producer costs than under a stable price level if productivity is changing. If productivity is increasing, a stable price level requires expansion of money income, which (unless perfectly anticipated by all) must translate into a temporary, general swelling of firm profits. If productivity is falling, a stable price level requires contraction of nominal income, which (unless anticipated) translates into a temporary, but general, fall in profits.

As Bertil Ohlin (1937, p. 321) once observed, keeping revenues "from getting out of balance" with costs (and especially wages) so as to prevent "abnormally large or low profits and profit expectations" is more crucial to macroeconomic order in the short run than stability of the price level as such. It is in this sense that the productivity norm, and not price-level stabilization, can be said to be truly consistent with the preservation of monetary equilibrium, where the latter requires continuous validation of Say's law of markets. Only under the productivity norm will aggregate (effective) demand continue to be just adequate to buy the fruits of industry at prices covering their (money) cost of production, without causing that cost to alter over time except in response to growth in capital and population. In Wicksellian terms, the productivity norm manages, where stability of the price level fails, to keep interest rates at their natural levels.

The productivity norm and the optimal quantity of money

Minimizing departures of relative prices and output from their full-information levels is only one possible objective of monetary policy. Another is to maximize consumers' welfare from money holdings. In general this calls for allowing prices of final goods to decline at a rate roughly equal to "the" real rate of interest (Friedman 1969). The productivity norm, by allowing the price level to decline secularly as productivity grows, comes closer to this ideal than price-level stabilization. Moreover, if the real rate of interest is equal to the rate of growth of real income (as has been roughly true historically and as is implied by standard models of optimal growth, e.g., Phelps 1961), the rate of deflation that maximizes consumers' welfare from money holdings will equal the rate of increase in per capita output, and will imply that factor prices are held constant. The productivity norm and the optimal quantity of money norm will then coincide.

The productivity norm in practice

Though past upholders of the productivity norm agreed that it was tanta-mount to "stabilization of some average of the prices of the original factors of production" (Hayek [1933] 1984, p. 161), they differed in their views concerning how this stabilization could be achieved in practice.[14] It was generally admitted that a true index of prices of factors of production could not be constructed, because of the lack of market-price statistics for most factors of production apart from unskilled labor. But such an approach is by no means necessary or even appropriate: a productivity-norm policy can be implemented, or approximately implemented, by directly stabilizing some readily available measure of the flow of money payments or income such as nominal GNP or domestic final demand.[15]

Just how money income should behave if the productivity norm is to be enforced depends on the extent of changes in the quantity of factors of production – including both labor and capital. A common view emerged in the 1930s that money income per capita, rather than aggregate money income, should be stabilized. The stabilization of per capita income was meant to prevent growth in the labor force – assumed to be approximated by growth in population as a whole – from having a depressing effect on nominal wage rates. To this opinion Robertson (1957, p. 39) added that, if capital increases and, therefore, contributes a greater share to total produc-tion, then the part of money incomes imputable to rental payments should also increase. Thus, nominal income should grow at a rate sufficient to reflect changes in both the labor force and the capital stock. This would allow prices to fall in proportion to purely *intensive* improvements in output, but less than in proportion to any improvements of a partly extensive nature.

Viewed as a proposal for stabilizing nominal income, the productivity norm resembles a number of recent suggestions for targeting nominal GNP.[16] A major difference, however, is that many of these recent suggestions consider the targeting of nominal GNP as a means for achieving stability of the price level. Indeed, these suggestions have been criticized for being incompatible with price-level stability whenever supply shocks occur (e.g., Barro 1986, p. 26). The productivity norm, in contrast, does not value price-level or real-output stability *per se*; it seeks merely to avoid those price and output fluctuations that are likely to involve departures of economic activity from its full-information structure. This characteristic also distinguishes the productivity norm from proposals for an elastic price standard, such as those of Hall (1984b, 1986) and Taylor (1980).

Although our main concern in this essay is not with the practical problems of implementing various price-level policies, it is appropriate to remark here that a nominal income target is no more difficult to implement than any price-index target. On the contrary, as Haraf (1986, p. 659) observes, an income target would probably lead to quicker reaction by the monetary authorities to velocity disturbances than a price-level target, without inviting inappropriate responses to real (productivity) disturbances.

CONCLUSION

Theoretical considerations and assumptions identical to those used by proponents of a stable price level lead one to favor the productivity norm over price-level stability and also over other price-level policies as a means for promoting general welfare. The norm would require the monetary authorities to stabilize per capita nominal GNP or domestic final demand or some other measure of per capita money payments, allowing for more rapid growth of money payments when the share of income attributable to capital is increasing.

Some features of a productivity norm – based on nominal income targeting – that should contribute to the norm's overall appeal include the following:

1 The fact that the productivity norm, like other popular policies, allows full monetary accommodation of changes in the velocity of money, with less reaction lag-time than a stable price-level norm and, hence, with reduced velocity-shock-related variability of prices.
2 The long-run equivalence of a productivity norm to price-level stabilization under stationary output conditions.
3 The productivity norm's equivalence to a money growth-rate rule if velocity is stable.

4 The productivity norm's emphasis on stability of aggregate demand, which conforms well with natural rate theories of output and employment and with the rational-expectations view that macroeconomic instability is caused mainly by problems of "signal extraction."

5 The fact that the productivity norm is a more moderate policy than a policy of either price-level stabilization or full employment – that is, the productivity norm avoids extremes of price or employment variability possible under these other policies.

6 The greater symmetry of the productivity norm compared with other price-level policies: Those who plead for monetary "accommodation" of adverse supply shocks do not also recommend monetary contraction to counteract the real effects of positive supply shocks.

7 The relative ease of implementing the productivity norm.

8 The coincidence of the productivity norm with the optimum quantity of money norm when the real rate of interest is equal to the rate of growth of real output.

9 The ability of the productivity norm to provide protection from the monetary authorities' abuse of their powers equal to or greater than what could be achieved by other price-level norms.

A proposal for targeting nominal income (rather than any commodity price index) is neither novel nor necessarily controversial. Yet this particular form of the proposal may be controversial for the simple reason that it would allow the price level to *fall* in normal, progressive times. Though this approach was once widely endorsed by economists, it is now practically unheard of. Instead, mild inflation is taken to represent a normal and moderate condition, while price-level stability is regarded as a hard-line extreme.

It must be remembered, however, that policy itself is responsible for these views, because policy created the last four decades of inflation, which everyone now takes for granted. The policy in question was founded on the view that expansion of nominal (effective) demand can eliminate unemployment. We now know that this view is mistaken. Although unemployment may sometimes be due to a deficiency of effective demand, and although expansion of demand may temporarily reduce unemployment even when its ultimate cause is *not* deficient demand, the view that inflation as such reduces unemployment (i.e., that the long-run Phillips curve is negatively sloped) has been discredited. If policymakers are prepared to admit that inflation has no such benefit, then it is encumbent upon them to press beyond the simple analytics of a nonexistent "inflation–unemployment trade-off" in deciding how the price level ought to behave. Price-level stability is one answer; the productivity norm is another, better answer.

NOTES

1 A former Archbishop of Wales, in a letter to the London *Times*, as quoted in Robertson (1963, pp. 11–12n).

2 For example, Messrs. Johnson and Angell.

3 This chapter is only incidentally concerned, however, with problems of *implementing* various price-level policies (e.g., index-number and time-lag problems). These problems are well recognized and have been discussed recently elsewhere (e.g., in Garner 1985).

4 Irving Fisher remarked (1925, p. 261) that, in practice, a tabular standard "would never accomplish more than a small fraction" of what price-level stabilization could achieve.

5 See also Warburton ([1946] 1951, pp. 298–99). Many contemporary monetarists are skeptical concerning the importance of "first-round effects" of changes in the quantity of money. See the discussion in Friedman and Schwartz (1982, pp. 29–31). Of course, to insist on the importance of such effects is not necessarily to agree with the Keynesian view that long-run effects can be ignored. The position of price-level stabilizationists – and also of proponents of the productivity norm (discussed below) – is essentially a Wicksellian one, which acknowledges both short-run and long-run effects while recognizing the difference between them.

6 See Leijonhufvud (1984).

7 This fundamental point is overlooked by Grossman (1986) in his critical response to Yeager (1986b).

8 Chapter 8 treats the history of the productivity norm in some detail.

9 Among Robertson's better-known students, Harry Johnson (1972, p. 29) also endorsed the productivity norm.

10 Or, as Robertson (quoting Shylock) put it in *Money* ([1922] 1928, p. 121): " 'I'll have my bond, speak not against my bond' – is that a plea which should be listened to from a debenture-holder or Trade Unionist in a country shivering for lack of fuel or impoverished by chronic warfare?"

11 It is regrettable that many macroeconomic models adopt a one-commodity framework, with labor as a sole, distinct factor of production. Such models represent precisely the kind of exceptional circumstance in which a desired pattern of relative prices can be established with the same number of absolute price adjustments (following a change in productivity) regardless of whether a price-level stability or productivity norm is adhered to. To see how different price-level policies may take a different toll on the price system and thereby provide different opportunities for error, one must refer to a multi-commodity framework.

12 This seems to have been Keynes's view in the *General Theory* (1936). See also Okun (1981, passim).

13 On this point, see Okun (1981, pp. 169–70). Contrary to what Okun suggests, this is only one of several reasons accounting for the fact that "prices are much more responsive to changes in costs than to shifts in demand . . . even when demand is pulling in the opposite direction."

14 The goal of stabilizing the "average price of factors of production" is not equivalent to one of stabilizing total money costs of production unless the quantity of productive inputs – of labor and capital – remains fixed: the productivity norm requires that prices fail to reflect *intensive*, but not extensive, improvements in output. Monetary expansion or contraction involving

expansion or contraction of total money costs is required in connection with population growth and the accumulation of capital.

15 Haraf (1986) argues that targeting domestic final demand (DFD) (= GNP less changes in business inventories and net exports) is more advisable than targeting GNP. DFD may well be a superior measure of "consumers' outlay" or aggregate spending.

16 See, for example, McCallum (1984, 1985, 1987), Gordon (1985), Hall (1981, 1983), Haraf (1986), Tobin (1980, 1983), and Meade (1978). For critical discussions of some of these proposals, see Bean (1983) and Taylor (1985).

REFERENCES

Bailey, Samuel. *Money and Its Vicissitudes in Value*. London: Effingham Wilson, 1837.

Barro, Robert J. "Rules vs. Discretion." In *Alternative Monetary Regimes*, pp. 16–30. Edited by Colin D. Campbell and William R. Dougan. Baltimore: Johns Hopkins University Press, 1986.

Bean, C. "Targeting Nominal Income: An Appraisal." *Economic Journal* 93 (December 1983): 806–19.

Black, Robert P. "A Proposal to Clarify the Fed's Policy Mandate." *Cato Journal* 5 (Winter 1986): 787–95.

Caplan, Benjamin. "The Wicksellian School – A Critical Study of the Development of Swedish Monetary Theory, 1898–1932." Ph.D. dissertation, University of Chicago, 1942.

Edgeworth, F. Y. *Papers Relating to Political Economy*. London: The Royal Economic Society, 1925.

Fisher, Allen G. B. "Does an Increase in Volume of Production Call for a Corresponding Increase in Volume of Money?" *American Economic Review* 25 (June 1935): 197–211.

Fisher, Irving. *Stabilizing the Dollar*. New York: Macmillan, 1925.

Friedman, Milton. "The Optimum Quantity of Money." In *The Optimum Quantity of Money and Other Essays*, ch. 1. Chicago: Aldine, 1969.

Friedman, Milton, and Schwartz, Anna J. *Monetary Trends in the United States and the United Kingdom: Their Relation to Income, Prices, and Interest Rates, 1867–1975*. Chicago: University of Chicago Press, 1982.

Garner, C. Alan. "Commodity Prices and Monetary Policy Reform." *Federal Reserve Bank of Kansas City, Economic Review* 70 (February 1985): 7–21.

Gordon, Robert J. "The Conduct of Domestic Monetary Policy." In *Monetary Policy in Our Times*. Edited by A. Ando, et al. Cambridge, MA: MIT Press, 1985.

Grossman, Herschel I. "Money, Real Activity, and Rationality." *Cato Journal* 6 (Fall 1986): 401–8.

Haberler, Gottfried. "The Different Meanings Attached to the Term 'Fluctuations in the Purchasing Power of Gold' and the Best Instrument or Instruments for Measuring such Fluctuation." Geneva: League of Nations. March 1931.

Hall, Robert E. "Lowering Inflation and Stimulating Economic Growth." In *Politics and the Oval Office: Toward Presidential Governance*, pp. 207–27. San Francisco: Institute for Contemporary Studies, 1981.

Hall, Robert E. "Explorations in the Gold Standard and Related Policies for Stabilizing the Dollar." In *Inflation*. Edited by Robert E. Hall. Chicago: University of Chicago Press, 1982.

Hall, Robert E. "Macroeconomic Policy under Structural Change." In *Industrial*

Change and Public Policy. Kansas City: Federal Reserve Bank of Kansas City, 1983.

Hall, Robert E. "A Free-Market Policy to Stabilize the Purchasing Power of the Dollar." In *Money in Crisis.* Edited by Barry N. Siegel. San Francisco: Pacific Institute, 1984a.

Hall, Robert E. "Monetary Policy with an Elastic Price Standard." In *Price Stability and Public Policy*, pp. 137–59. Proceedings of a symposium sponsored by the Federal Reserve Bank of Kansas City, 1984b.

Hall, Robert E. "Optimal Monetary Institutions and Policy." In *Alternative Monetary Regimes*, pp. 229–39. Edited by Colin D. Campbell and William R. Dougan. Baltimore: Johns Hopkins University Press, 1986.

Haraf, William S. "Monetary Velocity and Monetary Rules." *Cato Journal* 6 (Fall 1986): 641–62.

Hayek, F. A. "On 'Neutral Money.'" 1933. Reprinted in *Money, Capital, and Fluctuations: Early Essays*, pp. 159–62. Chicago: University of Chicago Press, 1984.

Hetzel, Robert. "A Mandate of Price Stability for the Federal Reserve System." *Contemporary Policy Issues* (1985): 50–67.

Johnson, Harry G. *Inflation and the Monetarist Controversy.* Amsterdam: North-Holland, 1972.

Keynes, J. M. *The General Theory of Employment, Interest, and Money.* London: Macmillan, 1936.

Leijonhufvud, Axel. *Information and Coordination.* New York: Oxford University Press, 1981.

Leijonhufvud, Axel. "Inflation and Economic Performance." In *Money in Crisis*, pp. 19–36. Edited by Barry N. Siegel. San Francisco: Pacific Institute, 1984.

McCallum, Bennett T. "Monetarist Rules in the Light of Recent Experience." *American Economic Review* 74 (May 1984): 388–91.

McCallum, Bennett T. "On the Consequences and Criticisms of Monetary Targeting." *Journal of Money, Credit, and Banking* 17 (November 1985): 570–97.

McCallum, Bennett T. "The Case for Rules in the Conduct of Monetary Policy: A Concrete Example." *Federal Reserve Bank of Richmond, Economic Review* 73 (October 1987): 10–18.

Meade, J. E. "The Meaning of Internal Balance." *Economic Journal* 88 (September 1978): 423–35.

Meltzer, Allan H. "Some Evidence on the Comparative Uncertainty Experienced under Different Monetary Regimes." In *Alternative Monetary Regimes*, pp. 122–53. Edited by Colin D. Campbell and William R. Dougan. Baltimore: Johns Hopkins University Press, 1986.

Mints, Lloyd W. *Monetary Policy for a Competitive Society.* New York: McGraw-Hill, 1950.

Ohlin, Bertil. "Employment Stabilization and Price Stabilization." *Lessons of Monetary Experience*, pp. 318–28. Edited by Arthur D. Gayer. New York: Rinehart & Company, 1937.

Okun, Arthur. *Prices and Quantities: A Macroeconomic Analysis.* Washington, DC: Brookings Institution, 1981.

Phelps, Edmond. "The Golden Rule of Accumulation." *American Economic Review* 53 (September 1961): 638–43.

Reynolds, Alan. "The Trouble with Monetarism." *Policy Review* 21 (Summer 1982): 19–41.

Robertson, Dennis H. *Money.* Cambridge: Cambridge University Press, 1922, 3rd rev. edn, 1928.

Robertson, Dennis H. *Lectures on Economic Principles*. London: Staples, 1957.

Robertson, Dennis H. "A Memorandum Submitted to the Canadian Royal Commission on Banking and Finance." Princeton University, *Essays in International Finance* (May 1963): 241–74.

Taylor, John B. "Output and Price Stability: An International Comparison." *Journal of Economic Dynamics and Control* 2 (February 1980): 109–32.

Taylor, John B. "What Would Nominal GNP Targeting Do to the Business Cycle?" *Carnegie-Rochester Conference Series on Public Policy* 22 (1985): 61–84.

Tobin, James. "Stabilization Policy after Ten Years." *Brookings Papers on Economic Activity* 1 (1980): 19–72.

Tobin, James. "Commentary." *Industrial Change and Public Policy*. Federal Reserve Bank of Kansas City, 1983.

Warburton, Clark. "The Misplaced Emphasis in Contemporary Business-Fluctuation Theory." 1946. Reprinted in American Economic Association, *Readings in Monetary Theory*, pp. 284–318. Homewood, IL: Richard D. Irwin, 1951.

Yeager, Leland B. "Price-Level Stability as the Goal of Monetary Reform." *Cato Journal* 5 (Winter 1986a): 821–4.

Yeager, Leland B. "The Significance of Monetary Disequilibrium." *Cato Journal* 6 (Fall 1986b): 369–99.

Yeager, Leland B. "Injection Effects and Monetary Intermediation." Unpublished manuscript, 1990.

8

THE "PRODUCTIVITY NORM" VERSUS ZERO INFLATION IN THE HISTORY OF ECONOMIC THOUGHT*

The idea that general macroeconomic stability requires stability of output prices has a long history. It can be traced to preclassical economists such as John Law (1705) and is recurrent in classical writings (see Viner 1937, 185–200). The doctrine was especially popular in the decades prior to the Keynesian revolution, when it was championed by Knut Wicksell, Irving Fisher, J. M. Keynes, Carl Snyder, George Warren and Frank Pearson, and Gustav Cassel, to name just its more well-known proponents. Although price-level stability took a back seat to "full employment" as a policy goal after the appearance of Keynes's *General Theory*, it now once again has numerous adherents among both economists and policy makers. A stable price level or "zero inflation" goal became official policy in New Zealand in 1989 and has been endorsed by monetary authorities in several other nations since, including Australia, Canada, and the United States.[1] Reform proposals resembling Fisher's "compensated dollar" plan have also gained a new lease on life.

The zero inflation norm is, indeed, so popular today that, transition costs aside,[2] its superiority to other potential price-level norms is usually taken for granted. Contemporary proponents of zero inflation appear to be unaware of an alternative "productivity norm" for price-level behavior, which would allow price-level movements to reflect opposite changes in productivity.[3] The productivity norm once had many prominent proponents, who offered telling arguments in its favor and against the more popular alternative of stable prices. Although now largely forgotten, these arguments seem just as worthy of serious consideration today as when they were first offered. The purpose of this chapter is not to present a rigorous, updated case for the productivity norm, but to review past arguments for it in the hope of generating further critical discussion of the pros and cons of

*Reprinted, with permission, from *History of Political Economy*, Vol. 27, No. 4 (Winter 1995).

zero inflation. In particular, readers are invited to consider: first, whether arguments made in the past against price-level stabilization and in favor of the productivity norm were sound when first offered; and second, whether the same arguments are equally damaging to the modern case for "zero inflation."

ARGUMENTS FOR ZERO INFLATION AND THE PRODUCTIVITY-NORM ALTERNATIVE

Three arguments for zero inflation have been prominent in the history of economic thought.[4] One is that unanticipated changes in the price level lead to unfair transfers of wealth: when prices rise unexpectedly, the argument goes, debtors gain at the expense of creditors because nominally fixed debts can be repaid in money having less purchasing power than when the debts were originally contracted (cf. Keynes 1920, chs. 1 and 2). When prices fall, creditors profit at the expense of debtors. Price-level stabilization supposedly prevents such unjust transfers.[5]

The second argument for zero inflation is related to David Hume's view that a gently *rising* price level will encourage entrepreneurs and stimulate industry. While not accepting Hume's argument in its positive form, many proponents of price-level stabilization have argued that *falling* prices must discourage industry and entrepreneurship and so should be avoided whenever necessary through expansionary monetary policy.

The third and final argument for zero inflation holds that price-level changes interfere with the price system's ability to allocate resources. Because "menu costs" are involved in adjusting individual money prices, relative price changes are most efficiently and accurately signaled when they involve a minimum number of money price changes. Otherwise incomplete or incorrect money price adjustments are likely to lead to economic waste. Some proponents of zero inflation have claimed that it allows the price system to do its job with a minimum of money price changes by eliminating any need for *general* price changes to offset changes in the supply of, or demand for, money.

Past proponents of the productivity norm did not question the validity of the above arguments for the case of an economy with stable productivity, that is with stable unit costs of production. Nor did they question the common premise that price-level movements often would not be accurately anticipated. Nevertheless, they did deny the applicability of arguments for zero inflation to economies experiencing changes in productivity due to secular changes in technology or supply shocks. In such circumstances, the productivity norm called for price-level movements mirroring changes in unit costs of production: prices should rise in response to any decline in productivity and fall in response to improvements in productivity. The productivity norm thus resembled a norm of *money-income*

164

stability, except that it would allow aggregate income to fluctuate with changes in total real factor employment. A policy of price-level stabilization applied to a circumstance of changing productivity would, according to proponents of the productivity norm, lead to the very disruptions of economic activity that price-level stabilizationists sought to avoid.[6]

Although groups of economists from various countries offered very similar arguments against price-level stability and in favor of a productivity norm, their similar views appear to have developed independently. For this reason, I review contributions by region, starting with the earliest and most extensive contributions, which were made by British writers.

THE PRODUCTIVITY NORM IN BRITISH ECONOMICS

Although reference has already been made to classical writings upholding a zero inflation deal, Will Mason (1982) argues cogently that classical (Ricardian) value theory was still more closely associated with the productivity norm, which treated labor as an ideal measure of value. The classical defense of the gold standard in particular was based on the view that gold maintains a relatively stable value *in terms of labor*. As Mason notes, this "classical" rationale for the gold standard "implied a relatively stable money-wage level and a falling price level as technological improvements increased labor's productivity" (Mason 1982, 548, n. 11). Proposals to stabilize the price level in the face of changes in productivity were therefore viewed as "a degradation of 'the standard'" by such a representative of classical orthodoxy as John Stuart Mill (1909, 548, n. 11).

It is ironic, therefore, that one of the earliest detailed arguments for the productivity norm was offered by Samuel Bailey, who is best remembered as a critic of Ricardo's labor theory of value.[7] In *Money and Its Vicissitudes in Value* (1837), Bailey makes use of a distinction, introduced by John Wheatley (1807) and adopted by many later proponents of the productivity norm, between changes in the value of money "originating on the side of money" and changes "originating on the side of other commodities" (Bailey 1837, 16). Whereas the former changes stem from alterations in the money supply or in the demand for money relative to income, the latter are due to changes in the "facility of supplying" other commodities, including "the discovery of shorter and more economical processes in the arts, and invention of machinery, [and] the abolition of monopolies and taxes" (16).

Equipped with this distinction, Bailey proceeded to consider the effects of changes in the price level, first, "on the industry of a country" and then "on pecuniary contracts" (1837, 45). Concerning the former, and in reply to Hume's claims in his *Essay on Money*, Bailey agrees that a fall in the price level originating on the side of money could depress industry. He also concedes that a rise in the price level originating on the side of money might stimulate industry, but he holds that this was mainly a result of unjust transfers of income and wealth in favor of entrepreneurs and speculators. Bailey's overall conclusion is that price changes stemming from monetary causes should "be regarded as an evil and not as a good" (81). Bailey does not believe, however, that this conclusion applies to price-level changes originating on the side of goods (86). Although Bailey does not discuss the effects of the latter kind of price-level changes on "industry" in detail, he implies that they would neither stimulate nor depress it. We shall encounter other, more detailed arguments as to why this is so later on.

Bailey's discussion of the different effects of the two kinds of price-level changes on pecuniary contracts is, in contrast, very complete. In an argument that was to be replicated by several later writers, Bailey endeavored to show that, although changes in the price level due to monetary causes involve unjust transfers of wealth, those reflecting changes in productivity do not involve any unjust transfers. Suppose, Bailey said, that A lends £100 to B for one year, and that prices in the meantime fall 50 per cent. If the fall in prices is due to an increased demand for money (with constant real income) or to a fall in the money supply, A obtains a real advantage, and B suffers an equivalent loss. But if, instead, the fall in prices is due to a general improvement in productivity, A's gain is not matched by any corresponding loss by B, because the enhanced, real value of B's repayment corresponds with the enhanced ease with which B (and other members of the community) are able to produce a given amount of real wealth (1837, 115–17). Likewise, if the price level rises due to a decline in productivity "both A and B would lose nearly half the efficiency of their incomes" (118). However,

> this loss would arise from the diminution of productive power, and not from the transfer of any advantage from one to the other. The fund out of which they both drew would be diminished, and they would both consequently draw less.
>
> (118)

Bailey could not see why creditors should not "bear their share of the loss arising from increased difficulty of production" any more than they "should not partake in the advantages derived by the community at large from improvements in production, in which [their] capital is in truth one of the instruments" (121). Bailey's conclusion, therefore, was that such cases provide "no pretext for interfering with the literal construction of [a fixed-money] contract, as a contract for quantity without reference to value" (121). It follows that overall justice should

> be effected by protecting both lender and borrower from all loss by [price-level] alterations originating on the side of money, and by

leaving them to their natural proportions of gain and loss from all alterations originating on the side of commodities.

(168)

Bailey was, however, far from believing that this ideal could be fully realized "with the present limited facilities of the human mind" (168). He was content to defend the gold standard as a practical approximation of his ideal.[8]

If (as Mason claims) the productivity norm was taken for granted by classical theorists, this was no longer the case after the 1870s. That decade marked the beginning of the end of classical value theory and its rationalization of both the productivity norm and gold monometallism. It also marked the onset of a secular deflation that lasted until the mid-1890s. Together these developments sponsored a shift in opinion concerning the ideal standard of value and also the corresponding ideal for general price-level behavior, with bimetallism (as well as Jevons's proposal for a "tabular standard") representing the first, tentative steps toward a popular policy ideal of zero inflation (Mason 1982, 549).

According to Mason, neoclassical champions of the gold standard did not explicitly defend the productivity norm, preferring instead to ignore the problem of deflation altogether or to engage in arbitrary semantics denying the monetary basis for falling prices. But a closer look suggests that prominent neoclassical theorists had not "forgotten the classical rationale" for gold, even if they did reject classical value theory and did occasionally resort to arbitrary semantics. Thus Alfred Marshall – who is more often remembered as a proponent of symmetallism as a scheme for stabilizing prices – came close to defending the productivity norm in his 1887 testimony before the Gold and Silver Commission. Asked whether gold had appreciated, Marshall replied that the term "appreciation" applied to gold should refer not to a mere rise in the value of gold relative to commodities but to an "increase in the power which gold has of purchasing labor of all kinds" ([1887] 1926, 33). Because productivity had risen, the greater bundle of commodities an ounce of gold could buy represented the same quantity of embodied labor. Therefore, gold had not appreciated relative to labor. Judged by Marshall's criterion, the post-1873 deflation was fully consistent with the existence of a "stable" standard of value. Marshall did at one time sympathize with the Humean doctrine that gently rising prices would stimulate industry. However, according to A. W. Flux (1930, 31–2), Marshall in his later lectures had changed his mind on this issue, claiming that only less capable and less discriminating entrepreneurs would require the stimulus of rising prices to engage in new undertakings. On the basis of this new view, Marshall even went so far as to argue that *falling* prices might provide the best psychological stimulus to enterprise, by weeding out all but the most capable and vigorous entrepreneurs.

Like Marshall, Frances Edgeworth also denied that falling prices were an "unmitigated evil" insofar as they reflected "the increased production of goods per head in the civilized world during the last twenty-five years" (1925, 427). Distinguishing a "consumption" standard of deferred payments such as is implicitly embodied in the zero inflation norm from a "labour" or "production" standard (the latter still having roots in Ricardian value theory), Edgeworth also observed, in an 1889 memorandum to the Committee to Investigate Variations in the Value of the Monetary Standard, that while many persons might unhesitatingly defend a consumption standard for circumstances of increasing prosperity (like the 1880s), the same persons "might be embarrassed if the principle were extended to the case of declining prosperity" (222), such as an adverse supply shock. In the latter case, the maintenance of zero inflation would require a *reduction* of money incomes and wages, which must necessarily add to debtors' burdens, perhaps making it impossible for some debtors to meet their nominal obligations.[9]

Sir Robert Giffen also threw the weight of his authority against the "Great Depression" thesis, reporting that as early as 1877, although the "common impression" was that a depression of unprecedented severity was in progress, "the common impression is wrong, and the facts are entirely the other way" (1904, 108). Returning to the topic a decade later, Giffen observed (174, 178) that the "depression" did not appear to involve any fall in nominal income or wages per head and, indeed, that Bowley's (1920) statistics for the years after 1880 showed a distinct *upward* trend in both per capita taxable incomes and per capita nominal wages. Later statistics confirm this (Table 8.1). The "Great Depression" was, in few words, a depression of the price level only, and hence no cause for any alteration of the monetary standard.[10]

Still later, Giffen offered a more explicit defense of the productivity norm in his criticism of Aneurin William's "Value of Bullion Standard" (1892), which closely resembled Irving Fisher's (1925) proposal for a "compensated dollar." "It is just as important," Giffen wrote,

> that the average money incomes of a community and still more the average money wages of the wage earning part of the community per head, should not fluctuate greatly over short periods, as it is that the average prices of commodities should not fluctuate.
>
> (1904, 173)

Indeed, Giffen continued, it is preferable for improvements in productivity to take "the shape of stationary money wages with a fall in prices" than for them to take the shape of rising wages with constant prices (174).

Although gold discoveries in the 1890s put a stop to secular deflation, ending that particular stimulus to arguments for and against the productivity norm, the wartime abandonment of the gold standard once again

168

Table 8.1 Real and nominal income and prices, United Kingdom, 1871–99*

Year	Population (millions)	Nominal income (Y) (millions £)	Y/cap	Real income (y) (million £)	y/cap	Price deflator (1929 = 100)
1871	31.556	972	30.80	1682	53.50	57.8
1872	31.874	1037	32.53	1689	52.99	61.4
1873	32.177	1111	34.53	1750	54.39	63.5
1874	32.501	1084	33.35	1763	54.24	61.5
1875	32.839	1072	32.64	1811	55.15	59.2
1876	33.200	1056	31.81	1827	55.93	57.8
1877	33.576	1047	31.18	1863	55.49	56.2
1878	33.932	1015	29.91	1839	54.20	55.2
1879	34.304	994	28.98	1883	54.89	52.8
1880	34.623	1037	29.95	1885	54.44	55.0
1881	34.935	1076	30.80	2000	57.25	53.8
1882	35.206	1116	31.70	2044	58.06	54.6
1883	35.450	1102	31.09	2041	57.57	54.0
1884	35.724	1073	30.04	2044	57.21	52.4
1885	36.015	1058	29.38	2070	57.48	51.1
1886	36.313	1082	29.80	2151	59.23	50.3
1887	36.598	1127	30.79	2232	60.99	50.5
1888	36.881	1204	32.65	2384	64.64	50.5
1889	37.178	1296	34.86	2531	68.08	51.2
1890	37.485	1326	35.37	2545	67.89	52.1
1891	37.802	1307	34.57	2518	66.61	51.9
1892	38.134	1268	33.25	2448	64.19	51.8
1893	38.490	1274	33.10	2474	64.28	51.5
1894	38.859	1362	35.05	2692	69.28	50.6
1895	39.221	1395	35.57	2796	71.72	49.9
1896	39.599	1431	36.14	2879	72.70	49.7
1897	39.987	1481	37.07	2950	73.77	50.2
1898	40.381	1563	38.71	3095	76.64	50.5
1899	40.773	1649	40.44	3221	79.00	51.1

*Including southern Ireland
Source: Friedman and Schwartz (1982, table 4.9)

brought the problem of price-level policy to the forefront of professional and popular debates. And, once again, despite the growing popularity of the zero inflation norm, the productivity norm had prominent defenders, including Ralph Hawtrey and Dennis Robertson, whose writings in favor of the norm demonstrate the independence of its merits from those of classical value theory or the gold standard.[11] Hawtrey embraced the norm implicitly throughout his Currency and Credit (1919), in which macroeconomic equilibrium is identified with stability of "consumers' outlay" – what we now call aggregate or effective demand. At one point, Hawtrey even invoked the productivity norm explicitly, observing that "if the consumers' outlay be constant, the [commodity price] index number will be raised by scarcity and depressed by abundance" and that this would be better than keeping the index number stable and having "consumers' outlay . . . raised by abundance and depressed by scarcity" (374). Hawtrey did allow, however, that consumers' outlay should expand with changes in population and additions to the stock of capital; he believed, in other words, that the price level should not have to fall because of *extensive* (as opposed to intensive) expansion of output. His ideal was a monetary unit with value fixed "in terms of human effort," in other words, what Edgeworth had termed a "labour" or "productivity" standard.

Years later, Hawtrey offered what was to be perhaps the best and most detailed defense of the productivity norm. Echoing Samuel Bailey, in "Money and Index Numbers" he stressed that, although every commodity price-index movement represents a monetary result – a change in the real value of the money stock – such a change may be due "*either* to a variation of real costs, *or* to a variation in the money value of the factors of production and exchange" (Hawtrey 1930, 69). In today's terminology, these correspond to shifts in aggregate supply and aggregate demand, respectively. Because the latter cause of general price movements involves a change in consumers' income and outlay, it represents a potential source of macroeconomic instability to be avoided by appropriate adjustments in the money supply. In contrast, it is entirely desirable that a price index should be allowed to reflect changes in unit costs, by falling or rising "just in proportion as output is increased or diminished" (70), as this is also consistent with stability of consumers' income and outlay. If productivity is rising, a stable price index will conceal swollen demand and swollen profits, setting the stage for a malinvestment boom. If productivity is falling, a stable price index will conceal shrunken demand and shrunken profits – a depression. Hawtrey gives an example of the latter case, adopting the standard view that "the elasticity of demand for all products taken together is unity" (70):

> Suppose, for example, that a consumer's outlay of £100,000,000 has been applied to 100,000,000 units of goods, and that producers who have hitherto received £20,000,000 for 20,000,000 units find their output reduced to 10,000,000 units, but the price of their product doubled. They still receive £20,000,000 and the other producers can continue to receive £80,000,000 for 80,000,000 units. But as £100,000,000 is now spent on 90,000,000 units the price level has risen by one-ninth. In order to counteract that rise, the consumers' outlay must be reduced from £100,000,000 to £90,000,000. Every group of producers will find the total proceeds of its sales reduced by 10 per cent. Wages, profits and prices will be thrown out of proportion, and every industry will have to face the adverse effects of flagging demand and falling prices. The producers whose prices

have been raised by scarcity will be no exception. Their total receipts are reduced in the same proportion, and they must reduce wages like their neighbours.

(79)

Nor, Hawtrey adds, does the argument depend on the assumption of a unitary elasticity of demand used in the illustration:

If the shortage is in a product of which the elasticity is greater than unity, the adverse effect on the producers of that product is greater and on the other producers less. If elasticity is less than unity the adverse effect on the former is less and may be more than counteracted, but what they gain their neighbours lose. Whatever the circumstances, the stabilization of the commodity price level in face of scarcity will always tend to cause depression.

(79)

Only a price index rising or falling along with changes in real costs of production, according to Hawtrey, would neither unwarrantedly encourage nor discourage dealers or producers (75–81). Significantly, Hawtrey's argument points to a flaw, not merely in policies aimed at achieving a zero growth rate for the price level but also in policies aimed at minimizing growth-rate variability. In a world where productivity shocks occur, the productivity norm succeeds better than either alternative policy in minimizing departures of the economy from its "natural" or "full-information" growth path.

Hawtrey's defense of the productivity norm, like Bailey's, was based on considerations of long-run debtor–creditor equity as well as short-run macroeconomic stability. Concerning equity, Hawtrey observed that "there is nothing in the idea of a fixed income to require that the possessor should be safeguarded against the effects of scarcity of natural products from which his neighbours with earned incomes suffer" (1930, 75). Similarly, if productivity increases generally, there is, in Hawtrey's view, no reason for recipients of fixed incomes to be excluded from the gain. Thus debtor–creditor equity is more a matter of stability of nominal income than of stability of commodity prices.

The other major British proponent of the productivity norm, Dennis Robertson, seemed to grow more convinced of its theoretical superiority as his career wore on. In the first edition of *Money* (1922, 119), Robertson was already inclined to think that the case for price-level stabilization was less self-evident than many others at that time believed. Citing Marshall's testimony before the Gold and Silver Commission, he observed that "from a standpoint of social justice and harmony," there was much to be said in favor of "a standard of value which should remain stable not in terms of goods in general, but in terms of productive power" (121–2). But Robertson at this stage was also impressed by the Humean argument that a gently rising price level would stimulate production "by adding to the money demand for goods" (123). He observed that it might well be "better that all should be busy, even though grumbling at the cost of living, than that some should be living cheaply and others left on the streets" (124). Unable to choose between two opposite views, Robertson concluded that, apart from "exceptional circumstances," it would probably be best to stick to a stable price level after all (125). Reading between the lines it is clear, however, that for those "exceptional circumstances," it was the productivity norm, rather than its converse, that Robertson wished to see prevail.

In *Banking Policy and the Price Level* (1926), Robertson took a much firmer stand against price-level stabilization; indeed, to reveal the defects of that policy was one of the book's main goals. Robertson endeavored to show how, in periods of technological change, price-level stabilization could "become a serious source of trouble" by causing "inappropriate additions to the quantity of Circulating Capital" (58). These would ensue in connection with the temporary lowering of interest rates below their "natural" (Wicksellian) levels – a particular instance of money illusion. Thus Robertson went beyond his former argument for the productivity norm, which had been based on consideration of equity only. The effects of this newfound understanding are apparent in Robertson's 1928 essay on "Theories of Banking Policy." Here the Humean argument for a rising price level is watered down considerably: inflation is seen as warranted only on rare occasions, to encourage, in Schumpeterian fashion, "discontinuous leaps in industrial technique" ([1928] 1940, 71). Moreover, the Federal Reserve System is accused of having "burgled the public" by stabilizing the general price level rather than "the price of labour" during the precrisis "years of rapidly advancing productivity" (68).

Around this time A. C. Pigou also came over to the productivity norm.[12] Although the first edition of Pigou's *Industrial Fluctuations* took a zero inflation norm for granted, the second edition (1929) – apparently influenced by both Hawtrey and Robertson – made numerous concessions to the productivity norm. In a new chapter eighteen, Pigou writes that, unlike price-level movements caused by changes in money supply or velocity, movements due to changes in "the productivity (per head) of a country's industry" will neither stimulate nor depress industry, nor cause any unjust redistribution of wealth between debtors and creditors (182). Elsewhere Pigou goes further by claiming that, when productivity is changing, macroeconomic stability and stable prices "are fundamentally incompatible with one another" (254). "On the whole" Pigou concludes,

> it would seem that, in a progressive community, the goal at which credit regulation can most usefully aim is not price stabilization in an absolute sense, but price stabilization adjusted to the trend of real

income per head; that is to say, a state of things in which prices fall in inverse proportion to the upward trend of *average* real income.

(256–7)

Two years after this – thanks to Hawtrey's latest effort and also to the events of 1929–30 – Robertson himself finally became a wholehearted convert. In "How Do We Want Gold to Behave?" (1931), he held it to be true prima facie "that the price level should fall *pari passu* with the increase of productivity per head" (21) – which meant, according to Robertson's estimate, by about 3 per cent a year in "normal" times (24). Robertson also noted the "growing recognition" being accorded to the productivity norm by other advocates of monetary stabilization, including Hawtrey and Pigou.

THE PRODUCTIVITY NORM IN SWEDEN

The appearance of the productivity norm in continental writings appears to have been independent of any direct British influence. However, the Swedish economist David Davidson, who defended the norm at length, developed his views on price-level policy while attempting to construct a neo-Ricardian, "objective" theory of value (Uhr 1971).[13]

Davidson first proposed and defended the productivity norm in the course of his critical appraisal of Wicksell's monetary writings. Davidson threw down the gauntlet in what was to become a protracted debate with Wicksell. In the last paragraph of his 1899 review of *Interest and Prices* (1898), Davidson took issue with Wicksell's claim – by then a commonplace – that stabilization of the price level would promote debtor–creditor equity. Although he agreed that stable prices would be consistent with equity in a stationary economy, Davidson – like Bailey, Hawtrey, and Robertson in England – claimed that this would not be so in an economy in which productivity was changing. In an example which by now will seem familar, Davidson argued that, were productivity to increase generally by 25 per cent with the price level held constant, non-fixed incomes such as wages and profits would also increase by 25 per cent, whereas fixed-money payments would stay the same in both nominal and real terms. In other words, lenders and other persons receiving contractually fixed incomes would not be allowed to take part in the improvement in productivity. In Davidson's view, this result would be less equitable than what would occur were the price level to fall by 25 per cent with all nominal incomes unchanged, for the latter policy would permit all persons to partake equally of improvements in productivity.

Wicksell offered no immediate reply to Davidson's criticism; in the second volume of his *Lectures*, which appeared in 1906, he repeated the substance of his earlier views, adding merely that he did not accept Davidson's claim that creditors and other recipients of fixed incomes should be allowed to enjoy a share of the gains associated with improvements in productivity. This prompted a longer article by Davidson, devoted entirely to a defense of the productivity norm and including a demonstration of the norm's greater consistency (as compared with price-level stabilization) with monetary equilibrium. This response drew Wicksell into the debate, which was fought over the next three years in the pages of the *Ekonomisk Tidskrift*.

Despite his efforts throughout this long exchange, Davidson never did manage to convince Wicksell of the superiority of the productivity norm. In part, Davidson himself was to blame for his failure, as he at one point conceded to Wicksell the validity of Wicksell's most forceful counter-argument, which was that the productivity norm would be impossible to implement in practice because it required the use of a (non-existent) measure of changes in productivity over time. In fact, Davidson need not have yielded so readily on this issue, for to implement his norm is not as difficult as he (and Wicksell) believed: as Robertson and others later suggested, the productivity norm can be implemented or approximately implemented by stabilizing some measure of per capita nominal income.[14]

At Wicksell's suggestion the formal debate was broken off in 1909. Davidson continued, however, to champion the productivity norm in other forums, including his astute, critical review of Fisher's plan for stabilizing the dollar. This review helped inspire Wicksell's own critical remarks on the Fisher plan in the second, 1911 edition of his *Lectures* (Thomas, 1935, 40n.).

This critique of Fisher was the first sign of a change in Wicksell's views. Nevertheless Wicksell in 1911 was still far from endorsing the productivity norm. Then the war came. Where Davidson alone had failed despite three long years of debate, the war succeeded, or nearly succeeded, in changing Wicksell's mind. Gustav Cassel (1923, 79–100, 129–36), himself a Wicksellian, maintained after the war that the wartime inflation had been a purely monetary phenomenon, which ought to have been prevented by a policy of higher interest rates and reduced note issues by the Riksbank (the bank of the Swedish parliament). Davidson demurred. He countered that the inflation had at least in part been a reflection of increased scarcity and fallen per capita output, which should be allowed to manifest themselves in higher output prices. Davidson even went so far as to support his argument with a table (reproduced here as Table 8.2) purporting to show the extent to which the wartime inflation was due to increased real scarcity as opposed to monetary expansion.[15] Almost despite himself, Wicksell was inclined to agree with Davidson against Cassel. Eventually Wicksell went so far as to explicitly concede the need for increased prices at times of substantially reduced per capita output "so that pesons with fixed incomes . . . have their share of the general calamity" (cited in Caplan 1942, 206n.). Davidson's victory was only partial, however, as Wicksell continued to insist (with

Table 8.2 Real and monetary causes of inflation in Sweden, 1914–22, according to D. Davidson

Year	Index of wholesale prices (1)	Index of commodity scarcity (2)	'Monetary' inflation (1)−(2)	%
1914	100	100	0	0
1917	244	162	82	57
1918	339	151	188	79
1919	330	132	198	86
1920	340	126	221	92
1921	211	106	105	95
1922	162	101	61	98

Source: Adapted from Uhr (1975, 297)

uncharacteristic inconsistency) on the desirability of zero inflation in "normal" times, including times when productivity was advancing.[16]

Several Swedish theorists in the 1930s, including Bertil Ohlin, Eli Heckscher, Gunnar Myrdal, and especially Eric Lindahl, followed Davidson in preferring the productivity norm (or the "Davidson norm," as they termed it) to the norm of zero inflation. Lindahl, an employee of the Riksbank in the 1930s, observed that a policy of strict price-level stabilization in the face of adverse supply shocks would entail a contraction of nominal spending, which could render nominal contracts unfulfillable (cited in Caplan 1941, 210). Ohlin argued that a policy of money-income stabilization to keep money revenues in "balance" with money costs of production would serve better than price-level stabilization to avoid "abnormally large or low profits and profit expectations" (1937, 321).

Myrdal's reasons for favoring the productivity norm differed from those of other Swedish writers. According to Myrdal, price-level policy must take into account the "different degrees of stickiness of various prices," its aim being to minimize the need for changes in the least flexible prices ([1939] 1965, 139n.). Davidson's productivity norm was preferable to a policy of price-level stabilization not, in Myrdal's view, by dint of any considerations of pure theory but because wages are (or were) in fact generally more sticky than commodity prices.[17]

Other Swedes, including Cassel and Eric Lundberg, continued to favor Wicksell's norm of price-level stabilization throughout the 1930s. Immediately after going off the gold standard in September 1931, the Riksbank declared its intent to stabilize the domestic purchasing power of the *krona*. According to Lars Jonung (1979b, 469), this declaration was probably drafted by Cassel. In October, the Riksbank secretly solicited the opinions of three economists, including Cassel as well as Heckscher and Davidson, on the matter of price-level policy (Jonung 1979a). In their separate reports, both Heckscher (who had been Davidson's student) and Davidson expressed strongly their desire to see the *krona* rejoined to an international monetary standard. As long as Sweden retained its independent standard, however, Heckscher believed that the Riksbank should aim at Davidson's norm of "a price level varying inversely with the growth in productivity" (Jonung 1979a, 90). Surprisingly Davidson, then 77 years old, did not come out explicitly in favor of the norm for which he was famous, referring only vaguely to an alternative to price-level stabilization which, according to Jonung (96), was probably the productivity norm. Of the three theorists, Cassel alone came out firmly and unambiguously for a policy of domestic price-level stabilization, which he had favored even prior to the collapse of the gold standard (92).[18] In the end, the "Swedish experiment" continued through the mid-1930s along Wicksellian, rather than Davidsonian, lines, reflecting Cassel's dominating influence.

THE PRODUCTIVITY NORM IN EUROPE AND NEW ZEALAND

In Europe outside of Sweden, although Davidson's work remained largely unknown, arguments favoring the productivity norm became increasingly popular during the first decades of this century. By the 1930s the norm had been widely accepted among Austrian, German, and Dutch economists who embraced it in their writings on "neutral money." Austrian and German writers, including Ludwig von Mises ([1928] 1978), F. A. von Hayek, Gottfried Haberler, and Wilhelm Roepke (1936), persistently criticized central bankers and the US Federal Reserve Board in particular during the 1920s for sponsoring what the economists termed "relative inflation" – growing nominal incomes masked (thanks to increasing productivity) by a stable price level (see Table 8.3). Von Mises in particular predicted on several occasions that this policy would lead to a crash.

Table 8.3 Real and nominal income and prices, United States, 1921–9

Year	Population (millions)	Nominal income (Y) (billion $)	Y/cap	Real income (y) (billion $)	y/cap	Price deflator (1929 = 100)
1921	108.538	61.793	569	59.567	549	103.7
1922	110.049	62.996	572	63.859	580	98.6
1923	111.947	74.095	662	73.460	656	100.9
1924	114.109	75.235	659	75.559	662	99.6
1925	115.829	78.602	679	77.343	668	101.6
1926	117.397	84.566	720	82.807	705	102.1
1927	119.035	83.104	698	83.623	703	99.4
1928	120.509	84.980	705	84.918	705	100.1
1929	121.767	90.320	742	90.308	742	100.0

Source: Friedman and Schwartz (1982, table 4.8)

J. G. Koopmans was another early champion of the ideal of "neutral money" as well as the founder of the school of thought now known as Dutch monetarism. Koopmans's criterion for "neutral" money was the absence of either excess aggregate demand (*Reine Nachfrage*) or deficient aggregate demand (*Nachfrage Ausfall*) (Fase 1989, 192). Koopmans insisted, though, that neutral money should *not* be identified with stability of the price level: in the face of improvements in productivity, neutral money would require falling prices, whereas in the face of adverse supply shocks, neutral money would require increases in the price level. Up to this point, Koopmans's views are identical to those of other productivity-norm advocates. However, unlike most of these other writers, Koopmans refrained from offering any concrete guideline for monetary management (190). Indeed, Koopmans denied that neutral money could be equated with the stability of any term or set of terms in the equation of exchange, thus rejecting Robertson's view, later adopted by Hayek as well, that the productivity norm for monetary equilibrium could be implemented or approximately implemented by stabilizing some measure of the flow of money income or aggregate demand – MV. In his 1930s correspondence with Robertson (Fase 1983) as well as in his later writings, Koopmans argued that a change in *relative* demands for various goods could cause an increase in the *general* price level with a larger flow of money income but no disruption of real equilibrium relationships. The particular scenario Koopmans has in mind was one involving three traders and what J. Ziljstra terms a "triangular money effect." Robertson responded to Koopmans by pointing out that he (Koopmans) had smuggled into his argument an unstated assumption about a changed velocity of money without indicating *why* velocity should change, conflating a change in the relative demands for various goods with a change in the demand for money relative to income (Fase 1983, 307).

Robertson's view favoring stability of MV as a criterion for monetary equilibrium and for implementing the productivity norm was shared by most other Dutch monetarists. Thus, G. M. Verrijn Stuart, who had been an advocate of price-level stabilization when working on his dissertation in 1919, later put forth a distinction between the "extrinsic" value of money, as reflected in the level of output prices, and its "intrinsic" value. Stability of the latter would, according to Verrijn Stuart, be consistent with monetary equilibrium and could be accomplished not by stabilizing prices but by stabilizing the flow of money income, MV (Fase 1989, 190).[19]

Among the Austrians, Haberler devoted several works to the topics of index numbers and monetary stability (1927; 1931; and 1932). In each, he questioned the desirability of a stable price level and defended (along lines similar to those taken by Davidson, Hawtrey, and Robertson) the idea of a price level adjusting in response to changes in real unit costs of production. Hayek, in contrast, was slower in coming around to the productivity norm.

Although from the start he rejected price-level stabilization, his alternative proposal at first was that the money supply should be kept *constant* ([1929] 1933; 1931). This opinion was based in part on the view, which Hayek took from von Mises, that "*every* new issue of circulating media brings about a lowering of the money rate of interest in relation to the natural rate" ([1929] 1933, 119n.). Here Hayek was guilty of an error opposite to the one he accused price-level stabilizationists of committing. Whereas proponents of zero inflation treated every price-level movement as if it represented a change in the supply or velocity of money, ignoring the possibility of changes in the (natural) rate of output, Hayek had entirely ignored the possibility of changes in velocity. Thus his recommendation would have permitted the price level to change along with changes in the demand for money even when productivity remained constant.

By the time of the appearance of the second edition of *Prices and Production* in 1935, Hayek had come around to the productivity norm. Citing a number of other proponents of the norm including Marshall, Edgeworth, Robertson, and Haberler, he wrote that "there is no harm in prices falling as productivity increases" (1935, 106) and, more significantly, that this result would be borne out by a policy of keeping "not the prices of consumers' goods, but incomes, or the prices of the factors of production constant" (105). To accomplish this "any change in the velocity of circulation would have to be compensated by a reciprocal change in the amount of money in circulation" (124). In other words, the product MV, rather than M itself, had to be kept stable. Hayek admitted that his earlier approach had "excluded considerations of changes in the velocity of circulation or the cash balances held in the different stages" of production (xiii).[20]

One of the last important articles to be devoted exclusively to defending the productivity norm was an article by the New Zealand economist Allen G. B. Fisher. In response to proposals for stabilizing the price level by Irving Fisher, Cassel, and others, A. G. B. Fisher (1935) maintained that to keep prices from falling in the face of improvements in productivity would generate false profit signals, causing resources to be misallocated. Like Hayek, Fisher insisted that only changes in the velocity of money warranted offsetting changes in its nominal quantity, so as to preserve a constant level of aggregate demand. In contrast, when real income increases, "the increased real purchasing power which is necessary" is best provided "through the use of the same number of units of currency" at a lower price level (204). "Not only" Fisher wrote, "is a fall of prices which is the result of increased productive efficiency not a bad thing, but efforts to check such a fall will inevitably lead to disequilibrium and depression" (209).

THE PRODUCTIVITY NORM IN THE UNITED STATES

In the United States, the productivity norm also had many champions. Like their British counterparts Marshall, Giffen, and Edgeworth, a number of American economists, including J. L. Laughlin (1887; 1893), Simon Newcomb (1893), and Frank Taussig (1893), attacked the norm of price-level stability as embodied in proposals for bimetallism, free silver coinage, and a "tabular standard" for deferred payments. Responding to the complaint that the gold standard, by allowing prices to fall steadily after 1873, had punished debtors and discouraged industry, these authors pointed to large increases in productivity rather than a "shortage" of gold as the true cause of falling prices.[21] According to Newcomb, "constant improvements in labor-saving machinery, the division of labor, [and] establishments on a large scale, which cheap transportation has rendered possible, have all contributed to the productiveness of human labor" (1893, 505). "Relative to labor rather than commodities," Newcomb said, gold had, not appreciated, but *depreciated*; indeed, if anything, prices had "fallen less than should have been expected" in response to improvements in productivity (507). Because it reflected improvements in real output, the downward trend in prices, rather than harming debtors, merely served to bestow upon creditors real interest returns commensurate with the enhanced productiveness of capital (507–8).

Unlike Newcomb and some other apologists for falling prices, neither Taussig nor Laughlin denied that gold had "appreciated." It was, Taussig said, pointless to debate whether falling prices were due to the appreciation of gold, the two things being, in fact, "two names for one and the same thing" (Taussig 1893, 106) rather than cause and effect. The question was not whether gold had appreciated, which was indisputable, but whether the appreciation had been harmful to debtors and industry generally. Responding to the Humean argument, revived in the United States by the bimetallist Francis Walker, that falling prices must discourage entrepreneurship, Taussig pointed to the fact that, while prices had been falling in the United States since 1873, money incomes and wages had steadily risen (105), giving no basis for the discouragement even of entrepreneurs suffering from money illusion:

The money incomes of the managers of industry have shown the same upward movement as the money incomes of other classes in society. So long as this is the case, it is idle to talk of a depressing effect on enterprise from the fall in prices, or of strangling of the industrial organism from insufficiency of the circulating medium. In fact, the immediate cause of the fall in prices has been the pushing on the market for sale of larger and larger quantities of commodities, produced with profit at lower and lower cost: a state of things fortunate for the community, and surely not depressing for the business man.
(111)[22]

Taussig's arguments against the charge that falling prices were unjust to debtors closely resembled those of Bailey, Davidson, and Haberler. "It is true," Taussig observed,

> that the money [the debtor] repays the creditor will buy more goods than it did when the loan was contracted; but [the debtor's] own money income has risen, or at least has not fallen, and the repayment of the loan can cause him no special hardship, – none greater than he must have expected.
>
> (109)

This, said Taussig, was a far cry from a situation where both wages and prices – and, hence, money incomes – have fallen, in which "the debtor really pays back more than he got, not only in terms of commodities, but in terms of labor or sacrifice in income" (109).

Taussig's appeal to a labor or "sacrifice" standard of value is reminiscent of the views of Giffen, Newcomb, and, ultimately, Ricardo; the appeal was most effectively employed by Taussig to defend the deflation-related gains of creditors against socialist opponents of the gold standard:

> Applying [the labor standard] test to the relations of debtor and creditor in the case supposed, we find it not one of hardship to the debtor, but apparently one of justice to both parties. It is true the creditor gets more commodities than he gave[23]; but he gets the product of the same amount of labor as he devoted[24] to the commodities originally lent; and why should he not share with the rest of the community the benefits of a general increase in the productiveness of labor?
>
> (107)

Besides defending falling prices, Taussig also argued that any effort to *prevent* prices from falling despite improvements in productivity would be harmful insofar as it must involve an artificial increase in money incomes, which would debar creditors "from that participation in the improvements in production which the present conditions give them" (121). Taussig concluded in view of this that a tabular or multiple standard of value as well as other schemes for stabilizing or raising the price level "do not seem . . . to be called for by any serious exigency not met by the maintenance of the gold standard" (125).

The debates of the early 1890s came to a halt with McKinley's election victory in 1896, which at the time assured retention of the gold standard (and which happened to coincide with the Klondike gold discoveries and the consequent end of secular deflation). The next endorsements of the productivity norm by US economists came in the 1930s from John Williams of Harvard, Benjamin Anderson of Chase Manhattan Bank, and James W. Angell of Columbia University. Along with Hayek, Robertson, and A. G. B. Fisher, Williams (1932, 149–50) and Anderson (1929) believed that the 1920s had been an era of "relative" inflation, with excessive money-income growth masked by a stable price level. Angell in turn argued that the ultimate objective of monetary policy should be "to prevent substantial changes in average money income per capita" and *not* stability in the price level (1933, 58).

THE PASSING OF THE PRODUCTIVITY NORM

By 1935 the productivity norm had been endorsed by prominent economists of many schools; it even appeared to be on the verge of unseating zero inflation as the most popular monetary policy ideal. Yet only a few years later, the norm fell once again into neglect. The main reason was the advent of Keynesianism. Although *The General Theory* at one point appeared to argue in favor of zero inflation, with nominal wages rising in response to improvements in productivity (Keynes 1936, 270–1), the work's main effect was to detract attention from price-level policy altogether, making such policy subordinate to the achievement of full employment. Subsequently, the proto-Keynesian belief that the Phillips curve represented an exploitable policy trade-off spelled a partial revival of price-level policy in the form of a proto-Humean defense of inflation (Laidler 1990, 139).

Many previous champions of the productivity norm, including most British economists, abandoned it in favor of some version of Keynesianism. A notable exception was Robertson, who by the end of his career found himself a lone defender of the norm. In his *Lectures*, Robertson continued to insist upon the need for such a norm to avoid "a windfall profit to entrepreneurs" when productivity increases or, conversely, windfall losses to entrepreneurs when productivity declines (1957, ii, 40). He also observed that the correctness of this view (except in industries in which workers are paid piece rates)

> is generally admitted in regard to individual commodities and only disputed when the argument is generalized; e.g. nobody was surprised at the fall in the price of motor cars between 1900 and 1939 or supposed that it meant that car manufacturers were all along on the point of being driven out of business.
>
> (41)

Robertson was, however, forced for pragmatic reasons to become "somewhat more tolerant" (42) than he had been in the 1930s of the popular goal of stabilizing the price level:

> I suppose I must concede that the huge growth of national debts as a proportion of national income on the one hand, and the fear of Communist overbidding on the other, render it unlikely that, in present

circumstances, a price-level falling in full proportion to increases in productivity will be unequivocally adopted in western countries as an objective of policy. And while in my heart I still hanker after that – the ideal Marshall-Hawtrey policy, I shall be pretty well content if fifty years hence I look round and find the price-level no higher than it is today!

(43–4)

In his final publication – a report to the Canadian Royal Commission on Banking and Finance – Robertson "with a twinge of conscience" confessed his temptation "to throw perfectionism to the winds, and to accept for practical purposes what to many people seems, though in practice it is not, the most 'natural' objective of all, namely, stability of the final price level" (1963, 11). Yet despite this pragmatic inclination, Robertson stood fast to the productivity norm as a theoretical ideal, which he noted would be roughly equivalent to a policy of stabilizing per capita money income.[25]

Outside of Britain, the ascent of Keynesianism was still less complete, so that the productivity norm continued to have some following. In Sweden, Davidson's influence continued well into the 1940s. According to Jonung (1979b), "the goal of price stabilization was . . . gradually relaxed" (479) in response to other demands upon the Riksbank in the course of that decade. Then, during World War II and partly as a result of Dag Hammerskjöld's influence, Davidson's productivity norm won the approval of the Swedish parliament and central bank, inspiring attempts to stabilize money income instead of the domestic price level (Hammerskjöld 1955, 145–6; Jonung 1979a, 101, n. 20). Dutch monetarists also kept the productivity norm alive into the 1960s (Fase 1983, 308). Hayek, finally, continued to uphold the productivity norm toward the end of his career, alongside his proposals for free choice in currency. In *Denationalization of Money*, he wrote that "a currency stable in terms of raw material prices is probably . . . the nearest approach we can hope to achieve to one conducive to stability of general economic activity" and that such a currency would also allow earners of fixed incomes to secure "an automatic share in an increase in industrial productivity" (1978, 71).

The vast majority of economists, however, either ignored or were ignorant of the productivity norm by the time Keynesian views began to be discredited by the advent of stagflation. As a result, Keynesian policy ideals gave way, not to the productivity norm, but to renewed calls for zero inflation. This turn of events was due in part to the pre-eminent role monetarists played in challenging Keynesian beliefs. Although some prominent monetarists of the post-Keynesian era did at least recognize the productivity-norm alternative, all were committed to a zero inflation ideal. Thus Lloyd Mints (1950, 132–3) conceded that price-level stability is not clearly preferable to the productivity norm for preserving debtor–creditor equity when productivity is changing. He also admitted that a productivity norm alone would guarantee the stability of aggregate demand and therefore prevent any "disturbance of equilibrium by the monetary system" (134). However, he viewed the productivity norm as requiring in practice the stabilization of an index of wages, which he felt would be unreliable as a signal of disequilibrium due to the stickiness of wages compared to prices; like Davidson and Wicksell, Mints failed to realize that the norm could be put into effect by targeting some measure of nominal income rather than by targeting any price or wage index. Despite this oversight, Mints concluded that the productivity norm "represents . . . one of the extreme limits of the range within which a reasonable policy must fall" (135). Had Mints followed Edgeworth in considering the implications of *falling* as well as rising productivity, he might not have characterized the productivity norm as an "extreme" policy compared to price-level stabilization.

Another monetarist who recognized the productivity norm as a potential rival to the norm of zero inflation was Clark Warburton.[26] Citing A. G. B. Fisher's article, Warburton ([1946] 1951) stated that a "possible exception to price-level stability without disturbance to the savings-adjustment mechanism is a gradual fall in prices in accord with increased productivity" (308n.). Warburton noted that a productivity norm would also allow the benefits of progress to be "more quickly and fairly distributed among the entire population" (308n.). However, echoing Robertson and Hume, Warburton claimed that a stable price level would provide "more incentives to business to make full use of improved techniques of production" (308n.). Here again, like Mints and other proponents of price-level stabilization, Warburton failed to consider the relative merits of the productivity norm and stable prices under conditions of *fallen* productivity.

As inflation worsened during the 1970s, monetarism with its ideal of zero inflation gained further ground against Keynesianism. However, this renewed support for zero inflation as a policy *ideal* was tempered by the widespread belief that accomplishment of this ideal would involve high short-run costs of inflation abatement. Roughly speaking, this perspective meant that, although zero inflation might be the best policy once it was an accomplished fact, a compromise (positive inflation) policy would be best *given* the reality of high inflation. Under the circumstances, the productivity norm with its implied ideal of secular *de*flation could not be expected to garner much support.

While fewer and fewer older economists bothered even to acknowledge the productivity-norm alternative, new generations emerged that were entirely unaware of the norm's presence in the history of economic thought.[27] One post-1970s reference to the norm also highlights the reasons for the norm's absence from current discussions. Writing at the peak of the inflation, Mason asked rhetorically whether "either side of the industrial bargaining table" was prepared to accept a productivity-norm-based policy of deflation. "The answer," Mason wrote, "is clearly negative. Indeed, at a time when inflation appears to be out of control and unions are playing catch-up plus, the question sounds ludicrous" (1982, 555–6).

But that was over a decade ago. Today, inflation is, arguably, no longer "out of control," and the goal of zero inflation is clearly within reach. Perhaps the time is now right, therefore, for monetary economists to proceed beyond the usual arguments for eliminating inflation by reconsidering the productivity norm.

NOTES

1 Strictly speaking, "zero inflation" and price-level stability are distinct, in that only the latter policy would require the "rolling back" of prices following some upward deviation from an original target. However, I assume here that both policies uphold continuous price stability as an *ideal* and therefore treat them as being identical. Contemporary proponents of price-level stabilization include Robert J. Barro (1986), Robert P. Black (1986), Kevin Dowd (1992), Robert Hetzel (1990), and Leland B. Yeager (1986a; 1986b). See also the articles collected in Lipsey (1990) and York (1990). Freedman (1991) discusses the Canadian debate.

2 Many theorists who might otherwise view zero inflation as an ideal believe that transition costs of achieving zero inflation in inflationary economies could outweigh any long-term gains. On this issue, see Howitt (1990), Scarth (1990), and Carlstrom and Gavin (1993).

3 Thus a recent editorial in the *Economist* (End of Inflation?, 1992, 11), in attempting to establish "the virtue of zero" inflation, argues simply that "anything higher" interferes with the smooth operation of the price system. The alternative of secular deflation, as implied by the productivity norm, is not considered. The same is true of recent scholarly arguments for zero inflation, including those cited in note 1.

4 For a more detailed review of theoretical arguments for price-level stabilization and the productivity-norm alternative, see Chapter 7.

5 This and the following arguments assume that changes in the price level are not perfectly anticipated. The same assumption is also taken for granted in arguments for the productivity norm occurring later in the text. Of course authors on both sides recognize that even anticipated inflation can have real effects, for example on money holders.

6 Proponents of the productivity norm implicitly rejected Laidler's assumption (1990, 134) that sector-specific productivity shocks "tend to cancel one another out with the passage of time," placing greater emphasis on what the literature today refers to as "hysteresis effects" of such shocks.

7 According to Thomas Humphrey (1990), Henry Thornton argued in favor of allowing adverse supply shocks to be reflected in temporary, upward movements in the price level. Thornton's stance hints at, but does not really encompass, a full-blown productivity-norm policy.

8 For the most part, neither classical nor later proponents of the productivity norm discussed its implications for international exchange. John Stuart Mill (1909, 593–606) was an exception in this regard. Broadly, it can be said that the arguments for adhering to a productivity norm in the international context are the same as those applicable to the closed-economy context: although national price-level changes consistent with the norm would facilitate the international sharing of productivity gains, they would not (unlike price-level changes having "monetary" origins) lead to any other unintended redistributions of wealth. According to Mill, a productivity norm is perfectly compatible with the

maintenance of an equilibrium of international payments given a fixed rate of exchange. By implication, then, a policy of price-level stabilization strictly observed despite changes in productivity would *not* generally be consistent with the preservation of international equilibrium under a fixed exchange-rate regime. Friedrich von Hayek ([1932] 1984) later stressed this implication, blaming the post-World War I breakdown of the gold standard on efforts to stabilize domestic price levels in the face of improvements in productivity.

9 Of course, if labor markets are characterized by *real* rather than nominal wage rigidity, then the productivity norm will be no more successful than zero inflation (or any other price-level policy) at avoiding short-run unemployment in consequence of negative productivity shocks.

10 Much later A. E. Musson concluded that, during the Great Depression, "prices certainly fell, but almost every other index of economic activity . . . showed an upward trend" (1959, 199).

11 As Mason correctly observes, "the question as to whether the [monetary] unit should be fixed in terms of labor (stable money wage rates or per capita money income) or commodities (stable price level) remains unanswered and unaffected by the conflict between the so-called cost and utility schools of value theory" (1982, 552).

12 Robertson refers to Pigou as a "recent convert" (1931, 21).

13 Because I do not read Swedish I have relied entirely on discussions of Davidson's work by Benjamin Caplan (1942, ch. 2), Carl Uhr (1960, 279–327; 1971), Brinley Thomas (1935), and Dag Hammerskjöld (1955).

14 The productivity norm is, however, distinct from modern suggestions for nominal gross national product targeting, which aim at establishing a stable average or long-run price level. If real output is a random walk, a consistent nominal GNP target is, in fact, not consistent with any pre-chosen rate of inflation. To this extent at least, the productivity norm represents the more coherent policy.

15 How Davidson constructed his "index of commodity scarcity" is not clear. It appears, however, that he assumed the velocity of money to be constant, and then proceeded to compare changes in the supply of money to changes in the price level along quantity-theoretic lines, inferring a change in "scarcity" from any departure from strict proportionality of changes in money and prices. Thus if the money supply increased 20 per cent, and prices increased 30 per cent, the "index of scarcity" was assumed to have increased 10 per cent.

16 But Carl Uhr (1971) maintains that Davidson "eventually succeeded in convincing Wicksell [that] the appropriate policy was to permit the price level to vary inversely with changes in productivity" (68).

17 Some other advocates of the productivity norm, including Hawtrey (1930, 75) and Robertson (1957, 40) – but not Davidson – also emphasized the stickiness of wages relative to output prices.

18 It is difficult to understand Jonung's assertion (1979b) that the three economists whose views were solicited by the Riksbank "exhibited great unanimity" in suggesting that the Riksbank aim at "stabilization of the price level according to Wicksell's norm" (469). Jonung's own summary of the contents of the three reports suggests that Cassel alone viewed such a policy as ideal. One also must bear in mind that the Riksbank did not, after all, seek the economists' opinion on *whether* it should aim at domestic price-level stability; its question to them was, rather, *how* such stability should be achieved and according to what price index.

19 G. Verrijn Stuart's father, C. A. Verrijn Stuart, also an economist, rejected the productivity norm, arguing instead (as his son had prior to 1929) in favor of price-level stabilization (Fase 1989, 191).

20 Hayek had already referred favorably to writings of past productivity-norm theorists in his 1931 essay "The 'Paradox' of Saving" ([1931] 1939, 254), originally published in German in 1929. However, he had not yet come around to favoring money stock changes to offset opposite changes in the velocity of money. The first evidence of a change in this aspect of Hayek's thinking appeared in his essay on "Saving" in the 1933 edition of the *Encyclopedia of the Social Sciences* ([1933] 1939, 157–70), in which he writes that "unless the banks create additional credits for investment purposes to the same extent that holders of deposits have ceased to use them for current expenditure, the effect of such saving is essentially the same as that of hoarding and has all the undesirable deflationary consequences attaching to the latter" (165).

21 In his modern discussion of the 1873–96 deflation in the United States, Roger Shields (1969) concludes that the episode contradicts the usual view linking deflation with depression.

22 Elsewhere (for example, 108), Taussig argues that depression could be avoided even with constant or falling money wages, so long as money wages increase or remain high *relative* to commodity prices.

23 The argument here refers to the gain on the loan principal, that is, *net* of nominal interest.

24 Perhaps Taussig should have said "as was devoted."

25 "Roughly" because allowance ideally should be made for growth of the capital stock as well as labor supply. Among Robertson's better-known students, Harry Johnson apparently adopted the productivity norm. Johnson once observed that, compared to it, price-level stabilization is merely a "popular approach" based upon "theoretical simplifications with no comparable theoretical justification" (1972, 29).

26 Milton Friedman's (1969) "Optimum Quantity of Money" argument superficially resembles arguments for the productivity norm in calling for a rate of deflation linked to the real rate of interest, which in equilibrium reflects the marginal product of capital.

27 Two noteworthy exceptions are David Glasner (1989, 237–41) and Earl A. Thompson (1981; 1986) who propose to revise the nineteenth-century idea of a labor standard of value, which is more or less equivalent to a productivity norm. Glasner (1989, 238) also acknowledges some earlier advocates of this ideal.

REFERENCES

Anderson, Benjamin. 1929. Commodity Price Stabilization: A False Goal of Central Bank Policy. *Chase Economic Bulletin*, May.

Angell, James W. 1933. Monetary Control and General Business Stabilization. In *Economic Essays in Honour of Gustav Casse*. London: George Allen & Unwin.

Bailey, Samuel. 1837. *Money and Its Vicissitudes in Value*. London: Effingham Wilson.

Barro, Robert J. 1986. Rules vs. Discretion. In *Alternative Monetary Regimes*. Edited by Colin D. Campbell and William R. Dougan. Baltimore: The Johns Hopkins University Press.

Black, Robert P. 1986. A Proposal to Clarify the Fed's Policy Mandate. *Cato Journal* 5.3: 787–95.

Bowley, Arthur L. 1920. *The Change in the Distribution of the National Income, 1880–1913*. Oxford: Clarendon.

Caplan, Benjamin. 1942. The Wicksellian School – A Critical Study of the Development of Swedish Monetary Theory, 1898–1932. Ph.D. diss., University of Chicago.

Carlstrom, Charles T., and William T. Gavin. 1993. Zero Inflation: Transition Costs and Shoe Leather Benefits. *Contemporary Policy Issues* 11.1: 9–17.

Cassel, Gustav. 1923. *Money and Foreign Exchange after 1914*. New York: Harcourt Brace.

Dowd, Kevin. 1992. The Case for Price-Level Stability. Unpublished manuscript, University of Nottingham.

Edgeworth, F. Y. 1925. *Papers Relating to Political Economy*. London: The Royal Economic Society.

End of Inflation? 1992. *Economist*, 22 February: 11–12.

Fase, M. M. G. 1983. The 1930 Correspondence between Koopmans, Robertson and Gregory, *De Economist* 131.3: 305–43.

————. 1989. Dutch Monetarism in Retrospect. *Perspectives on the History of Economic Thought* 2: 187–98.

Fisher, Allen G. B. 1935. Does an Increase in Volume of Production Call for a Corresponding Increase in Volume of Money? *American Economic Review* 25.2: 197–211.

Fisher, Irving. 1925. *The Purchasing Power of Money*. New York: Macmillan.

Flux, A. W. 1930. Comment on Robertson's "How Do We Want Gold to Behave?" In *The International Gold Problem*. Oxford: Oxford University Press.

Freedman, Charles. 1991. The Goal of Price Stability: The Debate in Canada. *Journal of Money, Credit, and Banking* 23.3: 613–18.

Friedman, Milton. 1969. The Optimum Quantity of Money. In *The Optimum Quantity of Money and Other Essays*. Chicago: Aldine.

Friedman, Milton, and Anna J. Schwartz. 1982. *Monetary Trends in the United States and the United Kingdom*. Chicago: University of Chicago Press.

Giffen, Sir Robert. 1904. *Economic Inquiries and Studies*, vol. 2. London: George Bell & Sons.

Glasner, David. 1989. *Free Banking and Monetary Reform*. Cambridge: Cambridge University Press.

Haberler, Gottfried. 1927. *Der Sinn Der Indexzahlen*. Tübingen: Mohr.

————. 1931. The Different Meanings Attached to the Term "Fluctuations in the Purchasing Power of Gold" and the Best Instrument or Instruments for Measuring such Fluctuations. League of Nations, March.

————. 1932. Money and the Business Cycle. In *Gold and Monetary Stabilization*. Edited by Quincy Wright. Chicago: University of Chicago.

Hammerskjöld, Dag. 1955. The Swedish Discussion of the Aims of Monetary Policy. *International Economic Papers* 5: 145–54.

Hawtrey, R. G. 1919. *Currency and Credit*. London: Longmans, Green.

————. 1930. Money and Index-Numbers. *Journal of the Royal Statistical Society* 93.1: 64–85.

Hayek, F. A. [1925] 1984. The Monetary Policy of the United States after the Recovery from the 1920 Crisis. Extracted in *Money, Capital, and Fluctuations: Early Essays*. Chicago: University of Chicago.

————. [1929] 1933. *Monetary Theory and the Trade Cycle*. Translated by N. Kaldor and H. M. Croome. New York: Harcourt, Brace.

————. 1931. *Prices and Production*. London: Routledge & Kegan Paul.

————. [1931] 1939. The "Paradox" of Saving. In *Profits, Interest, and Investment*. London: George Routledge & Sons.

————. [1932] 1984. The Fate of the Gold Standard. In *Money, Capital, and Fluctuations: Early Essays*. Chicago: University of Chicago Press.

————. [1933] 1939. Saving. In *Profits, Interest, and Investment*. London: George Routledge & Sons.

————. 1935. *Prices and Production*. 2nd edn. London: Routledge & Kegan Paul.

————. 1978. *Denationalisation of Money–The Argument Refined*. London: Institute of Economic Affairs.

Hetzel, Robert. 1990. A Mandate for Price Stability. *Federal Reserve Bank of Richmond Economic Review* (March/April): 45–51.

Howitt, Peter. 1990. Zero Inflation as a Long-Term Target for Monetary Policy. In Lipsey 1990.

Humphrey, Thomas M. 1990. Ricardo versus Thornton on the Appropriate Monetary Policy Response to Supply Shocks. *Federal Reserve Bank of Richmond Economic Review* 76.6 (November/December): 18–24.

Johnson, Harry G. 1972. *Inflation and the Monetarist Controversy*. Amsterdam: North-Holland.

Jonung, Lars. 1979a. Cassel, Davidson and Heckscher on Swedish Monetary Policy: A Confidential Report to the *Riksbank* in 1931. *Economy and History* 22.2: 85–101.

————. 1979b. Knut Wicksell's Norm of Price Stabilization and Swedish Monetary Policy in the 1930s. *Journal of Monetary Economics* 5: 459–96.

Keynes, John Maynard. 1920. *A Tract on Monetary Reform*. London: Macmillan.

————. 1936. *The General Theory of Employment, Interest and Money*. London: Macmillan.

Laidler, David. 1990: The Zero-Inflation Target: An Overview of the Economic Issues. In Lipsey 1990.

Laughlin, J. L. 1887. Gold and Prices Since 1873. *Quarterly Journal of Economics* 1 (April): 319–55.

————. 1893. The Appreciation of Gold. *Journal of Political Economy* 1.2: 278–80.

Law, John. 1705. *Money and Trade Considered*. Edinburgh: Andrew Anderson.

Lipsey, Richard G., ed. 1990. *Zero Inflation: The Goal of Price Stability*. Toronto: C. D. Howe Institute.

Marshall, Alfred. [1887] 1926. Evidence Given before the Royal Commission on Gold and Silver. In *Official Papers of Alfred Marshall*. London: Macmillan.

Mason, Will E. 1982. The Labor Theory of Value and Gold: Real and Nominal Standards of Value – and Implications for the Current Reconsideration of the Gold Standard. *HOPE* 14.4: 543–58.

Mill, John Stuart, 1909. *Principles of Political Economy*. Edited by W. J. Ashley. London: Longmans, Green.

Mints, Lloyd W. 1950. *Monetary Policy for a Competitive Society*. New York: McGraw-Hill.

Mises, Ludwig von. [1928] 1978. Monetary Stabilization and Cyclical Policy. In *On the Manipulation of Money and Credit*. Edited by Percy C. Greaves, Jr. Dobbs Ferry, NY: Free Market Books.

Musson, A. E. 1959. The Great Depression in Britain, 1873–1896. *Journal of Economic History* 19.2: 199–228.

Myrdal, Gunnar. [1939] 1965. *Monetary Equilibrium*. New York: Kelley.

Newcomb, Simon. 1893. Has the Standard Gold Dollar Appreciated? *Journal of Political Economy* 1.4: 503–12.

Ohlin, Bertil. 1937. Employment Stabilization and Price Stabilization. In *Lessons of Monetary Experience*. Edited by Arthur D. Gayer. New York: Rinehart.

Pigou, A. C. 1929. *Industrial Fluctuations*, 2nd edn. London: Macmillan.

Robertson, Dennis H. 1922. *Money*. Cambridge: Cambridge University Press.

————. 1926. *Banking Policy and the Price Level*. London: P. S. King.

————. 1931. How Do We Want Gold to Behave? In *The International Gold Problem*. Oxford: Oxford University Press.

————. [1928] 1940. Theories of Banking Policy. In *Essays in Monetary Theory*. London: Staples.

————. 1957. *Lectures on Economic Principles*. London: Staples.

————. 1963. A Memorandum Submitted to the Canadian Royal Commission on Banking and Finance. *Essays in International Finance*. Princeton, NJ: Princeton University International Finance Section.

Roepke, Wilhelm. 1936. *Crises and Cycles*. London: William Hodge.

Scarth, William. 1990. Fighting Inflation: Are the Costs of Getting to Zero Too High? In *Taking Aim: The Debate on Zero Inflation*. Edited by Robert C. York. Ottawa: C. D. Howe Institute.

Shields, Roger Elwood. 1969. Economic Growth with Price Deflation, 1873–1896. Ph.D. diss., University of Virginia.

Taussig, Frank N. 1893. *The Silver Situation in the United States*. New York: G. P. Putnam's Sons.

Thomas, Brinley. 1935. The Monetary Doctrines of Professor Davidson. *Economic Journal* (March): 36–50.

Thompson, Earl A. 1981. Free Banking under a Labor Standard. Unpublished manuscript, UCLA.

————. 1986. A Perfect Monetary System. Paper Presented at the Liberty Fund/ Manhattan Institute Conference on Competitive Monetary Regimes, New York, March 13–14.

Uhr, Carl G. 1960. *Economic Doctrines of Knut Wicksell*. Berkeley, CA: University of California Press.

————. 1971. Davidson's Theory of "Objective Value": A "Transformation" Problem. *HOPE* 3.1: 56–91.

————. 1975. *Economic Doctrines of David Davidson*. Stockholm: Almqvist & Wiksell.

Viner, Jacob. 1937. *Studies in the Theory of International Trade*. New York: Harper & Brothers.

Warburton, Clark. [1946] 1951. The Misplaced Emphasis in Contemporary Business-Fluctuation Theory. In American Economic Association *Readings in Monetary Theory*. Homewood, IL: Irwin.

Wheatley, John. 1807. *An Essay on the Theory of Money*. London.

Wicksell, Knut. 1898. *Geldzins and Güterpreise*. Jena: Gustav Fisher.

Williams, Aneurin. 1892. A "Fixed Value of Bullion" Standard. *Economic Journal* 2.2: 280–9.

Williams, John Henry. 1932. Monetary Stability and the Gold Standard. In *Gold and Monetary Stabilization*. Edited by Quincy Wright. Chicago: University of Chicago Press.

Yeager, Leland B. 1986a. Price-Level Stability as the Goal of Monetary Reform. *Cato Journal* 5.3: 821–4.

————. 1986b. The Significance of Monetary Disequilibrium. *Cato Journal* 6.2: 369–99.

York, Robert C., ed. 1990. *Taking Aim: The Debate on Zero Inflation*. Toronto: C. D. Howe Institute.

Part III

THE REGULATORY SOURCES OF MONETARY DISORDER

9

ARE BANKING CRISES FREE-MARKET PHENOMENA?*

INTRODUCTION

What causes banking crises, involving a general loss of confidence in banks? Practically everyone believes that they are an inherent part of fractional-reserve banking, and that government agencies alone are capable of preventing them. Even many persons who otherwise believe in free markets and who are critical of government regulation of banks generally accept the need for some kind of government intervention to prevent or otherwise deal with occasional banking crises. This view of banking crises is so generally accepted that its truth is often simply taken for granted by policy makers, who seldom bother to examine it critically. Nevertheless, a close look at the theory underlying it highlights certain empirical implications that turn out to be quite at odds with reality.

THE CONVENTIONAL THEORY OF BANKING CRISES

A banking crisis erupts when many or all banks in a banking system are confronted by large-scale demands to redeem their liabilities in cash, which demands the banks are unable to satisfy. In attempting to satisfy the demands, banks in a fractional-reserve banking system must undertake large-scale reductions in their balance sheets, shrinking available supplies of money and credit.

If banks held 100 per cent reserves, they could redeem all their liabilities at once if they had to without precipitating a crisis. A 100 per cent reserve banking crisis is an impossibility. Some conservative thinkers, including past Chicago-school economists Henry Simons and Lloyd Mints,[1] view this fact as reason enough for condemning fractional-reserve banking and for recommending its replacement with some 100 per cent reserve alternative.

*Reprinted, with permission, from *Critical Review*, Vol. 8, No. 4 (Fall 1994).

Such a stance takes for granted not only that fractional-reserve banking systems are inherently unstable, but also that fractional-reserve banking is not a source of potential welfare gains to society. Both claims are of doubtful validity, the first for reasons to be made clear in the text, and the second because it overlooks the benefits fractional-reserve banking provides in harnessing money holdings as a vehicle for funding investment. Under competitive conditions the latter benefits are partly enjoyed by money holders themselves, whose gain takes the form of explicit interest payments, lowered bank service charges, or some combination of each.

A second feature of the banking system upon which the conventional theory relies is that bank deposit contracts are serviced on a "first-come-first-served" basis: when persons come to redeem their deposits in cash, their banks pay them in the order of their arrival. Those who are first in line therefore face the highest probability of getting their deposits cashed, while those who are last in line face the lowest probability. This assumption is important, because it serves to motivate runs on individual banks. Such runs play a crucial part in the conventional theory of systemwide banking crises.

Granting these basic assumptions, how does a crisis occur? According to the conventional theory, the crisis is triggered by some "shock" to the banking system. This shock may exist only in the minds of some depositors, making the crisis a kind of self-deflating financial "bubble," or it may be a real event.[2] In either case, the shock must be assumed to threaten at least one bank's liquidity or solvency and, hence, its ability to satisfy its customers' demands for cash. The perception that any bank is having difficulties by itself is sufficient to trigger a run on the bank, for reasons that are obvious enough in light of the "first-come-first-served" way in which withdrawals are handled.

This conventional explanation of how a run against a single bank might occur is still a long way from a plausible story about a banking *crisis* involving simultaneous runs on all or many of a nation's banks. Clearly it is such a crisis, and not runs on single banks or small numbers of banks, that matters: if only a small number of banks is affected by runs, then persons running on those banks would have no reason to abandon the banking system altogether by hoarding cash. Such persons would instead merely transfer their savings (or as much of them as they have been fortunate enough to recover) to other, unaffected banks. Such limited runs, unlike a true banking crisis, do not end in a collapse of money and credit, and so are really no more important than a loss of market share by some limited group of firms in any industry.

How, then, may individual bank runs and failures be transformed into a true banking crisis? One possibility is an external shock that threatens to undermine the solvency of most or all banks simultaneously. It is difficult, though, to imagine a shock that could have such an effect on a large and heterogeneous banking system. Assuming that the banking system as a whole, if not individual banks within that system, is well diversified, it would seem that only a foreign invasion, a civil war, or some massive monetary shock not originating in the private banking system itself could have such a devastating effect. The conventional theory of crises does not, however, portray banking crises as a wartime phenomenon only or as one linked to any particular monetary policies. The theory must, therefore, rely on some mechanism other than wars and monetary policy shocks to account for "typical" crises.

It is here that the conventional view resorts to a "contagion effect" hypothesis, which holds that a run on any bank is likely to spread like an infectious disease to other banks, eventually undermining confidence in all. Why are bank runs contagious? The most popular explanation appeals to what are technically referred to as "information asymmetries" in the market for bank deposits. Although each banker knows the contents of his or her asset portfolio, most depositors do not, so they are inclined to assume that all banks are more or less alike. Because of this assumption, whenever any one bank is seen to be in difficulty, either because it has already failed or because it is being run upon by its customers, other ill-informed depositors immediately begin to worry that their own banks may also be in trouble. Rather than take a chance, and realizing that if they are to recover their deposits, they must redeem them before others have received all the cash, they run on their banks. A crisis thus ensues, with the shadow of distrust cast simultaneously upon all banks.

It is important to realize that, according to the conventional view, contagions are not extraordinary events but are likely to take place in any banking system unprotected by deposit insurance or a vigilant and dependable central bank. A presumption exists, therefore, that the authorities must guard against each and every bank failure if they are to succeed in avoiding banking crises, or must otherwise insulate the banking system from contagions by offering comprehensive insurance to depositors. Otherwise, individual bank runs or failures will occasionally lead to breakdowns of the whole system of money and credit.

SOME EVIDENCE AGAINST THE CONVENTIONAL THEORY

The conventional theory of banking crises has guided banking policy in the United States and elsewhere for many decades. It has been used to rationalize many kinds of restrictions on banking, ranging from minimum reserve and capital requirements to various interest rate and bank portfolio restrictions. It has also led to the proliferation of government-run deposit insurance schemes, despite the well-known hazards associated with them. Finally, it has helped justify the extension and consolidation of central bank powers and privileges, encouraging those few nations still lacking their own central banks to view their arrangements as inherently unsafe and economically backward.

Yet for all its wide-ranging influence, the conventional theory of banking crises appears to fail the most elementary kind of empirical test. The theory implies not only that crises are likely in any fractional-reserve banking system, but that they are especially likely in systems lacking any public lender of last resort or government deposit insurance. Readily available historical evidence, however, contradicts both claims. Tables 9.1 and 9.2, derived from the only international surveys of banking crises of which I am aware, suggest that genuine banking crises (each marked by an "x") have been rare in most well-studied fractional-reserve banking systems and entirely absent in several. Moreover, many of those systems that appear

Table 9.1 Banking panics, 1793–1933: "Unfree" banking systems

Year of panic	United States	England	France	Germany	Italy
1793	x	x	–	–	–
1799	x	x	–	–	–
1810	x	x	–	–	–
1815	x		–	–	–
1819	x		–	–	–
1825	x	x	–	–	–
1833	x		–	–	–
1837	x	x	–	–	–
1839	x		–	–	–
1847	x	x	x	–	–
1848			■	–	–
1857	x	x	x	x	–
1864			x		–
1866		x			–
1873	x			x	–
1875				■	–
1882			x[a]		–
1884					–
1889			x		–
1890					–
1891					x
1893	x				x
1894					■
1901				x	
1907	x				
1913				x	
1914	x■				x
1921					x
1930	x		x		
1931	x			x	
1933	x				

[a]Large bank failure.
Sources: Bordo, "Financial Crises," n4 below; Schuler, "World History," n6 below; and Schwartz, "Financial Stability," n4 below

Table 9.2 Banking panics, 1793–1933: "Free" banking systems

Year of panic	Canada	Scotland	Sweden	Australia	China	South Africa
1793	–		–	–	–	–
1797	–	x[a]	–	–	–	–
1810	–		–	–	–	–
1815	–		–	–	–	–
1819			–		–	–
1825			–[b]		–	–
1833					–	–[c]
1837	x[d]				–	
1839					–	
1845		■			–	
1847					–	
1857					–	
1864					–	
1866					–	
1873					–	
1882					–	
1884					–	
1889					–	
1890					–	
1891						
1893				x		
1901			■			
1907			x			
1911				■		
1914	x[c]■					
1920						x[f]■
1923	x[g]					
1930						
1931						
1933						

[a]Restriction of payments.
[b]Swedish free banking era begins.
[c]South African free banking era begins.
[d]Listed as a crisis year by Schuler, but not by Schwartz.
[e]Minor runs caused by binding capital requirements for note issuance.
[f]Inflation follows abandonment of gold standard during World War I.
[g]Major bank failure accompanied by minor runs on other banks.
Sources: Same as Table 9.1; also Lars Jonung, "The Economics of Private Money: The Experience of Private Notes in Sweden, 1831–1902," unpublished working paper, Stockholm School of Economics, 1989; and Lawrence H. White, *Free Banking in Britain: Theory, Experience and Debate, 1800–1845* (Cambridge: Cambridge University Press, 1984).

to have had few or no banking crises also lacked both deposit insurance and a lender of last resort.

I am not aware, furthermore, of any reason for suspecting that these relatively crisis-free banking systems were subject to fewer or less severe shocks than relatively crisis-prone ones. For example, it appears that in most respects Canada was just as "shocked" as the United States was by the post-1929 collapse of prices and incomes. Yet while the United States banking system soon suffered its worst banking crisis ever, Canada suffered no banking crisis – indeed, no bank failures – at all. Likewise, while the English banking system was battered by numerous shocks throughout the nineteenth century, Scottish banks seemed relatively immune. Because it can account for cross-country differences in the incidence of crises only by appealing to corresponding differences in the incidence of fundamental shocks (or perceptions of shocks), the conventional theory of crises seems hard pressed to explain the actual incidence of crises in various times and places.

Faced with this evidence of the conventional theory's failure, one cannot help wondering how it managed to become so popular in the first place. Another look at the historical incidence of banking crises suggests an explanation. As the tables show clearly, banking crises appear to have been a US specialty, with England earning second place in the banking crisis marathon. Most of our economic theories, including the conventional theory of banking crises, come from British and especially American economists, who know much more about the economic histories of their own countries than they know about experiences elsewhere. It is no wonder, therefore, that the received theory of banking crises appears, superficially at least, to fit the historical record of the United States and England, while bearing little connection to the experiences of many other nations. Even critics of the received theory have played into the hands of its proponents by relying solely on US experience to refute conventional assumptions, when evidence from other nations would make their task much easier.[3] On the other hand, the few writers who have actually surveyed international experience tend to focus too much on comparing the United States with the "United Kingdom" (meaning England) in drawing general conclusions from their surveys.[4] These writers are thus led to offer the presence of an "effective" or "dependable" public lender of last resort as the most important reason for the relative infrequency of panics in certain countries during certain periods, ignoring the more numerous cases (including those shown in Table 9.2) in which panics were avoided despite the *absence* of a public lender of last resort.

Behind our first empirical observation – that banking crises have not been equally frequent everywhere – lies another: that bank failures typically have not been contagious, or have been only mildly contagious. All banking systems have seen individual banks fail, but such failures have only rarely led to runs on most other banks. (Even in the United States, whose banking system has suffered more bank failures and experienced more crises than any other, wide-ranging bank contagions have been few and far between.)[5] This observation is supported both by direct evidence concerning the extent of bank runs and by statistics on the demand for legal tender, which should, other things being equal, increase whenever panic becomes general.

In fact, of well-studied episodes, only the US crisis of 1933 appears to have involved a truly systemwide panic. Apparently this single episode has inspired the conventional view of banking crises. Yet I shall argue later that even it does not lend any real support to conventional views concerning the nature of banking crises.

These considerations suggest that the conventional theory of banking crises is seriously inadequate. Yes, banking crises do occasionally occur, and at least one appears to have involved a nation's entire banking system. But far from being a typical or likely consequence of isolated bank failures or runs, genuine banking crises appear to be relatively unusual events, and events that are more unusual in some banking systems than in others. Clearly, there is a need for some alternative theory capable of shedding light on why banking crises have occurred in certain times and places, but not in others, despite the common ingredient of individual bank failures.

Another casual look at the evidence suggests the basic outlines of such an alternative theory by revealing, perhaps counterintuitively, that banking crises have been *more* frequent in heavily regulated banking systems than in relatively unregulated ones. Drawing on a survey by Kurt Schuler,[6] Table 9.1 lists banking systems which, throughout their histories, have been subject to at least two "major" regulatory restrictions, while Table 9.2 lists systems that were, for a time at least, characterized by no more than one major restriction. Although "free" for a while, the Table 9.2 systems were all eventually rendered unfree by additional major restrictions, usually consisting of restrictions on competitive note issuance anticipating or inaugurating the establishment of central banks.[7] Such restrictions are indicated in the table by black squares showing dates when the new restrictions were imposed. Similar squares in Table 9.1 mark dates when privileged banks of issue capable of serving as "lenders of last resort" were established in previously "unfree" (but nonetheless decentralized) banking systems. No square appears in the column for England because the Bank of England already possessed unique note issue privileges there before 1793 – the first crisis date recorded on the table.

This grouping of banking systems reveals clearly the positive connection between the extent of legal restrictions on various banking systems on one hand and the number of banking crises experienced by those systems on the other. Of forty eight recorded crises, all but seven (one of which is listed as a crisis in only one of two surveys employed) occurred in unfree systems. Furthermore, nearly half of the crises took place in systems having priviledged banks of issue that might, in principle, have served as lenders of last resort. This suggests that the presence of a public lender of last resort has, after all, been neither necessary nor sufficient to prevent the occurrence of banking crises. Of course, defenders of central banking might still insist that the presence of an "effective" or "dependable" lender of last resort is sufficient to prevent crises. Such a stance appears, however, to require an overly convenient definition of "effectiveness" or "dependability."

That is the big picture. Underlying it are smaller portraits of individual crises connecting them to particular institutional and legal circumstances. The common features present in these portraits can be summed up by observing that it is quite difficult, if not impossible, to give a coherent account of any single banking crisis anywhere without acknowledging a crucial role for some form of government interference or "legal restriction" in helping to make the crisis come about.[8]

A "LEGAL RESTRICTIONS" THEORY OF BANKING CRISES

An alternative theory of crises, based on the last observation, would hold that banking crises are not free-market phenomena, but are rather consequences of government intervention in banking and currency systems.

Many kinds of "legal restrictions" have played a role in historical banking crises, so that it is not possible to treat all crises as having identical causes: unlike the conventional theory of crises, the "legal restrictions" theory proposed here is multicausal rather than unicausal. The conventional theory's unicausal view of crises is, indeed, one of its clear weaknesses. Unicausal explanations of complex though recurrent economic events may be elegant and neat, but they are often also simplistic and wrong. While the conventional theory of banking crises accounts only for a "typical" crisis that has no historical counterpart, the legal restrictions theory is really a collection of distinct explanations for particular crises – all of which, however, share a common basis in misguided government policies.

Although one cannot construct a "general theory" of banking crises based on legal restrictions, one can present a catalogue of legal restrictions, showing how each may help bring about a banking crisis and offering illustrations from various historical episodes. I offer such a catalogue in the next chapter so I will not do more than summarize its contents here.[9] The kinds of legal restrictions that have made past banking crises possible are those that (1) have increased individual banks' exposure to shocks of various kinds; (2) have themselves been sources of important shocks; (3) have created an environment conducive to "contagion" effects, so that individual bank failures are more likely to lead to systemwide runs; and (4) have obstructed private market mechanisms for avoiding or averting crises.

1 Restrictions rendering banks more vulnerable to shocks include regulations artificially limiting banks' ability to diversify their assets and liabilities against relative price shocks. The most important examples of such restrictions are those artificially limiting the size of private

banking firms, either by restricting branching or by limiting access to capital. Direct portfolio restrictions (like those once embodied in many bank charters) also limit diversification, exposing banks to unnecessary risks. Restrictions on interest rates like those once enforced by Regulation Q have exposed banks unnecessarily to interest rate shocks.

Some legal restrictions increase individual banks' exposure to risk by actually subsidizing risky undertakings while allowing banks to reduce their own capital holdings. Examples of this include government deposit insurance and the presence of any lender of last resort willing to rescue insolvent banks.

2 Among restrictions that provide a basis for shocks that would otherwise not occur, the most important are laws supporting discretionary money-supply management by central banks. These laws – including both legal tender laws that enable the issuance of fiat money, and legal restrictions on private note issuance – are the fundamental basis for major interest rate and price-level swings which, according to Anna Schwartz,[10] have been the root causes of both past and recent waves of financial firm insolvencies.

3 Restrictions have also made contagion effects more likely. As noted previously, contagion effects have been the exception rather than the rule in economic history. That in itself contradicts the conventional theory of banking crises. But there is more: where contagions have taken hold in the past, they too have been encouraged by government interference. For example, government-erected barriers to branch banking in the United States have sponsored the artificial growth of correspondent relationships among banks, making confidence in banks a function of confidence in their correspondents. Another, more widely practiced form of legal interference – interference with private note issuance – has obstructed an important "secondary" market for bank liabilities. This market might otherwise have served to price bank-specific risks efficiently, eliminating information asymmetries. Other forms of interference, including bank holidays and manipulations of the monetary standard, have also helped produce contagions of panic, as will be seen below in reviewing the crisis of 1933.

4 Perhaps the worst way in which governments have helped expose banking systems to crises has been by interfering with banks' own devices for avoiding or otherwise dealing with such crises. By restricting private note issuance, governments have made it impossible for private banks to accommodate even routine changes in the demand for currency.[11] Governments have also prevented banks from undertaking "restrictions" of payments as a private means for coping with major shocks.[12] Finally, governments have artificially encouraged reliance on central bank lending in place of private interbank lending: all too often, central banks have functioned, not as lenders of last resort, but as lenders of *first* resort.

This makes them appear more essential in rescuing illiquid but solvent banks than they really are. Central bankers are loath to pass up any opportunity to present themselves as white knights coming to the rescue of an illiquid private bank – the damsel in distress.

Of course, branching restrictions and other devices that discourage the development of large, private banks also undermine opportunities for private assistance, for the simple reason that it is much more difficult for a clearinghouse or other private bankers' "club" to put together a large emergency loan package that relies on many small banks than it is to put together a similar package involving fewer, large banks. Restrictions on mergers, finally, rule out other potential private rescue efforts, and thereby increase the likelihood of depositors suffering losses and staging runs.

THE ROLE OF CURRENCY MONOPOLY

One legal restriction seldom discussed in the literature – the inability of private banks to issue their own notes – enhances the likelihood of banking crises in at least three important ways. First, it prevents banks from relying on their own resources to accommodate routine changes in the public's demand for currency. Second, it eliminates the secondary note market that could otherwise do away with information asymmetries in the market for bank money. Finally, monopolization of the supply of currency has been the basis for central banks' discretionary control of the stock of bank reserves. Through such control, central banks have been able to expand their own balance sheets recklessly, causing otherwise impossible gyrations in the price level, interest rates, and exchange rates – the most severe shocks to which private banks have ever been subjected.

That currency monopoly is the basis for central banks' discretionary manipulations of the money stock is, I trust, obvious enough: as long as all banks have equal rights to issue notes, none ever thinks of holding a rival's notes as reserves. Instead, rivals' notes are actively returned for redemption in some basic money. Historically, this was gold.

The awarding of monopoly privileges in note issuance changes all this. Suddenly one bank becomes the system's sole source of convenient paper currency. Other banks begin to covet its notes, which (being, at first, still redeemed in gold) are in widespread demand. Soon these notes are being treated as a reserve in place of gold – which is, in turn, placed on deposit with the privileged bank. At this point the privileged bank no longer has to worry about its own issues being redeemable by rivals. Its sole concern becomes the balance of international gold payments, which eventually turns against it if it expands too much, as it is inevitably tempted to do. (Under free banking, in contrast, it is simply not possible to have a balance of payments crisis initiated by excessive domestic money creation.) But there is a way around the balance of payments constraint that limits even monopoly bank expansion under a gold standard: the suspension of gold payments. What no bank would have dared to do in a system in which all banks enjoyed equal rights is now done with impunity by the privileged bank of issue, thereby making its notes a fiat money, first temporarily, then for good.

The establishment of fiat money, in turn, means unlimited scope for a privileged bank to further abuse its powers in pursuit of narrow political and financial ends. Such was, broadly speaking, the history of the growth of central banks and fiat money throughout much of the world during the present century. This history has set the stage for price level, interest rate, and exchange rate movements such as were never seen under the gold standard. These fluctuations have spelled doom to thousands of private banks. The link between central banking and the abandonment of commodity money is particularly worth stressing, because so many past economists wrongly perceived central banks as devices for securing monetary stability. The evidence presented here suggests, on the contrary, that central banking is incompatible with monetary stability. Free banking grounded in strict rules of contract and bankruptcy law would have provided a much stronger bulwark against the flood of paper money.

One lesson in this is, to use the language of game theory, that the central banking "game" does not have a positive sum: the unique powers enjoyed by central banks have not been costlessly acquired. They are, rather, powers that would, under free-market circumstances, have been more widely shared among all private banks. The consequence of regulations concentrating these powers in a single, government-favored bank has been to make other banks weaklings dependent on central banks for their protection. Today, unfortunately, few observers (banking experts included) appreciate how the rise of central banking has served to weaken private banks.

THE BANKING CRISIS OF 1933

It is of course impossible, within the confines of a short essay, to offer a "legal restrictions" theory of every historical banking crisis, or even of the forty one crises listed in Table 9.1. I will attempt, however, to apply the theory to one important banking crisis, namely the US crisis of 1933. That crisis is particularly important because, of all crises, it best appears to fit the conventional view. That is not surprising as the conventional view was, to a large extent, shaped by the events of 1933.

The basic features of the crisis, consistent with the conventional view, were as follows. Large numbers of bank failures in the early 1930s triggered massive withdrawals of currency from the banking system which, in turn, led to the system's failure in March 1933. That failure might have been avoided had the Fed played the part of lender of last resort, either in the traditional manner (by making loans to solvent though illiquid banks), or by otherwise expanding the monetary base to compensate for changes in the currency–deposit ratio.

Whereas the conventional view blames government for failing to respond appropriately to the crisis, treating the crisis itself as originating in market conditions, the legal restrictions approach identifies a more fundamental role of government interference. To begin, consider the large numbers of bank failures preceding the systemwide failure of March 1933. Although bank failures accelerated in the early 1930s, they had been common during the 1920s, when nearly 6,000 US banks failed. Most of the failures, both then and throughout the first two years of the Great Depression, were of small-unit banks in agricultural regions. These banks suffered from a decline in the relative price of agricultural products that predated the crash. Had the United States enjoyed nationwide branch banking, it might have avoided many or most of these relative-price-induced bank failures. Canada, which had branch banking, did avoid bank failures both before and after 1929, except for a single failure in 1923 involving fraud.

US bank failures rose after 1929 in part because of an increase in the public's desired currency–deposit ratio, which tends to move inversely with changes in real income.[13] Had US banks been free to issue their own notes, as Canadian banks still could, they might have accommodated much of this initial increase in the currency ratio by issuing more of their own notes in exchange for deposits. Indeed, national banks did manage to increase their note issues, from $691 million in February 1932 to $922 million in May 1933, thanks to a minor relaxation in otherwise binding note issuance restrictions.[14] This increase was, however, only a fraction of what was needed to accommodate the wants of the public. The remaining adjustment had to be provided through greater issues of Federal Reserve Notes and clearinghouse certificates and, in the absence of either, by means of a depletion of bank reserves.

Clearinghouse authorities in New York and elsewhere sought the Treasury's permission to issue clearinghouse certificates as substitutes for bank notes, as they had done during earlier crises. But they were refused permission on the grounds that such a private response was no longer needed: the Fed was capable of issuing "plenty of money that looks like real money."[15] In the event, of course, the Fed's response proved far from adequate.

Despite large numbers of bank failures, and legal restrictions precluding a secondary market in banknotes, bank runs prior to 1933 appear to have been confined to banks that either were insolvent before the runs or, owing to branching restrictions, were correspondents of insolvent banks. Even the dramatic run against the Bank of United States in December 1930 was not contagious.[16] Widespread panic did not become a feature of the US banking crisis until February 1933, when it was provoked by two ill-conceived government policies. These policies were the state-declared bank holidays, commencing with Michigan's on February 14; and the federal government's plan to devalue the dollar, which became a subject of widespread rumors around the same time.

Bank holidays became a potent cause of contagion effects by encouraging currency withdrawals by depositors in nearby states, who feared the holidays themselves might spread. Holidays therefore exacerbated the very problem of bank runs they were intended to forestall.[17] Bank holidays were also unnecessary: as bankers urged at the time, mere "restrictions" of payments of reserve money, such as were undertaken during previous panics in 1893 and 1907, could have served the purpose of protecting banks' liquidity without closing the banks and thereby entirely depriving depositors and borrowers of access to funds.[18]

Rumors that gold would be devalued led to a run on the dollar, the burden of which was felt mainly by the Federal Reserve Bank of New York. According to Barry Wigmore, it was the Federal Reserve, rather than commercial banks, that needed and pleaded for a bank holiday, which was finally declared by New York's Governor Lehrman on March 4, precipitating the national bank holiday on March 6. Gold was, in fact, devalued soon afterwards. Although by the time of its accomplishment this devaluation may have appeared necessary as a means for restoring monetary stability, devaluation was certainly *not* necessary earlier in the year, when it was first proposed as a means of supporting the prices of farm commodities to placate the farm lobby.[19]

Other federal policies, including increased postal rates and a two-cent tax on checks, both adopted in mid-1932, also contributed to the banking crisis by encouraging public withdrawals of currency from the banking system. Such errors of commission, rather than the Federal Reserve's equally destructive errors of omission, warrant calling the crisis of 1933 a product of legal restrictions rather than a free-market phenomenon. This seems to be the case with banking crises in general.

NOTES AND REFERENCES

1 Henry C. Simons, *Economic Policy for a Free Society* (Chicago: University of Chicago Press, 1948); Lloyd W. Mints, *Monetary Policy for a Competitive Society* (New York: McGraw-Hill, 1950).
2 Several recent studies favor the real-shock or information-based view of crises over the "bubble" alternative. See, for example, Frederic S. Mishkin, "Asymmetric Information and Financial Crises: A Historical Perspective," in R. Glen Hubbard, ed., *Financial Markets and Financial Crises* (Chicago: University of Chicago Press, 1991), 69–108; and Charles W. Calomiris and Gary Gorton, "The Origins of Banking Panics: Models, Facts, and Bank Regulation," in ibid., 109–73.

3 See, for example, George Kaufman, "Bank Contagion: A Review of the Theory and Evidence," *Journal of Financial Services Research*, 8, no. 2 (April 1994): 123–50.

4 See Michael D. Bordo, "Financial Crises, Banking Crises, Stock Market Crashes and the Money Supply: Some International Evidence, 1870–1933," in Forrest Capie and Geoffrey E. Wood, eds., *Financial Crises and the World Banking System* (London: Macmillan, 1986), 190–248; and Anna J. Schwartz, "Financial Stability and the Federal Safety Net," in William S. Haraf and Rose Marie Kushmeider, eds., *Restructuring Banking and Financial Services in America* (Washington, DC: American Enterprise Institute, 1988), 34–62.

5 Kaufman, n3 above.

6 Kurt Schuler, "The World History of Free Banking: An Overview," in Kevin Dowd, ed., *The Experience of Free Banking* (London: Routledge, 1992), 7–47.

7 In most cases the major change marking the transition from free to unfree banking was the establishment of a central bank enjoying exclusive note issue privileges.

8 This conclusion relies on readily available secondary accounts of the incidence of banking crises. Regrettably the extent of such evidence, especially for "free" banking systems, is quite limited. Ideally, one would want to have detailed survey evidence from a larger sample of both free and unfree systems. The conclusions reached here are, therefore, tentative ones. They do, nonetheless, at least attempt to come to grips with the evidence already at hand.

9 See also George Benston, "Does Bank Regulation Produce Stability? Lessons for the United States," in Forrest Capie and Geoffrey E. Woods, eds., *Unregulated Banking: Chaos or Order?* (London: Macmillan, 1991), 207–32.

10 Schwartz, n4 above.

11 George Selgin, "Accommodating Changes in the Relative Demand for Currency: Free Banking vs. Central Banking," *Cato Journal* 6, no. 2 (Fall 1986): 617–34.

12 Hugh Rockoff, "Institutional Requirement for Stable Free Banking," *Cato Journal* 6, no. 2 (Fall 1986): 617–34.

13 Phillip Cagan, "The Demand for Currency Relative to Total Money Supply," *Journal of Political Economy* 66, no. 1 (August 1958): 303–28.

14 Benjamin Anderson, *Economics and the Public Welfare* (Indianapolis: Liberty Press, 1979), 289.

15 Helen M. Burns, *The American Banking Community and New Deal Banking Reforms, 1933–1935* (Westport, CT: Greenwood, 1974), 75.

16 Elmus Wicker, "A Reconsideration of the Banking Panic of 1930," *Journal of Economic History* 40, no. 3 (September 1980): 571–83.

17 George Benston et al., *Perspectives on Safe and Sound Banking* (Cambridge, MA: MIT Press, 1986), 52; E. C. Colt and N. S. Keith, *28 Days: A History of the Banking Crisis* (New York: Greenburg, 1933). Nevada was actually the first state to declare a banking holiday, in November 1932.

18 Gerald P. Dwyer, Jr. and R. Anton Gilbert, "Bank Runs and Private Remedies," *Reserve Bank of St. Louis Review* 71, no. 93 (May/June 1989): 43–61; see also Rockoff, n2 above. The success of restriction would have depended on banks' (or clearinghouses') ability to issue notes (or clearinghouse certificates) as substitutes for legal tender currency and bond-based national banknotes. As noted, the federal government refused to give banks or clearinghouses permission to issue such substitute currencies.

19 Barry A. Wigmore, "Was the Bank Holiday of 1933 Caused by a Run on the Dollar?," *Journal of Economic History* 47, no. 3 (September 1987): 739–55.

10

LEGAL RESTRICTIONS, FINANCIAL WEAKENING, AND THE LENDER OF LAST RESORT*

It is not unlikely that the bolstering up of banking systems by their Governments is a factor which makes for instability.

Vera Smith (1936, p. 5)

INTRODUCTION

A popular defense of central banks and fiat money claims that they are needed to protect the payments system against the peril of financial crises. A central bank can act as a "lender of last resort" to other banks, assuring depositors that they need never fear a general banking collapse; fiat money in turn guarantees that the lender of last resort itself will never go broke.[1]

A crucial assumption behind the lender of last resort argument is that fractional-reserve banking is inherently "fragile" and crisis prone – that central banking and fiat money are an unavoidable response to market failure. According to Minsky (1982, p. 17), "conditions conducive to financial crises emerge from the normal functioning of a capitalist economy." In a free market, says Minsky, such conditions will occasionally produce "wide and spreading bankruptcies" that could, however, be prevented by "an alert lender of last resort" (p. 13).[2]

In this chapter I take issue with the lender of last resort argument by showing that its underlying assumption is false: fractional-reserve banking systems are *not* inherently weak or unstable. They are weak and unstable because legal restrictions have made them that way. The collapse of a fully deregulated banking system would be highly improbable if not impossible. It follows that central banks and fiat money are at most "second best" solutions to problems peculiar to regulated banking.

The chapter proceeds in two parts. The first concerns the role of more familiar legal restrictions in fostering financial fragility and crises. It focuses especially on banking problems in the United States. The second

*Reprinted, with permission, from the *Cato Journal*, Vol. 9, No. 2 (Fall 1989).

shows how restrictions on private *currency* issue in particular have historically been an especially significant cause of financial weakening; its focus is more on developments in Great Britain. Because central banking presupposes a monopoly in currency supply, the existence of central banks itself turns out to be a crucial cause of financial crises.

A "FINANCIAL WEAKENING" HYPOTHESIS

Why should banks, unlike other profit-maximizing firms, evolve in a manner that exposes them lemming-like to periodic waves of bankruptcy? I believe the answer is that they do not evolve that way at all but have been weakened by legal restrictions ultimately aimed at generating revenue for the government or at propping up special interests within the banking industry. In the United States the adverse effects of particular restrictions are well understood. What is not appreciated is how their cumulative effects have led to the present reliance upon a lender of last resort.

Were an evil dictator to set out purposefully to weaken a fractional-reserve banking system and to increase its dependence upon a lender of last resort, that dictator would (1) increase the risk exposure of individual banks to enhance their prospects of insolvency; (2) create an environment conducive to "spillover" or "contagion" effects, so that individual bank failures can lead to systemwide runs; and (3) obstruct private-market mechanisms for averting crises. Banking regulations in the United States and elsewhere have unintentionally done all three things. All that can be said in these regulations' favor is that some help to mitigate the unfortunate consequences of others.

Individual bank insolvency

Anti-branching laws

Legal restrictions subject individual banks to a higher risk of becoming insolvent by reducing their opportunities to avoid risk and by actually subsidizing bank risk taking. Of restrictions having the first effect, by far the most destructive have been laws against branch banking. Such laws account for the fact that the United States has more than 14,000 banks and more than 3,000 "thrift" institutions, most of which are small and localized. According to Mullineaux (1987, p. 77), even the largest US banks "are not large in relation to the size and wealth of the population," and only one of them is among the world's top ten. The smallness and lack of diversification of so many US depository institutions has made them chronically failure-prone: unit banks in the farm belt have been overexposed to farming losses, and Texas and Oklahoma banks have suffered from their involvement in oil-industry loans and in local real-estate development. In the Northwest, banks have relied excessively upon loans to the timber industry. Such overexposure of loan portfolios reflects the fact that banks' lending opportunities are to a large extent bound by their location. Even larger money-center banks have been adversely affected by anti-branching statutes, which by restricting their domestic business opportunities

> have encouraged them to be outward-looking. Because of their size and their presence in the major money centers they were well placed to help in the recycling of the OPEC surpluses, especially as Latin America developed a voracious appetite for funds. Many of them consequently developed an exposure to Latin America that far exceeded their capital bases.
>
> (Mullineaux 1987, p. 41)

As White observes (1986, pp. 895–6), restrictions against branch banking increase a bank's exposure to liability-related as well as asset-related risks. Branched banks typically rely upon a broad cushion of retail deposits gathered by local offices as their principal source of funds. Unexpected withdrawals at some branches can often be compensated for by a transfer of reserves from others. In contrast, unit banks, particular in large money centers, have relied heavily in recent years upon "liability management," attracting wholesale deposits as an alternative means for persons far removed from the money centers to take advantage of better investment opportunities there. The danger of this approach is that, in contrast to retail deposits, wholesale deposits are much more likely to be withdrawn in response to adverse rumors, not just because their size often makes them ineligible for insurance, but because their owners are less able to verify the truth of a rumor and are less bound by considerations of conveniences than retail depositors are to remain loyal to any particular bank. The dramatic collapse of Continental Illinois was to a large extent due to its heavy reliance upon liability management – a by-product of Illinois' strict anti-branching laws – though Continental would no doubt have become insolvent anyway as a result of its unwise and excessive energy loans.

No episode illustrates more dramatically the weakening effect of anti-branching laws than the Great Depression. Between 1931 and 1933 several thousand US banks – mostly small unit banks – failed. In contrast Canada's branch-banking network did not suffer a single bank failure even though in other respects Canada was just as hard hit by the depression – it could hardly have escaped all of the adverse effects on Canadian business of a 33 per cent fall in the US money supply. (The Canadian money supply fell by about 13 per cent.) Ironically the United States at the time *did* have a lender of last resort, whereas Canada did not.[3]

This comparison of US and Canadian experience has by now been made so often that it is in danger of becoming a cliché. Yet the comparison bears repeating because it suggests that branch banking alone would go far in rendering the US banking system immune to financial crises.[4] As branching laws are liberalized the US banking system will be progressively strengthened, and its reliance upon a lender of last resort will be correspondingly reduced.

A defense of restrictions on branching is that they prevent the banking industry from becoming overly concentrated and uncompetitive. This view misconstrues both the likely effects of full interstate branching and the meaning of competition. In O'Driscoll's estimate (1988, p. 673) without branching restrictions the United States might still have more than 4,000 independent banking firms. But even 400 banks with far-reaching branch networks would be a more than adequate guarantee against collusive behavior. More importantly, branch banks could really compete with one another by freely entering any locality. In contrast the present system is one of numerous, local monopolies. Competition is not just a matter of numbers.

In addition to exposing banks to risk, anti-branching restrictions have weakened them in other, less direct ways. During the nineteenth century they encouraged the growth and "tiering" or "pyramiding" of interbank deposits, with country banks remitting surplus funds to a dozen or more "reserve city" banks, and the latter sending funds to banks in New York City (Smith 1936, pp. 138–40). By this process the same dollar of high-powered money could be reckoned as part of several banks' reserves – a practice formally sanctioned by national banking law. This – along with legal restrictions on note issue – contributed greatly to the severity of the great money panics of 1873, 1884, 1893, and 1907 by causing illiquidity in any part of the country to have adverse repercussions everywhere else. Anti-branching laws have also stood in the way of bank mergers and acquisitions – the least disruptive way of dealing with troubled banks. Finally, anti-branching laws have indirectly weakened the financial system by providing a rationale for other legal restrictions – patchwork remedies that the supervisory authorities have embraced as a substitute for needed structural reform, but that have ultimately served to further weaken the banking system.

Activity restrictions

Just as anti-branching laws have subjected banks to increased risks by limiting their geographical diversification, other legal restrictions have done the same by limiting activity diversification. Laws like the Glass–Steagall Act of 1933 – designed to prevent banks from holding high-risk, high-return assets – actually serve (in an otherwise deregulated setting) to *increase* the probability of bank failures.[5] As Blair and Heggestad explain

(1978, p. 92), even the taking on of intrinsically riskier assets by a bank reduces the overall variance of returns on the bank's portfolio if fluctuations in the earnings of the riskier assets are negatively correlated to fluctuations in the earnings of the less-risky assets. Empirical evidence suggests that this has indeed been the case in recent years (Litan 1987, pp. 84–96). It appears to have been true, moreover, between 1930 and 1933. As Shughart (1988, pp. 600–2) relates, despite all the rhetoric used to justify Glass–Steagall "securities affiliates were identified as a proximate cause of failure only in the case of the Bank of United States," which was also guilty of fraud; in general "the presence of an affiliate appears to have reduced the probability of bank failure." The real motive behind Glass–Steagall, according to Shughart, was not to increase bank safety but rather to shield both banks and investment companies from the rigors of competition.

Other legal restrictions have increased the riskiness of bank portfolios, not by restricting the investments banks can engage in, but by actually *requiring* them to make potentially risky investments. A relatively recent instance of this is the Community Reinvestment Act of 1977. Before the Civil War, so-called "free banking" laws in numerous states forced banks to invest in state and local bonds as collateral for their note issues; in several states the required bonds proved to be very poor investments, becoming the major cause of free bank failures (Rolnick and Weber 1984). Nor have banks been the only financial institutions to suffer from such requirements: prior to 1981 most thrifts were restricted to mortgage lending, which overexposed them to declining real-estate prices.

One especially desirable activity banks might undertake in the absence of Glass–Steagall-type restrictions would be to compete with investment companies in offering checkable mutual fund accounts. As Goodhart (1987) explains, because the nominal value of mutual funds varies with the value of their underlying assets, they are (unlike bank deposit accounts) invulnerable to runs. Moreover, bank mutual fund accounts could offer distinct advantages over similar accounts offered by other firms, because bank customers could conveniently make transfers to and from their mutual fund accounts to other accounts offering different advantages (e.g., absence of minimum balance or minimum check-size requirements). Finally, were mutual fund accounts to displace deposits to any substantial degree, the burden borne by deposit-insurance schemes would be proportionately lightened, and the prospects for reforming deposit insurance – by replacing it with private insurance or by repealing it altogether – would be greatly improved.

Deposit-rate ceilings

Still other legal restrictions that have served to weaken banks and to create an artificial need for a lender of last resort are restrictions on deposit and loan rates of interest. Deposit-rate ceilings, also introduced by the Banking Act of 1933 (and extended by the Banking Act of 1935) were ostensibly aimed at guarding against banks bidding for customers by offering high rates on deposits, offsetting the higher cost of funds by engaging in unsafe investments with high-gross yields. But studies in recent decades, summarized in Mingo (1981), have challenged this rationale by showing a lack of evidence of any correlation between rates paid on deposits and the quality of a bank's assets. Furthermore if a correlation did exist, it could be because high-yielding assets lead to high deposit rates (as standard economic analysis would suggest) rather than the other way around. A more likely reason for imposing rate ceilings on banks was to preserve the market position of "thrifts," which had evolved to specialize in home finance – a market position that was itself a result of prior restrictions on mortgage lending by national banks (removed in 1914 by the Federal Reserve Act). Rate ceilings also served to prop up banks with a lucrative price-fixing scheme.

Rather than reduce banks' likelihood of failure, deposit-rate ceilings have tended to have just the opposite effect by limiting their ability to bid for funds when threatened by a disintermediation or other liquidity crisis. This was dramatically evident in the 1960s, when banks and later thrifts were racked by a series of disintermediation crises. The trouble started in October 1959, when (as a result of slowly mounting inflation) Treasury bill rates rose to 5 per cent – well above the 3 per cent Regulation Q limits on time deposits. Banks then faced a disintermediation crisis that was a portent of further troubles to come. As inflation and short-term money rates continued to rise (in part as a result of the escalating costs of the Vietnam War), the Fed found it necessary to allow one-step increases in rate ceilings on CDs for every year from 1962 to 1965 to avoid a recurrence of the 1959 crisis. This policy left the thrifts stranded, however, their own rates being fixed at 4 per cent (Wojnilower 1980, pp. 286–7). At last, to protect the thrifts, the Fed in 1966 refused to lift bank deposit-rate ceilings again, while simultaneously putting the brakes on monetary expansion. The result was an even more severe bank "credit crunch." Finally in August the Fed reversed its monetary policy again, this time to "rescue" the banks *from its own misguided policies.*

The banking crisis of 1966 – the first "financial crisis" (to adopt the conventional, hyperbolic vernacular) in the United States since the Great Depression – was a direct consequence of Regulation Q restrictions combined with erratic Fed monetary policy. This was also true of later disintermediation crises, including the thrift crisis of 1969. If rate restrictions had been absent then as they are today, these crises would not have happened and there would not have been any need for "last resort" lending by the Fed.

Deposit insurance

The absence of crises is, however, not necesarily evidence of a strong banking system: weak and even insolvent banks (and thrifts) can also be propped up by subsidies, which tend to encourage them to take on added risks causing them, more often than not, to become even weaker and more insolvent. Deposit insurance and central bank loans have increasingly had these effects in recent years, particularly in the thrift industry where hundreds of bankrupt "zombie institutions" have been kept afloat at tax-payers' expense instead of being allowed to succumb to the Darwinian forces of the market. (Thrifts received their first direct Federal Reserve support on February 23rd, 1989.)

The ill-effects of government deposit insurance are, as is well known, due to its lack of risk-adjusted premiums. This leads to moral hazard whereby the insured firms pursue risks that they would not pursue in an uninsured state.[6] Depositors, in turn, no longer feel any need to be concerned about the safety of particular depository institutions, and are tempted to supply funds to wherever rates are highest. According to McCulloch (1986, p. 82), thanks to federal deposit insurance

> banks and thrifts have engaged with impunity in all manner of excessive risks – foreign exchange speculation (Franklin National), speculative energy loans (Penn Square), inadequately investigated loans (Continental Illinois), insider loans (the Butcher banks), uncollectable Third World loans (almost every top ten bank) and so forth.

According to Short and Gunther (1988) the present weakness of Texas banks and thrifts is a result, not just of unit banking, but also of "policies that have removed incentives for depositors to reallocate their funds." Encouraged by the FDIC's decision to insure even large deposits at First City Bankcorp and at the First Republic Bank Corporation, depositors actually shifted funds into those troubled firms and out of stronger banks and thrifts. In the same way insurance has been helping bad banks to drive out good banks throughout the United States. As long as such subsidies continued (together with mergers) to provide *de facto* full coverage, the effects of this progressive financial weakening were not apparent; but with mounting bank and thrift losses, with insurance funds themselves facing bankruptcy, and with mergers subject to increased scrutiny, the cat has been let out of the bag. The present thrift and LDC-debt crises are poignant proof of this weakening. According to Kane (1985, pp. 120–1) the latter crisis is fundamentally due to "the turning on and off of deposit insurance subsidies." To the extent that the Fed is called upon to resolve these crises by acting as a lender of last resort, it will be addressing, not market failure, but the failure of legal restrictions on banks and thrifts including restrictions it itself has imposed.

The present deposit-insurance crisis suggests that the argument, popularized by Friedman (1960, pp. 37–8), that deposit insurance makes a lender of last resort unnecessary can be the opposite of the truth. For as long as insurance is underpriced, it makes depository institutions more rather than less failure-prone. As failures increase, the insurance funds themselves are threatened by bankruptcy. A lender of last resort is then needed to bail out the funds directly or to bail out and subsidize mergers of insolvent banks. Not to do so could lead to panic, as many depositors have no reason to trust their banks apart from the guarantees that insurance provides. The 1985 Ohio and Maryland S&L crisis bears this out quite clearly.

The lender of last resort itself

By the same token, though, the Fed is also one of its own worst enemies (I am tempted to say one of its own best excuses), because it also encourages banks to take on excessive risks, leading to trouble. That lenders of last resort can also be a source of moral hazard is, of course, recognized even by their most ardent supporters (e.g., Kindleberger 1984, p. 280). According to Garcia and Plautz (1988, p. 112),

> Lender-of-last-resort assistance can be viewed as a form of subsidized government intervention. If potential recipients interpret such assistance to mean that the central bank would step in to bail out any institution in difficulty, the available assistance could encourage (even subsidize) additional risk-taking among institutions with lender-of-last-resort access.

This problem, which has been called "The Bagehot Problem" (after Walter Bagehot, who drew attention to it in *Lombard Street*) would be avoided if the lender of last resort followed Bagehot's advice – in offering support only to solvent institutions at penalty rates. But Bagehot's advice is violated by most central banks in practice, as the rescue of Franklin National glaringly demonstrated (see Garcia and Plautz 1988, pp. 217–28).

The "contagion effect" myth

The preceding review suggests that legal restrictions have played a role in many, though by no means all, bank failures. Obviously failures – including failures due to outright fraud – would also occur under *laissez-faire*. Such failures should not have to be regretted, though. On the contrary, in banking as in other industries, failures are needed to discipline and weed out bad managers; furthermore, if they lead to takeovers (or if banks are well capitalized), *isolated* failures need not cause bank customers to suffer large losses. The great fear of failure that affects regulatory authorities today reflects the widespread belief that failures, instead of being limited to poorly managed banks, will have undesirable "third-party" effects, causing panic to spread indiscriminately to other banks in the system.

Indeed, a lender of last resort is needed only when such "contagion, spillover, or domino effects" threaten "the stability of the entire monetary system" (Humphrey and Keleher 1984, p. 278), for otherwise runs and failures at one or several depository institutions would result in a transfer of funds to others, strengthening rather than weakening the latter. Only if panic becomes general – if depositors lose confidence in the entire banking *system* – will depositors switch to holding high-powered money, weakening all depository institutions in the process.[7] Thus a crucial (though often implicit) assumption in the pro-lender-of-last-resort literature is, to quote Solow (1982, p. 238), that "any bank failure diminishes confidence in the whole system," leaving no private banks in a position to stem a panic.

This is a very strong assumption, especially in view of the paucity of support one finds for it in history. In US experience Rolnick and Weber (1986) found no evidence of any contagion effects from bank runs during the "free banking" era (1837–60). Reviewing the national banking era (1863–1913), Kaufman (1988, p. 16) found only limited evidence of contagions in the panics of 1878, 1893, and 1907; and the evidence is weak except for 1893. Even during the "Great Contraction" of 1930–3 – the episode from which contemporary authorities still seem to draw all of their conclusions – contagion effects appear to have been limited regionally until late 1932; prior to 1932, moreover, runs were confined for the most part to banks suffering from prerun insolvency or to banks affiliated with insolvent firms (Wicker 1980). Even the failure of the Bank of United States in December 1930 did not provoke any panic runs in New York City, according to Wicker (p. 580). Finally, in their study of more recent experience, Aharony and Swary (1983) found no evidence of any contagion effect (measured by a fall in bank stock prices) following the failures of the United States National Bank of San Diego or the Hamilton National Bank of Chattanooga; they did find evidence of a very limited contagion (involving banks known to be heavily involved in the foreign-exchange market) stemming from the failure of Franklin National. Their overall conclusion (p. 321) was that the "failure of a dishonestly run banking institution, even a large one, need not cause panic and loss of public confidence in the integrity of the banking system as a whole."[8]

Still more recently the failure of Continental Illinois in 1984 also led to a slight and short-lived stock-price contagion; but it (like all previous, recent failures of large banks) did not lead to any net withdrawal of high-powered money by noninsured depositors (Benston et al. 1986, p. 66). The run on Home State Savings and Loan in Ohio in 1985 did involve some withdrawals of currency and did spread to other Ohio S&Ls covered by the same insurance scheme (as well as to privately insured S&Ls there and in

Maryland); however, it also did not involve any general panic but only a limited panic based upon depositors' (justified) concern over the condition of their accounts' insurers together with uncertainty as to the Fed's likely response.

In Canada also, bank runs usually do not seem to have been contagious. According to Schuler (1988, pp. 37, 54), the only exceptions have been the panic on Prince Edward Island in 1881, which spread from the insolvent Bank of Prince Edward Island to other local banks owed money by it, and runs in 1985 on several small western banks following the failures of the Canadian Commercial and Northland banks.[9] In neither incident did runs affect any of Canada's nationwide banks. "[I]mmunity to runs," Schuler concludes, "apparently depends greatly on bank size."

All of this evidence adds up to one crucial fact: that the public generally knows more about the state of the banking system than the supervisory authorities give it credit for knowing. When certain banks or groups of banks get into trouble (or are suspected with good reason of being in trouble), depositors transfer funds from those banks into other, safer banks. They do not lose confidence in the banking system as a whole. This suggests that last resort assistance by a central bank, particularly to institutions suffering from pre-run insolvency, is unnecessary except on *very* rare occasions.

What about those "rare occasions"? Don't they supply a sufficient rationale for having a lender of last resort? The answer depends on what *causes* have given rise to contagion effects. One possible (and popular) explanation can be readily dismissed: this is the "random" or "bubble" theory of panics as entertained by Kindleberger (1978), Bryant (1981), Diamond and Dybvig (1983), Waldo (1985), and many others. According to this theory, panics need not be based upon any real shock with preditable, adverse effects on bank earnings, but may occur even in response to intrinsically irrelevant events, such as sunspots. All of the evidence reviewed above, as well as the findings of Gorton (1986), dispute this view, supporting instead the alternative hypothesis that panics are based on prior, real shocks with predictable adverse repercussions on bank earnings.

Under what circumstances, then, might such shocks expose an entire banking system to contagious runs, as they seem to have done in 1933 and (perhaps) in previous crises? One possible circumstance is when banks are involved in one another's assets through correspondent relationships. As Garcia and Plautz (1988, p. 19) point out, the failure of a correspondent "can bring down a chain of its respondent banks." This was one justification given by the Fed for rescuing Continental Illinois. But the depth and breadth of correspondent relationships in US banking is itself, as was explained earlier, a consequence of unit banking, which should become less and less important as branching restrictions are lifted. Even as matters stand, moreover, correspondent relationships are hardly extensive enough to be likely to cause a flight to currency.

Another cause of contagion effects – one that also played a crucial role in the 1933 panic – is resort to bank holidays. As Benston et al. explain (1986, p. 52), fears of widespread panic that inspire government officials to declare a bank holiday can easily become a "self-fulfilling prophesy": a holiday freezes up part of the money supply, reducing incomes generally and encouraging withdrawals by clients of otherwise solvent banks that fear the holiday will spread. In this way Nevada's bank holiday in October 1932 had its own "domino effect," culminating (with the help of depositors' apprehensions concerning FDR's fidelity to the gold standard) in the national bank holiday in March 1933. In the same way, Maryland depositors were inspired to run on their S&Ls in part because they feared Maryland would follow Ohio's example by declaring a holiday.

Resort to bank holidays is particularly unfortunate in that it is a substitute for a more effective but less dangerous alternative. This is a "restriction" or "suspension" of high-powered money payments of the kind resorted to by private banks (with the government's acquiescence) in the pre-Federal Reserve era, and that Herbert Hoover was prevented from implementing in February 1933 owing to Roosevelt's refusal to cooperate. Because a restriction allows banks to remain open to conduct lending operations and also to receive deposits and settle accounts with one another (or even, perhaps, with banks not affected by the restriction), it constitutes less of a "freeze" on the money supply and hence less of a reason for depositors at other banks to panic. Later I will argue that such suspensions are also consistent with maximizing banks' earnings and consumers' utility, so that they could play a role even in a fully deregulated banking system.

A third likely cause of a banking contagion is a macroeconomic shock so severe as to place all or most banks in danger of insolvency despite their best efforts to diversify. All that needs to be said about this is that its most likely cause would be irresponsible behavior by a central bank.[10] Thus it hardly constitutes a good reason for giving central banks extra leeway (including the right to issue inconvertible money) to allow them to serve as lenders of last resort.

A final and most important potential cause of contagion effects in response to real shocks is an "information externality." Such an externality may be present whenever bank depositors are unable to inform themselves of the riskiness of their own banks, and so are forced to generalize from the troubles experienced by others. To the extent that such externalities are present, the evidence reviewed above suggests that their effects are limited. Depositors do seem to know *something* about their banks, so that, at worst, trouble spreads from insolvent banks to others that are, if not insolvent themselves, in some nontrivial way "similar" to the insolvent banks.

Moreover, it will be argued below that information externalities are themselves yet another by-product of legal restrictions, which would be absent (or much less severe) under *laissez-faire.*

Market support mechanisms

Private last resort lending

Another implicit assumption in the lender of last resort literature is that, if a central bank does not avert a financial crisis, private agents will not, either: the rendering of aid to troubled banks to avoid a systemic banking collapse is regarded as a "public good" (e.g., Solow 1982, p. 241ff.). Here again the assumption has little foundation in fact: although bank runs and failures may have third-party effects, these do not necessarily imply market failure. As long as some private banks are not threatened by runs (and are indeed receiving money withdrawn from other institutions), it will be in their interest to aid their solvent but illiquid rivals. Nor is there any basis for the claim, made by Guttentag and Herring (1983, p. 5) and implied elsewhere, that a government lender of last resort "may have better information than the private markets . . . and may know that [a] bank is solvent when the private market does not."

In fact private providers of last resort assistance are much more likely than any central bank to conform to the "classical" recipe of lending only to solvent institutions at penalty rates, in part because doing so is entirely consistent with profit maximization. As will be seen below, by refusing last resort assistance central banks in the past have managed to reinforce their own privileged status – a status that rendered them peculiarly immune to confidence externalities. More recently, on the other hand, central banks have been inclined to extend aid at subsidy rates and often to insolvent institutions (Garcia and Plautz 1988, p. 54; Sprague 1986, *passim*). In doing so they in effect act as lenders, not of last, but of first resort. Such behavior allows central banks to create an exaggerated impression of their importance. It serves, at the same time, to further weaken the banking system by creating another "moral hazard" and by discouraging the development of private arrangements for responding to crises.

Central bank aid to *insolvent* institutions is especially harmful: last resort aid fulfills its purpose when it serves to signal the public that an institution is indeed viable. Aid to insolvent banks undermines this purpose, as the public discovers that a bank – even though it has received assistance – may still fail. Thus an offer of last resort aid may no longer suffice to end a run and may not suffice even if the stricken institution really is solvent, because the offer of aid no longer serves to convince a skeptical public that the recipient is sound. For this reason the Fed alone was unable to end runs at First Pennsylvania Bank in 1980 and at Continental Illinois in 1984. As

Garcia and Plautz explain (1988, p. 168), private assistance had to be included in the rescue packages to those banks "to demonstrate that those with their own monies at risk were confident that the crises would be resolved without losses being incurred by uninsured depositors."

Although the rendering of emergency assistance by private banks has been quite common throughout history, legal restrictions have hampered it in numerous ways, all of which generate an artificial need for central bank assistance. The fact that central banks often underbid would-be private rescuers has already been mentioned. Branching restrictions are also to blame, for by encouraging the proliferation of small banks, such restrictions – in addition to making banks more failure-prone to begin with – also hinder the assembly of large, wholly private rescue packages. Even an overnight loan backed by plenty of collateral, if very large (like the Fed's $23 billion loan to the Bank of New York in 1985) poses a tremendous, if not insuperable, challenge to numerous small banks that could easily be met by a group of larger banks acting in concert.

Takeovers and mergers

Bank regulatory authorities generally agree that the best way to dispose of an insolvent bank or thrift is not to liquidate it but, if possible, to have it taken over by a solvent bank or bank holding company. Yet although they are pleased to take credit for frequently arranging such takeovers, the fact is that legal restrictions and policies sanctioned by the authorities themselves are the main impediments to takeovers, which could otherwise proceed in such a way as to permit greatly reduced reliance upon the central bank as a lender of last resort. Kareken (1986, p. 11) sums up the situation nicely:

> If a bank is, for instance, constrained to have no branches, then neither can it acquire another bank and . . . keep the acquired bank in existence . . . Bank acquisitions and mergers are, then, to an extent limited by state branching restrictions or, more fundamentally, by the McFadden Act. But that is not all. Under present day federal bank regulatory policy, no bank with FDIC-insured balances can go ahead with an acquisition or merger until it has gotten the approval of the appropriate federal bank regulatory agency, whether the OCC, the FDIC, or the Federal Reserve Board (FRB), all of which are, as it were, special antitrust agencies.[11]

As if this were not enough, the Bank Merger Act of 1966 allows the Department of Justice to challenge any bank acquisition or merger approved by the above listed agencies (Kareken 1986, p. 12), while Federal Reserve restrictions make bank holding company acquisitions of thrifts unattractive. All of these impediments to takeovers reflect the authorities' "bigness paranoia" – their obsession with concentration ratios in banking – which prevails despite the fact that banking in the United States is a long way from being as concentrated as banking elsewhere. Somewhat ironically, the shortage of big banks in the United States is itself a barrier to takeovers, because bigger banks can much more readily absorb the business of smaller banks than other small banks can.

Another unfortunate aspect of present policy is that, until very recently, it has permitted takeovers only of insolvent or nearly insolvent banks and thrifts. This clearly lowers the odds of finding eligible bidders for a bank or, alternatively, makes it necessary for the authorities to sweeten the pot by assuming some of the bad assets of a failed institution or by providing subsidized "leverage." Indeed, Kane (1985, p. 11) reports that, for large banks especially, the regulatory authorities "ordinarily make a tenacious effort through subsidizing lending to keep troubled institutions afloat well past the point of market value insolvency" using "cosmetic accounting" to hide the practice. This policy of forbearance is the equivalent of adminis- tering a "poison pill" to failing institutions in its efficacy in discouraging potential acquirers. It also encourages insolvent firms to "go for broke" – taking on risky investments in a last-ditch effort to stay alive.

The very fact that would-be takeovers or mergers must be disclosed to the authorities before they can proceed makes voluntary (i.e., hostile but nonshotgun) takeovers of poorly managed banks less likely. As Jensen explains (1988, pp. 44–5), prior disclosure of a planned takeover of a publicly traded firm allows stockholders in the target firm to bid up the price of its stock to equal the full discounted value of any expected gain in net earnings from the takeover. Thus nothing is left for the would-be acquirer, which (unless offered a last minute subsidy) has every incentive to bow out.

In sum, the elimination of branch restrictions and a *laissez-faire* policy towards mergers and takeovers would have allowed many of today's problem banks and thrifts to have been quietly absorbed by sound institu- tions well before their net worth became negative, and would have done so without the need for "last resort" subsidies made at taxpayers' expense.

THE ROLE OF CURRENCY MONOPOLY

So far I have argued that restrictions on branch banking, portfolio diversi- fication, interest rates, and mergers, together with mispriced deposit insur- ance and "emergency" loans, have contributed to the fragility of the US banking system, making it crisis-prone and generating an artificial need for a lender of last resort. Yet this account seriously understates the case against having a central bank functioning as a lender of last resort, because it fails to reveal how *the very presence of even a well-behaved central bank is itself a fundamental cause of financial fragility*. This is so because central banking entails a monopoly in the supply of hand-to-hand currency, which has historically been a particularly destructive legal restriction on private banking as well as a crucial cause of monetary instability. Rather than being merely a *means* which allows central banks to act as lenders of last resort (Humphrey and Keleher 1984, p. 176), currency monopoly was the original *raison d'être* of central banks and a cause of the troubles central banks were called upon to correct only as an afterthought.

Currency monopoly directly contributes to financial fragility in three ways: (1) by preventing private banks from independently accommodating changes in the public's relative demand for currency; (2) by precluding a secondary market for demandable bank liabilities; and (3) by creating a new and unstable form of high-powered money.

Currency demand

A major part of the so-called "inherent instability" of contemporary fractional-reserve banking rests upon the fact that private banks cannot issue notes. An increase in the public's demand for currency relative to its demand for deposit balances under such circumstances must lead to withdrawals of high-powered money from banks' reserves. Unless the withdrawals are somehow neutralized, they will provoke a multiplicative contraction of deposits.[12] Insofar as an increase in the relative demand for currency does not reflect a loss of confidence in banks (as is typically the case), then redeemable banknotes (which like deposits are a claim against some ultimate money of redemption) can be perfectly adequate in satisfying it. Of course, as Rockoff (1986, p. 629) points out, freedom of note issue cannot prevent a crisis if deposit holders do lose confidence in the banking system and therefore choose to withdraw the ultimate money of redemption (an extreme possibility to be dealt with by separate means, discussed below). But restrictions on note issue only serve to increase the likelihood of this happening by causing even nonpanic-driven increases in currency demand to place a strain on the banking system, thereby helping to inspire a loss of confidence.

History is littered with instances that bear out these claims, a number of which are described in Selgin (1988, ch. 8). Perhaps the most notorious were the great "currency shortages" of 1893 and 1907 in the United States, which provided a rationale for the establishment of the Federal Reserve System. Although national banks were legally permitted to issue notes, they were hampered after 1882 by the growing scarcity of government securities, required by the National Banking Act as collateral for note issues. A seasonal stringency of credit emerged each year with the autumnal increase in demand for currency "to move the crops." On the aforementioned dates this stringency degenerated into full-scale panic. Private banks, clearinghouses, and other firms issued millions of dollars' worth of "currency substitutes" in partly successful efforts to stem the crises. Most of this ersatz currency was probably illegal, but its successful use helped to reveal the extent to which the crises were an avoidable consequence of legal restrictions on note issue. Here again Canada offers an interesting counterexample, for what were "crises" in the United States took the form there of mere increases in the outstanding stock of private banknotes, some of which crossed the border to provide relief to Americans suffering from a shortage of exchange media.

Another example is the role of the Fed's monopoly on note issue in helping to bring on the "Great Contraction" of 1930–3. As income falls, the demand for hand-to-hand currency increases relative to the demand for deposits independently of any loss of confidence in the banking system. Thus some of the post-1929 withdrawals of high-powered money which placed a strain on many banks might have been avoided had the banks been able to issue notes as well as create deposits.

A secondary note market

Previously I observed that a contagion effect could take hold in a system of unregulated deposit banks as the result of an "information externality." Because depositors lack knowledge of bank-specific risks, any real shock known to have rendered one bank insolvent may be regarded as a likely cause of serious damage to others. Thus bad news concerning one bank spills over to apparently similar banks.

It turns out that this potential cause of a banking contagion is another consequence of legal restrictions on private, competitive note issue. As Gorton (1987) explains, prices of financial assets for which secondary markets exist will – according to the efficient markets hypothesis – tend to reflect their relative riskiness. Thus a secondary market for bank money can, in theory, be a reliable source of information concerning bank-specific risks, which could serve to limit bank runs to truly insolvent firms. However, the secondary market for checkable deposits is too "thin" to be efficient, because checks drawn by different persons for the same amount and from the same bank are distinct assets. Therefore, freedom of note issue is necessary if market price signals are to be relied upon to stamp out a contagion.

A secondary banknote market is typically portrayed as involving professional nonbanknote "brokers" as well as banknote "reporters" – weekly publications with information on note discounts. If brokers do not request any risk-related discount (beyond transaction costs) to redeem a bank's notes, holders of those notes can rest assured that the bank is solvent and will not have any incentive to "monitor" its solvency by staging a run on it. On the other hand, holders of notes trading at a discount do not need to run, either, but can "walk" to a broker who charges them for assuming the risk that the notes' issuers may fail.

Though secondary note markets did indeed function this way in the United States and elsewhere in the early nineteenth century and before,[13] the tendency in a fully unregulated system is for brokers and banknote reporters to give way to banks with nationwide branch networks accepting one another's notes directly or through clearinghouses at par.[14] It has been suggested (e.g., Gorton 1987, p. 3) that this tendency also implies the abandonment of a secondary note market and the return of an information-externality problem. The truth is rather that there is still a "virtual" secondary note market in which banks and clearinghouse associations rather than brokers become "market makers" and where notes tend to be priced either at par or at zero (the latter being the case where a note is refused in payments by banks other than its issuer). The "binary" system of note pricing in this "virtual" market is sufficient to avoid a contagion effect. Noteholders have reason to stage a run only on banks whose notes are not being accepted at par by other banks. Because notes, unlike checks, are fungible, a person who deposits a note with a rival bank need have no fear that the bank will refuse to credit his or her account after (unsuccessfully) trying to redeem the note. Thus a bank's acceptance of a rival's note is, unlike its acceptance of a check, a definite token of its confidence in the rival's solvency. It is only when par acceptance of notes by rival banks is *required by statute* (as it was, for example, under the National Banking Act of 1864) instead of being voluntary that it ceases to be a reliable source of information about bank-specific risk. With freedom of note issue and exchange in *any* of its likely forms, a bank information externality would be extremely unlikely.[15]

High-powered money

It is widely believed that financial crises are most likely to occur in periods of tight money following longer periods of monetary ease (Kindleberger 1978; Minsky 1977, 1982; and many theorists of the "Austrian" school). Experience seems to confirm this view (Garcia and Plautz 1988, p. 7), which suggests yet another reason for viewing central banking and currency monopoly as a cause of, rather than a cure for, financial instability. The reason is that a currency monopoly makes possible much more erratic fluctuations in the money stock than can occur in banking systems where currency is issued competitively in the form of redeemable notes. When note issue is monopolized, the liabilities of the privileged bank of issue inevitably become high-powered money even though they themselves may still be redeemable in specie.[16] This high-powered money replaces specie as the principal bank reserve medium, the consequence being that the bank of issue is relieved from suffering any adverse clearings when it overissues.

Furthermore, an expansion or contraction of the privileged bank's liabilities leads to a multiple expansion or contraction of deposits at unprivileged banks, to be checked only when international specie flows force the bank of issue to alter its course. Obviously if a central bank suspends specie payments, or if a permanent fiat money system is established (something relatively easy to do once notes are issued monopolistically), the privileged bank's power to inflate or deflate will, in principle at least, be unlimited.

A central bank's power to unilaterally expand or contract a nation's money stock must be compared to the relatively limited potential for similar expansion or contraction in a free banking system. Elsewhere (Selgin 1988, chs. 3–6) I explain in detail why free banks, unlike a central bank, cannot unilaterally or collectively affect a change in the price level or in nominal rates of interest. For this reason, and also unlike a central bank, they cannot unilaterally deplete a nation's gold stock by overissuing. This makes them incapable of creating the circumstance most frequently to blame for both American and European financial crises under the gold standard: a rising domestic price level (with or without a speculative "mania") combined with a shrinking stock of specie.[17] Needless to say, free banks would also be incapable of the hyperinflations and secular stop-and-go inflations that distinguish fiat money regimes and are the most important cause of financial crises in more recent history.

To a remarkable extent, the literature on financial crises has turned a blind eye toward these fundamental truths. Thus Kindleberger (1978, p. 52) lists the growth of private banking and financial instruments, gold discoveries, and (p. 17) the ability of competitive banks to "stretch" their reserves as causes of excessive monetary expansion,[18] while treating privileged (central) banks as sources of stability:

> Central banking arose to impose control on the instability of credit. The development of central banking from private banking, which is concerned to make money, is a remarkable achievement. By 1825, division of labor had been agreed upon: private bankers of London and the provinces financed the boom, the Bank of England financed the crisis.
>
> (Kindleberger 1978, p. 77)

This is a truly incredible interpretation of the history of banking in England. It would certainly have come as a surprise to the directors of the Bank of England, both in 1825 and for many years after, to learn that they, unlike private bankers, were not "concerned to make money" or indeed that their bank's privileged status was awarded to it so that it could "impose control on the instability of credit." They would probably have been inclined to think that the whole point of the Bank's possessing the powers and privileges it possessed was precisely to enable it "to make money" and, more importantly, to enable it to make money more easily than other banks could in return for its sharing some of the money with the government. As regards the alleged "division of labor" in 1825, we have already seen how it is theoretically suspect. Moreover, in voicing a view made famous by the Bank directors during the Restriction, Kindleberger ought to know that he is standing on thin ice. Just as some participants in the bullionist controversy blamed the Bank of England rather than the country banks for depreciation of the pound during the Restriction (White 1984, pp. 55–8), later writers including Parnell and Mushet (cited in White, p. 63) laid blame for the 1825 crisis squarely on the shoulders of the Bank of England and its overissues of 1824–5.[19] Their view is also upheld by more recent authorities including Nevin and Davis (1970, p. 43), who note that the country banks had been *contracting* their note issues and accumulating reserves locally and in London after 1819 in anticipation of resumption. Their policy changed after 1822, when the Bank of England – encouraged by a last minute decision of the government to allow a continuance of country small-note circulation until 1833 (Thomas 1934, p. 42) – imprudently decided to employ the large reserves it had gained from the countryside by reducing its lending rate to 4 per cent and extending the maturity of eligible bills from 65 to 95 days. "The country banks," according to Nevin and Davis "could hardly do other than follow these changes in the credit situation" by expanding their own issues.

For some later episodes (when the "division of labor" should have been even more firmly established) the evidence against the Bank is still more conclusive. A recent case in point was the "fringe bank" crisis of 1973–4. According to Reid (1982) that crisis was based on a boom willfully engineered (with the Bank of England's help) by the Heath government in its "dash for growth." Nor has the Bank of England been the only central bank to be guilty of errors of commission (and not merely of omission) in modern times. As Garcia and Plautz observe (1988, p. 111), the Fed on several occasions has set "the stage for real and financial sector insolvencies and liquidity crises." Excessive expansion of money made possible by the existence of central banks exposed financial institutions to wider and more frequent swings in nominal interest rates than could or would have occurred otherwise. An example of this cited by Kindleberger himelf in a fairly recent article was the Fed's attempt to assist Nixon's 1972 re-election by expanding the money stock in the hope of lowering interest rates (Kindleberger 1988, p. 176). To suggest as Kindleberger does elsewhere that such behavior contradicts the true purpose of central banks "arose" to fulfill is to ignore their historical origins entirely. It is like suggesting that lions "arose" in order to perform circus acts. The real surprise is not that central banks often inflate but that they have been trained occasionally *not* to do so.

To conclude, monopoly in currency supply is more a cause of, than a cure for, financial fragility. This fact helps to account for the stability of past, decentralized banking systems such as those of Scotland (White

1984), Canada (Schuler 1988), Sweden (Jonung 1985), and Switzerland (Weber 1988) in the nineteenth century – a success that must appear paradoxical to those who regard fractional-reserve banking as inherently unstable and in need of a lender of last resort.[20]

The political economy of central bank "hierarchy"

There is yet another, more subtle way in which restrictions on private currency issue have contributed to the perceived need for a lender of last resort. This is by indirectly fostering the view that private banking is *naturally* hegemonic or "hierarchical" (Gorton 1987; Gorton and Mullineaux 1987; Goodhart 1988). This view suggests that free development of a banking system would naturally lead to its being dominated by a single firm, from which other banks would borrow in times of stress, and to which they would send their reserves in normal times. What this view neglects is that the extent of hierarchy observed in contemporary banking systems is not consistent with private bankers' pursuit of their selfish interests in an unregulated setting (Selgin 1988, ch. 2). Such hierarchy is another consequence of legal restrictions, including especially restrictions on note issue, that have allowed particular banks to dominate and control their rivals while also weakening the latter.

By far the most important example of this in history has been the rise to dominance of the Bank of England. The Bank's emergence as a central bank was the result of its receiving a series of legal privileges in return for large loans to the government (Smith 1936, pp. 9, 129; Bagehot [1873] 1915, pp. 90–7). Among the Bank's more important privileges prior to 1826 were (1) its monopoly of note issue within a 65-mile radius of London, (2) its monopoly of limited liability and joint-stock banking, and (3) its status as exclusive holder of the government's deposits. The prohibition of limited liability and joint-stock banking outside of London was especially injurious, as it forced most of England to depend upon small, undercapitalized "country" banks as a source of currency.[21] According to Lord Liverpool (quoted in Dowd 1989, p. 125), this arrangement was

> one of the fullest liberty as to what is rotten and bad, but one of the most complete restrictions as to all that is good. By it a cobbler or cheesemonger [may issue notes] while, on the other hand, more than six persons, however respectable, are not permitted to become partners in a bank with whose notes the whole business of the country might be transacted.

According to Parnell (quoted in White 1984, p. 40), it was the presence of so many "cobblers and cheesemongers"[22] in English banking that caused hundreds of banks there to fail in 1826. In contrast, the relative freedom of

Scottish banking had endowed it with several strong joint-stock banks, with nationwide branches, all of which were unharmed by the crisis in England.

The Bank of England's privileges also caused other banks to keep their specie reserves with it and to treat its liabilities as their ultimate source of liquidity.[23] This situation only served to enhance the subservience of the weaker banks to their privileged rival, causing the system to be still more top heavy and "hierarchical." The Bank had learned, furthermore, that in the event of a crisis it could rely upon the government to protect it from bankruptcy by sanctioning its suspension of payments. Thus while other banks were unnaturally dependent upon the Bank, it could refuse to assist them with impunity – a kind of moral hazard opposite the kind most associated with central banking today. A relatively late example of this may have been the Bank's refusal to extend aid to Overend, Gurney and Company in 1866 (De Cecco 1975, pp. 80–2). A better example, perhaps, was the Bank of France's willful destruction of rival, provincial banks of issue in 1847–8 (Kindleberger 1984, pp. 104–7). Such conduct by central banks only serves, of course, to further strengthen their command over remaining, underprivileged rivals.

The exalted status of the Bank of England did not just make other English banks depend on it. For London was also the financial capital of Great Britain and, indeed, the world; to dominate the London money market was, therefore, to dominate the world money market. The consequence of this was that non-English banks, including the Scottish banks during the free banking era, occasionally looked upon the Bank of England as a potential source of emergency short-term funds.

This fact has led several writers (Cowen and Kroszner 1989; Rockoff 1986, p. 630; Rothbard 1988; Sechrest 1988; Goodhart 1988) to deny that banking in Scotland was ever truly free after all because it, too, depended upon access to a central bank. In arguing thus they confuse a banking system's reliance upon access to a financial center with its reliance upon access to a privileged bank of issue. Had banking in England been free, there is no doubt that London would still have been Great Britain's (as well as the world's) financial center. In that case Scottish banks might have relied upon any of several large, English joint-stock banks to gain access to the central money market or, better still, would simply have located their own branches (if not their headquarters) there. To really appreciate the irrelevance of this criticism of free banking, though, one should contemplate what would have happened if Scotland had set up a monopoly bank of issue while England allowed its banks to develop free of legal restrictions. Then economists might have been treated to the spectacle of a privileged central bank having to rely upon several competitive banks of issue as "lenders of last resort" and as conduits to the national and world money markets. What conclusions would they have drawn from this? What conclusions should be drawn from the fact that large Canadian banks have sometimes relied upon private banks in New York City both prior to and after 1913? Finally, what should one conclude from the experience of the Swedish *enskilda* banks prior to 1900 – which were as a matter of policy refused assistance by the more privileged Riksbank but which were free of failures nonetheless – or from the similar experience of Switzerland's cantonal banks of issue in the years preceding the Franco-Prussian War? None of the latter systems can be said to have depended even indirectly upon assistance from a privileged central bank.

Thus the "hierarchy" enjoyed by central banks is not a natural development but rests on "a combination of political motives and historical accident" (Smith 1936, p. 2), the most important motive being governments' desire to gain financial favors from particular banks. Far from being consistent with the healthy development of private banking, such hierarchy is a cause of financial weakening: the strength enjoyed by central banks is strength sapped from their would-be rivals. Moreover, the central-banking "game," in which strength is transferred from several banks to one bank, has a negative sum.

Significantly, Walter Bagehot – the "high-priest" of central banking – understood all of this. The Bank of England's special responsibilities stemmed, in his view, from its holding "the ultimate banking reserve of the country." But this fact, far from being natural, was due to the Bank's "accumulation of legal privileges . . . which no one [sic!] would now defend" ([1873] 1915, pp. 66, 90–7). Far from wanting to defend "the monarchical form of Lombard Street," Bagehot (pp. 65–7) called it "dangerous" and contrasted it unfavorably to the "natural" system "of many banks of equal or not altogether unequal size [that] would have sprung up if Government had let banking alone":

> In all other trades competition brings the traders to a rough approximate equality. There is no tendency to a monarchy in the cotton world; nor, where banking has been left free, is there any tendency to a monarchy in banking . . . A monarchy in any trade is a sign of some anomalous advantage, and of some intervention from without.

Present-day defenders of central banking have neglected this part of Bagehot's teachings, twisting his "second best" argument for central banks into a "first best" argument.[24]

Panic-proof free banking

I have tried to suggest above that the maximization of banking efficiency and the avoidance of fragility and crises are not conflicting goals, one of which demands competition and financial liberalization and the other of which demands regulation and control. A liberalized and hence competitive banking system is likely to be both more efficient *and* less fragile and crisis-prone.

Nevertheless, even such a free banking system would not necessarily be panic proof. As long as banks continue to have liabilities unconditionally redeemable on demand, while holding only fractional reserves, the possibility of a systemic collapse would still exist. The system could still be exposed to a sudden increase in the public's demand for the ultimate money of redemption, prompted by an invasion or revolution; or it might be threatened by a major computer malfunction (like the one that caused the Bank of New York's $23 billion default in 1985). An important question, then, is whether a lender of last resort would be necessary even in a deregulated system to guard against such rare events.

The answer, I think, is that it would not, the reason being that the widespread reliance upon bank liabilities unconditionally convertible on demand is itself an artificial consequence of legal restrictions. As Rockoff points out (1986, p. 623), the Act of 1765 imposed a fine of £500 on any Scottish bank failing to redeem a note on demand; likewise free banking laws in the United States required state authorities to redeem *all* of a bank's notes from the proceeds of sales of deposited bonds in the event that the bank failed to redeem a single dollar on demand.[25] Such laws prevented banks from offering alternative, contingent-convertibility contracts to their customers, thereby needlessly exposing them to a higher risk of default and panic.

Contingent-convertibility contracts – contracts that make the redemption of a bank note or deposit credit contingent upon the *total value* of redemptions being requested at any moment – may take either of two forms. One allows a bank under special circumstances to "suspend" or "restrict" convertibility of deposits into high-powered money. A bank while suspending convertibility may still engage in other types of banking business, by issuing notes, accepting deposits, and making loans. It may also make special arrangements for continuing its settlements with other banks, thereby ensuring that notes and checks drawn from it can still be used for payments generally. The other kind of contingent-convertibility contract provides for the issuance of "option-clause" notes, which can, at the issuing bank's discretion, be redeemed either on demand or after a predetermined delay, with interest paid to the notes' holders as compensation in the latter case. Both option-clause notes and suspension of deposit convertibility have been observed in history. The former were issued by Scottish banks prior to 1765; the latter were resorted to on several occasions by national banks in the pre-Federal Reserve era.[26] Moreover, as Dowd (1988), Gorton (1985), and others have observed, their use is entirely consistent with the interests of both banks and their customers, so that legal restrictions alone have stood in the way of their more widespread use in place of unconditionally convertible liabilities. It would be only in banks' interest to exercise their option to suspend cash payments in situations where such payments become physically impossible (Postlewaite and Vives 1987, pp. 490–1). According to Gorton (1985, p. 190) suspension in such circumstances prevents bank liability holders from engaging in behavior that could force their banks to suffer "fire-sale" losses: "Suspension circumvents the realization of suboptimal depositor withdrawals which are based on (rational) fears of capital losses" but which could lead to even *greater* losses than a more orderly process of liquidation. More importantly, perhaps, the mere prospect that suspension may be resorted to will, according to Dowd (1988, p. 327), "suffice to stabilize [a] panic and protect the banking system from collapse." Thus contingent-convertibility contracts can provide an effective substitute for a lender of last resort or deposit insurance or other government-imposed devices for containing a banking panic.[27]

CONCLUSION

Despite frequent claims to the contrary, fractional-reserve banking systems are not inherently fragile or unstable. The fragility and instability of real-world banking systems is not a free market phenomenon but a consequence of legal restrictions. This does not mean that deregulation is without its dangers. Dismantling bad bank regulations is like cutting wires in a time bomb: the job is risky and has to be done in carefully ordered steps, but it beats letting the thing go on ticking. Once the fuse – the legal restrictions – is dismantled, the payload – central banking and fiat money – can safely be disposed of.

NOTES

1 According to Barth and Keleher (1984, p. 16) "to function as a lender of last resort [a central bank] must have authority to create money, i.e., provide *unlimited* liquidity on demand" (emphasis added).
2 Minsky even tries to rule potential criticisms of his "financial-instability hypothesis" out of court by declaring (1982, p. 16) that "No theory of the behavior of a capitalist economy has merit if it explains instability as the result either of exogenous policy mistakes or of institutional flaws that can be readily corrected."
3 Canada turned to central banking in 1935, for reasons that had little to do with securing financial stability. See Bordo and Redish (1986).
4 Relative freedom of note issue and activity diversification also contributed to the greater strength of Canadian banking.
5 That, at least, would certainly be true in the absence of deposit insurance, which by subsidizing risk taking may encourage banks to diversify in ways that would increase their overall exposure to risk (Litan 1987, pp. 84, 103–4). This implies that deposit insurance itself may have to be reformed or repealed *before* all

portfolio restrictions (except those that concern clear conflicts of interest) can safely be lifted.

6 Thus the problems of Glass–Steagall and Regulation Q were supposed to prevent *can* exist in the presence of federal deposit insurance.

7 This contradicts a statement in Guttentag and Herring (1983, p. 6). Depositors may also switch into high-powered money despite their continuing confidence in banks, because their payments plans demand greater use of hand-to-hand money. As will be shown below, such behavior would not pose any threat to a fully deregulated banking system.

8 Goodhart (1987, p. 85) reaches the same conclusion with respect to recent runs in the United Kingdom.

9 O'Driscoll (1988, p. 672) observes that these failed banks "were more like the typical US rather than the typical Canadian bank. Neither . . . was widely branched, and they were specialized energy banks."

10 Reasons for this are given below.

11 Fairly recent changes in the law, including the Garn–St. Germain Act of 1982, provide for only limited relaxation of branching restrictions in the absence of similar reforms of state laws.

12 Even Lloyd Mints (1950, p. 186) – one of the original proponents of this "inherent instability" thesis – admits that it "is due in part to a wholly unnecessary legal restriction," namely restrictions against note issue. He goes on to say that, to be consistent, "the defenders of fractional-reserve banking should propose [to give banks] the privilege of note issue with the same required reserve ratio for notes and deposits" (p. 188).

13 On the functioning of the secondary note market in the United States prior to 1845, see Knodell (1988).

14 For an account of how and why this happens, see Selgin (1988, ch. 2).

15 That deposits would still lack a distinct secondary market (or virtual secondary market) of their own does not matter if they are backed by the same general assets as notes are. This has always been the case for unregulated banks, though it was not true for the banks of the so-called "free banking" era in the United States or for national banks afterwards. For this and other reasons, these banks were subject to information externalities despite being able to issue notes. See Selgin (1988, pp. 138–9).

16 See Selgin (1988, pp. 48–9).

17 Humphrey and Keleher observe (1984, p. 279): "Crisis situations involving the LLR [lender of last resort] frequently followed excessive credit expansions. Such credit expansions often were large and prolonged enough to produce outflows of specie and to foster doubts about the ability of commercial banks to redeem their paper in gold."

18 For critical remarks on these alleged causes of monetary overexpansion, see Selgin (1988, ch. 6 and pp. 129–33), and Chapter 12 below.

19 It is worth noting that not a single Scottish bank failed or felt the need to apply to the Bank of England for assistance during the 1825 crisis. See White (1984, p. 47).

20 See above, Chapter 9. There are, of course, many criticisms of competitive note issue – including the claim that it is inconsistent with a generally well-behaved money supply – which I am not able to consider here. For a fairly comprehensive discussion, see Selgin (1988).

21 For many years the Bank itself did not feel compelled to establish branches for the issue and redemption of its notes beyond the city. An 1826 campaign led by Thomas Joplin resulted in a new law allowing the establishment of joint-stock

banks outside of London; but the law did not permit the new joint-stock banks to issue notes, and it encumbered them with a variety of "irksome" restrictions. Although many of the latter were eventually removed, the prohibition against joint-stock banknote issues remained in place. See Nevin and Davis (1970, pp. 59–60).

22 It is not clear whether Parnell borrowed this expression from Lord Liverpool or vice versa.

23 This practice was officially sanctioned by the Bank Act of 1833, which made Bank of England notes legal tender for payments among other banks.

24 Kindleberger (1978, p. 164) even declares that Bagehot "thought it proper that the Bank of England, and not the banks themselves, should hold the reserves necessary to get the country through a panic" – the exact opposite of the truth.

A well-known British economist who shared Bagehot's critical views on central banking was Sir Robert Giffen (1905, pp. 175–6).

25 Enforcement of the law was another matter. There are plenty of stories, including ones that are probably true, about note brokers and private individuals being "run out of town" both in Scotland and in the United States for daring to request cash in exchange for notes. Ideally, the law should allow banks to engage freely in all manner of contractual agreements with their customers, enforcing those agreements as written. In practice the law did neither.

26 Although it is true that suspension of payment by national banks could not be based upon prior, contractual consent of their customers, Gorton (1985, p. 177) observes that "neither banks, depositors, nor the courts opposed it at any time."

27 Diamond and Dybvig (1983) claim that contingent-convertibility contracts may be inferior to deposit insurance because suspension under the former will harm the interests of depositors who wish to withdraw high-powered money for the purpose of increasing their consumption expenditures even as it safeguards the interests of depositors who "panic." This argument neglects the fact that high-powered money is not needed for normal expenditures, particularly if bank notes can be issued freely. A suspension of payments, unlike a bank holiday, need not interfere with depositors continuing to make purchases by check or bank note. Historically, banks (and hence the public generally) have frequently agreed to accept notes and checks of suspended (even failed) rivals at par. See below, Chapter 11.

REFERENCES

Aharony, J., and Swary, I. "Contagion Effects of Bank Failures: Evidence from Capital Markets." *Journal of Business* 56 (July 1983): 305–22.

Bagehot, Walter. *Lombard Street: A Description of the Money Market.* 1873. Reprint. London: John Murray, 1915.

Barth, James R., and Keleher, Robert E. "Financial Crises and the Role of the Lender of Last Resort." *Federal Reserve Bank of Atlanta Economic Review* (January 1984): 58–67.

Benston, George J.: Eisenbeis, Robert A.; Horvitz, Paul M.; Kane, Edward J.; and Kaufman, George G. *Perspectives on Safe and Sound Banking.* Cambridge, MA: MIT Press, 1986.

Blair, Roger D., and Heggestad, Arnold A. "Bank Portfolio Regulation and the Probability of Bank Failure." *Journal of Money, Credit, and Banking* 10 (February 1978): 88–93.

Bordo, Michael D., and Redish, Angela. "Why Did the Bank of Canada Emerge in 1935?" Paper presented at the Economic History Association, September 1986.

Bryant, John. "Bank Collapse and Depression." *Journal of Money, Credit, and Banking* 13 (November 1981): 454–64.

Cowen, Tyler, and Kroszner, Randall. "Scottish Banking before 1844: A Model for Laissez–Faire?" *Journal of Money, Credit, and Banking* 21 (May 1989): 221–31.

De Cecco, Marcello. *Money and Empire: The International Gold Standard, 1890–1914.* Totowa, NJ: Rowman and Littlefield, 1975.

Diamond, Douglas W., and Dybvig, Philip H. "Bank Runs, Deposit Insurance, and Liquidity." *Journal of Political Economy* 91 (June 1983): 401–19.

Dowd, Kevin. "Option Clauses and the Stability of a Laisser Faire Monetary System." *Journal of Financial Services Research* 1 (1988): 319–33.

Dowd, Kevin. *The State and the Monetary System.* Oxford: Philip Allan, 1989.

Friedman, Milton. *A Program for Monetary Stability.* New York: Fordham University Press, 1960.

Garcia, Gillian, and Plautz, Elizabeth. *The Federal Reserve: Lender of Last Resort.* Cambridge, MA: Ballinger, 1988.

Giffen, Sir Robert. "Fancy Monetary Standards." In idem, *Economic Inquiries and Studies,* pp. 186–77. London: George Bell and Sons, 1905.

Goodhart, C.A.E. "Why Do Banks Need a Central Bank?" *Oxford Economic Papers* 39 (March 1987): 75–89.

Goodhart, C.A.E. *The Evolution of Central Banks.* Cambridge, MA: MIT Press, 1988.

Gorton, Gary. "Bank Suspension of Convertibility." *Journal of Monetary Economics* 15 (March 1985): 177–93.

Gorton, Gary. "Banking Panics and Business Cycles." Unpublished ms., 1986.

Gorton, Gary. "Incomplete Markets and the Endogeneity of Central Banking." Unpublished ms., 1987.

Gorton, Gary, and Mullineaux, Donald J. "The Joint Production of Confidence: Endogenous Regulation and 19th Century Commercial-Bank Clearinghouses." *Journal of Money, Credit, and Banking* 19 (November 1987): 457–68.

Guttentag, Jack, and Herring, Richard. "The Lender-of-Last-Resort Function in an International Context." *Essays in International Finance.* Princeton, NJ: Princeton University Press, 1983.

Humphrey, Thomas M.; and Keleher, Robert E. "The Lender of Last Resort: A Historical Perspective." *Cato Journal* 4 (Spring/Summer 1984): 275–318.

Jensen, Michael C. "Takeovers: Their Causes and Consequences." *Journal of Economic Perspectives* 2 (Winter 1988): 21–48.

Jonung, Lars. "The Economics of Private Money: The Experience of Private Notes in Sweden, 1831–1902." Paper presented at the Monetary History Group Meeting, London, 1985.

Kane, Edward J. *The Gathering Crisis in Federal Deposit Insurance.* Cambridge, MA: MIT Press, 1985.

Kareken, John H. "Federal Bank Regulatory Policy: A Description and Some Observations." *Journal of Business* 59 (January 1986): 3–48.

Kaufman, George G. "The Truth about Bank Runs." In *The Financial Services Revolution: Policy Directions for the Future,* ch. 2. Edited by Catherine England and Thomas Huertas. Boston: Kluwer Academic Publishers, 1988.

Kindleberger, Charles P. *Manias, Panics and Crashes: A History of Financial Crises.* London: Macmillan, 1978.

Kindleberger, Charles P. *A Financial History of Western Europe.* London: Allen & Unwin, 1984.

Kindleberger, Charles P. "The Financial Crises of the 1930s and the 1980s: Similarities and Differences." *Kyklos* 41(2) (1988): 171–86.

Knodell, Jane. "Interregional Financial Integration and the Banknote Market: The Old Northwest, 1815–1845." *Journal of Economic History* 48 (June 1988) 287–98.

Litan, Robert E. *What Should Banks Do?* Washington, DC: The Brookings Institution, 1987.

McCulloch, J. Houston. "Bank Regulation and Deposit Insurance." *Journal of Business* 59 (January 1986): 79–85.

Mingo, John J. "The Economic Impact of Deposit Rate Ceilings." In *Regulation of Consumer Financial Services*. Edited by Arnold A. Heggestad. Cambridge, MA: Abt Books, 1981.

Minsky, Hyman P. "A Theory of Systemic Fragility." In *Financial Crises: Institutions and Markets in a Fragile Environment*. Edited by Edward I. Altman and Arnold W. Sametz. New York: John Wiley & Sons, 1977.

Minsky, Hyman P. "The Financial-Instability Hypothesis: Capitalist Processes and the Behavior of the Economy." In *Financial Crises: Theory, History, and Policy*, pp. 13–39. Edited by Charles P. Kindleberger and Jean-Pierre Laffargue. London: Cambridge University Press, 1982.

Mints, Lloyd. *Monetary Policy for a Competitive Society*. New York: McGraw-Hill, 1950.

Mullineaux, A.W. "Why Is the US Banking System so Unstable?" *Royal Bank of Scotland Review* 153 (March 1987): 36–52.

Nevin, Edward, and Davis, E.W. *The London Clearing Banks*. London: ELEK Books, 1970.

O"Driscoll, Gerald P. "Deposit Insurance in Theory and Practice." *Cato Journal* 7 (Winter 1988): 661–75.

Postlewaite, Andrew, and Vives, Xavier. "Bank Runs as an Equilibrium Phenomenon." *Journal of Political Economy* 95 (June 1987): 485–91.

Reid, Margaret. *The Secondary Banking Crisis, 1973–75*. London: Macmillan, 1982.

Rockoff, Hugh. "Institutional Requirements for Stable Free Banking." *Cato Journal* 6 (Fall 1986): 617–34.

Rolnick, Arthur J., and Weber, Warren E. "The Causes of Free Bank Failures." *Journal of Monetary Economics* 14 (October 1984): 267–91.

Rothbard, Murray N. "The Myth of Free Banking in Scotland." *Review of Austrian Economics* 2 (1988): 229–45.

Schuler, Kurt. "Evolution of Canadian Banking, 1867–1914." Unpublished ms., University of Georgia, 1988.

Sechrest, Larry J. "White's Free-Banking Thesis: A Case of Mistaken Identity." *Review of Austrian Economics* 2 (1988): 247–57.

Selgin, George A. *The Theory of Free Banking: Money Supply under Competitive Note Issue*. Totowa, NJ: Rowman & Littlefield, 1988.

Short, Genie D., and Gunther, Jeffrey W. "The Texas Thrift Situation: Implications for the Texas Financial Industry." Federal Reserve Bank of Dallas, 1988.

Shughart, William F., II. "A Pubic Choice Perspective of the Banking Act of 1933." *Cato Journal* 7 (Winter 1988): 595–613.

Smith, Vera. *The Rationale of Central Banking*. London: P.S. King & Son, 1936.

Solow, Robert M. "On the Lender of Last Resort." In *Financial Crises: Theory, History, and Policy*, pp. 237–48. Edited by Charles P. Kindleberger and Jean-Pierre Laffargue. London: Cambridge University Press, 1982.

Sprague, Irvine. *Bailout: An Insider's Account of Bank Failures and Rescues.* New York: Basic Books, 1986.

Thomas, S. Evelyn. *The Rise and Growth of Joint-Stock Banking.* London: I. Pitman & Sons, 1934.

Waldo, Douglas G. "Bank Runs, the Deposit-Currency Ratio and the Interest Rate." *Journal of Monetary Economics* 15 (March 1985): 269–77.

Weber, Ernst Juerg. "Currency Competition in Switzerland, 1826–1850." *Kyklos* 41(3) (1988): 459–78.

White, Lawrence H. *Free Banking in Britain: Theory, Experience, and Debate, 1800–45.* London: Cambridge University Press, 1984.

White, Lawrence H. "Regulatory Sources of Instability in Banking." *Cato Journal* 5 (Winter 1986): 891–97.

Wicker, Elmus. "A Reconsideration of the Causes of the Banking Panic of 1930." *Journal of Economic History* 40 (September 1980): 571–83.

Wojnilower, Albert M. "The Central Role of Credit Crunches in Recent Financial History." *Brookings Papers on Economic Activity* 2 (1980): 277–326.

11

IN DEFENSE OF BANK SUSPENSION*

INTRODUCTION

The recent Japanese banking and US S&L debacles appear to have been brought about in part by government deposit insurance (e.g., Kane, 1989). A reconsideration of alternatives to such insurance as a means for coping with banking panics is therefore warranted. I believe that resort to occasional bank suspensions or private contracts allowing such suspensions is one alternative worth reconsidering.

Many persons are inclined to reject bank suspension because it brings to mind images of a bank "holiday," like that of March 1933 in the United States, in which bank debt ceases altogether to be exchangeable for goods and services. Such an image of suspension is also conveyed in Diamond and Dybvig's (1983) influential analysis of bank runs, which links suspensions with the large-scale interruptions of consumption, thereby drawing the conclusion that government deposit insurance is preferable.

However, popular opinion concerning the necessary costliness of bank suspension is mistaken. When legally permitted to do so, banks can avoid many of the costs typically associated with suspension by "restricting" payments of high-powered money while continuing to receive and issue bank notes or checks. The Diamond and Dybvig model cannot allow for this possibility because it does not allow for the use of bank debt (in the form of checkable deposits or notes) as a medium of exchange. Here I extend the Diamond–Dybvig (D–D) model to show how bank suspensions may proceed without causing significant welfare losses due to the interruption of consumption. Historical evidence supports the implications of this extended D–D model. The same evidence also suggests that high welfare costs suffered in past bank suspensions have been due to legislative interference in banking rather than suspension *per se*. In the absence of

Reprinted, with permission, from the *Journal of Financial Services Research*, Vol. 7, No. 4 (December 1993).

such legislative interference suspension might well prove less costly than government-based insurance schemes.

THE DIAMOND–DYBVIG MODEL

Diamond and Dybvig examine banking panics using a model designed to explain the role of banks.[1] The D–D economy starts out with N consumers endowed with equal quantities of the economy's single consumption good, e.g., following Wallace (1988), a bushel of corn. There are three periods, 0, 1, 2 – a "planting" period, an "intermediate" period, and a "harvest" period. A bushel of corn planted in period 0 yields $R > 1$ bushels in period 2, but only one bushel in period 1. Because consumers may meet with emergencies in period 1, investment in corn production is risky. Unlucky "type 1" consumers will have to liquidate their corn investments prematurely, realizing a net return of zero. In contrast, lucky "type 2" consumers can afford to delay consumption until the harvest, enjoying a positive return. All consumers feel vulnerable as of period 0, however, because they do not learn their types until period 1.

According to Diamond and Dybvig, a bank is a device that allows optimal risk sharing by pooling investments and dividing anticipated returns among type 1 and type 2 consumers. Assuming that the fraction, t, of type 1 consumers is less than one, risk sharing takes the form of (nontransactable) deposit contracts entitling depositors to a preset payoff of r_1 bushels of corn per bushel deposited in period 0 for period 1 withdrawals ($R > r_1 > 1$) and to a residual payoff of r_2 ($< R$) bushels of corn per bushel deposited in period 0 for period 2 withdrawals, where r_2 represents a pro rata share of corn harvested in period 2 (Diamond and Dybvig, 1983, p. 408).[2] A "good" banking equilibrium with optimal risk sharing occurs when deposit contracts are taken advantage of *and* type 2 consumers behave like type 2 consumers, delaying their withdrawals until the harvest.

Unfortunately, Diamond and Dybvig demonstrate that such a "good" equilibrium is only one of two possibilities. A "bad" equilibrium may also occur in which type 2 agents panic and join type 1s in withdrawing their deposits prematurely. Because the D–D model assumes a single bank, such panic-based withdrawals are the equivalent of systemwide panic in a multibank system. A panic spoils the risk-sharing arrangement because, with $r_1 > 1$, the value of the bank's assets in period 1 ($= N$ bushels of corn) falls short of the promised period 1 redemption value of bank deposits ($= Nr_1$). Assuming that the bank has zero net worth and that a "sequential [first-come-first-served] service constraint" is in effect, depositors who recover their initial deposits *plus* interest in period 1 leave the rest with less than their initial deposits.[3] It follows that "anything that causes [type 2 consumers] to anticipate a run will lead to a run" (Diamond and Dybvig,

1983, p. 410), including intrinsically irrelevant random events such as sunspots.[4]

ALTERNATIVE MEANS FOR
SHORT-CIRCUITING RUNS

Diamond and Dybvig consider a private arrangement which can protect a bank from runs. This arrangement is a modified demand-deposit contract allowing the bank to "suspend" convertibility of its deposits in the event of a panic.[5] Unlike a "pure" demand-deposit contract, a suspension contract prevents consumers from withdrawing their deposits in period 1 "after a fraction $f < r_1^{-1}$ of all deposits" has been withdrawn (Diamond and Dybvig, 1983, p. 410.)[6] When t (the fraction of type 1 consumers) is known, this type of contract is "incentive compatible," resulting in a unique Nash equilibrium with $f = t$ (Diamond and Dybvig, 1983, p. 411). A suspension contract succeeds, in other words, in preventing runs "by removing the incentive of type 2 agents to withdraw early" (Diamond and Dybvig, p. 410).[7]

However, suspension contracts also have a serious shortcoming. This shortcoming becomes apparent when the fraction of type 1 consumers, t is a random variable. Then, although suspension contracts can still prevent runs, convertibility may be suspended before all type 1 agents have made their withdrawals. Such a result is inconsistent with optimal risk sharing because it precludes emergency consumption by some type 1 consumers. A fundamental source of the problem is the bank's inability to discriminate between period 1 withdrawals by persons motivated by emergencies (type 1 consumers) and period 1 withdrawals by persons motivated by a loss of confidence (panicking type 2 consumers).[8]

This defect of private suspension contracts provides a rationale for government deposit insurance, which, according to Diamond and Dybvig (p. 404), "can improve on the best allocation that private markets provide." The conclusion is biased by the authors' acknowledged failure to address the problem of moral hazard, which they believe can be overcome "by some sort of bank regulation" (p. 417). The remainder of this chapter reassesses Diamond and Dybvig's conclusion by showing how the inclusion of *transactable* bank debt ("bank money") in a D–D economy alters the social costs of suspension.

A DIAMOND–DYBVIG ECONOMY WITH MONEY

A peculiar feature of the D–D model and of later elaborations of it by Chari (1989), Engineer (1989), and Wallace (1988, 1990) is that, despite including a "bank," the model lacks distinct media of exchange such as currency or checkable deposits. Consumers deposit "corn" directly in the bank in period 0, withdrawing corn in periods 1 and 2. The bank, in turn, plants the corn for what it hopes will be a period 2 harvest. Alternatively (although Diamond and Dybvig do not allow for this possibility), the bank might be assumed to resist planting a fraction of its corn deposits equal to its expected period 1 withdrawals to avoid unnecessary planting and harvesting costs. Either way, the bank's "liquid" asset is also the economy's sole consumption good. As Wallace (1990, p. 15) states, "the bank is like a cash machine, except that it dispenses the consumption good, not cash."

This peculiarity of the D–D bank makes it impossible to conceive of a "suspension" of bank payments that does not pose a threat to consumption: A suspension of payments in the D–D model has the same effect that closing all retail outlets for real goods would have in an actual economy. In particular, suspension risks interfering with the consumption plans of some type 1 agents because the D–D bank, besides providing intermediation services to its customers, is also the economy's sole source of consumable commodities. The D–D framework is thus unable to distinguish disturbances to consumption that are *indirect* consequences of *media of exchange shortages* from disturbances to consumption that stem directly from the unavailability of consumption goods themselves. That such a distinction should be allowed for is obvious in view of the undisputed empirical fact that past banking panics have typically involved media of exchange shortages but *not* shortages of real commodities. In what follows the distinction is allowed for by incorporating monetary exchange into Diamond and Dybvig's model in a transparent manner that alters (non-panic) equilibrium allocations of the original model as little as possible.

Outside money

The simplest way to add money to the D–D model while retaining the model's underlying spirit is to introduce a new asset, e.g., "gold," which functions as a medium of exchange and is, therefore, more "liquid" than corn. To give gold an exchange role to perform without altering equilibrium allocations of the original D–D model, let us assume that the economy's N consumers have no corn endowment in period 0, but are instead endowed with one ounce of gold each. Next, let us add a set of infinite-lived competitive "corn merchants" to the economy, endowing the merchants with an inventory of at least N bushels of corn (but no gold) in period 0. While the bank in our model continues to provide intermediation (and production) services, it no longer serves as consumers' primary source of corn. Instead, consumers as well as the bank must purchase corn from corn merchants, whose function is to buy, stock, and sell corn at an exogenously given "world" price of one gold ounce per bushel.[9] A "cash-only" payments technology is assumed so that gold must be employed in purchasing corn and in making and redeeming bank deposits. Gold and bank deposits are, therefore, not substitutes: whereas deposits remain nontransactable but are preferred as a store of value, only gold functions as a medium of exchange. Note that the cash-only "constraint" employed here differs from cash-in-advance constraints in other monetary exchange models in that its presence alone has no bearing on equilibrium allocations of real goods.

The above changes in the model, besides allowing for the use of money, also reflect the reality of the division of labor between sellers of finished goods and intermediaries. In the real world, consumers buy finished goods from retail firms, e.g., supermarkets, and not directly from producers or intermediaries. Intermediaries, moreover, do not engage in production, but lend investible funds to specialized producers. (We retain, however, the Diamond and Dybvig assumption that the bank is also a producing firm: corn merchants do not have direct access to the corn production technology.) A formal motivation for such division of labor and for the existence of a distinct medium of exchange is not attempted here, since such a motivation would be beyond the scope of this chapter as well as contrary to the goal of leaving equilibrium allocations unaltered by the proposed modifications. Our sole aim is to make the D–D model consistent with the real-world separation of intermediaries from retailers together with the employment of money as an exchange medium in a manner that preserves as much as possible the underlying D–D analysis of bank panics.[10]

Because consumers' utility functions are unchanged from the original D–D model, consumers continue to obtain utility through the consumption of corn only; gold, the medium of exchange, is noninterest bearing and "intrinsically useless." The corn "production technology" is likewise the same as before, with the bank still serving a double role as both a corn "producer" and a provider of risk-sharing (liquidity-transformation) services.[11] What is altered is the structure of transactions in the economy as well as the structure of bank assets, for now a "circuit flow" of money is added to the original model's pattern of transactions involving real goods only: bank deposits are both received and paid in gold, which both banks and depositors must use to purchase corn. For simplicity, assume for the moment that t, the fraction of type 1 consumers, is known. In period 0 consumers, instead of depositing corn with the bank, deposit N ounces of gold. The bank then uses $N(1 - t)$ ounces of gold to buy an equal number of bushels of corn from the corn merchants and retains Nt ounces of gold as a reserve in anticipation of period 1 (gold) withdrawals. (The "gold-only" cash constraint prevents the bank from trading deposit credits for corn.) Bank deposits thus become fixed claims to gold, yielding zero gold interest but promising $Nt(r_1 - 1)$ bushels of (net) corn interest in period 1 and $N(1 - t)(r_2 - 1)$ bushels of (net) corn interest in period 2.[12] At the onset of period 1 bank assets consist of $N(1 - t)$ bushels ("ounces worth") of corn and Nt ounces of gold; the latter item constitutes the bank's liquid reserve medium.

At the onset of period 2, if type 2 consumers have not panicked, the bank's assets will consist of a "harvest" of $N(1 - t) + N(1 - t)(r_2 - 1)$ bushels of corn only (all gold reserves having been paid out in period 1). To "liquidate" its assets the bank sells $N(1 - t)$ bushels of corn to the corn merchants, thereby acquiring gold with which to redeem its remaining $N(1 - t)$ deposits. The other $N(1 - t)(r_2 - 1) = N(1 - tr_1)R - N(1 - t)$ bushels of corn go directly to remaining (type 2) depositors, as interest. The depositors, finally, use their gold to buy $N(1 - t)$ bushels of corn from the merchants. Consumption and risk sharing thus follow the same pattern as in the deterministic-t D–D model, with all gold ending up in the hands of merchants. Were a new generation of consumers lucky enough to have another N bushels of corn sprout up in their backyards, they could sell the new corn to the merchants who, in buying this corn, would dispose of the gold received from consumers of the previous generation. A new bank could then be formed, and the investment process could be repeated.

The difference between our extended D–D model and the D–D original may be more easily grasped through a comparison of bank balance sheets for both models, showing bank assets and liabilities for each of the three periods (Table 11.1).

A "bad" D–D equilibrium with outside money

In our extended model, even with a known value of t, a "bad" equilibrium exists just as in the original D–D model, with type 2 consumers losing confidence in period 1 and attempting to withdraw their deposits prematurely. Optimal risk sharing then breaks down, since some depositors are

Table 11.1 Bank assets and liabilities, by period, original and modified D–D models

Period 0		Period 1		Period 2	
A	L	A	L	A	L
I. Original model					
Corn: N bushels	Deposits: N bushels	Corn: N bushels	Dep's due: Ntr_1 bu.*	Corn: $N(1 - tr_1)$. R bu.	Dep's due: $N(1 - tr_1)$. R bu.
II. Modified model					
Gold: N oz.	Deposits: N oz.	Gold: Nt oz.	Dep's due: Nt oz.	Gold: $N(1 - t)$ oz.	Dep's due: $N(1 - tr_1)$ $R - N(1 - t)$ bu.
		Corn: $N(1 - t)$ bu.	Interest: $Nt(r_1 - 1)$ bu.*	Corn: $N(1 - tr_1)R - N(1 - t)$ bu.	

*Period 1 interest is treated here as being financed out of bank capital.

bound to realize negative (corn) returns. Indeed, the "bad" equilibrium in our extended model is, if anything, worse than its nonmonetary counterpart, since the bank not only must abandon corn production but must also sell its existing corn holdings to corn merchants before it can redeem its deposits. In reality this process of liquidation might take time, exacerbating losses to depositors (cf. Engineer, 1989; Calomiris and Kahn, 1991).

Note that, in the new model as in the old, with t known a suspension contract exists that can prevent runs while preserving optimal risk sharing. Suppose that deposit contracts allow payments to be suspended once $f = t$, i.e., once the fraction of deposits withdrawn in period 1 is equal to the (known) fraction of type 1 consumers, which determines the bank's period 1 fractional gold-reserve ratio. This contract satisfies the D–D suspension-contract requirement that $f < r^{-1}$ provided that $r_1^{-1} > t$. The later conditions will hold for all $r_2 > 0$, i.e., for any situation in which a "good" risk-sharing banking equilibrium is feasible.[13]

Finally, suppose that t, the fraction of type 1 consumers, is random so that the bank must plan according to an estimate $\hat{t}$. Here again, the result resembles that obtained in the original D–D model: suspension can still forestall a panic, but not without upsetting the consumption plans of some type 1 consumers whenever $\hat{t} < t$. In such cases, some type 1 agents are prevented from redeeming their deposits in gold in period 1. Without gold, consumption of corn in period 1 (excluding corn received in net bank interest payments) is impossible *even though corn merchants may have unsold inventories of corn*. The harmful consequences of suspension follow, not from the fact that all "goods" are locked away in bank vaults – as in the original D–D model – but from the existence of a (gold) cash constraint that in the event of suspension prevents type 1 agents from trading their bank deposit contracts directly for *available* corn. This result is more consistent with the "stylized facts" of historical banking crises, which typically have involved shortages of money but *not* shortages of consumption goods.

Thus many of Diamond and Dybvig's original results can be recovered in an extended and more realistic model incorporating outside money. It is especially worth noting that the inclusion of outside money and of merchants holding corn inventories has been accomplished in a transparent manner that does not alter the original model's main conclusions. This suggests that the original model's portrayal of the costs of suspension does *not* depend strictly on its nonmonetary nature. However, we shall see below how that portrayal *does* depend on the assumption that bank debt is nontransactable and therefore cannot serve as a medium of exchange.

Bank money

Our extended D–D model, though more realistic than the original, is still unrealistic in one important respect. Although it allows for "outside" money, it does not allow the use of transactable bank debt or "bank money" as a substitute medium of exchange. The introduction of bank money allows us to treat the bank in our model, not just as a "transformer" of liquid assets, but also as the provider of a low-cost payments technology. It also allows us to consider an alternative approach to the "suspension of convertibility" not possible in a pure outside-money system and not considered by Diamond and Dybvig. This alternative approach can avoid the previously noted welfare costs of suspension.

We can introduce bank money into our model in a straightforward way by assuming that demand deposits are both "checkable" and freely convertible into paper banknotes used in making change or in exchanges where checks are unacceptable. To allow bank money to serve in place of outside money in all payments, we can assume that corn merchants usually treat bank debt as a perfect or superior substitute for gold, accepting bank checks and notes routinely at par.[14] Merchants, in other words, behave like type 2 consumers in "normal" times. The economy's cash-only constraint is thus relaxed.[15] To make nominal magnitudes in the model with bank money conform with those in the pure outside-money case, we will assume that corn merchants "import" the N bushels of corn sold to the bank in period 0, paying for them in gold (bank money being unacceptable in foreign payments). This assumption disallows any "multiplication" of the domestic stock of bank money relative to the original stock of gold. It does not, however, preclude corn merchants' holding corn inventories beyond the initial N bushels.

As before, consumers in period 0 deposit N ounces of gold with the bank. Because bank money is a perfect substitute for gold in transactions after period 0, the bank can use all of its gold to buy N bushels of corn from the corn merchants. So long as it does not anticipate a panic the bank does not have to restrict its corn purchases to $N(1 - t)$ bushels as before, because it will not need to maintain any gold in anticipation of period 1 withdrawals.[16] The relaxed cash constraint makes it unnecessary for type 1 consumers to withdraw gold for making corn purchases in period 1. Instead "impatient" consumers can write checks or pay banknotes to the corn merchants, transferring their holdings of bank debt to them. Deposit transfers do not result in any actual gold withdrawals in a one-bank system.

To extend the realism of the model a step further, we can assume the existence of a multibank system in place of a single bank. Individual banks must keep gold reserves for settling interbank balances from the exchange of checks and (bank-specific) notes in period 1. In equilibrium overall net balances would be zero, but precautionary reserves equal to βN, with $0 < \beta < 1$, are still needed if subgroups or transactions are settled according to a random sequence. Finally, if gold and bank money are not perfect substitutes, so that some fraction of "normal" period 1 transactions (e.g. "imports" of some special variety of corn not directly available from domestic corn merchants) requires payment in gold, the banking system will keep additional fractional reserves of $\alpha t N$, where α represents the fraction of "imports" in period 1 consumption.

In a "pure" ($\alpha = \beta = 0$) bank-money version of the D–D economy, a "good" equilibrium exists in which $N[1 - t(r_1 - 1)]$ bushels of corn (original N bushels minus period 1 interest) remain in the bank after period 1, yielding $RN[1 - t(r_1 - 1)]$ bushels in period 1. This equilibrium contrasts with the pure outside-money case in which only $N[1 - t(r_1)]$ bushels of corn remain planted until the harvest, yielding $RN[1 - t(r_1)]$ bushels. The difference, RNt, includes interest paid on corn merchants' deposits held from period 1 to period 2.[17]

PANIC AND SUSPENSION IN A D–D ECONOMY WITH BANK MONEY

The "normal" use of bank money in the above economy does not preclude the possibility of bank runs in the absence of suspension contracts: type 2 agents can still panic and stage a run on the banking system, realizing that sufficient period 1 withdrawals would leave latecomers with negative returns. As in the pure outside-money case, a panic can occur whenever type 2 agents fear for any reason that other type 2 agents will lose confidence and demand redemption of their deposits prematurely. Significantly, and unlike previous cases, type 1 consumers can also panic now, by attempting to redeem their deposits in gold instead of continuing to write checks or offer banknotes which might be refused to corn merchants. In the original D–D model, in contrast, a type 1 person who lost confidence in the banking system in period 1 would not act differently from any other type 1 person. If banks hold zero (or fractional) gold reserves, and are restricted to unconditional demand-deposit contracts, any panic must necessarily force them to liquidate their assets prematurely, destroying the risk-sharing arrangement.

Once again suspension contracts can preclude panic by limiting period 1 withdrawals and thereby eliminating the prospect of negative period 2 returns. Unlike in the previous models, though, several sorts of suspension are conceivable:

1 First, full suspension or a "bank holiday." Here, all bank activity ceases until period 2 if the fraction of deposits withdrawn in gold in period 1, f_g, reaches αt. When a bank holiday is declared, deposits cease to be convertible into either notes or gold and banks cease to receive checks. In a multibank system, interbank transactions also come to a halt. Bank money therefore eases to serve as a reliable substitute for outside money even for "normal" transactions among nonpanicking agents.

2 Second, partial external suspension, which Friedman and Schwartz (1963, p. 330) call a "restriction" of cash payments to the public. For example, over-the-counter gold payments may be discontinued once $f_g = \alpha \hat{t}$, yet deposits may remain fully convertible into banknotes, checks and notes may continue to be received at full value by banks, and banks may remain open for other activities, e.g., renewing loans, not represented in the D–D framework.

3 Third, "internal" suspension, which is a one-period suspension of *inter-bank* gold payments, requiring interbank consent only. Banks can then make additional gold available to type 1 consumers on occasions when they collectively underestimate period 1 demands for "imports."

With these possibilities in mind, consider what happens if an external suspension (either a "holiday" or a "restriction") occurs at $\hat{t} < t$ when t is random. Evidently, either of the two types of external suspension can protect banks from failing and thereby eliminate the motive for panic by type 2 agents (who in the D–D framework are residual claimants of bank earnings). But whereas resort to a bank holiday prevents consumption by some type 1s, as in the original D–D model, resort to restriction avoids this undesirable side effect. Restriction (but *not* holiday) contracts assure corn merchants that bank money can always be regarded as a safe substitute for gold, just as they assure other type 2 depositors of the future value of their deposits.[18] Actual resort to restriction is for this reason fully consistent with the continued employment of bank money as a domestic medium of exchange. Potential restriction-related welfare losses to type 1 consumers are thus limited to those few instances in which their emergency consumption plans called for "imports." These losses would tend to be spread among *all* type 1 consumers by means of a slight discount applied to bank money relative to gold. As α approaches 0, so also do suspension-related welfare losses to type 1 consumers regardless of the magnitude of $t - \hat{t}$. In the limiting case, where either notes or checks are a perfect substitute for gold in all transactions, restriction involves no discount on bank money and hence no welfare loss.[19]

Furthermore, if banks hold liquid gold reserves equal to βN for period 1 interbank settlements in addition to gold held in anticipation of withdrawals for "imports" then, for any $N\beta \geqslant N\alpha(t - \hat{t})$, an internal suspension of interbank gold payments, with interbank IOUs substituted for intermediate cash settlement until period 2, would enable the banks to pay gold to importers despite having underestimated t, avoiding welfare losses even with $\alpha > 0$. The restriction of gold payments to the public might in this case involve bankers' efforts to undertake nonprice rationing of gold in favor of depositors ("importers") capable of demonstrating a special need for outside money.

These advantages of restriction over a bank holiday in a bank-money economy point to another advantage. Recall that in a bank-money economy type 1 consumers can also "panic" if they lose confidence in the bank-money payments mechanism. This panic will manifest itself in type 1 consumers' decision to withdraw gold for all of their planned consumption expenditures in period 1, and not just for a fraction, α, of such expenditures. The possibility of a bank "holiday," unlike that of a mere restriction, actually provides a basis for such a panic among type 1 consumers by threatening to shut down the bank-money payments mechanism. Because of this difference, bank holiday deposit contracts, unlike restriction contracts, are not incentive compatible in a world where bank money is commonly employed as a medium of exchange: contracts that threaten bank holidays may actually make banks more vulnerable to panic in addition to resulting in more *ex post* damage to type 1 consumers. *One would, for this reason, expect to observe occasional low-cost bank restrictions, but not bank holidays, in unregulated banking.* One should also find more panics in systems where it is feared that holidays may be legally imposed.

To conclude, in an extended D–D model with bank money, a special kind of suspension contract allowing the "restriction" of payments is both feasible and effective in preventing runs. Such a contract may – in connection, perhaps, with an internal suspension – avoid the social costs associated with suspension in the original D–D model and in its extended counterpart with outside (but not bank) money. If bank money is a perfect substitute for outside money, the welfare losses from suspension that provide a rationale for deposit insurance in the original Diamond and Dybvig study can be entirely avoided.[20]

BANK SUSPENSIONS IN HISTORY

According to our extended D–D model, bank suspension contracts may be a low-cost alternative to deposit insurance where (1) bank money is able to serve in place of outside money in most payments and (2) banks are contractually free to "restrict" payments (without shutting down entirely) to protect themselves from runs. Historical episodes in which both conditions have been met have, however, been rare. The reason for this has been not some intrinsic shortcoming of bank money or resort to restriction but rather legal interference with both of these. In all of the better-known episodes of bank suspension, legal restrictions hindered the use of bank-money substitutes in place of outside money while preventing banks from restricting payments. Because of this, historical bank suspensions have involved higher than necessary welfare costs.

Legal resort to restriction

Throughout history governments have denied banks the right to make use of explicit restriction clauses in their deposit or banknote contracts, insisting instead that deposits and notes be unconditionally redeemable in outside money on demand (Rockoff, 1986, pp. 618–623). The few exceptions include Scotland from 1730 to 1765, Sweden from 1864 to 1903, and Canada throughout most of the nineteenth century (Dowd, 1989, pp. 12–14). Bank runs were unknown in all three episodes. Furthermore, although the notes of some smaller Scottish banks occasionally bore a discount relative to gold, notes of the more well-established Scottish banks and of Canadian and Swedish private banks appear to have circulated at par throughout the periods in question. This fact suggests that occasional resort to restriction or the threat thereof did not result in any substantial disruption of payments or associated welfare losses in any of these arrangements.

Other bank suspensions have been sanctioned by governments on an *ad hoc* basis only, often after panic had begun to take its toll. In such cases the beneficial, deterrent effect of suspension *contracts* could not be realized, and some welfare losses stemming from interrruptions of investment and production were incurred before suspension was invoked. Postsuspension losses were, however, typically limited by resort to restrictions rather than holidays. In the United States prior to the Civil War, banks were allowed to suspend in response to emergencies in 1814, 1837, 1839, and 1857. In every case, suspension took the limited form of restriction of specie payments, and banks in various regions of the country went to great lengths to prevent any disruption of payments by engaging in agreements to continue accepting each other's notes at par (Redlich, 1951, pp. 248ff.). Typically these agreements involved provisions for regular note exchange with interest charged on accumulated balances in lieu of immediate settlement as well as stipulations limiting loan expansion for the duration of the restriction. In some cases new deposits were accepted on the understanding that the depositor could receive payment of checks or drafts in notes but not in specie, and merchants formally agreed to continue receiving banknotes at par (Redlich, 1951, pp. 248–250, 259–261, 268–269). The complete success of such measures in avoiding welfare losses from suspension depended on the measures' being adopted uniformly throughout regions of the country affected by the emergency. Such success was no doubt hampered by the peculiar unit banking structure of the US banking industry. Nevertheless, in those areas (mainly large cities) where cooperation was possible, welfare losses were largely avoided. After 1857 clearinghouses played a crucial role in organizing and supervising restrictions of payment. As banks became more limited in their ability to issue notes in the 1880s, this supervisory role of clearinghouses during restrictions became supplemented by their role as issuers of emergency currency (discussed below).

In some later episodes in the United States, government-sanctioned suspensions, in addition to being declared belatedly, were also made to take the extreme form of bank holidays. Because such holidays entail a complete shutdown of bank operations and not just a "restriction" of over-the-counter payments of outside money, they could not help but involve massive welfare losses of the kinds stressed by Diamond and Dybvig. During the Panic of 1907 the governors of Oklahoma, Nevada, Washington, Oregon, and California declared a series of bank holidays, against the wishes of many bankers, instead of sanctioning a less complete restriction of payments (Sprague, 1910, p. 286). Such holidays severely hindered the use of checks as substitutes for outside money in normal payments, frightening depositors in neighboring states into running on their banks. The same, misguided policy of declaring bank holidays instead of allowing mere restrictions of payment was repeated on a nationwide scale in 1933, again against bankers' wishes (Anderson, 1979, p. 290; Burns, 1974, pp. 38, 45). With the declaration of a nationwide holiday on March 6, deposits ceased to be of much use as a medium of exchange. The contrast with previous bank-organized suspensions was substantial. During the 1907 crisis, for example, most banks restricted cash payments without impeding the use of checks:

> A depositor could not go to his bank and get all the cash he wanted, but he could withdraw a check on his bank and pay a debt with it. And the recipient of the check could deposit that check in his own bank and have it honored through the clearinghouse, and could draw checks against the deposit thus created to make his own payments.
>
> (Anderson, 1979, p. 286)

The main effect of the 1933 holiday was to make demands for currency more acute than ever, impeding the course of exchange (Freidman and Schwartz, 1963, pp. 328–330). As had been the case in 1907, but to a much greater extent, previous statewide holidays provided a motive for panic by impatient ("type 1") consumers who might normally have relied on their checkbooks for making purchases.

In their brief reference to US experience, Diamond and Dybvig (1983, p. 410) observe that the government-sponsored bank holiday of 1933 was "more severe than any of the previous suspensions." However, they fail to note that a "suspension" in their own model has effects more akin to those of a "holiday" with a large-scale curtailment of consumption than to any mere "restriction" of payments. The crucial difference is that a bank restriction permits the continued use of bank money – checks or notes – in payments, whereas a holiday shuts down the bank-money payments mechanism entirely.

Restrictions on bank money

Government sponsorship of bank holidays has not been the only factor contributing to the costliness of historical bank suspensions. Regulations restricting or prohibiting the issuance of certain kinds of bank money, notably banknotes, have also added to the welfare costs of suspension by reducing the substitutability of bank money for outside money, forcing a greater than necessary reliance on outside money in "normal" payments. In many historical banking systems competitively issued banknotes, being a hand-to-hand currency, served in place of outside money in transactions for which checks were unacceptable. Such notes played a crucial part in allowing payments to proceed during restrictions. Scotland's experience after 1765, when both suspension contracts and the issuance of notes under £1 were outlawed, illustrates this point. In 1797, following rumors of a French invasion, the British government authorized the Bank of England and Bank of Ireland to suspend gold payments. Although no such authority was given to any Scottish bank, the banks of Scotland decided collectively (and illegally) to restrict gold payments on their own initiative. Although the Scottish business community generally abided by this decision, large numbers of depositors and note holders at first crowded the banks to make unusual requests for gold or silver. According to Checkland (1975, p. 221):

> These persons were alarmed at the prospect that silver might wholly disappear, leaving no unit of payment under the one-pound note. They feared that, if this happened, street trading and indeed all retail trading by the lower orders would cease, together with payment of their wages. The master tradesmen, too, earnestly appealed to the bankers for a little silver to pay their workers.

To meet the shortage of small change, private tokens of various kinds were issued, and £1 notes were torn into quarters. The banks for their part paid out small sums of specie in secrecy. Finally in April the government reauthorized the issuance of small notes of Scottish banks. By such means the interruption of normal, domestic purchases by bank depositors, made necessary in the first place by legal restrictions, ended, and Scotland "settled to a new regime of inconvertibility" (Checkland, 1975, p. 223).[21]

Elsewhere more severe restrictions on private note issuance led to still higher costs of bank suspension. In England notes under £5 were prohibited by an act of 1777. This act also had to be relaxed during the Bank Restriction to reduce disruptions of trade. In the United States, state banks were entirely prohibited from issuing notes by a 10 per cent tax effective as of mid-1866, while national banknotes had to be delivered from Washington after first being secured by deposits of federal securities. During the 1880s and 1890s, the rising price of federal securities made note issuance increasingly unprofitable. Because of such legal barriers to note issue, restrictions of bank payments in connection with the crises of 1873, 1893, and 1907 included restrictions on payments of banknotes as well as legal tender. Fearing that such restrictions would deprive it of hand-to-hand money necessary in small payments, the public hoarded currency, and currency premiums of up to 5 per cent developed in New York and elsewhere (Dwyer and Gilbert, 1989, pp. 48–49). In every case these premiums were soon "largely removed by means of substitutes for money, such as certified checks and local script [sic] of various kinds" as well as clearinghouse certificates, which allowed the economy "to adjust itself to suspension . . . sufficiently well to permit the continuance of ordinary business payments" (Sprague, 1910, pp. 71, 200, 203).[22] Lingering currency premiums and associated depositor welfare losses reflected the limited usefulness of local currency substitutes in interregional transactions (Sprague, 1910, pp. 75, 291), which might also have been avoided had banks been permitted to establish nationwide branches and to issue notes secured by their general assets, as was the case in Canada.[23]

Internal suspensions could, of course, ease the strain of meeting interregional payments by making legal-tender bank reserves available for the public's use. Such internal suspensions were marked in the United States by the temporary use of clearinghouse loan certificates in interbank settlements (Timberlake, 1984). Internal suspensions complemented the use of emergency (nonbank) currencies and certified checks in minimizing depositor welfare losses in 1873, 1893, and 1907; they were, nevertheless, inadequate to avoid welfare losses altogether. Although bankers undertook nonprice rationing of legal tender in favor of persons (e.g., importers) for whom it was "absolutely necessary" (Anderson, 1979, pp. 286–287), some price rationing still occurred.

During the banking crisis of 1932–1933, artificial limits on banks' powers of note issue aggravated welfare losses caused by the immobilization of deposits. Small-denomination currency was in especially short supply (Roberds, 1990, p. 17; Burns, 1974, p. 44), and nonbank enterprises resorted once more to issuing scrip. In some poorer communities in Georgia accustomed to conducting business on a cash basis, bank holiday scrip issues alone were sufficient to prevent "any significant disruption of normal activity" (Roberds, 1990, p. 18).[24]

These historical findings have an important bearing upon the practicability of the suspension alternative today. They show that, insofar as payments today continue to require hand-to-hand money, the potential for low-cost bank suspensions will be limited by banks' inability to issue circulating notes legally.

CONCLUSION

Past banking systems avoided suspension-related welfare costs by "restricting" outside-money payments only, while continuing to supply money in the form of banknotes or checkable deposits, which were close substitutes for outside money for most payments. However, legislative interference added to the costs of suspension by limiting banks' powers of note issuance (forcing them to resort to less acceptable "currency substitutes") or by imposing bank "holidays" instead of sanctioning more limited restrictions of payment. In the absence of such interference bank suspension may in fact be a less costly means than government deposit insurance for coping with banking panics.

NOTES

1 A number of recent papers extend the D–D model but retain the basic features of it criticized here. See Engineer (1989), Wallace (1988, 1990), and Chari (1989). The summary of the basic D–D model that follows draws on all of these studies.

2 Specifically, $r_2 = \max \{R(1 - r_1 t)/(1 - t), 0\}$ where t is the fraction of type 1 consumers. A positive period 2 return results so long as $t < r_1^{-1}$. The assumption that r_2, unlike r_1, is a pro rata rather than a preset payoff amounts to treating type 2 consumers as residual claimants, bypassing issues related to bank solvency. This aspect of the D–D model is criticized in Dowd (1992).

   Another peculiar feature of the D–D bank is that it is a corn-producing firm and not just a saving-investment intermediary. The bank's assets therefore include corn but not loans. Both simplifications are retained in the present study.

3 As Wallace (1988) has shown, this argument rests upon the implicit assumption that consumers are "isolated" from the banking system so that the bank cannot retrieve interest paid to early withdrawers.

4 Gorton (1985, 1988) criticizes the treatment of panics as random events in the D–D model.

5 Diamond and Dybvig (1983, p. 410) refer to contracts allowing the suspension of convertibility "of deposits to cash." However, since no distinct "cash" is present in the D–D model, suspension therein really refers to suspension of convertibility of deposits into corn, i.e., goods. Later we shall modify the D–D model so as to allow "suspension" to take on its historical meaning.

6 If there are N deposits in period 0, and impatient consumers receive r_1 bushels of corn for each bushel deposited, then, if f is the fraction of deposits withdrawn in period 1, any $f > r_1^{-1}$ would require a total period 1 payoff of $Nfr_1 > N$, leaving nothing for the remaining $N(1 - f)$ type 2 agents.

7 On the potential Pareto-superiority of suspension contracts relative to pure demand-deposit contracts see Gorton (1985), Dowd (1988), and Wallace (1990). A recent defense of pure demand contracts is Calomiris and Kahn (1991). Engineer (1989) shows that suspension does not necessarily prevent runs in a three-period version of the D–D model.

8 In Wallace's (1990) version of the D–D model, potential welfare losses from suspension are limited compared to losses in the D–D original. This result follows from Wallace's special assumption that "aggregate risk" (i.e., uncertainty respecting the value of t) is limited to a subgroup of those persons who attempt to make period 1 withdrawals, where the subgroup is always "last in

251

line." The bank can then limit suspension-related welfare losses to type 1 persons in the subgroup, who receive less corn in period 1 than other type 1 persons if suspension is invoked.

9 The assumption that corn merchants live for ever is consistent with viewing them as enterprises rather than as individuals, and serves to allow money to be valued positively beyond period 2, when the original generation of consumers has no more use for it but can pass it on, via the merchants, to a later (nonoverlapping) generation of consumers.

Of course, a more complete model would allow merchants to earn a commission, contracting to purchase corn in the "wholesale" market at some price $x < 1$ sufficient to pay an expected gross rate of return of R on their period 0 corn inventory. This return is the merchants' reward for serving as a reliable source of corn. For convenience merchants' commissions are left out of the present account.

A reader has argued that the addition of merchants with corn inventories to the D–D model is tantamount to the addition of a "lender of last resort." This view would have some force in the absence of a medium of exchange distinct from corn itself; but in the model with money, a true lender of last resort would have to be some agency capable of serving as an emergency source of *money*, not goods. Otherwise supermarkets would have to qualify in the real world as lenders of last resort, implying that their existence alone could render central banks and deposit insurance unnecessary. As shall be shown, in the present model with outside money and no restriction of payments the presence of corn merchants, even with abundant inventories of corn, is *not* sufficient to prevent a banking crisis.

10 In Alan Musgrave's (1981) terminology, our goal is to take what D–D implicitly treat as a "negligibility assumption," namely that the welfare costs of bank suspension do not depend on the presence or absence of monetary exchange and nonbank goods merchants, and treat it instead as a "heuristic assumption" that must be relaxed to assess the theory's applicability to real-world banking systems.

Loewy (1991) also modifies the D–D model by exogenously imposing a role for (fiat) money, by way of assuming that agents must satisfy a legal fiat money "reserve requirement." This approach does not attempt to capture money's market role as a medium of exchange.

11 Thus, our revised model still does not include a role of bank loans in the usual sense.

12 The assumption that bank interest is paid directly in the form of corn is admittedly unrealistic and contrary to our assumptions of a cash-only payments technology and of corn merchants specializing in providing corn to consumers. It is adopted here for the sake of simplicity only, because it allows us to retain the original D–D rate-of-return scheme without abandoning the convenient assumptions of a fixed price of corn and a fixed stock of gold.

13 The proof is the same as in note 6.

14 The potential superiority of bank money to gold rests on the former's greater convenience.

A reader claims that, in the presence of uncertainty as regards the value of bank assets (which is excluded from the D–D framework), banknotes and checks would circulate at varying discounts rather than at par, so that consumers would suffer a welfare loss from using them instead of gold in corn purchases. This argument is inconsistent with historical episodes of relatively free note issuance, such as those of Scotland, Canada, and the US Suffolk system, in which banknotes did routinely circulate at par, notwithstanding the uncertain value of their issuer's assets. In these and many other episodes banknotes were routinely treated by consumers as superior substitutes for specie. The US experience with "free banking" does, on the other hand, appear to support the reader's claim. That experience, however, reflected the peculiar riskiness of notes based on limited bond portfolios as well as high redemption costs encountered in unit banking. On forces leading to routine par exchange of checks and notes under (unregulated) free banking, see above, Chapter 2.

15 A more realistic approach might explicitly require that banknotes or some other hand-to-hand currency be used in certain payments e.g., for making small change. Then checks alone would not be perfect substitutes for gold, though a combination of checks and notes would. One could also allow *some* merchants to behave as type 1s, consuming their inventories in period 1, without altering the chapter's main conclusions.

16 The bank is constrained to purchase only N bushels of corn despite its ability to "create deposits" in exchange for additional bushels by the knowledge that it must be prepared to redeem all of its liabilities in gold in period 2.

17 Note that r_1 and r_2 in the present model will generally be higher than r_1 and r_2 in the previous models owing to an increase in bank wealth.

18 Gorton (1985) shows that banks will resort to suspension or restriction of payments only when such a strategy is in the interest of depositors, i.e., when there is no *prerun* danger of insolvency. Dowd (1988) shows, furthermore, that payment of competitively determined interest on suspended bank liabilities is sufficient to guard against inflationary bank lending during suspension. In the D–D framework prerun insolvency is ruled out by the assumed corn production technology, which abstracts from aggregate (returns) uncertainty.

19 It is not true, as a reader has claimed, that "only certified checks" can circulate during a suspension and that these must be discounted. In fact certified checks have circulated historically only when banks have been legally restricted in their ability to bearer notes. In some past suspensions notes also remained at par. Some examines are discussed in the next section.

The D–D framework does, however, fail to allow for one possibility that might cause bank money to be discounted during a restriction of payments. This possibility involves public fear that banks will take advantage of restriction to expand unduly their balance sheets, thereby reducing the likelihood of future resumption. Historical banks allayed such fear by offering "penalty" rates of interest to holders of their suspended liabilities or by formally agreeing not to expand their balance sheets prior to resumption.

20 Once again, an implicit assumption here is that corn merchants' period 1 inventories are adequate to provide for the wants of type 1 consumers. Otherwise a liquidation of bank assets would have to be undertaken to avoid period 1 welfare losses. As I suggested previously, it seems desirable to distinguish a "banking" crisis, involving shortages of money and money-related intermediation services, from a crisis due to shortages of consumer goods.

21 The Act of 1797 permitting small notes to be issued was rescinded on December 31, 1800.

22 On the use of substitutes, including clearinghouse certificates, for banknotes and legal tender during the crises of 1893 and 1907, see Andrew (1908), Horwitz (1990), Timberlake (1984), and Warner (1895).

23 Chari (1989) also argues that branch banking along Canadian lines might have prevented suspension-related welfare losses under the national banking system. His argument differs substantially from that proposed in the present essay,

however. Rather than disputing the D–D claim that suspensions must leave some type 1 consumers "empty handed" if banks underestimate the value of t, Chari observes that branch banking would have permitted banks to participate in an efficient market for interbank loans while simultaneously diversifying withdrawal risks. In that case t could in effect be regarded as a nonrandom (and hence predictable) variable (Chari, 1989, p. 11). Our point is the complementary one that, even if t were to remain unpredictable under branch banking, suspension costs to impatient consumers could be avoided through the use of nationally accepted checks in interregional payments.

24 New York bankers had planned to reintroduce clearinghouse certificates during the 1933 crisis, but were prevented from doing so by Treasury Secretary Woodin. Woodin insisted that private currency substitutes would be superfluous in light of the Fed's ability to issue "plenty" of "money that looks like real money" (Burns, 1974, p. 45).

REFERENCES

Anderson, Benjamin M. *Economics and the Public Welfare*. Indianapolis: Liberty Press, 1979.

Andrew, A. Piatt. "Substitutes for Cash in the Panic of 1907." *Quarterly Journal of Economics* (August 1908), 497–519.

Burns, Helen M. *The American Banking Community and New Deal Banking Reforms, 1933–1935*. Westport, CT: Greenwood Press, 1974.

Calomiris, Charles W., and Charles M. Kahn. "The Role of Demandable Debt in Structuring Optimal Banking Arrangements." *American Economic Review* 81(3) (January 1991), 497–513.

Chari, V. V. "Banking Without Deposit Insurance or Bank Panics: Lessons from a Model of the US National Banking System." *Federal Reserve Bank of Minneapolis Quarterly Review* (Summer 1989), 3–19.

Checkland, S. G. *Scottish Banking: A History, 1695–1973*. Glasgow: Collins, 1975.

Diamond, Douglas W., and Philip H. Dybvig. "Bank Runs, Deposit Insurance, and Liquidity." *Journal of Political Economy* 91(3) (June 1983), 401–419.

Dowd, Kevin. "Option Clauses and the Stability of Laissez-Faire Monetary System." *Journal of Financial Services Research* 1 (1988), 319–333.

————. "Option Clauses and Bank Suspension." Unpublished manuscript, University of Nottingham, 1989.

————. "Models of Banking Instability: A Partial Review of the Literature." *Journal of Economic Surveys* 6(2) (1992), 107–132.

Dwyer, Gerald P., Jr., and R. Anton Gilbert. "Bank Runs and Private Remedies." *Federal Reserve Bank of St. Louis Review* 71(3) (May/June 1989), 43–61.

Engineer, Merwan, "Bank Runs and Suspension of Deposit Convertibility." *Journal of Monetary Economics* 24(3) (November 1989), 443–454.

Friedman, Milton, and Anna Jacobson Schwartz. *A Monetary History of the United States, 1867–1960*. Princeton, NJ: Princeton University Press, 1963.

Gorton, Gary. "Bank Suspension of Convertibility." *Journal of Monetary Economics* 15 (1985), 177–193.

————. "Banking Panics and Business Cycles." *Oxford Economic Papers* 40 (December 1988), 751–781.

Horwitz, Steven. "Competitive Currencies, Legal Restrictions, and the Origins of the Fed: Some Evidence from the Panic of 1907." *Southern Economic Journal* 56(3) (January 1990), 639–649.

Kane, Edward. *The S & L Insurance Mess: How Did It Happen?* Washington, DC: The Urban Institute, 1989.

Loewy, Michael B. "The Macroeconomic Effects of Bank Runs: An Equilibrium Analysis." *Journal of Financial Intermediation* 1 (1991), 292–256.

Musgrave, Alan. "Unreal Assumptions in Economic Theory: The F-Twist Untwisted." *Kyklos* 34(3) (1981), 377–387.

Redlich, Fritz. *The Molding of American Banking.* New York: Harper Publishing Company, 1951.

Roberds, William. "Lenders of the Next-to-Last Resort: Scrip Issue in Georgia During the Great Depression." *Federal Reserve Bank of Atlanta Economic Review* (September/October 1990), 16–30.

Rockoff, Hugh. "Institutional Requirements for Stable Free Banking." *Cato Journal* 6(2) (Fall 1986), 617–634.

Sprague, O. M. W. *History of Crises under the National Banking System.* Washington, DC: National Monetary Commission, 1910.

Timberlake, Richard H. "The Central Banking Role of Clearinghouse Associations." *Journal of Money, Credit, and Banking* (February 1984), 1–15.

Wallace, Neil. "Another Attempt to Explain an Illiquid Banking System: The Diamond and Dybvig Model with Sequential Service Taken Seriously." *Federal Reserve Bank of Minneapolis Quarterly Review* 12(4) (Fall 1988), 3–16.

———. "A Banking Model in Which Partial Suspension Is Best." *Federal Reserve Bank of Minneapolis Quarterly Review* 14(4) (Fall 1990), 11–23.

Warner, John DeWitt. "The Currency Famine of 1893." *Sound Currency* 2(6) (February 1895), 1–11.

12

BANK-LENDING "MANIAS" IN THEORY AND HISTORY*

Before economists relegate a speculative event to the inexplicable or bubble category . . . we must exhaust all reasonable economic explanations . . . [Our method requires] that we search intensively for market fundamental explanations before clutching the "bubble" last resort.
(Garber, 1990, p. 35)

INTRODUCTION

Traditional accounts of economic "manias" have been questioned in recent years by Peter Garber and like-minded skeptics who deny the usefulness of identifying speculative episodes with "outbursts of irrationality." In one area, however, such accounts still prevail. Banking theory and history have so far escaped Garber-type revisionism. The traditional view, whose modern exponents include Pope (1989), Goodhart (1988), Lawlor and Darity (1989), Barclay (1978), and Kindleberger (1978, 1984, 1990a, 1990b), holds that commercial banks – especially unregulated ones – are prone to become involved in speculative "manias." Encouraged by a boom they themselves may set in motion, banks fuel the boom by expanding the stock of bank money, allowing their reserve ratios to decline. The banking system thus weakens itself and sets the stage for a crisis. Market forces, and the bank-money clearing mechanism in particular, are considered powerless to check expansions of bank money when all banks tend to expand in concert. A rationale is thereby found for legal restrictions on banking, including statutory reserve requirements and government monopolization of currency. Without such restrictions, even with a limited stock of high-powered money, the stock of bank money is believed to exhibit multiple short-run equilibria or even a continuum of such equilibria.

In this final chapter I plan to show that traditional "mania" scenarios of credit expansion (1) exaggerate the role of "confidence" or "optimism" as a

Reprinted, with permission, from the *Journal of Financial Services Research*, Vol. 6, No. 3 (September 1992).

factor in bank lending and (2) are not supported by evidence from past, unrestricted banking systems.

RATIONAL AND IRRATIONAL BANKING BOOMS

A long-standing view of banking crises, elaborated and popularized in recent years by Minsky (1982), Goodhart (1988), and Kindleberger (1978, 1984, ch. 15, 1990a), sees them as consequences of prior speculative booms that bankers either initiate or are drawn into. Inspired by a prevailing mood of business optimism, banks may undertake "pervasive credit expansion" until their "credit positions are extended beyond some limit sustainable in the long run" (Kindleberger, 1984, p. 270). Eventually euphoria gives way to distress, followed by panic and a crash – the bank-money "bubble" bursts. Banks are thus implicated for being "procyclical in operation" at best and "directly responsible for severe fluctuations" at worst (Goodhart, 1988, p. 50).[1]

Unrestricted banking systems, and ones possessing freedom of note issue in particular, are assumed to be especially prone to reckless overexpansion (Goodhart, 1988; Lawlor and Darity, 1989; Kindleberger, 1978, p. 54). According to Kindleberger (1990a, p. 18), while speculative manias may occur even under centralized and regulated banking, "short-run profit making will go much further to destabilize the system under . . . unregulated free banking."[2]

In evaluating the mania hypothesis, it is necessary to distinguish manias involving increased nominal bank lending from ones involving decreasing credit standards. Only the former kind of lending mania will be critically considered here. It is also necessary to distinguish a banking "mania" from a "rational" banking boom. A banking boom can be rational in the broad sense of being strictly consistent with maximizing behavior conditioned by "objective" variables. Such a boom might be driven by changes in market fundamentals, such as the supply of high-powered money or the market-clearing loan rate of interest. A true banking mania, in contrast, is not justified by changes in any exogenous, fundamental determinants of banking profits, but is driven by purely subjective variables, such as bankers' "optimism" or "confidence."[3] When such subjective variables become relevant, "maximizing behavior" may fail to have a well-defined meaning.

"Optimism" and bank lending

The above separation of banking booms into booms stemming from fundamentals and booms exemplifying true "manias" omits a third possibility that has been prominent in recent economic literature. This is the possibility of a "rational" bank-lending "bubble." Unlike a true mania, a rational bubble is consistent with maximizing behavior in the special sense of being based upon bankers' expectations of profit from lending that are somehow (temporarily) *self-fulfilling*. The omission of rational bubbles has not been inadvertent. As Blanchard and Watson (1982) make clear, self-fulfilling price and profit expectations may arise only in connection with variable price assets, such as land, stocks, and perpetuities. Historical banks, in contrast, have typically invested in assets, including loans, with predetermined nominal payoffs and payoff dates, and have held reserves also bearing a fixed nominal price. The maximum (default-free) value of yesterday's loans is independent of the quantity of loans made today. It follows that credit bubbles driven solely by bankers' self-fulfilling price and profit expectations can generally be ruled out. Famous exceptions, like John Law's Banque Royale, have been products of peculiar regulatory circumstances.[4]

The above argument does not mean that bankers' expectations have *no* bearing on forecasted rates of profit. Bankers' optimism may, for example, incline them to expand credit by causing them to lower their estimates of future loan losses. However, because anticipated loan losses typically amount to a small fraction only (e.g., less than 1 per cent) of the book value of a bank's loans, even a dramatic reduction in bankers' estimations of such losses can inspire only a modest increase in bank lending. This is especially true if the supply schedule for bank loans is interest inelastic, as is generally true in reality.

Although bankers' optimistic profit expectations are unlikely to be self-fulfilling, the expectations of bank *borrowers* are another matter. An increase in borrowers' optimism will lead to an outward shift in the demand schedule for bank loans until the equilibrium loan rate of interest conforms with the anticipated rate of return on investment. A rise in the equilibrium loan rate will imply some expansion of credit so long as the loan supply schedule is not perfectly interest inelastic. But this possibility refers to the influence of an exogenous market "fundamental" rather than to any autonomous developments within the banking industry. It is therefore left for critical consideration in a later part of this chapter.

True manias and in-concert expansion

In the course of a true mania bankers, although they may continue to *believe* that they are maximizing profits, lose sight of the requirements for long-run maximization. It is obviously not possible to have an economic "theory" of manias so defined. Nevertheless, it is possible to examine critically the claim that bankers are more likely to lose sight of the requirements for long-run profit maximization than managers of other firms. It is widely held, for instance, that banks are subject to "herding behavior" (Lawlor and Darity, 1989, p. 25), which causes them to expand,

and to overexpand, in concert.[5] In such situations, it is argued, optimal reserve ratios for individual banks and the equilibrium money multiplier cease to be well defined. As Barclay (1978, p. 3) puts it, "The banking business does not have a certain outcome but, instead, a number of possibilities which might, at best, be represented by a probability distribution." The possibilities include "upsurges of activity" driven by bankers' "overeagerness to exploit [available] profit opportunities" (Barclay, 1978, pp. 1, 5). Such upsurges differ from "rational" bubbles insofar as they are not at all consistent with maximizing behavior. Indeed, one implication of such possibilities for bank-credit growth is that market forces, including growing risks of bankruptcy, may be unable to restrain banks' irrational "overeagerness."

The alleged failure of the clearing mechanism

One reply to the above view points to the bank-money clearing mechanism, through which competing banks' claims on one another are settled in some outside reserve asset, as a sufficient check against overexpansion. Given determinate market shares for the deposits or notes of individual banks, any bank that expands its balance sheet independently of its rivals will suffer a loss of reserves through adverse clearings. The reserve losses will eventually cause the overexpanding bank to default, and should quickly discourage any excessive lending based solely on subjective considerations (White, 1984, ch. 1 and pp. 87–101; Selgin, 1988, ch. 3).

Critics of unregulated banking reply that the clearing mechanism cannot limit the growth of bank money when banks expand in concert, as they will tend to do during a speculative mania. When banks expand together at similar rates, all are confronted with like increases in gross clearing debits *and credits*, with no new adverse clearings to encroach upon bank reserves. There is, then, no well-defined "optimal" expansion either for individual banks or for the banking system as a whole: various levels of bank-credit expansion will all be consistent with the same level of perceived bank liquidity and safety, as measured by the frequency and value of bank reserve deficits.

The in-concert expansion argument has been traced by Mints (1945, pp. 104–105) to Doubleday (1826, pp. 30–31) and by Wood (1939, pp. 38–39) to Pennington (1829, pp. 121–122). It has been accepted by most twentieth-century writers. Thus Keynes (1930, p. 27) observed that "[e]very movement forward by an individual bank weakens it but every such movement by one of its neighbors strengthens it: so that if all move forward together no one is weakened on balance." Mints (1945, p. 205) in turn complained that earlier theorists "greatly overemphasized" the importance of the clearing mechanism "as a means of controlling the aggregate of bank credit."

Similar views are expressed in the writings of present-day critics of free banking (Bordo and Schwartz, 1989, p. 4; Lawlor and Darity, 1989, p. 24; Pope, 1989; Goodhart, 1988). According to Goodhart (1988, p. 30),

> the clearinghouse mechanism tends to lead all banks to expand, or to contract, at a broadly similar rate, but does not itself determine what the average growth might be, nor whether it would be stable, or subject to sharp fluctuations.

A systemwide overexpansion of bank money can, according to these writers, be checked only by actual leakages of high-powered reserves from the banking system.[6] In a closed banking system such leakages must take the form of public "withdrawals of [high-powered] cash over the counter" (Phillips, 1921, p. 83). Yet such withdrawals cannot be relied on where notes of private banks are routinely employed as hand-to-hand currency (as they have been in the past) and where holders of bank money cannot directly monitor their banks' liquidity (Cothren, 1987). The optimal bank reserve ratio may therefore be indeterminate, and the actual ratio may fall to arbitrarily low values without provoking disintermediation. Rather than nip overexpansion in the bud, "leakages" might only serve to prick an (irrational) "bubble" long overdue for bursting.

CRITIQUE: THE MICROECONOMIC LIMITS OF IN-CONCERT EXPANSION

Despite their widespread acceptance and distinguished adherents, the in-concert overexpansion thesis – and, hence, the concept of bank-lending manias as a whole – are theoretically weak. Both contradict generally accepted conclusions concerning the microeconomic determinants of bank reserve demand, which suggest strict limits to bank expansion when reserves are limited even if subjective considerations incline bankers to expand in unison.

The theory of optimal reserve holding recognizes, apart from statutory reserve requirements, two distinct sources of bank reserve demand, each a function of bank clearings. The first is "net average" reserve demand (Olivera, 1971; Baltensperger, 1974). This reflects the deterministic pattern or expected value of net bank clearings. The other is "precautionary" reserve demand. It reflects the stochastic or random element in clearings. When banks expand in unison, none suffers any increase in net average reserve demand, as the expansion does not lead to any change in the mean or expected value of net clearings for any of the expanding banks. This has been correctly noted by proponents of the in-concert overexpansion thesis. However, because the precautionary demand for reserves of each bank *does* increase with any growth in *gross* bank clearings, it does not follow that systemwide expansion is unchecked. The presence of a precautionary demand for reserves suggests a determinite and finite value for the money multiplier in unrestricted banking. This means that bankers driven to expand together by some purely subjective stimulus will experience a countervailling, objective stimulus in the form of deficient reserves.

Let $f(X)$ represent the distribution of net clearings facing a representative bank, conditional on the quantity and the turnover of the bank's liabilities, and let $E(X) = 0$ – an assumption consistent with the absence of any secular "leakage" of reserves from the bank and also with any extent of in-concert expansion of bank liabilities. Assuming (as is usually done) that $f(X)$ is approximately normal, the representative bank's optimal reserve will equal some multiple, b, of the standard deviation of X,

$$R^d = b\sigma_x$$

where b varies inversely with the exogenously given opportunity costs of reserve holding and directly with the penalty costs of (unanticipated) reserve deficiencies. Assuming further that there are n identical banks and that the banking system has a fixed endowment of high-powered reserves R^S, the equilibrium stock of bank money M^* must generate a value of σ_x such that $nb\sigma_x = nR^d = R^s$. Because net bank clearings are governed by a stochastic process, any increase in *gross* clearings (occasioned either by an in-concert expansion in the stock of bank money or by an increase in its velocity) causes σ_x, hence R^d, to increase.

Empirical studies of banks' demand for excess reserves support the theory described above. Although these studies typically employ deposits as a scale variable and proxy for the variability of clearings (Frost, 1971, pp. 813–814), the authors clearly recognize turnover of deposits as a positive determinent of reserve demand, implying that clearings or debits (deposits times turnover) would be a better scale variable. Thus Morrison (1966, p. 7) states that "If transactions costs are positive, the amount of cash banks desire to hold might be expected to vary directly ... with the rate of deposit turnover." A test of this proposition, performed by regressing bank excess reserves on deposits and the Treasury bill rate (as in Frost, 1971) and adding a deposit turnover variable, produces the expected results (Table 12.1). The turnover coefficient is positive and significant at a 95 per cent confidence level after adjusting for first-order autocorrelation. This result suggests that reserve demand depends on the activity of deposits as reflected by their turnover and not merely on the *level* of deposits. It also suggests, contrary to Goodhart and other proponents of the mania hypothesis, that turnover does not proxy confidence or optimism and so act to stimulate *pro*cyclical bank lending.

The positive relation of precautionary reserve demand to bank deposits implies that, even given fixed values for the turnover of bank money and the nominal stock of high-powered reserves, in-concert expansion must lead to a systemwide shortage of (precautionary) reserves even though no

Table 12.1 Excess reserve demand regression, US banks monthly data, 1948–1968
(*t*-values in parentheses)

Intercept	D	TOVER	TBR	T
0.83599	0.00449	0.003346	−0.06814	−0.00208
(53.6)	(2.872)	(2.019)	(−5.512)	(−19.484)
R^2 = 0.8449				

Notes: TBR = Treasury bill rate; D = net demand deposits; TOVER = demand deposit turnover; T = linear trend variable; other RHS variables are detrended. The sample period ends in September 1968, when lagged reserve accounting began. Estimates have been corrected for autocorrelation by the Yule–Walker method

bank actually suffers a sustained reserve outflow.[7] Indeed, only *one* bank has to realize that, in expanding along with the rest, it has overstepped well-defined bounds of safety, for the system as a whole to be driven back to equilibrium. This is because contraction by any one bank acting in isolation *will* generate positive net-average reserve demands that will force remaining banks to contract.

BANKING "FUNDAMENTALS"

The theory just reviewed suggests that the demand for bank reserves in an unrestricted banking system free of "leakages" is not a function homogeneous of degree 0 in the size of individual bank balance sheets. Given values for the stock of outside-money reserves, the turnover of bank money, interest rates, and penalty costs of default, equilibrium values for the stock of bank money and the optimal bank reserve ratio exist that should be more or less invariant to changes in bankers' "optimism."

This conclusion casts doubt upon the popular view that bank money is subject to mania-driven growth, by showing that the optimal banking system reserve ratio is not ill-defined. Unless bankers are "irrational" to the point of courting bankruptcy, a fundamentally unjustified expansion of bank money would probably be checked by perceived reserve shortages before gaining mania-like proportions. This conclusion suggests that banking manias have been less common historically than is often supposed. Many alleged manias may actually have been "rational" booms driven by changed market fundamentals. We next consider how some of these fundamentals may influence bank behavior, to see which ones are likely to inspire booms, and how.

Velocity

It has been observed that booms typically involve a "movement out of liquid assets such as money into long-term or equity assets" (Kindleberger,

1990b, p. 71). This suggests a rise in the velocity of bank money, occasioned by a fall in its perceived relative yield. Conventional theory suggests, however, that, far from encouraging banks to expand their balance sheets, a rise in velocity should lead, *ceteris paribus*, to an increase in banks' optimal precautionary reserve ratios, entailing as it must an increase in the rate of turnover of bank money. Maximizing behavior would then require a *countercyclical contraction* in bank balance sheets (Selgin, 1990).

Goodhart (1988, p. 30) and Lawlor and Darity (1989, p. 25) observe that unregulated banks may expand their balance sheets by taking measures to enhance the public's willingness to hold bank money. An extreme version of this possibility is considered by Minsky (1982) in his description of "Ponzi finance" – a financial scheme where interest payments exceeding income receipts are financed through further debt issuance. That bankers may take steps to encourage more public holding of bank money cannot be denied; but this possibility offers no support for the claim that unrestricted banks will expand credit excessively. Holding the aggregate stock of bank reserves constant, banks may (presumably at rising marginal cost) exert a *downward* influence on velocity which they can then safely offset by expanding their balance sheets. No overall increase in nominal expenditures, hence no fueling of a speculative boom, is implied by such behavior. Alternatively, banks may attract more deposits of high-powered money, sponsoring a general increase in the money stock and nominal expenditures, but with no necessary decline in the ratio of bank-money expenditures to reserves. Here again the scenario does not imply any obvious weakening of the banking system.

The rate of interest

An increase in loan or bond rates of interest raises the opportunity cost of reserve holding. It is often assumed that higher loan rates must lead to a fall in the optimal bank reserve ratio, so that an intense demand for loans during booms will inspire banks to "stretch" their reserves. Reality is more complicated. Penalty costs of default may also be positively related to interest rates (which influence the terms of "emergency" borrowing). The optimal reserve ratio will then depend in a complicated manner on the relationship between various borrowing and lending rates without being related in any definite way to their absolute values (Olivera, 1971, p. 1103). Empirical studies confirm this, showing that the demand for bank reserves is relatively interest inelastic except perhaps at unusually low rates of interest (Frost, 1971; Morrison, 1966; Rasche, 1972; Sushka, 1976; Hancock, 1985). Moreover, as will be seen later, historical banking booms have typically involved *falling* rather than rising rates of interest until their final stages. This means that banking booms have usually been driven, not by changes in the demand for credit, but by rightward shifts in bank-credit

263

supply schedules. Assuming that such shifts have not been due to banks irrationally allowing their reserve ratios to fall, they must have been due either to financial innovations allowing banks to keep smaller reserves, or to increased supplies of high-powered money (Minsky, 1982, p. 33).

Panics

Banks keep higher reserve ratios in the immediate aftermath of runs and panics than they keep in "normal" times. A number of explanations have been offered to account for this, none of which appeals to irrational bank behavior either before or following the onset of panic. According to Frost (1971), high post-panic reserve ratios may reflect a "kinked" demand function for bank excess reserves – one that becomes interest elastic at very low interest rates. At such low rates of interest banks' costs of adjusting their reserve position may exceed the opportunity costs of holding excess reserves. Significantly, Frost's kinked demand curve hypothesis does *not* support the contrary view (discussed in the previous subsection) that *high* interest rates will lead banks to *expand* credit while skimping on reserves.

Other theorists, including Friedman and Schwartz (1963, pp. 534–542) and Morrison (1966), attribute high post-panic reserve ratios to bankers' anticipations of further runs and associated extraordinary reserve leakages. Thus, while leakages are not essential to pin down the money multiplier, an increase in the expected value of leakages will reduce the multiplier's value. All of these explanations imply discrete changes in bank reserve ratios in response to changed business conditions. In normal times reserve ratios are lower than in periods immediately following a crisis. This alone may account for the occasional observation of countercyclical movements in bank reserve ratios. It does not, however, necessarily imply that banks during "good" times will progressively and imprudently reduce their reserve ratios and fuel speculative booms.

HIGH-POWERED MONEY

Bank expansion may, of course, be driven by an increase in high-powered bank reserves, which the clearing mechanism cannot neutralize. The high-powered money may be a commodity money such as gold, the stock of which depends on such "fundamentals" as the balance of international payments and the profitability of gold mining; or it may be a fiat money, which will typically be issued in inflationary amounts if the issuer is guided by an increased desire for seignorage. Lastly, the notes and deposits of a monopoly bank of issue will serve as high-powered money even when the monopoly bank itself must redeem them at a fixed price in some still more "basic" money. For this reason a monopoly or quasi-monopoly bank of issue is not subject to the usual clearing-mechanism discipline, but must ultimately be constrained by internal or (in an open system) external leakages of the ultimate money of redemption (Selgin, 1988, pp. 48–49). Such leakages (unlike leakages to other banks arising in connection with the operation of the clearing mechanism) may have to await a rise in prices – too late, perhaps, to prevent a surge of speculative activity which then becomes difficult to check. It follows that the scope for speculative booms is widened in the presence of monopoly banks of issue even where the latter are constrained by a commodity standard. This view, which is applicable to both "private" and "public" monopoly banks, runs counter to the conventional view, endorsed by proponents of the mania hypothesis, of central banks as instruments of monetary restraint. For obvious reasons, speculative booms based on growth in bank reserves should not be cited as evidence of banking manias or attributed to any irrational behavior on the part of (competitive) bankers.

The next section will show that several historical banking manias were actually based on injections of high-powered money, sometimes due to expansion by a central bank of issue. Contrary to the conventional view, these episodes offer no clear evidence of any irrational behavior by competitive bankers and hence provide no valid rationale for restrictions on competitive banks' powers of money creation.

BANK-LENDING MANIAS IN HISTORY:
A SAMPLING

Despite frequent references in the literature to bank-lending manias, few have been documented in the least-restricted banking systems, that is in systems lacking central banks, statutory reserve requirements, or other extra-market sources of monetary control and therefore dependent solely on the clearing mechanism as a source of restraint. This void is surprising in light of the standard view that such systems ought to be most prone to reckless overexpansions of money and credit. Some attempts have been made to explain away this incongruity. For example, Bordo and Schwartz (1989, p. 9), and Goodhart (1988, pp. 51–52), in attempting to account for the relative stability of the Canadian banking system in the nineteenth century, attribute the system's stability not to its clearing mechanism, but to branch banking, competitive private note issue, and the convertibility of banknotes.[8] Similar features, plus the presence of unlimited liability for many note-issuing banks, are also supposed to account for the stability of free banking in Scotland in the first half of the same century. Such "explanations" are question-begging for two reasons. First, they fail to recognize that branch banking, competitive note issue, and the convertibility of banknotes are all typical of unrestricted banking systems, not special consequences of regulation. To the extent that any of them reduces banking system instability, the instability is not an inherent feature of *unregulated* banking. Second, the explanations fail to explain how these features prevent bank manias from occurring. Branch banking and competitive note issue alone pose no check on credit expansion; indeed, the conventional view (not challenged by the authors in question) is that freedom to issue notes gives bankers *more* opportunities to expand their balance sheets.

Unlimited liability might be viewed as a device that would cause bankers to behave more conservatively, but the facts suggest otherwise. In Scotland the chartered, limited liability banks were just as conservative as unlimited liability banks; in fact the only clear example of wreckless behavior by a Scottish bank involved the Ayr Bank (discussed below), whose owners had unlimited liability. (Canadian banks, incidentally, were subject to double, but not unlimited, liability.) Finally, because public requests for the redemption of notes ("internal reserve leakages") were quite unusual in both systems (White, 1984; National Monetary Commission, 1910), the convertibility of banknotes into specie (or, in Canada, Dominion notes) was irrelevant for much of Scottish and Canadian experience except insofar as such convertibility was taken advantage of by rival banks in the settlement of clearing balances. It follows that the clearing mechanism functioned in both arrangements as an almost exclusive source of short-run monetary restraint which, contrary to the standard view, prevented lending manias from occurring.

Other, relatively free banking systems, such as those of nineteenth-century Sweden and Switzerland, were also noteworthy for their apparent freedom from bank manias (Jonung, 1985; Weber, 1988). In a few instances, though, decentralized systems do appear to have become embroiled in speculative booms. Relying on the same limited evidence available to proponents of the mania hypothesis – evidence that admittedly may involve some "window dressing" insofar as it consists of publicly reported bank statistics – I will consider four cases, all involving relatively unrestricted banking systems, of supposed bank-lending manias: (1) the boom preceding the Ayr Bank crisis in Scotland in 1772; (2) the country banking boom leading to the English Panic of 1825; (3) the US boom that led to the Panic of 1837; and (4) the land and banking boom prior to the Australian crash of 1893.

The Ayr Bank crisis

Despite the widely accepted general immunity of Scottish free banking from manias and crises, manias are alleged to have occurred even in Scotland, the most spectacular being the one preceding the Ayr crisis of 1772 (Boase, 1867, pp. 213–241).[9] According to Checkland (1975, p. 214), in the months preceding that crisis "[e]very banker extended his credits and his note issue as confidence grew" knowing full well "that a liquidity crisis must develop." Instead of "acting in the light of that level of advances and note issue that would have been optimally related to the stability and growth needs of the time," the Scottish banks allegedly fueled a speculative boom by offering "relatively easy credit" (Checkland, 1975, p. 215). No less an authority than Adam Smith – himself an Ayr Bank shareholder at the time of the crash – opined that Scottish banks as a whole had been "carried away by the optimism and aggressiveness of the merchant community" (cited in Checkland, 1975, p. 268).

The evidence, however, contradicts the view that all or even a majority of Scottish banks participated in the pre-Ayr-crisis boom. The Ayr Bank (Douglas, Heron and Co.) was established in November 1769 in response to its founders" peculiar belief that the Scottish banking system was "failing to do its duty by liberally expanding credit" (Checkland, 1975, p. 260; Munn, 1981, p. 30). The new bank proceeded at once to embark upon "a policy of indiscriminate lending" where "those in charge showed no apparent sign of having thought out the basis of their operations" (Checkland, 1975, p. 261). By mid-1772, just prior to suspending, the Ayr had £220,000 of its notes in circulation – down from a peak of £450,000 but still more than the circulation of the next two largest banks put together – with over £1 million in total liabilities and only £12,956 of specie on hand (Boase, 1867, pp. 88, 106; Checkland, 1975, p. 129). This represented a reserve ratio approximately one-tenth that of other Scottish banks at the time (Munn, 1981, p. 141).

The Ayr Bank's expansion does appear to have been irrational or at least ill-informed and may have helped place Scotland "in the grip of a speculative frenzy" (Checkland, 1975, p. 129). But, notwithstanding assertions to the contrary, the expansion was almost entirely a solitary undertaking of the Ayr Bank, in which other Scottish banks did not participate. Indeed, while the Ayr Bank energeticaly expanded its liabilities, other banks of issue not only kept aloof from the boom but *contracted* their liabilities in anticipation of trouble. Ironically, it was a policy instituted by the Ayr Bank itself upon its founding that sealed its fate. The Ayr had agreed from the start to accept rival banks' notes at par, compelling the formation of a biweekly note exchange for all Scottish banks of issue (Checkland, 1975, p. 126). As the Ayr's circulation grew, so did adverse clearings against it. The Ayr went to unusual lengths to avoid immediate default, first by rediscounting bills at a loss in London, and then by obtaining emergency loans from other banks of issue (Checkland, 1975, pp. 127–128; Munn, 1981, pp. 29–32). Nevertheless, adverse clearings eventually caught up with it.

When the Ayr finally collapsed on the 25th of June, 1772, 13 small, private, nonissuing banks also failed. Like the Ayr, these banks had had extensive dealings with the London banking house of Neale and Co., which failed on the 8th of June (Hamilton, 1956, p. 412). But of the 17 large banks of issue, only one – the Merchant Banking Company of Glasgow – was forced (temporarily) to suspend. The others, including both the Bank of Scotland and the Royal Bank, successfully "weathered the storm," a few "having never had a larger store of coin ... in proportion to their circulation and other liabilities" (Boase, 1867, p. 88). Ironically, Checkland himself (1975, p. 269) acknowledges this, contradicting his own earlier remarks by noting how many Scottish banks "stood aside, curtailing their lending and notes issues" as the Ayr expanded so that, with the Ayr's collapse, "the credit excess was purged from the Scottish system." All of this suggests that the clearing mechanism was effective in disciplining the Scottish banking system as a whole (White, 1984, pp. 31–32).

The Panic of 1825

The English Panic of 1825 has been called "an almost classic case of the 'boom that ran away'" (Scammell, 1968, p. 131n). At that time the English currency system was largely decentralized. The Bank of England still enjoyed a monopoly of joint-stock banking and was sole bank of issue in the London area; but the rest of England was serviced by numerous "country" banks of issue, legally limited to six partners or less.

No legal restrictions (apart from gold convertibility) limited the issues of country banks prior to 1844, and numerous writers, including a few modern ones (Scammell, 1968, pp. 131–133; Barclay, 1978, pp. 9–10; Kindleberger, 1978, p. 52), have blamed the country banks for bringing on disaster. As Kindleberger concisely asserts (1978, p. 77), "private bankers of London and the provinces financed the boom" whereas "the Bank of England financed the crisis."

Theory, in contrast, supports another view – one argued by Bullionist writers during the Bank Restriction, the Free Banking School between 1825 and 1850, and more recently by Wood (1939), Pressnell (1956), Nevin and Davis (1970), and Dowd (1989). Of all English banks, only the Bank of England with its special privileges enjoyed having its notes treated as a cash reserve by other banks. Continuing a practice adopted during the Restriction, country banks settled local clearing balances in Bank of England notes and kept accounts with London private banks to settle nonlocal clearings (Coppieters, 1955, pp. 44–45). London private banks, in turn, also settled their internal clearing balances with Bank of England notes (Coppieters, 1955, p. 92; Kindleberger, 1984, p. 78). Thus the Bank of England, by altering the volume of its notes and by standing ready to rediscount bills for London private bankers, was indirectly able to influence the volume of note issues and advances in the countryside (Pressnell, 1956, p. 220).

These arrangements also made the Bank of England immune to the discipline of domestic adverse clearings. Disregarding domestic, nonmonetary demands for specie (which were of relatively minor importance), the

Bank was subject only to the eventual discipline of an external drain of specie, which would come into play only after a lag of uncertain length encompassing a rise in prices.[10] The Bank of England's freedom from internal restraints suggests that speculative booms and busts were more likely to be sponsored by it than by the country banks. If the Bank of England expanded, other banks as a whole would follow suit, whereas no country bank or group of country banks wielded any similar influence.

Available quantitative evidence, unfortunately limited to annual data, is consistent with the above interpretation. The ratio of country note circulation to Bank of England issues remained within the narrow range of 0.64 to 0.663 for most of the years 1818 to 1825.[11] The sole exceptions were 1823 and 1824 – the two years preceding the crisis – when the ratios were 0.572 and 0.588, respectively. These figures suggest that, insofar as country banks behaved unusually in the years just prior to the crisis, they did so by becoming more *conservative* than usual, resisting any impulse to extend their liabilities beyond levels consistent with available, liquid reserves of Bank of England notes.

The Bank's circulation (and hence the reserves of country banks) did, however, grow after 1822 as part of "a general plan for cheap money and credit expansion" (Wood, 1939, p. 82; also Pressnell, 1956, pp. 478–479). The plan encompassed a lowering of the Bank rate of discount to 4 per cent from its traditional value of 5 per cent and an extension of the maximum maturity of eligible bills from 65 to 95 days (Thomas, 1934, p. 42). As the Bank expanded its liabilities, its stock of bullion reached a peak of close to £14 million in May 1824 and then fell continuously and rapidly to £1.26 million by the close of 1825 (Boase, 1867, pp. 330, 340), when the Bank rate was restored to 5 per cent. The country banks, having been kept in the dark about the status of the Bank's bullion reserves (Coppieters, 1955, pp. 95–99), could hardly be expected to do other than respond positively to the increased abundance of their own reserves, by reducing their own discount and deposit rates. The evidence does not, on the other hand, provide any convincing support for the view that country banks pushed beyond limits justifed by the Bank of England's policies, notwithstanding the "insane speculation" (Boase, 1867, p. 338) that is said to have inspired them recklessly to disregard their liquidity.[12] Critics of free banking who have felt obliged to appeal to a country-banking mania to account for the events of 1825 have simply failed to appreciate adequately the Bank of England's special influence (Boase, 1867; also Gilbert, 1837, pp. 108–169; Wood, 1939, p. 27; Coppieters, 1955, p. 177). As Pressnell has observed (1956, p. 496), lapses by a few country bankers were "hardly more striking than those of a minority of men in business communities during most periods." That so many (80 in all) suspended in the ensuing crisis is also no proof that country banks on the whole were reckless or irrational beforehand. It reflects, rather, the debilitating effects of the six-partner rule, which impaired country banks' ability to withstand shocks stemming from the Bank of England's inconsistent policies.

The Panic of 1837

Traditional accounts of the US Panic of 1837 hold it to have been a consequence of banks "expanding their notes and deposits without a corresponding increase in their specie reserves" (Temin, 1969, p. 17). The dismemberment of the Bank of United States after 1832 is supposed to have paved the way by leaving state banks free to engage in an "unprecedented expansion of bank credit" (Matthews, 1954, p. 49).

Even in New England, where the Suffolk bank operated an efficient clearing system, bankers are supposed to have fanned the flames of over-speculation. From 1830 to 1837 the number of New England banks rose from 173 to 324 (Fenstermaker, Filer, and Herren, 1984, Table 4). This growth was accompanied by expansion of the money stock as well as by rising prices after 1834 (Temin, 1969, p. 68). Despite its acknowledged ability to restrain individual banks, the Suffolk clearing system supposedly failed to restrain expansion by New England banks taken as a whole (Anderson, 1926, pp. 48–49; Lake, 1947, p. 190; Bordo and Schwartz, 1989, p. 4; Fenstermaker and Filer, 1986). Rather than keeping them in check, the Suffolk system is alleged to have allowed New England bankers to expand in concert to unsafe and unsustainable levels.

This traditional view has been challenged by Sushka (1976) and by Temin (1969). Temin argues that the credit "boom" of the mid-1830s was due to an increase in the US specie stock, mainly in connection with capital inflows from Britain that were reversed abruptly in early 1837. Although reserve ratios in New England were lower than elsewhere in the country, this reflected the exceptionally high public reliance on bank notes in that part of the country (Temin, 1969, p. 75). Thanks to the Suffolk's redemption facilities, New England banknotes traded at par throughout the region, so that gold offered no special advantage in inter-state exchange. That New England banks were the last in the nation to suspend in 1837 also suggests that they were not especially unsafe.

More significant still is the fact that the aggregate reserve ratio for New England did not decline in the boom years preceding the panic. Figures from Fenstermaker and the US Treasury, cited in Temin (1969), show a stable (Fenstermaker) or slightly rising (Treasury) ratio for 1834 to 1837. More recent data from Fenstermaker, Filer, and Herren (1984) confirm these earlier results. Table 12.2 summarizes New England bank reserve-ratio data for the years 1834 to 1837.

In Table 12.2, one figure only – the last in the third column – suggests expansionary behavior on the part of New England banks. Yet even that figure actually reflects a loss of specie in connection with the changed

Table 12.2 Ratio of specie to banknotes and deposits at New England banks

Year	US Treasury	Fenstermaker	Fenstermaker et al. I	Fenstermaker et al. II
1834	0.06	0.10	0.10	0.45
1835	0.07	0.11	0.09	0.48
1836	0.07	0.10	0.10	0.55
1837	0.09	0.12	0.07	0.51

Sources: First two columns from Temin (1969, p. 75); third and fourth columns from Fenstermaker, Filer, and Herren (1984, Table 4). The ratios in the third column are calculated the conventional way, with specie reserves divided by the money stock (banknotes and deposits). Those in the fourth column are based upon Fenstermaker's alternative approach, where reserves include balances due from other banks as well as notes of other banks (the latter also being deducted from the money stock figures).

balance of payments in 1837. The stock of bank money in New England actually fell that year from $42.3 million to $41 million. At no point does the evidence suggest any mania-like, in-concert expansion by the banking system or any failure of the Suffolk clearing mechanism to pin down the money multiplier. The evidence from New England agrees with Sushka's conclusion (1976, p. 833), based upon econometric results for the United States as a whole, that "the Panic of 1837 cannot be attributed to speculative banking practices."

Fenstermaker and Filer (1986) provide a novel argument for the proposition that the Suffolk system failed to restrain New England banks. Comparing figures from before and after 1825, when the Suffolk first established note redemption accounts for other New England banks, they find no significant decline in the money multiplier, and a significant increase in the proportion of banknotes in the total money stock (Fenstermaker and Filer, 1986, pp. 39–40). But rather than suggest a lack of any restraining influence on the part of the Suffolk Bank, these findings illustrate certain economies from centralized note redemption, which reduced New England's overall need for specie reserves. Prior to 1825, the Suffolk was aggressively redeeming country notes directly at their issuers' counters, forcing the issuers to keep large specie reserves. The widened range of acceptance of notes at par after 1825 merely added to economies from centralized note redemption by encouraging persons to use notes instead of gold and silver coin in interregional exchanges. As greater efficiencies in the use of specie were realized, reserve ratios fell. This parameter change did not show, therefore, that New England banks were at any point "unrestrained" in their ability to grant credit or issue notes.

The Australian Crash of 1893

Banking in Australia was largely unregulated in the nineteenth century. Entry was practically unrestricted, banks were free to issue notes, and no statutory reserve requirements were enforced. Until the mid-1880s, the system prospered, displaying admirable stability compared with more restricted banking systems elsewhere. Then a fall in real estate prices caused many banks to suffer heavy losses. Finally, in January 1893, a dramatic collapse occurred: half of Australia's 26 trading banks suspended, with their depositors forced to bear heavy losses. The crisis forever "tarnished the image of bankers as responsible guardians of society's savings" (Pope, 1989, p. 61).

Modern discussions of the crisis blame it on a lack of governmental restrictions on bank lending. According to Pope (1989), Merrett (1989), and Boehm (1971), Australian banks in the 1880s were led to overexpand credit in response to rising real estate prices. As the land boom progressed, banks were supposedly encouraged to expand together in proportion to the rising value of collateral securities (Merrett, 1989, p. 71). According to Pope (1989, p. 15), the Australian clearing mechanism, though undoubtedly effective in restraining individual banks, "never prevented all banks from expanding in unison." Thus the banks were allegedly able to take part in a "Gadarene race to ruin" (Pope, 1989, p. 30), allowing their reserve ratios to fall to exceedingly low levels (Pope, 1989; Merrett, 1989, p. 75).

Once again, however, the facts provide no evidence of a banking mania. Merrett (1989, p. 75) reports that the aggregate reserve ratio (specie to notes and deposits, including time deposits) fell from 0.3217 in 1872 to 0.2188 in 1877; but his figures for later five-year intervals show no further downward trend. Although the ratio declined to 0.1687 in 1882, it returned to 0.2158 in 1887, falling once more to 0.1656 in 1892. Even the lowest figure compares favorably to those from other banking systems, both regulated and free. It is much higher than Scottish bank reserve ratios for the mid-nineteenth century, which were often as low as 0.01 or 0.02, and about the same as ratios for free Canadian banks in the late nineteenth century and for heavily regulated US banks today. Of course, conditions may have warranted a much higher reserve ratio for Australian banks than was typical elsewhere, so that the above cross-country comparisons do not necessarily show that Australian banks were not reckless.

Pope's annual data, presented graphically (1989, p. 20, fig. 8), are more plainly inconsistent with the overexpansion hypothesis. According to Pope's chart, in the seven years preceding the crisis the average reserve ratio of the 13 banks that survived the crisis varied from about 0.17 to about 0.19, with no apparent trend. The average ratio of the 13 suspended banks actually *rose* steadily from about 0.15 to about 0.16. These figures are consistent with the decline in Australian lending rates during the period in question. They also show that Australian banks on the whole did *not* allow their reserve ratios to fall to extend their involvement in the real estate market. The boom was financed, not by any increase in the bank money multiplier, but by injections of high-powered money from Australian gold mines and from the British capital market.[13] When injections from Britain came to a sudden end with the Barings Crisis of 1890, many Australian banks were obviously unprepared; but this did not make them guilty of having lent excessively and "irrationally" during the boom years.

CONCLUSION

Available evidence from less restricted banking systems does not support the banking mania tradition. Banks not subject to legal limits on their issues have not taken advantage of this to allow their reserve ratios to fall during booms. Banks *have* tended to hold *higher* than usual reserve ratios in the aftermath of crises, perhaps in anticipation of extraordinary "leakages" of high-powered money. In short, if banks have behaved in any procyclical fashion, they have leaned in the direction of exceptional conservatism during slumps. When monetary expansion has "fanned the flames" of euphoria and planted the seeds of an eventual crisis, the expansion has generally been caused not by falling reserve ratios for competitive banks (as the mania thesis claims), but by exogenous injections of high-powered money. These injections have sometimes consisted of specie inflows; at other times they have consisted of the expanded liabilities of a central bank of issue freed from the normal discipline of domestic adverse clearings.

The empirical evidence generally accords with the microeconomic theory of bank reserve demand. It suggests that, given some available stock of high-powered reserves, bank clearing arrangements are able to restrain systemwide expansion by competitive banks. On the other hand, the clearing mechanism cannot prevent expansions based upon injections of high-powered money. For competitive banks to resist expanding in response to such injections would be maniacal indeed.

NOTES

1 In correspondence Kindleberger observes that booms stemming from "euphoric lending" do not *always* lead to a crisis: some "subside with a whimper instead of a bang."

2 These authors do not deny that some legal restrictions, such as deposit insurance, may actually encourage banking manias.

3 Matthews (1954, pp. 207–208) links manias to "a sudden rise in profit expectations and weakening of normal standards of business caution unjustified (or not fully justified) by current changes in the objective rate of profit." In this Matthews is closely followed by the previously cited authors.

4 The note issues of the Banque Royale were aimed at supporting the price of its own stock. The result was a very peculiar banking bubble that began to deflate as soon as wary investors tried to realize capital gains by converting shares into notes and notes into gold (Garber, 1990, pp. 42–47).

273

5 For a critical examination of the "herding behavior" hypothesis in international lending, see Jain and Gupta (1987).

6 Goodhart (1988, p. 48) asserts that even an actual reserve leakage "might not itself lead to more cautious behavior." As will be seen, there is some truth to this claim as regards privileged banks of issue, but none supporting it with respect to competitive issuers.

7 Sir John Hicks (1967, p. 51), calling this a "liquidity pressure" effect, observed that it ought to lead to a general contraction of credit: as individual banks perceive that their reserve endowments no longer provide adequate protection against adverse clearings in any single clearing session, all are driven to reduce their loans and liabilities until the aggregate demand for reserves no longer exceeds the aggregate reserve endowment. Chapter 6 presents a detailed analysis of the comparative statics of money supply under free banking. Under central banking, liquidity pressure might be offset by accommodative expansion of the stock of base money.

8 Kindleberger (1978, p. 117) notes that financial crises occurred in Canada in 1879, 1887, and 1908. But there is no evidence of a speculative boom preceding any of these crises. The crisis of 1908 was brought about by legal restrictions on the note issues of Canadian banks, which led to a harvest-season "currency shortage" similar to but much less severe than those routinely experienced in the United States in the same era.

9 An earlier, alleged mania, the "small note mania" of the early 1760s, is critically examined by Rockoff (1986, pp. 619–622).

10 This argument conforms with the classical price-specie-flow theory of international gold movements.

11 Calculated using Burgess's estimates of country banknotes outstanding, as cited in Coppieters (1955, p. 151), and excluding Bank of England notes under £5. Burgess's estimates were based on data from a survey of 122 country banks. An alternative series by Sedgwick was based on stamp returns and therefore reflects banks' *preparations* rather than actual *issues* of notes. Sedgwick's series declines dramatically from 1818 to 1822, reflecting an 1819 resolution by the House of Commons requiring the redemption of all country notes under £5 before 1825. This resolution made it uneconomical for banks to prepare new small notes after 1819 except to replace those too worn for further use. A subsequent act of 1822 extended the legality of small notes until 1833, thereby prompting renewed note preparations. Many of the new notes were used to replace those that had been allowed to wear out through repeated reissuance from 1819 to 1822 (Wood, 1939, p. 15).

   August Bank of England circulation figures are reported in Boase (1867, p. 340). Bank of England notes under £5 are excluded because they were neither used in the settlement of bank clearings nor (outside of London) held as bank till money. Demand deposits did not become an important component of the English money stock until after the introduction of joint-stock banking in 1826.

12 Interest rates were low during the boom, so that banks had no opportunity-cost motivation for reducing their reserve ratios.

13 Banks may, of course, also have fueled the real estate boom by reducing nonreal-estate-related loans.

REFERENCES

Anderson, M. D. "A Note on the Elasticity of the Currency." *American Economic Review* 16(1) (March 1926), 47–50.

Baltensperger, Ernst, "The Precautionary Demand for Reserves." *American Economic Review* 64(1) (March 1974), 205–210.

Barclay, Christopher R. "Competition and Financial Crises, Past and Present." In: Jack Revell, Ed., *Competition and Regulation of Banks*, Bangor, UK: University of Wales Press, 1978, 1–23.

Blanchard, Oliver J., and Watson, Mark W. "Bubbles, Rational Expectations, and Financial Markets." In: Paul Wachtel, ed., *Crises in the Economic and Financial Structure*. Lexington, MA: Lexington Books, 1982, 295–315.

Boase, C. W. *A Century of Banking in Dundee*. Edinburgh: R. Grant and Son, 1867.

Boehm, E. A. *Prosperity and Depression in Australia*. Oxford: Oxford University Press, 1971.

Bordo, Michael D., and Schwartz, Anna J. "The Performance and Stability of Banking Systems under 'Self-Regulation': Theory and Evidence." Australian National University Joint Economic Conference on Regulating Commercial Banks, 1989.

Checkland, S. G. *Scottish Banking: A History, 1695–1973*. Glasgow: Collins, 1975.

Coppieters, Emmanuel. *English Bank Note Circulation, 1694–1954*. The Hague: Martinus Nijhoff, 1955.

Cothren, Richard. "Asymmetric Information and Optimal Bank Reserves." *Journal of Money, Credit, and Banking* 19(1) (February 1987), 68–77.

Doubleday, Thomas, *Remarks on Some Points of the Currency Question*. 1826.

Dowd, Kevin. "The Evolution of Central Banking in England, 1821–1890." Unpublished manuscript, 1989.

Fenstermaker, J. van, and Filer, John E. "Impact of the First and Second Banks of the United States and the Suffolk System on New England Bank Money." *Journal of Money, Credit, and Banking* 18(1) (February 1986), 28–40).

Fenstermaker, J. van, Filer, John E., and Herren, Robert S. "Money Statistics of New England, 1785–1837." *Journal of Economic History* 44(2) (June 1984), 441–453.

Friedman, Milton, and Schwartz, Anna J. *A Monetary History of the United States, 1867–1960*. Princeton, NJ: Princeton University Press, 1963.

Frost, Peter A. "Banks' Demand for Excess Reserves." *Journal of Political Economy* 79(4) (July/August 1971), 805–825.

Garber, Peter M. "Famous First Bubbles." *Journal of Economic Perspectives* 4(2) (Spring 1990), 35–45.

Gilbert, James W. *The History of Banking in America*. London: Longmans et al., 1837.

Goodhart, C. A. E. *The Evolution of Central Banks*. Cambridge, MA: MIT Press, 1988.

Hamilton, Henry. "The Failure of the Ayr Bank, 1772." *Economic History Review* 8(3) (1956), 405–417.

Hancock, Diana. "The Financial Firm: Production with Monetary and Nonmonetary Goods." *Journal of Political Economy* 93(s) (October 1985), 859–880).

Hicks, John. "The Two Triads, Lecture 1." In: *Critical Essays in Monetary Theory*. Oxford: Oxford University Press, 1967, 1–16.

Jain, Arvind K., and Gupta, Satyadev. "Some Evidence on 'Herding' Behavior of U.S. Banks." *Journal of Money, Credit, and Banking* 19(1) (February 1987), 78–89.

Jonung, Lars. "The Economics of Private Money: The Experience of Private Notes in Sweden." Unpublished manuscript, 1985.

Keynes, J. M. *A Treatise on Money*, vol. 1. London: Macmillan, 1930.

Kindleberger, Charles P. *Manias, Panics, and Crashes*. New York: Basic Books, 1978.

Kindleberger, Charles P. *A Financial History of Western Europe*. New York: George Allen and Unwin, 1984.

Kindleberger, Charles P. "Free Minting." Unpublished manuscript, 1990a.

Kindleberger, Charles P. "The Panic of 1873." In: Eugene N. White, ed., *Crashes and Panics: The Lessons From History*. Homewood, IL: Dow Jones-Irwin, 1990b, 69–84.

Lake, Wilfred S. "The End of the Suffolk System." *Journal of Economic History* 7(2) (November 1947), 183–207.

Lawlor, Michael S., and Darity, William A. "Letting Banks Be Banks, Letting Bankers Be Bankers? A Critical Survey of Bank Reform." Unpublished manuscript, 1989.

Matthews, R. C. O. *A Study in Trace-Cycle History: Economic Fluctuations in Great Britain, 1833–1842*. Cambridge: Cambridge University Press, 1954.

Merrett, D. T. "Australian Banking Practice and the Crises of 1893." *Australian Economic History Review* 29(1) (March 1989), 60–85.

Minsky, Hyman P. "The Financial Instability Hypothesis: Capitalist Processes and the Behavior of the Economy." In: Charles P. Kindleberger and Jean-Pierre Laffargue, eds., *Financial Crises: Theory, History, and Policy*. Cambridge: Cambridge University Press, 1982, pp. 13–47.

Mints, Lloyd, *A History of Banking Theory*, Chicago: University of Chicago Press, 1945.

Morrison, George R. *Liquidity Preferences of Commercial Banks*. Chicago: University of Chicago Press, 1966.

Munn, Charles W. *The Scottish Provincial Banking Companies, 1747–1864*. Edinburgh: John Donald, 1981.

National Monetary Commission. *Interviews on Canadian Banking*. 1910.

Nevin, Edward, and Davis, E. W. *The London Clearing Banks*. London: Elek, 1970.

Olivera, J. H. G. "The Square-Root Law of Precautionary Reserves." *Journal of Political Economy* 79(5) (September/October 1971). 1095–1104.

Pennington, James. "Paper Communicated by Mr. Pennington." In: Thomas Tooke. *A Letter to Lord Grenville*. Appendix 1. 1829. 117–127.

Phillips, Chester Arthur. *Bank Credit*. New York: Macmillan, 1921.

Pope, David. "Free Banking in Australia before World War 1." Unpublished manuscript. 1989.

Pressnell, L. S. *Country Banking in the Industrial Revolution*. Oxford: The Clarendon Press. 1956.

Rasche, Robert H. "A Review of Empirical Studies of the Money Supply Mechanism." *Federal Reserve Bank of St. Louis Economic Review* 54(7) (July 1972). 11–19.

Rockoff, Hugh. "Institutional Requirements for Stable Free Banking." *Cato Journal* 6(2) (Fall 1986). 617–634.

Scammell, W. M. *The London Discount Market*. London: Elek. 1968.

Selgin, George. *The Theory of Free Banking*. Totowa, NJ: Rowman and Littlefield. 1988.

Sushka, Marie Elizabeth. "The Antebellum Money Market and the Economic Impact of the Bank War." *Journal of Economic History* 36(4) (December 1976). 809–835.

Temin, Peter. *The Jacksonian Economy*. New York: Norton. 1969.

Thomas, S. Evelyn. *The Rise and Growth of Joint Stock Banking*. vol. 1. London: Sir Isaac Pitman and Sons. 1934.

Weber, Ernst J. "Currency Competition in Switzerland, 1826–1850." *Kyklos* 41(3) (1988). 459–478.

White, Lawrence H. *Free Banking in Britain*. New York: Cambridge University Press. 1984.

Wood, Elmer. *English Theories of Central Banking Control, 1819–1858*. Cambridge, MA: Harvard University Press. 1939.

NAME INDEX

Aharony, J. 215
Anderson, Benjamin M. 180–1, 206n, 248, 250
Anderson, M.D. 270
Andrew, A. Piatt 74n, 253n
Angell, James W. 180, 181
Aschheim, Joseph 115n, 125n
Axelrod, Robert 65

Bagehot, Walter 3, 46, 73, 78–9, 82, 214, 226, 228
Bailey, Samuel 146, 165–7, 170
Baltensperger, Ernst 21, 68, 125–6n, 132, 260
Barclay, Christopher R. 256, 259, 268
Barro, Robert J. 142, 157, 184n
Barth, James R. 230n
Bean, C. 148, 160n
Benston, George J. 11n, 25, 26, 68, 206n, 215, 217
Berlin, Mitchell 28
Bisschop, W.R. 61, 67
Black, Fischer 36–7, 43, 48n, 71, 72, 73n, 114n, 125
Black, Robert P. 142, 184n
Blair, Roger D. 210–11
Blanchard, Oliver J. 258
Boase, C.W. 266, 267, 268, 269, 274n
Boehm, E.A. 272
Boot, Arnoud W. 26
Bordo, Michael D. 24, 26, 32, 33, 74n, 196, 230n, 260, 265, 270
Bowley, Arthur L. 168
Brennan, H. Geoffrey 46
Brown, H.G. 115n
Brunner, Karl 126n
Bryant, John 43, 44, 216
Buchanan, James M. 46

Burns, A.R. 47n, 59, 60, 61, 73n
Burns, Helen M. 206n, 248, 250, 254n

Cagan, Phillip 116n, 206n
Calomiris, Charles W. 28, 135, 205n, 242, 251n
Cameron, Rondo 31, 84, 91, 93n
Cannan, E. 97, 115n, 116n, 125n, 137
Cannon, James G. 68, 69, 74n
Caplan, Benjamin 150, 174, 175, 185n
Carlisle, William 73n
Carlstrom, Charles T. 184n
Carr, Jack 31
Cassel, Gustav 163, 174, 175, 176
Chari, V.V. 238, 251n, 253–4n
Chase, Samuel B., Jr. 119, 126n
Checkland, S.G. 31, 64, 65, 68, 130, 249, 266–7, 268
Christ, C. 24, 130, 134, 139n
Clower, Robert W. 18, 48n
Coase, Ronald H. 35
Coghlan, Richard T. 126n
Coleman, Andrew 49n
Cooley, T.F. 116n
Coppieters, Emmanuel 268, 269, 274n
Cothren, Richard 260
Cowen, Tyler 2, 3, 27, 31, 41, 42, 48n, 227
Crick, W.F. 125n
Cyril, James F. 68

Darity, William A. 256, 257, 258, 260, 263
Davidson, David 146, 173–6, 182
Davis, E.W. 225, 232n, 268
Davis, R.G. 116n
De Cecco, Marcello 227
De Roover, Raymond 60, 73n

278

SUBJECT INDEX

activity restrictions: banks 210–11
adverse clearings, law of *see* clearings
assets: unregulated banks 70–1
Australia: banking crises 197; crisis of 1893 271–3; zero inflation 163
Austria: productivity norm 146, 176–8, 182
Austrian economics 17
Ayr bank crisis (1772) 266–8

Bagehot Problem 214; *see also* central banks: aid for banks
bailments 98
balance of payments crisis: and free banking 202–3
Bank Act (UK)(1844) 78
bank holidays 201, 236, 244; US 25, 205, 217, 248
Bank Merger Act (1966) 219–20
bank money: added to Diamond–Dybvig model 242–4; and commercial banks 119–28; and credit 101–3, 106; demand for 103–5, 112–14; demand-accommodating changes in 121–5; efficiency of supply 110–11; evolution of 98–9; and monetary deregulation 97–118; reserve ratio to 105–7; restrictions on 249–50; stability of monetary unit 108–10; *see also* currency; demand deposits
Bank of Canada 33
Bank of England 33, 46, 81, 87, 88; crisis of 1825 268–70; dominance of 226–7; establishment of 82–3; as lender of last resort 31, 83; privileges 3, 78–9, 80, 199, 226, 228; relationship with Scottish banks 31;

role of 224–5; suspension of gold payments 249
Bank of France 91, 227
Bank of Ireland 249
Bank of New York 219, 229
Bank of Prince Edward Island 216
Bank of Scotland 64, 65, 268
Bank of the United States 204, 211, 215, 270
banknotes: brokerage 64; central bank monopoly 73, 221–2; duelling 65, 66; issued by clearinghouses 69; issued by free banks 6–7, 30–3, 69–70; modern free banking school 18–24; origins 62–3; par acceptance 19, 63–7, 223; redemption 99–101; restrictions 136–7, 199, 201, 202–3, 204, 249–50; secondary markets 25–6, 86, 202, 204, 222–3; *see also* clearing mechanisms
banks and banking: aid from central banks 26, 89–90, 214, 218–19; and clearinghouses 68, 202; globalization 9; goldsmith 60–1, 98; origins 60–1; warehouse 61
Banking Acts (1933, 1935) 212
Banque Royale 258
Barings Crisis (1890) 273
barter 58–9, 72
base money 2; competitive systems without 16, 36–44; free banking with 16, 18–30; historical episodes 30–3
bearer notes 62–3
booms: rational and irrational 257–60; *see also* manias
branch banking 63; Canada 204, 209–10; and clearinghouses 80–2; and crises 201; restrictions on 26, 73,

Genoa 60

Germany: banking crises 196; productivity norm 146, 176–8

Glass–Steagall Act (1933) 210–11

gold standard: compared with pure accounting systems 38–9; displacement of 66; and price levels 179–80; value in labor terms 165–7

goldsmith banking 60–1, 98

Goodhart, Charles: *The Evolution of Central Banks* 77–93

governments: coinage monopolies: 59–60; establishment of central banks 33; involvement with money 44–6; role in banking 2; *see also* legal restrictions

Great Contraction (1930–3) 25, 167–8, 204, 209, 215, 222

guarantee, money back: fiat-type money 36

Hamilton National Bank of Chattanooga 215

herding behavior: banks 258–9

high powered money 223–30; and manias 10, 264–5, 273

hoarding: bank money 108

holidays *see* bank holidays

Home State Savings and Loan 215–16

Hong Kong and Shanghai Bank 88

Hoover, Herbert 217

hyperinflation 224; and fiat-type money 34–5

income: and productivity norm 156–8

in-concert expansion 22, 107–8, 134; and manias 258–60; microeconomic limits of 260–2

industry: effects of price levels 164, 165–6, 167–8, 179

inflation 17, 109, 145, 172; and employment 147, 158; England 83; and free banking 224; and productivity norm 183–4; relative 176, 180–1; Sweden 174–5; *see also* zero inflation

information 216; from clearinghouses 68; and contagion effects 217–18, 222–3; and crises 195; free banking 85–8; knowledge surrogates 113–14; and legal restrictions 25–6, 45, 201, 202

inside money 36–7, 45, 58; acceptance of 63–7; establishment 62–3; free banking 69–70

interest 98–9; on banknotes 18, 70; and productivity norm 156; warehouse banking 61

interest rates: and booms 263–4; ceilings on 26, 211–12; and money supply 109; restrictions on 201

investments: role of commercial banks 119–28

Italy: banking crises 196

joint-stock banking: England 80, 226–7

Keynesianism 181–3

knowledge surrogates 113–14

labor: as measure of value 165–7; and price level 148

legal restrictions: development of central banks 72–3; and free banking 26–30, 136–8; and information problems 87; relationship with crises 7–8, 25–6, 199–205; and suspension 236–7; theory 42–4; weakening effects of 207–20

lenders of last resort 24; aid to banks 214; Bank of England as 31, 83; central banks as 26, 88–9, 201–2, 207; clearinghouses as 32; and contagion effects 45, 88–9, 215; and crises 198, 199–200, 201; private 218–19; weakening effects of legal restrictions 207–20; *see also* specific banks

liabilities, bank: secondary markets 86–7, 201

liability management: US 209

macroeconomics *see* commercial banks; control, monetary; price level policy; supply, money; productivity norm

manias, bank-lending: 9–10, 256–77; in history 265–73

market support mechanisms 218–20

McFadden Act 219

Merchant Banking Company of Glasgow 267–8

mergers 210, 219–20

metals: as medium of exchange 59

Printed in the United States
109189LV00003BE/1/A

9 780415 140560